MAUD GONNE

BY SAMUEL LEVENSON

James Connolly, *A Biography*

MAUD
GONNE

Samuel Levenson

Reader's Digest Press
Distributed by
Thomas Y. Crowell Company
New York   1976

Excerpts from *The Letters of W. B. Yeats*, edited by Allan Wade, copyright 1953, 1954, are reprinted with permission of Macmillan Publishing Co., Inc., and Anne Butler Yeats.

Excerpt from "The Lover Mourns for the Loss of Love," in *Collected Poems* by W. B. Yeats, is reprinted with permission of Macmillan Publishing Co., copyright 1906, renewed 1934 by W. B. Yeats.

Excerpts from "No Second Troy" and "Reconciliation," in *Collected Poems* by W. B. Yeats, are reprinted with permission of Macmillan Co., Inc., copyright 1912 by Macmillan Publishing Co., Inc., renewed 1940 by Bertha Georgie Yeats.

Excerpts from "September 1913" and "To a Child Dancing in the Wind," in *Collected Poems* by W. B. Yeats, are reprinted with permission of Macmillan Publishing Co., Inc., copyright 1916 by Macmillan Publishing Co., Inc., renewed 1944 by Bertha Georgie Yeats.

Excerpts from "The Second Coming" and "A Prayer for My Daughter" are reprinted with permission of Macmillan Publishing Co., Inc., from *Collected Poems* by W. B. Yeats, copyright 1924 by Macmillan Publishing Co., Inc., renewed 1952 by Bertha Georgie Yeats.

Excerpts from "A Bronze Head," "The Circus Animals' Desertion," "Beautiful Lofty Things," and "The Municipal Gallery Revisited" are reprinted with permission of Macmillan Publishing Co., Inc., from *Collected Poems* by W. B. Yeats, copyright 1940 by Georgie Yeats, renewed 1968 by Bertha Georgie Yeats, Michael Butler Yeats and Anne Yeats.

For rights outside the U.S. to quote from *Collected Poems* of W. B. Yeats and *The Letters of Yeats*, edited by Allan Wade, I am grateful to A. P. Watts and Son, Ltd., London.

Excerpts from *Yeats, the Man and the Masks*, by Richard Ellmann, are reprinted with permission of Macmillan Publishing Co., Inc., copyright 1948 by Macmillan Publishing Co., Inc., and the author.

Excerpts from "*Scattering Branches*," edited by Stephen Gwynn, are reprinted with permission of Macmillan Company of London and Basingstoke.

Excerpts from *Memoirs* by W. B. Yeats, edited by Denis Donoghue, are printed with permission of M. B. Yeats, Miss Anne Yeats and the Macmillan Company of London and Basingstoke.

Excerpts from *Flowering Dusk*, by Ella Young, are used with permission of the publishers, Longmans Green and Co., Inc., a division of David McKay Co., Inc. Copyrighted 1945 by Longmans Green and Co., Inc.; renewed 1973 by J. R. Thompson.

Manufactured in the United States of America

LIBRARY OF CONGRESS CATALOGING IN PUBLICATION DATA

Levenson, Samuel.
  Maud Gonne.

  1. MacBride, Maud Gonne. I. Title.
DA958.M25L48   941.5082'1'0924   [B]   76-32
ISBN 0-88349-089-7

1 2 3 4 5 6 7 8 9 10

For
DOROTHY AND GRANVILLE HICKS

Contents

Author's Note

I acknowledge with gratitude the assistance provided me by the following individuals and institutions.

In Ireland: Sean MacBride, for allowing me to interview him and to use verbatim extracts from *A Servant of the Queen* and other material written by his mother. Mrs. Sean Mac-Bride imparted to me her memories of Maud and showed me through Roebuck House.

Jim Thomas, an American who was doing graduate work at Trinity College, displayed great initiative and acumen in examining numerous periodicals for references to Maud Gonne. Other individuals who provided information were:

W. J. Brennan-Whitmore, Catherine Burke, Basil Clancy, E. Ua Curnain, Murt Curran, Sidney Gifford Czira (deceased), H. J. P. Dillon-Malone, Denis Donoghue, Gladys Dunleavy, Marie Johnson (deceased), John Jordan, Harry Kernoff (deceased), Anthony Lennon, Charles McCarthy, F. X. Martin (OSA), Mary Murphy of Telefis Eireann, Michael J. Murphy, Gearoid O'Brien, Nora Connolly O'Brien, Leon O'Broin, Sheila O'Donoghue, Eithne Coyle O'Donnell, Andrée Sheehy-Skeffington, Francis Stuart, and Imogen Stuart.

The facilities and staff of the National Library of Ireland, under the directorship of Padraic Henchy, were, as always, an indispensable and invaluable resource. The National Gallery of Ireland gave me permission to reproduce some of the pictures in its collection. Edmund Ross, Dublin photographer, skillfully duplicated the MacBride family photographs used in this book.

In Britain: J. P. Brooke-Little, of the British College of Arms, provided me with a complete Cook family tree, as well as much related material. Others who provided generous assistance were Lt. Col. Howard N. Cole, Aldershot, Hampshire, a military historian; Sir Francis F. M. Cook, the present baronet; A. Norman Jeffares; L. Metcalfe, managing director, Cook and Watts, Ltd.; Clive Pawley, Vicar of Tongham, Surrey; Vera Ryder; and Geoffrey Sutton. I made good use of both the newspaper collection in Colindale of the British Museum, and the four-month membership that the London Library offers to foreign scholars upon application.

In the United States: W. W. Lyman, William M. Murphy, Thomas Parkinson, and B. L. Reid. Ready assistance was given me by the New York Public Library, the Library of Congress in Washington, D.C., and several libraries in Massachusetts (Boston Public, Worcester Public, Clark University, Worcester State College).

For the treatment of Yeats's relations with Maud Gonne, I have consulted most frequently Yeats's collected poetry, his autobiographies and other prose works, his letters as edited by Allan Wade; and the classic works by Joseph Hone, Richard Ellmann, A. Norman Jeffares, Virginia Moore, T. R. Henn, and John Unterecker. Several books appeared during the 1970s which gave new detail on this subject: primarily, Yeats's *Memoirs*, as edited by Denis Donoghue, but I also include Dominic Daly's life of the young Douglas Hyde and J. H. Natterstad's treatment of Francis Stuart.

For information about Irish politics, a matter in which Maud Gonne was deeply interested during her entire life, I have found most useful F. S. L. Lyons' marvelously detailed and accurate history, *Ireland Since the Famine*.

It is widely believed, and again asserted by Dr. Denis Donoghue in the *London Times* (February 16, 1973), that a treasure trove of Yeats-Gonne letters lies secreted in the vault of a Dublin bank. This opinion is almost certainly erroneous. It is true that there exist more than two dozen letters written by Maud Gonne which have never seen the light of day. At some earlier time they may indeed have been in a bank vault, but at present they are in the hands of one of Maud's descendants who steadfastly refuses to permit scholars to see them. The descendant contends that they are in a disorganized condition, impossible to read, and of trivial importance in any case. It is probable that in some of these letters Maud gave W. B. Yeats instances of her husband's drunkenness and brutality; though interesting, they are not likely to alter this biography in any important way.

The most valuable contributions to this book were made by my wife. Her encouragement and multifarious talents, which range from acute literary criticism to the ability to decipher illegible handwriting, were of first importance in improving the quality of my manuscript and speeding its completion.

SAMUEL LEVENSON
Worcester, Massachusetts
August 1976

CHAPTER I

The Cooks and the Gonnes

MAUD GONNE WAS ONE of the great English beauties of the Victorian period. That beauty remained a central fact of Maud's existence during much of her life. Six feet tall, with a willowy figure, soft hazel eyes, an apple blossom complexion, and hair of burnished bronze, she was the kind of woman whose appearance in a room, at a ball, or on the street caused heads to turn and conversations to cease. Her emergence from a hansom would prompt street urchins to cry out in astonished admiration, and more sophisticated observers to comment that she filled whatever room she entered with her sheer presence.

No one who knew her in the days of her glory is now alive. But many Irish men and women recall her in her later years as one of Dublin's most extraordinary personalities— part eccentric, part heroine. They remember her as a tall, gaunt woman in black robes speaking on Dublin street corners about her current political or economic obsession. And they have not forgotten the stories they heard from their elders about her unconventional life in Paris, her constant cigarette smoking, the dogs and birds with which she surrounded herself, her affair with a French politician, her illegitimate children, her marriage to Irish patriot John MacBride, and the scandal of her separation from him.

Some remember Maud Gonne's activities to house evicted tenant farmers, feed school children, aid political prisoners, find homes for Catholic refugees from Northern Ireland, establish a fully independent Irish Republic, and end partition between Northern and Southern Ireland. Few recall the names of the women's organizations and publications she founded, or the number of times she went to prison. And some confuse her with another tall Ascendancy woman who took up the Irish cause after a fling in Paris—the Gore-Booth girl, who came back with a Polish count named Markievicz. But they all know that the word "maudgonning" means agitating for a cause in a reckless, flamboyant fashion.

Maud herself wished to be thought of as an Irish patriot. She was hailed in her lifetime as an Irish Joan of Arc, and would have been happy to be remembered as such for all time. A quarter of a century after her death, controversy surrounds the importance of her contributions to the Irish nation and its people. The scandal that still hovers around her name has grown dim. But it is neither her activities in Ireland's behalf, her unconventionality, nor her striking beauty that give her a place in history. It is, rather, the obsessive pursuit of her by the greatest poet of the era, William Butler Yeats. Her steadfast rejection of his proposals bit so deeply into his soul that he never ceased to fashion glorious poetry about her beauty, her talents, and the mystery of her personality. She was to Yeats what Beatrice was to Dante. And thus, Yeats made her a permanent figure of romance and myth throughout the English-speaking world.

Few stories match hers in irony. Though Maud Gonne was deeply and energetically involved all her life in Irish public affairs, she is remembered because of her *private* affairs—and most of all for a private affair in which her participation was minimal. Her dream of a prosperous, independent Irish nation, and the effort she expended to make it a reality, proved in the long run to be less memorable than the frustrated passion of a poet.

The obverse side of Maud's love of Ireland was her intense hatred of England, an emotion that did not arise from either ignorance or personal oppression. Maud, born and largely nurtured in England, was in no way connected to the submissive English masses who, in those days, tilled the soil, manned the factories, and, in the great houses, polished their masters' boots. She was a member of the Cook family, part of the commercial-industrial-ecclesiastical-military class that ruled Britain in the nineteenth century.

The founder of the Cook dynasty was William Cook, born in 1784 in the little Norfolk parish of Suton near Wymondham. William grew up strong, healthy, and ambitious. When he came of age, he left his father's futureless sheep farm and went off to London, where he found a job in a linen store in Clerkenwell; his wages were five shillings a week, plus bed and board and a suit of clothes.

William did well. In two years his name went up over the shop beside that of his employer and in 1809 he courted and married an alderman's sister. In 1814 he became sole owner of the store.

Deciding that the wholesale side of the linen and drapery business would be more profitable than selling at retail to Clerkenwell housewives, Cook sold the little business and leased premises in the heart of London's famed commercial center, the City. By 1834, Cook, Son and Company, "Warehousemen," had become one of the largest firms of its kind in existence, manufacturing silk, linen, woolen, and cotton goods, and distributing throughout the world.

With his profits William bought Roydon, a sixteenth-century manor house at East Peckham, Kent, and installed his wife and children within its Tudor and Jacobean walls.

He died in 1869 at the age of eighty-five, leaving a fortune of over £2,000,000. From that time on no Cook had to work for a living.

The speed with which the children of this erstwhile sheep farmer and dry goods clerk were absorbed into Victorian society shows the power of money even in those caste-ridden days. Leaving aside for a moment the destiny of William Cook's oldest child, William II, Maud's grandfather, we find that the three daughters, Augusta, Caroline Louisa, and Mary Anne, all married well, as did his youngest son, Major Edwin Adolphus Cook, of the 11th Hussars.

The most remarkable of William Cook's children was the second son, Francis, who during a visit to Portugal when he was twenty-four married a woman from Lisbon named Emily Lucas. At twenty-six Francis joined the family firm and became its head when the founder died, but by then his interests were multiple. At the age of thirty-nine he had purchased Monserrate, a renowned palace at Cintra, near Lisbon, restored the building and its famous gardens, and acquired huge tracts of land in the area. Moreover, in recognition of his benevolence to the Portuguese poor, he had been created Viscount Monserrate by the King of Portugal.

Francis Cook's second great interest was his art collection. In 1860 he acquired for his residence Doughty House, in Richmond Hill, near London, and there assembled one of the finest collections of paintings of his time. Advised by J. C. Robinson, he bought important works by Van Eyck and other Flemish masters, by Dutch landscape and genre painters, by Rubens and Rembrandt, and French, Spanish, and Italian masters. Italian majolica, bronzes, ivories, tapestries, and antique statuary were also part of the collection. Doughty House was open to art students, and its paintings were lent generously to exhibitions throughout the country and overseas.

Francis was ever generous, except perhaps to his wife. In

1885 he established, as a tribute to the Princess of Wales, later Queen Alexandra, a house in South Kensington for women students of music and other arts. This gesture cost him £80,000, but the money was well spent since he was created a baronet in 1888.

Maud did not like her Uncle Frank. In her sometimes prejudiced autobiography, written long after these events, she says that Sir Francis inherited from her grandfather, his older brother William Cook,

> ... a marvelous collection of pictures and art treasures and had built two long picture-galleries on to his house to hang them.... He had married a very beautiful Portuguese lady, Aunt Emily, whom he treated abominably. She seems to have been the only one of the aunts Mama had loved and she was my godmother. She was old and faded when I knew her, and in her long black silk dress and mantilla moved about among all these riches and splendours like a neglected ghost. Uncle Frank would not allow her a carriage ... when she occasionally visited London, she had to go in a hired fly. Her excursions to London were generally to buy magnificent dolls for us children and she never forgot her godchild's birthday; but these extravagant presents had to be kept secret from Uncle Frank and the money to pay for them had to be craftily saved from the housekeeping accounts which Uncle Frank always examined every week himself....
>
> I do not know how Uncle Frank, who was Mama's guardian, managed to possess himself of all grandfather's art treasures, leaving Mama ... but one solitary unsigned picture, a beautiful Venus and Cupid which hangs to-day on my wall....

Maud goes on to relate that, following the death of Aunt Emily, "Uncle Frank married an enterprising American woman, imbued with distinct ideas on women's rights, who took over the keeping of accounts."

This was Tennessee Celeste Claflin, a forty-year-old divorcée whom Francis married when he was sixty-four, soon after she had brought him a message from his dead wife advising him to do so. Tennessee, who sometimes signed herself as Tennie C., had participated in most of the escapades that dotted the life of her older sister, Victoria

Claflin Woodhull, founder of a sensational journal called *Woodhull and Claflin's Weekly*, former Wall Street stockbroker, apostle of "free love" and spiritualism, and once People's Party candidate for the United States Presidency with the black abolitionist Frederick Douglass as her running mate.

When Frank died, Maud tells us, the publicity that Lady Cook received over the years in the pages of the society journals was "a just retribution!" Sir Francis, reputedly a tall, large man and slow of speech, had looked on genially when Tennessee gave a garden party at Richmond, where the crowd, drawn from all classes, was so great that workmen had to tear down the fences so that it could pour into the meadows.

He continued his daily trips to the City until his death at eighty-three. The heir to his title, to Doughty House, and to Monserrate was his oldest son, Frederick Lucas Cook, at the time a member of Parliament. His personal estate, valued at £1,500,000, he left to both of his sons and to his only daughter, the wife of a much-decorated major general.

From the first there has been a strong inclination on the part of Cook men to become military officers and of Cook women to marry officers, a trend that has continued into the fourth and fifth generations. There appears an occasional member of Parliament or a King's Counsel, but the new branches of the Cook family tree are still festooned with military ranks from all the services and with appropriate decorations: Knight Grand Cross of the Order of the Bath, Knight of the Order of the Garter, Victoria Cross, Companion of the Distinguished Service Order, and Order of the British Empire.

The present baronet, Francis Ferdinand Maurice Cook, represents in his single person the extinction of two family trends—he has shown no inclination for commerce or the military arts—and the culmination of two other trends—a passion for painting and an inclination toward multiple marriages. Divorces among the Cooks have been frequent from the beginning; but Sir Francis, who was sixty-eight in 1975, has carried the practice to an extreme. He has been divorced six times and married seven.

It is easy to say, but hard to prove, that many of Maud's traits—self-confidence, self-possession, the habit of command, the belief that she could accomplish anything by working at it, a sense of *noblesse oblige*—were inherited from the Cooks. They would doubtless have developed no matter what wealthy Victorian family she had been born into. It would seem inevitable, however, that the daughter of Edith Frith Cook and a professional soldier would be impelled by her genetic endowment to be a warrior—if not for England, then against it.

Maud's grandfather, William Cook II, the oldest son of the founder of the Cook fortune, was a sober, pious man, a true Victorian. He lived placidly with his wife, the former Margaretta Frith; and worked hard in the family business, unaware that he would not live to inherit it. In no way did he resemble his younger brother Francis; he showed no interest in collecting works of art, in other women, or in foreign countries. His wife, who died young, had lost her own mother at an early age and had been kept by her aunts in various boarding schools—an experience so detestable that before she died she made her husband promise that he would never permit their two daughters, Edith and Emma, to be sent to such schools or to fall into the clutches of their aunts.

William Cook did not long survive his wife. He died in 1852, at the age of thirty-eight, leaving the bulk of his estate in the custody of his brother Sir Francis and his brother-in-law Thomas Gribble, to be held in trust for his daughters until they were twenty-four or had married before then with their guardians' consent.

Edith Frith Cook did the latter, when, at the age of

twenty-one, she married a dashing captain of the 17th Lancers Regiment named Thomas Gonne (pronounced "gone").

In afteryears Maud liked to say that the Gonne family had some Irish blood, this being a matter of some importance to one who was so often called the Irish Joan of Arc. She conceded that the Cooks were entirely English, but quoted her Aunt Lizzie Gonne, who dabbled in genealogy, as saying that the Gonnes had originated in Mayo County before emigrating in the dim ages to Scotland. She also said that some Gonnes later returned to Mayo. At other times she felt that the whole matter "had better be left in oblivion."

The ranking authority on Irish surnames, Edward Mac-Lysaght, writes, rather inconclusively, that the name of Gonne may indeed be Irish—a variant of Gawne, meaning stunted or short, a name that appears in seventeenth-century papers from counties Cork and Kerry, or a variant of O'Gowan. On the other hand, he adds, it may be a synonym for the English or Scottish name of Gunn.

Not that it matters. Maud did not become an Irish patriot because she had Irish blood. She was simply proving once again, to quote Conor Cruise O'Brien, that "Irishness is not primarily a question of birth or blood or language; it is a question of being involved in the Irish situation."

There is no doubt at all, of course, that Maud's father, Thomas Gonne, was born in London on January 9, 1835, into a wealthy family of wine importers. Since his oldest brother, William, was running the firm by the time Thomas reached twenty-one, there was not much for him to do but to join the British army. Following the current custom, he bought a commission as cornet, a now extinct rank equivalent to second lieutenant, in the 2nd Dragoons or Royal Scots Grays, so called because the regiment was always mounted on gray horses.

After serving a year in Ireland, Thomas Gonne was promoted to lieutenant, and eager to see action, was transferred at his own request to the 17th Light Dragoons, a regiment under orders to move to India to suppress the Indian Mutiny. The 17th, whose regimental badge bore a skull and crossbones and the motto "Death or glory," participated in the battle of Bunker Hill in the American colonies in 1775, and more recently in the famous charge of the light brigade at Balaclava.

Lieutenant Gonne arrived in Bombay on December 17, 1857, won the India Mutiny Medal during his tour of duty, and returned to England in 1860 to take a two-year course at the staff college at Camberley that qualified him for promotion to captain. His whereabouts during the next few years are uncertain; but he must have spent a good deal of 1865 in East Peckham, Kent, for a financial settlement relating to his prospective marriage to Miss Edith Cook was signed there on December 18 of that year. The marriage, which is recorded in the General Register Office in London, took place at the East Peckham Parish Church on December 19, 1865.

There is a great deal of evidence to indicate that their daughter, Maud Gonne, was born on the following day, December 20, 1865. If true, it says a good deal about Maud's father, and about a society in which marriage settlements could continue to be heavily bargained when the birth of progeny was imminent. It also may indicate why Maud Gonne was so often vague about dates in her life.

There is certainly an astonishing *absence* of any record of Maud Gonne's birth at the official registry, Somerset House in London, or anywhere else. The Richmond Herald of Arms in London has said that it was "quite possible that care was taken not to register Edith Maud Gonne's birth," and that since "it was an offence not to record a birth," a nonregistration was almost more interesting from a historical point of view than an actual registration.

Most encyclopedias and biographical dictionaries give no date at all for Maud Gonne's birth. A few give the year

1866, but a reporter who visited Maud Gonne MacBride in 1935 received only a smile and no correction when he congratulated her on completing "the seventieth year of her eventful life." His story was published in the *Irish Times* on December 20, 1935, under the heading "Seventy Years To-Day." Similar articles were published in other years, without any complaint from Maud about dates.

Most convincing of all, perhaps, is the typescript of an unpublished article found in the morgue of a Dublin newspaper. The article was headed "Madame MacBride's Story, told in an interview," and started with the words, undoubtedly taken direct from Maud's lips, "I was born near Aldershot camp in 1865."

CHAPTER II

The Colonel's Daughter

🌿 WHATEVER THE DATE, Maud Gonne began her life in Tongham, a tranquil Surrey village thirty-seven miles from London, and a few miles from the huge army base of Aldershot where her father was stationed. The base had been established only a dozen years earlier, but Tongham was already a favorite place of residence for officers' families. Maud's parents must have been particularly fond of it, for both are buried in the churchyard of the parish church where Maud was baptized.

In 1868 Captain Gonne was posted to Ireland to fill the position of brigade major of the Dublin Division and of the Curragh, the military base in County Kildare on the west bank of the Liffey. He housed his wife, Maud, and Maud's infant sister, Kathleen, in Howth, a small fishing village on a promontory of the same name on the north side of Dublin Bay.

Maud remembered their home as an ugly little place opposite the Baily lighthouse. When Tommy, as she always called her father, came home for weekends, the children were taken in a one-horse carriage to meet him at the railway station at Sutton. On the way back, Maud writes in her autobiography, "Tommy's bags and exciting parcels of cakes and toys filled the well of the car and the drive home seemed very long till we could get opening them."

Maud and Kathleen played every day on the summit of the rocky hill that rises steeply above the sea at Howth. And sometimes their nurse, "a wonderful climber," would take them down the zigzag cliff path, the seagulls wheeling and crying above, to bathe in the little rock pools, where the waves come splashing in. "Kathleen and I boastfully declared that we were swimming, with our feet and hands firmly touching the bottom."

While Nurse, who was a sociable soul, had tea with the people who lived in the little cabins along the road, the two girls played with the barefooted Irish children and shared their fare of griddle cakes baked on turf fires and potatoes boiled in big iron pots. The hospitality was one-sided, for Maud and Kathleen were never allowed to bring their friends to their own meals, which were served in the sitting room by the housemaid, the silver christening mugs and spoons brilliantly polished.

The Gonne children had mixed feelings about these playmates. Their clothing was inferior, but oddly enough, their book knowledge was greater because they trudged every day to the faraway school house while Maud and Kathleen played house all day in the heather on the lee side of the hill. All the children were united in their admiration for Bobby, an older boy who gathered seagull eggs on cliffs where the others were not permitted to climb, and who told stories about the smugglers and rebels who had once occupied those cliffs and caves.

Eventually, the Gonne family moved to their second home in Ireland, a large rambling house called Floraville in Donnybrook, a Dublin suburb. Here the family portraits could be seen to better effect, in particular a large oil painting of Mrs. Thomas Gonne that reveals her to have been a slim, narrow-nosed, and thin-lipped woman. There was also a portrait of Maud, a light-haired, pink and white child, painted by a Dublin artist named Wall.

When Mrs. Gonne became ill with tuberculosis, Tommy took her to London, intending to go on to Italy where it was hoped that she could regain her health. Unfortunately, the disease was so far advanced that on June 21, 1871, Edith Frith Gonne died. Just turned twenty-seven, she was buried by the same East Peckham vicar who had married her only six years before.

Maud opens her autobiography with her memories of the deathwatch in London at the gloomy house of a relative, of her father kneeling beside the body of his wife, and of his telling her, in words she never forgot, "You must never be afraid of anything, even of death."

For a time their English nurse, Mary Anne Meredith, took care of the motherless girls, but when Captain Gonne received orders to leave Ireland, it was obvious that further arrangements would have to be made. The first decision was hastened by an event that occurred one Sunday when Captain Gonne, with his two daughters, had lunch with Lord Howth at Howth Castle, an impressive place, with a tower at each end. After lunch the girls dashed madly about the gardens eating giant strawberries, unmindful of the effects of their exertions upon their velvet frocks, their pink silk stockings, and the ostrich feathers that decorated their big straw hats and that Meredith periodically spent hours recurling. A woman playing croquet on the lawn was distressed by the sight, and told Tommy that it was disgraceful of him to let his children grow up without any schooling and running wild like savages. Her concern may have been partly motivated by the fact that it was obvious even then that Maud was going to be astonishingly beautiful.

In any case, Tommy decided to leave the children in Ireland under the tutelage of a proper governess, and in due time one arrived. The daughter of an English clergyman, she was willing enough to teach reading, writing, music, and all the other subjects proper for young ladies to learn; but since her own knowledge of these subjects was scanty, she proved ineffective.

The second decision was to move the girls to London and

place them in the care of Augusta Sophia Cook Tarlton, their mother's aunt, and widow of the rector of Lutterworth. Aunt Augusta lived alone in a huge house with enormously large rooms in Hyde Park Gardens, where several other Cooks had their homes. But, though her staff included a butler, a footman, a cook, a coachman, the children's governess, their nurse, Mary Anne Meredith, maids, and a stableboy, she was a penurious woman. Every afternoon Maud, aged eight, and Kathleen, five, both dressed in velvet, would accompany her in a yellow coach to the inexpensive Army and Navy stores, or to the markets at Hyde Park or Covent Garden, where she could buy fruit and vegetables more cheaply than at a greengrocer's.

At dinner, they were spared the discussion of food prices only because they were not brought downstairs until it was time for dessert. Dressed now in starched muslin with wide blue sashes, they were each served an apple or an orange and a biscuit or two on hand-painted pink plates.

After dinner the children followed Aunt Augusta to the drawing room to listen to the governess perform, quite badly, on the piano. Then, while Aunt Augusta played patience, they sat in bored silence until, at nine, their nurse arrived to take them up to bed.

This plan for raising Maud and Kathleen also proved unsatisfactory. Portuguese Aunt Emily was the most outspoken of the relatives in expressing her dissatisfaction with the children's musical education, their French accent, and Maud's health, which because of her mother's untimely death, was always a matter of great concern. A doctor was consulted about the state of her lungs, and subsequently Tommy removed the children to the south of France, where he had rented a cottage called Villa Fleurie on the road between Cannes and Grasse. It stood in fields of orange and lemon trees, carpeted with Parma violets, and in the garden there was an even greater source of delight to Maud and Kathleen—a tiny fountain filled with tiny green frogs.

The Frenchwoman who was placed in charge of their education—the only formal education they ever received—was intelligent and well schooled, with strong republican, equalitarian, and philanthropic sympathies. She made the history of mankind vivid for Maud and Kathleen, and instructed them well in the use of French and other subjects. They often went with her to inspect a little villa, still in the process of being built, to which she intended to retire. In its unfinished kitchen, she prepared delicious dishes, taught the children how easy it was to cook if one used one's mind, and picnicked with them under her fragrant mimosa trees. Because she was basically a happy woman, she made everyone around her happy. In her autobiography Maud wrote, "I owe to her most of the little education I possess. What was of more importance, she had given us the desire to learn; she made us love literature and took the trouble to discuss it with us. So, although Tommy had to leave to go to India, which was a heartbreak to us, he left us in good hands." As a specific consequence of this training, Maud could henceforth write letters in French as easily as in English, and sometimes more grammatically.

To Maud, the significant thing about these years was that Tommy "kept his promise to Mama." He never sent the children to school and he kept them from the clutches of their aunts. Actually, the most important result of her French education was that it liberated her from the ideas and customs that prevailed in the Britain of Queen Victoria's day. As a child she developed an interest in matters that were not then considered of concern to women; as she grew older she became interested in art; sympathetic with radicals of all kinds; tolerant of originality, individual life-styles, and eccentricities—and addicted to cigarettes. As a grown girl she was often in Paris during a period when, as Anais Nin has said, everything was forgiven to anyone who had talent—and the courage, one might add—to display it. It was almost inevitable that Maud

should emerge as a person difficult for either English Protestants or Irish Catholics fully to understand.

Some of this was undoubtedly due to her cosmopolitan
upbringing. For though Maud lived mainly in southern
France from the ages of ten to seventeen, she spent a good
deal of time in Switzerland during the summers and in Italy
during the winters. And because her father had become a
military attaché, she was able to meet him in many different European cities. In 1878 he was promoted to lieutenant colonel and placed in command of the 17th Lancers. He
held this post, which took him to South Africa and India,
for only a few years, returning then to his former career as
military attaché in St. Petersburg, where he was stationed
for another two years.

The same traits that made Tommy Gonne a successful
military attaché—vigor, curiosity, an interest in many aspects of life—made him an ideal companion for his daughter. With her he visited cathedrals, museums, picture gal-
leries, theaters, and opera houses. They spent much time in
antique shops, where Tommy often bought a piece of embroidery or a wood carving. He had taste and knowledge
and enjoyed collecting such objects.

With his dark eyes and regular features, he cut a dashing
figure at diplomatic balls in the resplendent uniform of the
17th Lancers. And because he looked young for his age and
treated Maud like a companion rather than a daughter, they
resembled, she thought, a honeymoon couple when they
went on excursions together. It is not hard to believe, for at
fourteen Maud was already five foot ten, had persuaded her
nurse to lengthen her skirts, and wore her gold-brown hair
in great coils on the back of her head.

Once, while they were briefly in Paris, Tommy took his
daughter to meet his twice-widowed Aunt Mary, the Comtesse de la Sizeranne. She was seventy years old and a
remarkable contrast to staid Cook aunts. Formerly a noted
beauty, she wore black velvet costumes, and her naturally

snow-white hair was dressed in the fashion of Marie Antoinette. Every age, she told Maud, has its beauty if the woman accepts it.

Aunt Mary lived in an exquisite little flat hung with red damask in the Place Vendome. There she was looked after by a manservant, a maid, and a young Englishman whom she addressed as Figlio (he called her Madre), though neither could speak Italian. His secretarial duties were nominal, serving only to explain his presence to a conventional world. He was a good musician, well off, and had a charming flat of his own in London, but was unable to live without her. Whenever they quarreled he would be back the following day seeking forgiveness.

Aunt Mary's hobby was launching beauties. Nothing delighted her more than to discover and present to the world a beautiful girl, and see her obtain the subsequent rewards. She decided at once that Maud was a find, but could not persuade Tommy to leave her in Paris. In the afternoon they spent together, the Comtesse took Maud to the shop of Guerlain, the famous perfumer, and had many shades of powder and a number of creams tried on her face. Then she waved them all away, saying, "The child's complexion can't be improved." Before the day ended she had given Maud a bottle of perfume, taken her to a milliner to buy her a black lace hat, and driven with her in the Bois de Boulogne at the fashionable hour, thus showing off her latest discovery.

All this Maud relates in her autobiography with amused detachment and no trace of vanity. But Tommy was not easy about the activities of his teenage daughter. When Maud was fifteen, he received a letter from a young Austrian who had seen her from a distance, exchanged a few words with her, and now sought permission to ask her hand in marriage. Tommy's answer was strongly worded and the young man disappeared in short order. A month later Maud learned about this and though she scarcely remembered the suitor, she resolved that never in the future would she permit her father to decide such matters alone.

Not long after the first episode, Maud and her father attended an affair in Vienna where a member of the English royal family noticed her sitting on a couch and sent an equerry to find out who she was and to ask if she would be willing to meet him. From this incident comes the legend that when King Edward VII was Prince of Wales he wanted to marry Maud and make her his morganatic wife.

At seventeen, Maud's entanglements grew more serious during a long stay in Rome with a friend of her mother. She was attracted to an American artist who was painting her portrait, but when a young Italian proposed to her in the Colosseum by moonlight, the time and place seemed so appropriate that she accepted him. Naturally, her hostess was disturbed, and wrote Tommy about the engagement in such terms that he cabled ordering Maud to come to Ireland, where he was then serving as assistant adjutant-general at Dublin Castle. When she left Rome, Maud writes in her autobiography:

The American artist brought me a wonderful armful of flowers to the station and the Italian a large bag of chocolates which the heat had rendered sticky. I regretted the American had not been in the Colosseum, but . . . I afterwards learned he had a wife in America . . . so he was not really to blame.

Once in Dublin, she kept receiving letters from the Italian, which Tommy confiscated and burned. Then her suitor took to using milk as ink, writing on the pages of fashionable papers and circulars which her father would unsuspectingly pass on to her. One morning after breakfast, when Tommy sat down before the fire to read his correspondence, Maud settled herself on a stool beside him, held a circular close to the flame, and showed him the impassioned message that emerged in brown letters. "Look, Tommy," she said. "You've given me a lot of circulars like this. Don't you realize how silly you're being? If I show you this trick, it's because I know a lot of others like it. So let's make a bargain. In three or four years I'll be of age and able to marry this man. But I won't. I'll tell him that he must not write to me for three years. But you must stop opening my letters so that people won't seem more interesting than they are."

At first her father was aghast, then burst out laughing and promised never again to open any letters addressed to her. He sealed the bargain by buying her an evening gown. Tommy enjoyed nothing more than giving presents.

At this time, no one could have foreseen Maud's future role. She came to Ireland as a stranger, completely ignorant of its long and sad history. She knew nothing about the years of sullen submission, punctuated by flashes of violence, that followed the expropriation of its land by English invaders and Scottish settlers, nor of persistent efforts to force the native Celts to relinquish their religion and language. She was ignorant of the devastation wrought by Oliver Cromwell's army two centuries before her birth; and of the penal laws which flourished for many subsequent decades, laws that prevented Catholics from exercising almost all forms of religious or civil liberty. They could not vote, become citizens of an incorporated town, hold a lease for more than a stated period, enroll at Trinity College, become lawyers or teachers, serve in the military, possess arms, ride a horse worth more than a stated amount, or carry a sword.

Late in the eighteenth century, British rule in Ireland began to crumble. The American and French revolutions, the formation of a volunteer militia that sought free trade for Irish goods, the impassioned oratory of Henry Grattan and Henry Flood in the ancient Irish parliament, and the organization in 1791 of a Society of United Irishmen contributed to this. The society's leader, Theobald Wolfe Tone, a dashing young Protestant lawyer, sought to abolish all religious distinctions and unite all Irishmen against the "unjust influence" of Britain.

When England and France declared war in 1795, Tone went to France to seek her help in asserting Ireland's claim to independence—and met with disaster. In December 1796, when he accompanied a French fleet to Bantry Bay in southwestern Ireland, high winds prevented the troops from landing. In 1798 the sporadic risings he fostered were so quickly suppressed by the British that when two more French fleets invaded Ireland that year, they found no insurrection to support. Tone cut his throat in prison to avoid the dishonor of being hanged.

The immediate consequence of Wolfe Tone's alliance with France was a redoubling of British efforts to bribe or intimidate members of the ancient Irish parliament into voting for its own extinction and for a union of the Irish and English parliaments. Success came in 1800 with the passage of a bill called the Act of Union. One hundred Irish representatives were permitted to sit in the House of Commons at Westminster where they were outnumbered five to one.

None of these Irish delegates was a Catholic until 1828, when Daniel O'Connell, a Kerry lawyer turned politician, succeeded in winning a seat. The "uncrowned king of Ireland," firmly supported by Catholic laymen and clergy, accomplished much in the way of freeing Catholics from paying tithes to the Established Church, extending popular education, and providing help for the poor. But when O'Connell turned his attention to repealing the Act of Union, he fell victim to his own aversion to violence. He called for a huge mass meeting to be held on October 8, 1843, on the shores of Clontarf, a Dublin suburb, where the Irish leader Brian Boru had vanquished the invading Danes eight centuries earlier. When the government banned the meeting, O'Connell gave way and never recovered his former dominance.

Before his death in 1847, O'Connell witnessed the rise of

a group of patriots who did not suffer from his constraint. Called "Young Ireland," they issued two influential period-icals, the *Nation* and the *United Irishman*, which had a last-ing influence. Their most important contributors were Thomas Davis, a Protestant barrister with a knack for writ-ing patriotic poetry; Charles Gavan Duffy, a Catholic jour-nalist from County Monaghan; and John Mitchel, a so-licitor from County Down. Fired by the words of these writers, by a revolution in France, and by their own de-plorable condition, some young Irelanders in County Tip-perary started a quickly squashed rising in 1848. There was no successor to it, for a great pall of death caused by the potato famine of 1845 had fallen on the country. In the next six years, Ireland lost one-fourth of its population through hunger, disease, and emigration.

The tenuous flame of rebellion was carried to Paris and New York by James Stephens and John O'Mahony, who founded a secret society of active rebels known as the Irish Republican Brotherhood, "the Organisation." Members were termed Fenians, a name derived from the *fian*, the band of warriors led by the legendary Celtic hero Finn MacCool. On September 18, 1867, three Fenians attacked a police van in Manchester, England, blew open the locked door, and freed two of their number. A police sergeant was killed in the fracas and the alleged perpetrators were hanged; but the "Manchester Martyrs" became a legend and a source of rebel inspiration for many decades thereaf-ter.

Since Maud was only two at the time, the names of these patriots meant nothing to her. But she was not long in Ireland before she became familiar with the name of the new uncrowned king, Charles Stewart Parnell. A Protes-tant landlord from County Meath, he entered Parliament in 1875, when he was not yet thirty. Tall, bearded, with haughty good looks, in 1877 he became president of the Home Rule Confederation of Great Britain, and in 1879 president of a recently founded Irish National Land League. The following year he took over leadership of the Irish group in Parliament and intensified his predecessor's campaign of obstructionism in a way that rocked the empire and won the wholehearted approval of the Irish people.

Even the advocates of violence and of radical land reform were impressed. So was William Ewart Gladstone, a prime minister with a Puritan conscience. In 1881 he guided through Parliament a law which reduced rents for the small Irish tenant and insured that he could not be evicted so long as he paid them. He was also given the rights to any improvement he made on his farm, and first right to buy it if it were put up for sale. These were the famous long-sought three F's—Fair Rent, Fixity of Tenure, and Free Sale.

Gladstone's progress toward offering Ireland Home Rule, a modicum of self-government for Ireland, was dramatically delayed when, on May 6, 1882, Lord Frederick Cavendish was assassinated on the very day he arrived in Dublin to assume his new position of chief secretary for Ireland. Cavendish and Under-Secretary T. H. Burke were both killed while walking in Phoenix Park by some freelance Fenians magniloquently termed "Invincibles." The subsequent shock and revulsion—Parnell offered to resign his seat in Parliament—inspired that body to pass immediately a new crime suppression act.

Maud, at seventeen, and far removed from Irish politics, took no notice of these events. She did watch the state entry of a new viceroy, Lord Earl Spencer, that occurred soon afterward, but stayed only long enough to observe that Lady Spencer, nicknamed the Faerie Queen, was much too old and portly to deserve the title. Her principal occupation during these first days in Dublin was meeting her father's friends. Invitations to teas, dinners, and balls piled up so high on the mantelpiece that Tommy promised to help her answer them and advised her to start keeping an engagement book.

At a tea party held in honor of the Gonnes, Maud was told that after she was presented at the coming viceregal court, the lord lieutenant, in accordance with old "Irish" custom, would kiss her, as he would all the debutantes. Maud created something of a stir by saying that she would not accept this honor, and made some remarks, borrowed from Mademoiselle, about the feudal origin of the *droit du seigneur* and the need for abolishing this and other relics of barbarism. There was no confrontation, however, because the Prince and Princess of Wales came to hold court, and the Prince, being neither king nor king's representative, had no right to kiss debutantes in public. Of course, everyone knew what he did in private.

Maud's presentation dress was embroidered with iridescent beads so as to look like a fountain. The white satin train trailed on the ground a full three yards. Though Maud refused to attend the special class given to instruct debutantes how to curtsy and manage their trains, she spent hours practicing in private before the long mirror in her room.

All went well at the presentation. On the following evening, dressed in the same shimmering gown but with the train removed, Maud attended the great court ball in St. Patrick's Hall. She had the honor of dancing with the Duke of Clarence, oldest son of the Prince of Wales, who managed not only to tread excruciatingly on her satin-slippered toes but to drop the remark that, though Dublin was celebrated for the number of its pretty girls, so far he had not seen any. Overhearing him, the Prince of Wales shoved him aside saying, "Get out, you young fool, saying such a thing to a beautiful woman," and himself escorted Maud to the royal dais.

The Comtesse de la Sizeranne, reminded of Maud's existence by seeing her picture in the society papers, sent her a diamond pendant and asked her to go with her to Germany in August. Tommy gave his consent, and in Hamburg

Maud received the full treatment of a professional beauty. Except in the morning, when Aunt Mary slept late in their fashionable hotel, she was continually on parade, in a dress carefully selected for each occasion. Aunt Mary always managed to obtain a table at the Casino or a box at the theater where Maud would be most noticed. She was permitted to dance only with celebrated men or very good dancers so that people would stop to watch them.

When the corpulent, aging Prince of Wales visited Hamburg, he saw Maud and the Comtesse on the promenade, remembered seeing Maud in Dublin, and spoke to her. Tommy, arriving that evening, was not pleased to hear about this chat and to learn that the Prince would probably ask his daughter to supper.

"An invitation from royalty is a command," he told the Comtesse. "If I refuse to let her go, my military career will suffer. I am taking her away immediately, before any invitation is received."

When Maud entered the room, her father told her that, by a great stroke of luck, he had obtained tickets for the performance of Richard Wagner's operatic tetralogy, *Der Ring des Nibelungen*, at Bayreuth. She could go with him if she could start early the following morning. Maud was pleased at this opportunity to hear Wagner sung in his own opera house, and went off without the pretense of an apology to Aunt Mary.

On her return to Dublin in 1884 Maud made a serious attempt to run her father's household and act as his hostess. And though in the kitchen she found her advice unwanted, there were certain social tasks that she performed well. One of them was to call on wives of newly arrived officers and to entertain for them at least once. She found the work boring; the men dull, but presentable because of their uniforms and their military training; the women hopeless. For once her comment betrays class bias: "Some were vulgarly pretentious; others, decent, drab little creatures struggling with children and household difficulties."

Maud's favorite couple was the Canes (a name she occasionally spelled with a "K"). Captain Claude Cane was a tall, handsome artillery officer with interesting philosophical ideas. He later became a high-ranking Freemason, which signified, Maud wrote in her autobiography, "that we were in opposite camps." Eva, his pretty wife, came from Malta; she had Maud's own un-English way of speaking frankly about the dullness of garrison life.

As a way of combatting boredom, and proving that she was grown up, Maud took pains to make friends with the upper ranks, including the generals. They had all traveled, some had read a good deal, and most could tell interesting stories about their adventures, while the young officers generally talked of nothing but sports and racing. Maud was a good listener, and there is no reason to disbelieve her statement that her afternoon teas attracted many elderly generals and became a garrison institution. Her activities even smoothed the way for Tommy to settle some differences with these dignitaries on the best way to utilize the troops in Ireland. They could hardly quarrel with the assistant adjutant-general while being on friendly terms with his lovely daughter.

As a diversion Maud visited the stables and rode with her sister. At other times, both would watch the frequent parades and field demonstrations, taking a malicious delight in guessing which fat infantry colonel would come tumbling off his horse first. Maud had a striking empathy with the horses, and her feelings were hurt when Tommy said she was not as good a horsewoman as Kathleen. While riding to hounds, moreover, she could not bear to see the foxes torn apart.

Maud was nearing her twenty-first birthday when her family made plans to visit the Canes at their country house.

On the morning set for departure, however, Colonel Gonne felt ill and sent the girls off without him, promising to join them the following day. Instead, he sent a telegram saying he was still not well. When the girls returned to Dublin, Tommy was in bed but the doctor was not at all alarmed.

A week later, at the age of fifty-two, Colonel Gonne was dead. Maud missed him for the rest of her life.

The *London Times* gave typhoid fever as the cause of his death and implied that his contracting it was due to the well-known unsanitary condition of the Royal Barracks in Dublin. The same paper described the nineteenth-century pomp and splendor of his military funeral cortege in its issue of December 3, 1886. Every regiment, battalion, and corps quartered in the Dublin District was represented, the 17th Lancers with arms reversed. The coffin, placed on a gun carriage drawn by six horses, was

literally covered with rarest flowers... above them being laid the cocked hat and sword of the deceased officer. Next came the charger, led by two troopers of the 4th Dragoon Guards, all its trappings in mourning, and boots reversed in stirrups. Alongside the gun-carriage walked the pall-bearers.... All the men were cloaked, as the afternoon was bitterly cold, the long cloaks of the cavalry and the dark plumes of the Lancers lending a particularly sombre aspect.... Leaving the Royal Barracks, the troops marched in slow time... but a short distance down the quays they broke into quick time. When nearing the steamer the band of the Welsh Regiment played the Dead March....

In this way Colonel Gonne's body was carried to the steamer *Banshee*, then taken to England, and buried in the family plot beside that of his wife. The name Gonne can still be read on the stone cross above the graves.

After the funeral, William Gonne, Tommy's oldest brother, brought his orphaned nieces to his London home at 11 St. Helen's Place. There, in the months that followed, Maud's life was crammed with characters found mostly in Victorian melodrama. We have a rich crusty uncle, despotic guardian of two beautiful orphans; a pious, Bible-reading aunt who wishes to adopt them; a devoted and sympathetic nurse; and even a tearful fallen woman.

About six weeks after Colonel Gonne's death, when Maud came down to the drawing room to pour afternoon tea, she found a young woman, "pale and rather beautiful if her face had not been disfigured with tears," trying to tell Uncle William that his brother, Colonel Thomas Gonne, was the father of her infant child.

When Maud asked, "Are you Mrs. Eleanor Robbins?" the stranger and Uncle William were equally astonished. But Maud knew the name well. The day before Tommy died she had helped him write a check for this woman, and had addressed the envelope containing it.

Mrs. Robbins, taking heart, told Maud that the baby was named Daphne, that she wanted nothing but to keep the child until she could get work, that she had been deserted by her husband, that she had been ill, and that the Colonel would never have left her and the baby unprovided for.

Uncle William refused to believe that the child could be Colonel Gonne's and, indignant at the impropriety of the entire conversation, ordered the woman to leave. It took all of Maud's persuasiveness to convince him that, since her father had sent Mrs. Robbins a check despite his critical condition, he would have wanted to provide for her. The scene ended with Uncle William grudgingly giving Mrs. Robbins five sovereigns and promising more.

The following day Maud visited Mrs. Robbins at her flat on Edgeware Road but Daphne did not charm her, for Maud was unable to "see beauty . . . in fledglings till their feathers appear . . . or in babies till their eyes have expression and colour and their complexion grows flowerlike." She soon placed the mother with a Russian family, where she stayed twenty years, by saying that the woman had been her own governess. When Mrs. Robbins was unable any longer to have her daughter with her, Daphne was cared for by Nurse Mary Anne Meredith, who later retired to Farnborough. Eventually Daphne married and had many children; they never knew that their grandfather had been Colonel Thomas Gonne of the 17th Lancers.

Maud saw from the first that her situation in Uncle William's house was intolerable. During her childhood, when she had shared the English prejudice against the Irish, she had liked to think that Uncle William had a typical Irish face, and referred to him in secret as "William O'Gonne of Ballygonne Castle." Like the Cooks, he insisted on reading family prayers before breakfast, on everyone's attending church every Sunday, and on punctuality at all times. He required his wards to record every day in account books the way they spent their allowances.

Kathleen, a devotee of beauty, avoided disputes and rows because she considered them ugly. But Maud filled out her account book a month ahead, and the first time she plowed through a rain to attend Sunday services, she managed to develop a hacking cough. The doctor who was summoned cautioned Uncle William (Maud always could twist doctors around her finger) and she was freed from the burden of attending church on Sunday or rising early for morning prayers.

In the living room after dinner, while drinking the excellent port he dealt in, Uncle William would rail against the workers for seeking a ten-hour day and better working conditions. Perhaps because of this, Maud once slipped out of the house to witness a massive labor demonstration at Trafalgar Square. It was led by the fiery trade union organizer Tom Mann, whose advocacy of the doctrine that factories should be seized and operated directly by workers' organizations brought him several prison terms. The way the crowd melted away when a few policemen with nightsticks appeared indelibly impressed on her mind the conviction that the English were bred-in-the-bone cowards.

On occasion, Charles Gonne, Tommy's second brother, who lived in Ascot, would come to St. Helen's Place with his wife, Lizzie, and his daughters, gentle Chotie and spirited, fiery-haired May. The four cousins became fast friends, and would conspire in Maud's bedroom to circumvent parental restraints, with Nurse Meredith acting as a sympathetic chorus. Meredith thought that Maud's life depended on her release from that dreary London house.

The result of this constant plotting, accomplished with Aunt Lizzie's help, was that Maud and Kathleen were given permission to spend two months in Ascot. As they left Uncle William's house, he was standing in the hallway, saying goodbye, and holding £2 in his hand. He asked the girls to take out their account books and enter in them eight half-crowns on eight successive pages so that he would not need to mail them their weekly allowance. It was then that Maud's habit of listing expenditures several days before she made them was discovered. "In a trembling voice," he told her that he would assuredly find a method of dealing with such underhanded maneuvers.

In due time Uncle William rode out to Ascot to deliver his ultimatum. Since Thomas Gonne had not left enough money for his daughters to live on, and since they manifestly lacked the training and education to make a living on their own, their only course was to accept a generous offer from Aunt Augusta Cook to adopt them permanently. Maud, supported by May, promptly declined the offer. Chotie and Kathleen thought it was best to hedge.

After more conclaves, Maud and May decided to enter nurse's training, Maud because she had felt so inadequate when her father was ill, and May because she thought it was a glamorous profession. The girls applied secretly to the Charing Cross Nursing Institute for admission, and while on a shopping expedition with Lizzie took the necessary health examination. May passed, but Maud, owing to the condition of her lungs, failed.

Maud now thought of becoming an actress. She had studied elocution in Dublin and, after she had appeared in an amateur play, Herman Vezin, a well-known London actor, had told her that she could have a great stage career, and

should see him if she ever wanted it. She announced her
new intention at the next secret meeting but failed to make
the sensation she expected, for her sister Kathleen and
cousin Chotie announced simultaneously that they were
going to enroll at the famous Slade school of art and become
painters.

All these plans actually bore fruit. On the following day,
Maud, accompanied by Nurse Meredith, went from Ascot
to London and was told by Vezin that he could find a job
for her in a repertory company. In order to finance Maud's
stay in London, Meredith withdrew some of her savings.
This act of devotion on her part was only one of hundreds,
but Meredith is never mentioned in Maud's autobiography.
Was it because she was an Englishwoman, and a loyal one?
In any case, Maud and Kathleen later showed the extent of
their devotion. After Meredith's death in 1902 at the age of
seventy, they had her body exhumed from the cemetery in
Farnborough and reburied at Tongham, to rest beside the
Gonnes. Her grave bears the inscription, "Beloved nurse of
Colonel Gonne's children."

Ever resourceful and persuasive, Aunt Lizzie now convinced Uncle Charlie that it was quite sensible for May to
become a nurse, especially since she would probably marry
before she finished training; and that Chotie and Kathleen
should be permitted to attend the Slade school. "Not wanting to be far away from any of her chicks," she even persuaded her husband that a house in London would be better
for his health than Ascot.

As for Maud, within four months she had the satisfaction
of sending Uncle William a six-foot poster, printed with her
name in foot-high letters, announcing that she would have
the leading role in two plays to be offered by a touring
company. Uncle William's response was to ask that she
spare the family disgrace by assuming a stage name. Maud
retorted that the name Gonne belonged to her and that she
was honoring it by earning her own bread. But then, she
writes, ". . . disaster overtook me. I had worked very hard

at voice production and spent nights and days rehearsing in draughty, dismal, dusty halls and theatres. The day I was to have started on tour found me lying weakly in bed, after a haemorrhage of the lungs... and owing a large sum for breach of contract to the director of that ramshackle touring company, which I did not know how to pay...."

When the young rebels met at Maud's bedside it was clear that she was seriously ill, and that none of them was equipped as yet to make her own living. However, May seemed to be enjoying her work as a nurse in training while Chotie and Kathleen had amusing stories to tell about their days at Slade. One concerned Aunt Augusta, who had arrived to judge their progress. Glimpsing a nude male model through an open door, she was so shocked that she fled without making her inquiries.

As this juncture, like a liberating angel, Aunt Mary, the Comtesse de la Sizeranne, entered upon the scene. She informed Maud and Kathleen that there was no need for them to worry about making their own living; that dear William had been quite wicked to make up such stories about their father's poverty; that when they came of age, they would be well off. She herself would take Maud to southern France where the warm sun and sparkling sea would soon make her well.

This is Maud's own account, typically dramatized, of her victory in her war against Uncle William. More prosaic records show that it was won on April 17, 1887, when Colonel Gonne's will was probated. The bulk of his estate, including the substantial settlement he had received when he married Edith Cook, was left in equal shares to his two daughters, to be turned over to them when they turned twenty-one. Since Maud had reached that age four months earlier, she was now financially independent, and free of control by anyone. Shaking the dust of England from her feet, she returned to Europe with her aunt, the Comtesse. This decision changed the course of her life.

CHAPTER III

A Rebel Is Born

MAUD ALWAYS CLAIMED in countless spoken and printed words that she had been converted to the cause of freeing Ireland before she left there and gave as a major cause of her conversion the incidents of British oppression and terror she had seen as a child in Howth and Donnybrook and as a young girl in Dublin's military and social circles. As a minor cause, she listed filial loyalty.

She never forgot that her father had once rebuked her at a party when she had joined with other English guests in mocking the accents and attitudes of their native Irish hosts. Nor that he had reprimanded a young English captain for pretending that he had mistaken the master of the house for the butler. "If you accept a man's hospitality, at least behave like a gentleman," Tommy had said. And, shortly before he died, he had told Maud that he intended to resign from the army and run for Parliament as a Home Rule candidate. This conversation occurred on the terrace of the Royal Barracks in Dublin while they watched a parade of the Irish National League, an organization that differed from the Land League in putting Home Rule first on its program and relegating land reform to second place. As the banners and bands went by, Maud was astonished to hear her father say, "Yes, they are quite right. The Irish are entitled to govern themselves." Tommy had even gone so far as to write out his electoral speech; he now took it out of his pocket and read it to her.

An incident Maud liked to tell concerned a tall, red-faced landlord who had delivered a diatribe against the Land League while she was dining at his country home. The burden of his grievance was that the League was hindering the sport of hunting. "As I was coming home this evening," he said, "I saw Paddy Ward and his family lying in the ditch. I had warned him often enough that he would be evicted if he joined the Land League. His wife didn't look as if she was going to live till morning. I stopped and told him he would be responsible for her death. Now he had no roof to shelter his family, and that is what he deserves."

Maud was shocked. She asked, "And you did nothing about it?" "Let her die," he answered. "These people must be taught a lesson," and he resumed eating his dinner.

Many of the atrocities Maud mentions are vague and undocumented. No doubt she had seen numerous cases of poverty and injustice in Ireland; even for a person in her social class they would have been hard to miss. And any girl educated by Mademoiselle would have become indignant about them. But it is also true that her indignation became fervent only after she returned to Europe and met Lucien Millevoye.

He appears in Maud Gonne's autobiography, *A Servant of the Queen*, only as her partner in their joint war against perfidious Albion, never as her lover. Though Maud was in her seventies when the book was published, she still had reason not to divulge the affair. It would have damaged her reputation as a single-minded Irish patriot, injured her son Sean's budding legal career, and if people were not able to guess that Iseult Gonne was her illegitimate daughter by Millevoye, they did not deserve to be told.

Few details about Maud Gonne's romance with Lucien Millevoye are known. Not even when and where it was consummated.

It seems probable, though again there is no proof, that,

during most of their relationship of a dozen years, Lucien
was genuinely in love with Maud and would have married
her had he been able to obtain a divorce without injuring
his political career—something almost impossible in
Catholic France. We are left with the certainties that the
liaison occurred—two births attest to it—and that far from
interfering with their political life, the affair nourished and
stimulated it.

Lucien Millevoye, who was fifteen years older than
Maud, bore a surname that most intellectual Frenchmen
would recognize. His grandfather was the famed poet
Charles-Hubert Millevoye, whose work had anticipated the
melancholy and response to nature of the Romantic movement. Lucien was born in Grenoble in 1850. At the age of
twenty-five he became a magistrate in Lyons, and for a time
seemed likely to follow in the steps of his father, chief
justice of the Lyons appeals court. It was the French government's failure to take steps to recapture Alsace-Lorraine,
lost in 1870 to Germany, that turned his attention to the
right-wing politics to which he devoted his life. At the time
he met Maud he was watching, hopefully and eagerly, the
entrance on the political scene of a dashing young general,
Georges Boulanger. Appointed minister of war in 1886,
Boulanger was making major changes in the organization of
the French army, and seemed to be turning it into a force
that could meet the Prussians on even terms.

The accounts vary, but it seems probable that Maud and
Lucien first met at Royat, a village in the Auvergne
mountains of central France, famed for its curative springs.
Though it was feared that Lucien was consumptive, he had
another ailment; his marriage was falling apart.

"A tall man of between thirty and forty," he was introduced to Maud on the promenade while she was listening to
a band concert in the company of her sister Kathleen and
her Aunt Mary. When a thunderstorm broke the sultry
atmosphere, the group took refuge in their resort hotel,

where Aunt Mary's "secretary" proceeded to play the piano. But Maud, who loved storms, slipped through the drawn curtains onto the roofed-in terrace. As she put out her arms to feel the cool rain, she heard someone speak behind her. It was M. Millevoye telling her that her aunt had sent him to summon her back.

"How can one leave a storm like this?" Maud asked.

Millevoye agreed that it was difficult, then remarked that she was obviously not afraid of storms.

She shook her head. "No. One must never be afraid of anything—even death. But have we not met before? I feel that we have." Maud believed she had great powers of extrasensory perception.

"Because he was a Frenchman," Lucien thought the remark was an invitation, and kissed her dripping wet arm. She turned to go in. "You don't understand," she told him.

After that they met every day at the springs and promenades. While they walked together, Lucien taught her the intricacies of European politics. He was bitterly opposed to the French Republic, deriding its numerous ministerial crises, the emptiness of its debates, the corruption of its politicians. He did not believe in a hereditary monarchy but was convinced that "at times the genius of a nation incarnates itself in a man. That man has the right to rule despotically. . . ."

He saw in General Boulanger that very man, and he had good reason to believe that he would triumph. The right dominated the army, navy, diplomacy, and judiciary, and the machinery of public administration. The world of finance, the professions, and most of the newspapers were in its control. And it was supported by the Roman Catholic Church.

Millevoye's speeches before patriotic groups were a melange of superheated patriotic calls for unity, attacks on the supporters of Dreyfus, who was then being unjustly tried for treason, and invective against the appointed and

elected officials of the government. Millevoye wrote a
sinewy, eloquent French; was knowledgeable in all the fine
arts; and skilled in the use of sword and pistol—which was
fortunate since he engaged in several duels. In 1889 he
became a member of the House of Deputies from Amiens,
and from the 16th Arrondissement of Paris four years later.
On the way he developed an interest in the humane treatment of animals and anti-vivisection, feelings he shared with
Maud Gonne.

Among the Gonne family pictures are two photographs
of Lucien Millevoye. One, taken in Paris, shows him with a
General Grant type of beard and mustache, a thin face,
straight nose, small ears, thinning hair, and protuberant
eyes. He is wearing a polkadot cravat and a high, stiff
collar. In the other picture, taken in Dublin, his mustache
flares a bit more, his beard is less heavy, his hair a bit
thinner. In both pictures he resembles Maud's father. One
would never discern his many distinguished facets from
these photographs but Maud knew them all, and the touch
of possible tragedy lent him by his illness heightened the
fascination of his activist doctrines. He considered England
almost as great an enemy of France as Germany, for it was
England that had defeated the great Napoleon, and he believed that she had encouraged Bismarck to make Germany
replace France as the principal military power on the Continent.

One way to strike at England, Millevoye thought, might
be through Ireland. "Why don't you free Ireland as Joan of
Arc freed France?" he asked Maud. "You don't understand
your own power. To hear a woman like you talking about
going on the stage is infamous."

The appeal was irresistible. It was an era when strong-
minded Englishwomen were marrying Indian rajahs, crossing the Sahara on camels, crusading against corsets and for
women's suffrage; and when, to a beautiful, young, wealthy
woman, nothing seemed impossible. Swiftly a pact was

made. Lucien would help Maud free Ireland and she would help him regain Alsace-Lorraine for France. The pact was cemented when she was privileged to meet the great General Boulanger himself at a little country restaurant. She found him "good-looking with fair hair and clear steady grey eyes," but doubted that he had the resolution to play the part envisaged for him by Millevoye and by Paul Déroulède, an ultra-nationalist anti-Semite who had founded an organization called the League of Patriots.

While these new concepts were simmering in Maud's mind, she accepted an invitation to Constantinople from Lilla White, daughter of Tommy's old friend, the British ambassador to Turkey. Taking leave of her sister and her aunt, Maud went to Marseilles to embark, and when Millevoye appeared to say goodbye, spent a blissful day with him, lunching on bouillabaisse and strolling through the markets. Lucien gave her a marmoset, a squirrel-like furry creature they found in an animal shop, to act as her chaperone, and a small revolver for additional protection.

The first day of the trip was stormy. Maud was miserable. On the second day she felt better, and on the third, against the captain's instructions, she slipped off the boat when it stopped for a few hours at Syra, one of the Greek Cyclades Islands. The busy seaport was considered too dangerous for women to visit, but Maud persuaded a Greek who had come on board to sell trinkets to the tourists to take her ashore in his boat. She felt quite safe with her little chaperone snuggled on her shoulder, and her revolver in her pocket. Two hours later, when she wanted to return, the Greek had two other sailors with him and was slow in getting the boat started. After they had been rowing for some time, Maud noticed that they were moving away from the tourist ship. She pointed out the correct direction, but the Greek simply smiled, and told her in broken English that he wanted to show her some sights. Maud ordered him to turn at once. When he laughed in reply, she said, "Obey or I fire," and leveled her revolver at him. The men stopped rowing, there was some quick Greek conversation, and the boat headed for the ship. Maud covered the helmsman with her revolver until they reached the steamer; then she threw him a fifty-franc note, and scrambled up the ladder.

During a stopover in Smyrna, she explored the town with a German commerical traveler, who regaled her with his business exploits. "He was a very ordinary young man, but I was not bored. I can never understand boredom. Every human being is interesting and has a story to tell."

Maud spent a pleasant month in Constantinople with Lilla White, who had often visited her in France and had shared Mademoiselle's instruction. She found it difficult, however, to meet any Turks and she disliked having a uniformed flunky with a long staff vigorously clear the way for her and Lilla when they went shopping. Their principal source of amusement was to dress up as Turkish women and wander about in the embassy gardens. Sir William White eventually had to ban this diversion, since it was being whispered that the English ambassador was secretly keeping a harem.

When Maud landed at Naples on her way back to France, she found two letters waiting for her; one was from Millevoye, the other from Madame Edmond Adam, a woman Maud admired greatly and tried to emulate. Both wanted to see her in Paris as soon as possible.

Madame Adam, born in 1836 as Juliette Lamber, was called La Grande Française because she incorporated in her person so much of the French wit, charm, and chauvinism of the period. Juliette was a writer of popular fiction, and founder-editor of an influential bi-weekly magazine, *La Nouvelle Revue*. The mistress of a leading political salon, her friends included such important politicians as Leon Gambetta, a founder of the new French Republic, and such authors as Gustave Flaubert, Victor Hugo, and Alphonse Daudet.

An extreme nationalist, Madame Adam glorified the French military as the sole reliable instrument for regaining Alsace-Lorraine. She never doubted that Alfred Dreyfus had conveyed military secrets to the Germans; condemned British rule over Egypt, South Africa, and Ireland; shared the fears of Millevoye and the League of Patriots that England was trying to isolate France; and advocated an alliance of the French Republic with Russia, however unnatural such an alliance might appear.

Maud and Madame Adam were much alike—even in their personal characteristics. Juliette did not smoke cigarettes, to be sure, but she was convinced that soothsayers, palmists, and other practitioners of the occult sciences could foretell her future; she respected Louis Auguste Blanqui, whose ideas influenced Karl Marx, mainly because he was the kind of radical who returned blow for blow; and at all times displayed enormous energy, sociability, self-reliance, and love of controversy. Her biographer, Winifred Stephens, wrote, "Intensity is the dominant note of Mme. Adam's nature." The same words could fit Maud Gonne.

When Maud arrived in Paris, Juliette Adam gave her certain proposals for a treaty with Russia and asked her to take them secretly to St. Petersburg and deliver them to Popodonotzeff, head of the Holy Synod and the czar's chief advisor. These proposals were from the Boulangist party and the League of Patriots; the pro-English French government, which distrusted these groups, would certainly not want to transport them to Russia. Haste was essential, Madame Adam said, since Schuvaloff, the Russian ambassador in Berlin, was sending counterproposals intended to bind Russia to Germany instead of to France.

Maud set out at once. When her train reached Berlin she observed a man on the platform who was carrying an attaché case so carefully that she assumed he must be a diplomat. He looked back at her several times, which was not

strange in view of her height and beauty and of the long
black veil she was wearing, instead of a hat, to keep the dust
off her hair. It gave her the appearance of an extremely
beautiful nun.

At the Russian frontier it was discovered that Maud's
passport had not been countersigned in Paris, and she was
told she would have to remain four days at the frontier
while it was sent to Paris and returned properly signed.
Pretending not to understand the problem, she turned ap-
pealingly to the man she had noticed and asked him to do
her the favor of translating the words of the immigration
officer. Though she tossed the delay off lightly—she was
traveling only for fun, and in no hurry to reach St.
Petersburg—she indicated that she was sorry not to have
the pleasure of traveling the rest of the way with such a
courteous and helpful gentleman.

Since Maud could be extremely persuasive and charming
when her principles were not at stake, the man, who turned
out to be an official with the Russian embassy in Berlin,
took matters in hand, and induced the immigration officer
to telegraph the Foreign Office for permission to admit the
lovely Englishwoman at once. It was granted within the
hour, and Maud was profuse in her thanks. She became less
grateful when, right after they were seated in a private
carriage, the Russian knelt before her and started telling her
of his great joy in having met such a beautiful and accomplished lady.

Though Maud still had her revolver, she resorted to more
subtle methods of dissuasion. Taking his hand, she told
him how happy she was to be with a Russian, for everyone
knew that Russians, unlike Frenchmen and Englishmen,
did not look on women in a vulgar way but understood how
beautiful the relationship between men and women could
be. The official got off his knees, and, while still holding
her hand, discussed unsentimental matters with her until
they arrived in St. Petersburg. The next day he brought his

wife to visit her at the Hotel de l'Europe where she was staying.

In her autobiography Maud discloses that in the Russian's valise "were the very papers from Schuvaloff, Russian ambassador in Berlin, of which Madame Adam had spoken," but that hers were delivered first into the hands of grim old Popodonotzeff. She could hardly have known this for a fact, but there is no question that it improves the story.

Maud spent much of her two weeks in St. Petersburg in the company of the charming Polish princess Catherine Radziwill, to whom she had brought a letter of introduction from Madame Adam. The two women took to each other, and, at one of Catherine's salons, Maud met William Thomas Stead, perhaps the most famous journalist of the day. Then about forty-seven, he was editor of the *Pall Mall Gazette* and renowned as the investigator who had been imprisoned a few years earlier, in 1885, for his sensational attacks on the British government's failure to curb white slavery.

Because Princess Radziwill, who dabbled in politics, wanted to know what Stead was doing in Russia, Maud engaged him in lengthy conversations. He was happy enough to talk to someone he later described as the most beautiful woman in Europe. Maud found him "a curious type... with more than ordinary force and vitality, but little culture or literary background." She analyzed him as a man whose puritanical beliefs were constantly at war with his sensual temperament; hence, he was obsessed by sex. "He could talk of nothing else and... it made him rather repellent to a girl who hated such talk and I told him so, which led him to write me a very foolish and very amorous letter, endeavouring to explain."

Maud left this letter in her writing case in the drawing room, where, on returning from a drive, she found waiting for her the celebrated Madame Novikoff, who was rumored to be a Russian spy and very much interested in promoting better relations between Russia and England. Maud had looked forward to Madame's conversation but today she was untypically dull and Maud noticed that she soon made an obvious excuse to leave.

The next morning Stead arrived in a state of great agitation and accused Maud of having shown his letter to Madame Novikoff. "She repeated the very words I used," he said. Whereupon, being an emotional person, "he buried his head in his arms on the table and cried."

Maud was able to convince him that, while Madame Novikoff was alone in her drawing room, she must have opened the writing case and read the letter. Her action might well have been caused by jealousy, for Stead now revealed that Madame Novikoff, while living in England, had been the first cultivated woman to recognize his talents, had helped him to get his first job on a London paper, had shared his liberal ideas, and had stood by him in the fight that had landed him in jail. It was she who had brought him to Russia and introduced him to influential people at court. It seemed evident that, feeling betrayed by his obvious admiration for Maud, she had tried to make him believe that Maud was mocking his suit.

The talk ended on a more placid note, with Stead expressing his sympathy for Home Rule in Ireland, and his admiration for Michael Davitt, founder of the Land League. Stead thought him a greater man than Parnell, and promised to introduce Maud to him.

Though Maud and Stead met several times in later years, their friendship foundered. Stead helped to destroy Charles Stewart Parnell, when his liaison with a married woman, "Kitty" O'Shea, became known, whereas Maud took the opposite course. She had ample personal reasons, of course, for being tolerant of anyone who infringed on approved sexual behavior.

Maud did not wait for Stead to introduce her to Michael

Davitt. While Davitt was serving as a Home Rule member of Parliament, he was visited by a tall, beautiful, and well-dressed young Englishwoman who told him that she had been distressed by the conduct of Irish landowners, and wanted to know how she could help the situation. Brashly, Maud volunteered her opinion that whatever the Irish did in retaliation for their treatment by England should not be considered a crime, but an act of war, and perfectly justifiable. Was it not vital that foreigners should be made to understand this? She knew quite a few important people in France and Russia whom she might influence.

Davitt disagreed. He thought burnings and assassinations were only delaying the passage of a Home Rule bill. The most useful work she could perform among her foreign friends was to dispel the English propaganda that identified the Irish Party with crime and outrages. He gave her a ticket to the gallery so that she could watch the debates, and wrote her off as an obvious English *agent-provocateur*. (He told her this later, after they had become friends.)

Michael Davitt is one of the most admirable figures in the entire history of Irish rebellion. He was a thoroughgoing democrat, as energetic in fighting for women's rights, free public education, trade unionism, and the end of Jewish pogroms in Russia as he was in fighting for Irish national freedom and land reform. Unlike most of the earlier patriots he was free of the whiff of the Big House and Trinity College, for he was the son of Roman Catholic peasants who had been evicted from their County Mayo farm when Michael was five. At nine, while working in a cotton mill in industrial Lancashire, he lost an arm. Some Methodists in the area who became aware of this gave him shelter, food, and the beginnings of an education in a local Wesleyan school.

At fifteen Davitt became a bookkeeper in a printing shop, and soon after joined the Fenian movement. At twenty-four he was convicted of participating in a plot to raid a jail and seize its store of arms and ammunition. The next seven years he spent in English prisons picking oakum and breaking up granite blocks, with no concession being made for his lack of an arm.

Davitt emerged from prison with a new idea: that the Irish masses would rally around the cause of national freedom only if they believed it would guarantee them permanent possession of the farms they tilled. In 1879 he founded the Irish National Land League, which sought in the short run, to keep tenants from paying excessive rents and being unjustly evicted, and, in the long run, to make them owners of their farms. The League gave food and shelter to ousted families, organized demonstrations against evictions, and mobilized public opinion against any man who dared to take a farm which another had been forced to leave. It sought to give the peasantry not only protection but self-respect. The movement grew swiftly. Within a year after the League was founded it had 200,000 members and a thousand branches.

Charles Stewart Parnell was persuaded by Davitt to accept the presidency of the organization. But he could not embrace with any real warmth the collection of "communists, Garibaldians, atheists, and criminal conspirators" who reputedly made up its membership. A landlord himself, he disliked "the vague, half-militant, half-utopian tone of Davitt's language," and slowly the alliance between the two dissolved.

Maud's reason for visiting the British Isles in 1886 was not just to meet Davitt, nor was. it entirely political. She wanted to see some relatives in England, and to visit in Ireland her childhood friend Ida Jameson at Airfield, the luxurious Jameson home outside Dublin. Youngest of a large and noted liquor-distilling family and the only one still single, Ida had some "curious psychic faculties" that had been the basis for her friendship with Maud when both their families lived in Donnybrook.

In the rose garden at Airfield, Maud told Ida about her

new passion for freeing Ireland from English rule, and about her disappointing interview with Michael Davitt. Though Ida's family, like most Protestants, were unionists, dedicated to maintaining the bond with England, Ida promptly became an ally. She sealed their alliance by having two gold rings made with the word Eire engraved on them; the girls pledged themselves to wear them for the rest of their lives.

Ida did more. Without her family's knowledge, she arranged for them to have tea the next day with a student at Trinity, Charles Hubert Oldham, who, in that bastion of unionists, was suspected of being a dedicated Home Ruler. This was the first step that led to Maud's association with the movement to revive the literature, language, mythology, music, and sports of the ancient Celtic civilization and build upon them a viable Irish nation and culture.

Oldham was not only a Home Ruler but a staunch believer in the right and even the duty of intelligent women to participate in public affairs. He realized that their participation would also add to the aesthetic background of such affairs. After seeing Maud at tea a few times, he invited her to a meeting of the Contemporary Club, of which he was secretary and where he promised she would meet the famous separatist, John O'Leary. Oldham introduced Maud in this fashion: "Maud Gonne wants to meet John O'Leary. I thought you would all like to meet Maud Gonne."

Maud liked the cozy club rooms overlooking College Green, but suspected that the dozen men comfortably smoking and drinking tea would have preferred not to admit women. However, when a "tall, thin, strikingly handsome old man" rose from an armchair by the fire, with a puzzled frown on his face, and took her hands, she was sufficiently composed to say the right thing: "Mr. O'Leary, I have heard so much about you; you are the leader of revolutionary Ireland. I want to work for Ireland, I want you to show me how." Or so Maud alleges.

That evening Maud met several Irishmen who later be-

came famous as founders of the Celtic Revival. She also
learned something about the divisions that existed between
well-intentioned Irishmen. She was surprised to hear
O'Leary denounce the Land League and pour scorn on
the Irish parliamentary leaders, John Dillon and William
O'Brien, while Oldham vigorously defended them.

In the early hours of the morning, O'Leary and Oldham,
who later hung pictures of Maud all around the club walls,
took her back to Airfield. She was proud that they had
invited her to return to the club whenever she was in Dublin and that O'Leary had asked her to have tea with him and
his sister the following day.

O'Leary looked much older than his fifty-eight years.
His hair had turned white when he was sentenced in 1865,
the year Maud was born, to a twenty-year term in Portland
prison in England for alleged acts of terrorism. His real
crime had been to work for a Fenian publication, *The Irish
People*. After serving nine years, often in the prison's lime-
stone quarries, he was sent into exile, and spent the next
decade in Paris, returning to Ireland in 1885. To some
Celtic Revivalists, he seemed the very embodiment of militant, oppressed Ireland with his massive head, luminous
dark eyes, strong features, and white beard.

O'Leary was always on the lookout for recruits that could
form an intellectual backing for the separatist movement. In
1886 he observed that "one of the many misfortunes of
Ireland is that she has never yet produced a great poet. Let
us hope that God has in store for us that great gift." Not
long afterward, he found one—William Butler Yeats, who
was destined to play so great a part in Maud's life.

O'Leary soon discovered over the teacups that Maud was
not an intellectual, but since she was young and he was
hopeful, he took her education in hand, urging her to read
the new books of Celtic mythology and translated Gaelic
poetry that were being published, and lending her some
literature from the Young Ireland period of the 1840s.

Maud was impressed by the number of books in his room, carefully arranged and dusted, and by his gentle, self-effacing sister Ellen, "a charming little lady with the same aquiline features as her brother, only much softer; she was dressed in very unfashionable clothes which suited her."

When Maud learned from John O'Leary that Ellen had written some poems, she and Oldham subsidized the publication of a book of them. It was one of Maud's numerous but unpublicized good deeds; she much preferred to publicize her adventures. Ellen had the pleasure of holding in her hands the proofs of *Lays of Country, Home and Friends,* published in 1890, before her tragic death from cancer.

Maud saw a great deal of O'Leary and his friends, though her attempts to draw some of her unionist friends into his fold proved unavailing. She herself was not yet ready to relinquish other activities. Pursuing an earlier dream, she visited the City of Dublin Hospital and there began to learn the rudiments of nursing. Its matron, Miss Beresford, who shared her belief that every woman should have such information, allowed Maud to accompany her on ward visits and to lend an occasional hand.

In this way, Maud learned the extent of the hospital's financial problems and, recruiting Ida Jameson and Oldham, she organized a benefit concert. Though the idea was conventional, the execution was not. The three young people decided that music and poems by Irish authors only should be performed. This meant, among other things, that "Let Erin Remember" would replace "God Save the Queen."

The concert was a sell-out and a great success. Many of Maud's old friends from Dublin Castle were present, and her new friends from the Contemporary Club as well. Ida Jameson sang Irish ballads and rebel songs; Maud recited "The Banshee and Dark Rosaleen" by John Todhunter, a well-to-do doctor turned poet and playwright, and ended up with rebel poems. Though there was some indignant comment on the omission of "God Save the Queen," the press reports in general were favorable.

Other "engagements" followed. One was at a meeting of the Celtic Literary Society, a club that pleased Maud so much that she applied for membership. With some embarrassment young Willie Rooney, co-founder of the club with Arthur Griffith, explained that its rules forbade the admission of women.

Soon afterward she received the same answer from the Irish National League, whose offices were directly across the street from the Gresham Hotel, where she had moved from Airfield. In October 1886 the National League had launched a "Plan of Campaign" designed to lower rents for tenant farmers. It was far too new and complex a movement for Maud to understand; but since the organization had the word "national" in it, she felt impelled to visit the office and ask for membership. She was promptly rebuffed, but the following day was visited by the League's able, weather-beaten secretary, Timothy Harrington, accompanied by small, affable Patrick O'Brien, Member of Parliament, and T. P. Gill, "pale and lanky, a typical clerk."

The visitors first warned Maud that the Gresham was honeycombed with spies working as waiters and chambermaids. Maud said she had her own reasons for disliking the hotel, that "it was full of priests and men from the country talking loudly and eating and drinking more than was seemly, and of obsequious waiters and chambermaids. . . ." They told her that she, an Englishwoman, was an "object of much speculation on both sides," that they themselves did not believe that she was a British spy, but that they could not go against the provision in the League's constitution that barred women from membership. They listened amiably while she argued that Ireland needed her women for the work to be done. Tim Harrington replied with a proposition. There was plenty of work that she could do, he said. She could visit Donegal and publicize the evictions that were taking place. At the very least, her presence would raise the tenants' morale. He promised to give her letters of introduction to the Bishop of Raphoe and to priests through whose parishes she would be passing.

Pleased with the idea, Maud sent a long telegram to her first cousin, May Gonne, who had just passed her nursing examination, asking her to join her on a tour of the west. While waiting for her to arrive, Maud chose horses for the trip at a livery stable, selected a driver, and set up lodgings in a temperance hotel near Trinity College. Maud particularly appreciated its proximity to the National Library, where she could write letters and, when the time came, speeches and articles. Some of her companions in the attempt to revive national culture found her rooms, where there was always tea and coffee, a handy place for visiting after the library was closed, "for we all kept late hours in Dublin in those days, and . . . our talk was the wine on which we used to get satisfactorily drunk. . . . Many now famous poems and plays had their first reading in those rooms in Nassau Street, and many plots were hatched in them, plots for plays and plots for real life."

Dublin Castle, ever watchful, took note of this activity, became uneasy, and assigned two plainclothes men from the G Division of the Dublin Metropolitan Police to keep watch at the door. In her autobiography Maud referred to these men frequently, giving some people the impression that she coined the term "G men." Filled with youthful high spirits, she took great pleasure in making them miserable. At her direction, the fourteen-year-old lad who did odd jobs for the tenants of the Nassau Temperance Hotel repeatedly placed two camp stools on the sidewalk to indicate to the detectives that their mission was known. Once, in exasperation, they carried away the stools, whereupon Maud sent a letter to Dublin Castle requesting their return; the intention, she wrote, was to rent them to the Crown, not to donate them.

When the men were trailing her, she would suddenly hail the only available carriage and give them the slip. At other times she would direct her "jarvey" to go full speed, as if she were trying to lose them, but check the speed when it seemed likely that the detectives were being left behind. The senseless pursuit would conclude at the Gresham or the Shelbourne Hotel, where Irish conspirators were not likely to enter.

Once, when the police trailed her from counter to counter in a large department store, she informed a clerk that the gentlemen were making "unwelcome advances." At another time she entered a section devoted to the selling of "women's intimate apparel" and forced them either to depart or spend their time in the unlikely occupation of reading the advertisement for Erect Form corsets—"not only the most stylish of corsets, but their hygienic construction places the strain on the muscles of the hips and back, where they are most capable of bearing it."

Visiting County Donegal and other parts of the poverty-stricken west was a rich educational experience for Maud. For the first time she saw what farm homes were like, how ugly rural villages could be, how justice was administered, how tenants were evicted. She acquired some comprehension of the structure of the Irish Catholic Church and of the nature of individual priests.

The first person of importance the Gonne cousins met was the Bishop of Raphoe, the Most Reverend Doctor O'Donnell, the youngest and handsomest bishop in Ireland. He invited them to dinner, and since a diocesan conference was concluding, the girls had the odd experience of dining with ten priests. Maud was impressed by the simplicity of the arrangements, and by the fact that the bishop's sister helped the maid to serve. She was also grateful to the clerics for providing her with the names of inns, and sometimes farmhouses, where they could stay most comfortably. She thought them very kind and helpful to two young heretics. "I had not joined the Catholic

Church then," she wrote in her autobiography, "but I was never made to feel the difference; there is no intolerance or bigotry naturally in Irish people, it is only when politics succeed in exploiting religion that this devastating influence comes in. . . ."

Some of the priests had been educated at Le Collège Irlandais in Paris and enjoyed talking with her about France. When the subject of evictions came up, awkward mention was made of a Father McFadden of Gweedore, who had recently been released from jail following the murder by his infuriated congregation of a district inspector who had come to his church on Sunday to arrest him. A Father Peter Kelly was also mentioned, and one of the priests told Maud quietly but significantly, that she must see him when she passed through Dunfanaghy.

But most of the priests, Maud sensed, were upholders of law and order, supporters of the Irish Parliamentary Party in its peaceful struggle for Home Rule, and believers in the idea that peasants faced with eviction had no recourse. They could at least take a shot at the landlords, Maud thought. She dared not say the words and felt like a coward for not saying them.

The following morning was bright and sunny. The horses and Dagda, Maud's huge dog and inseparable companion, were in fine spirits as they started the run toward the coast of County Donegal. But as the party came near the ocean, a cold, heavy rain began to fall, and Dagda began to lag because the sharp stones were cutting his feet. Later Maud would have a cobbler make boots for him to wear on long journeys but now it was necessary to reduce speed and the cousins were almost frozen by the time their driver pulled up before Father Kelly's parish house in Dunfanaghy. The priest gave the girls a warm welcome, bringing them stiff drinks of rum and hot water, and insisting that Maud, who always looked deceptively frail, must sit in his own armchair by the fire.

Father Kelly knew John O'Leary and was an outspoken

sympathizer with the militant movement. As a priest, he could not shoulder a gun, but he supported the Land League, had little faith in the Irish parliamentarians, and considered it hypocritical to encourage peasants to refuse rent payments and eviction without arming themselves. He wanted the Irish people to organize and be ready to fight for a free Ireland whatever the consequences. To do that they needed weapons more powerful than boiling water and stones. Father McFadden, in nearby Gweedore, was equally patriotic but his ideas were different. He supported both the Irish Parliamentary Party and the merits of fighting bailiffs and soldiers with boiling water, sticks, and stones. He gave Colonel Olpherts, who owned most of the land in the area, a great deal of trouble.

On the following day, Father McFadden's curate, Father Stephens, a tall, thin young man with dark, anxious eyes, took the Gonnes to see how justice was administered in County Donegal. Some of his parishioners were being tried for stealing turf. The girls trudged through mud and dung from their hotel to the courthouse with Father Stephens clearing the way through a crowd of women in shawls and men in ragged frieze coats. The judge, a florid military type, was wearing tweeds and leggings. The accused were six men and boys, their rough fair hair and gray eyes contrasting with their thin, weather-beaten faces. The witness, "a foxy-looking gentleman in riding breeches," testified that he had seen them on Colonel Olpherts's mountain cutting turf and carrying it away in creels on their backs.

Maud and Father Stephens spoke in whispers. Who is the magistrate? "Colonel Olpherts." Who is the witness? "His agent. Olpherts is both judge and plaintiff." Will they be convicted? "Probably. They have no turf on their holdings and must get some to keep their families alive. Last week another group of men went to jail for gathering seaweed for fertilizer. All the seashore belongs to Olpherts; there is nothing free in Ireland but the air."

Maud thought of Dean Swift's words when he heard an English lady remark on the sweetness of the Irish air: "Madam, for God's sake don't say that or the English will tax it."

Father Stephens was proved right when the judge ordered the accused to pay the value of the turf and a fine of 10 shillings each. If they did not pay within a month, they would spend a month in prison. The accused men did not testify, since they knew no English; a policeman had to tell them the sentence in Gaelic.

Maud returned to the same area a bit later, having been invited by Father McFadden to witness some unusually large evictions. Over 150 decrees had been issued, which meant a thousand people would be homeless, many of whom would end up in workhouses. While she was sitting in Father Stephens's little parlor, Maud was told in a whisper that the evictions scheduled for the following day would not take place, that someone had obtained some noxious cow medicine from the veterinarian and put enough of it in the bailiff's drink to kill him. The information proved wrong. Though the bailiff seemed shaky, he did appear; a half-dozen homes were broken into with a battering ram, and the occupants placed, with their meager possessions, on the roadside. At one cottage, a woman with a one-day-old baby was carried out on a mattress, followed by a number of crying children and a white-faced man.

Father Stephens asked the woman if she had any place where she could stay.

She shook her head. "Anyone who takes us in will be evicted himself."

"But won't someone in the village give you shelter?"

"Falcarragh belongs to Olpherts too: they dare not."

At that, Maud turned to Father Stephens and told him to take a room for the woman at her hotel and in her name. This at least Olpherts could not prevent. Then she headed back to Dublin, disappointed that the bailiff had not died,

and convinced that "if I could have done anything to contribute to his death I would have done so and would have
felt I was committing no sin, since he was an essential cog
in the British war machine . . . it is the English who forced
war on us, and the principle of war is to kill the enemy."

Back in Dublin she found a better remedy for Ireland's
ills than praying for the death of a bailiff. She went to work
with Patrick O'Brien helping him to raise more of his Land
League huts for evicted families. Representing the effort of
an entire countryside, these huts were put up by boys and
girls who collected stones for the walls, farmers who
supplied straw for the thatch, skilled thatchers and masons
who worked without pay—as all did. And when a group of
huts were finished, a barrel of porter, home-made cakes, a
local fiddler, and blazing turf torches accompanied the
grandest housewarmings that Maud had ever attended.

Eithne Coyle O'Donnell, whose parents were among
those evicted in County Donegal in the black year of 1886,
remembers what they told her about Maud's repeated
visits. Maud Gonne, they said, "who dazzled everyone by
her beauty, charm, and humility," had given what money
she could spare to the evicted women with young children,
to buy food; had also collected clothes from her friends in
Dublin to cover the half-naked children who had no place
to go except the workhouse. Most of the time, they told
Eithne, "this noble-hearted woman" had come on horseback, sometimes she had got a lift on the local mail cart.

Later Maud asserted that every tenant she had advised to
join the Land League and refuse to pay exorbitant rent had
eventually been reinstated on his land. But she readily admitted that she had been dealing only with individual cases
where the landlords were weak, working only as a freelance on the fringe of a mighty movement. She had acted so
cautiously, she wrote, because of advice she had received
from Father Peter Kelly about the futility of unarmed resis-

tance and because of her woman's inherent sense of responsibility.

Maud would not have been surprised, perhaps, to hear
that she would go far as a revolutionary. But the future also
held a role for her—probably her most famous—of which
as yet she had no inkling. Her meeting with William Butler
Yeats was waiting in the wings.

To Maud that first meeting was a minor event; even had
she not already been taken up heart, body, and soul with
Lucien Millevoye, it would have meant only a rather insignificant addition to her expanding Irish circle. The important events of 1889 were her sister's wedding and the need
to sustain Millevoye when his idol, General Boulanger,
turned out to be a man of straw.

She would live long enough to understand that in the
world of literature the liaison of Maud Gonne and Lucien
Millevoye is of no importance when contrasted with the
unconsummated love of Maud Gonne and Willie Yeats.
She would accept the disparity. Yet there is little doubt
that, in her heart, she considered this ironic, and felt that
Willie, compared to Lucien, was a dolt.

CHAPTER IV

"When the Troubling of My Life Began"

To WILLIAM BUTLER YEATS, 1889 would always be the fateful year when he met Maud Gonne and "the troubling of my life began."

Yeats, whose parents had moved to London from Dublin in 1887, was then living with them at 3 Blenheim Road, in Bedford Park, a community of scholars, writers, and artists. Maud came there bearing a letter of introduction from John and Ellen O'Leary to John Butler Yeats, Willie's father, but his sister Elizabeth knew better. She wrote in her diary for January 30, 1889:

Miss Gonne, the Dublin beauty (who is marching on to glory over the hearts of the Dublin youths), called to-day on Willie, of course, but also apparently on Papa. She is immensely tall and very stylish and well dressed in a careless way. She came in a hansom all the way from Belgravia and kept the hansom waiting while she was here. Lily noticed that she was in her slippers.

On the evening of the following day, January 31, Yeats dined with Maud, her sister Kathleen, and an unnamed male cousin. The next day he wrote John O'Leary:

She is not only very handsome but very clever. Though her politics in European matters be a little sensational. . . . It was pleasant however to hear her attacking a young military man from India who was there, on

English rule in India.* She is very Irish, a kind of "Diana of the Crossways." Her pet monkey was making, much of the time, little melancholy cries at the hearthrug.... It was you, was it not, who converted Miss Gonne to her Irish opinions. She herself will make many converts.

On February 3 he wrote Ellen O'Leary, "Did I tell you how much I admire Maud Gonne? . . . If she said the world was flat or the moon an old caubeen tossed up into the sky I would be proud to be of her party."

More than twenty-five years later, Yeats wrote movingly about that fateful first meeting:

I was twenty-three years old when the troubling of my life began. I had heard from time to time in letters from Miss O'Leary, John O'Leary's old sister, of a beautiful girl who had left the society of the Viceregal Court for Dublin nationalism. In after years I persuaded myself that I felt premonitory excitement at the first reading of her name. Presently she drove up to our house in Bedford Park.... I had never thought to see in a living woman so great beauty. It belonged to famous pictures, to poetry, to some legendary past. A complexion like the blossom of apples, and yet face and body had the beauty of lineaments which Blake calls the highest beauty because it changes least from youth to age, and a stature so great that she seemed of a divine race. Her movements were worthy of her form, and I understood at last why the poet of antiquity, where we would but speak of face and form, sings, loving some lady, that she paces like a goddess.

He remembered little of her speech that day except that her words in praise of war vexed his father. The emotion remained. He felt that she had brought into his life "a

*Probably Maud's cousin Captain Edward Gonne. He subsequently became radical enough to favor women's right to vote. He once rebuked a fellow officer for striking a suffragette demonstrator with his sword. In November 1910 he gave directions to Mrs. James Cousins and other suffragettes on how to reach 10 Downing Street so that they might break some windows there. On another occasion he received "a severe spinal injury" when he was pushed off a platform while addressing a suffragette gathering. See Mary R. Richardson, *Laugh a Defiance*, p. 134.

sound as of a Burmese gong, an overpowering tumult that yet had many pleasant secondary notes."

He saw Maud on every one of the nine days she was in London. He never forgot the first dinner he had with her in her rooms in Ebury Street. She seemed:

so exuberant in her ways that it seemed natural she should give her hours in overflowing abundance . . . that she should give and take without stint. She lived surrounded by cages of innumerable singing birds, and with these she always travelled . . . and they and she were now returning to Paris where their home was.

They discussed many subjects during their early meetings. Maud spoke of her wish to find a play in which she might appear in Dublin. Yeats offered to write one for her based on an Irish tale he had recently read. The play when he wrote it was *The Countess Cathleen*.

When he noticed a book by Algernon Swinburne that contained a tribute to Victor Hugo, he felt impelled to confess his dream of becoming an Irish Hugo. He sensed early that, to make an impression on her, he would somehow have to become a public figure, "for her beauty . . . seemed incompatible with private, intimate life."

He discovered that Maud, like himself, had been drawn to the concept of a revived Irish nation and culture by the tutelage of John O'Leary. Then they spoke of the refusal of Nationalist leader William O'Brien to accept prison clothes during his term in jail, and of his making what he considered a political protest by going about naked. Yeats was amused, and perhaps a little shocked, when Maud said, "There was a time when men sacrificed their lives for their country, but now they sacrifice their dignity."

Not wanting to be thought too impressionable, Yeats tried for a time to conceal his infatuation from his friend Katharine Tynan, a woman he looked up to because she was four years older than he and her reputation as a poet was much greater. "Who told you that I am taken up with

Miss Gonne?" he wrote Katharine in March 1889. "I think she is very goodlooking and that is all I think about her. What you say of her fondness for sensation is probably true. I sympathise with her love of the national idea rather than any secondary land movement, but care not much for the kind of Red Indian feathers in which she has trapped out that idea."

Yeats added that Maud reminded him of his cousin and first beloved, Laura Armstrong, the girl who had awakened him from "the metallic sleep of science and set me writing my first play.... She interests me far more than Miss Gonne does."

In his recollections, Yeats thought that there was, even at their first meetings, something in Maud's manner that was declamatory, "Latin in a bad sense," and possibly unscrupulous. She seemed to desire power for its own sake, to win elections for the sake of winning. Her goals were unselfish, he recalled, but, unlike the Indian sage who said, "Only the means can justify the end," Maud was ready to adopt any means that promised to be successful.

He made two observations, which doubtless owe something to discoveries he made as their relationship progressed:

We were seeking different things: she, some memorable action for final consecration of her youth, and I, after all, but to discover and communicate a state of being.... Her two and twenty years had taken some color, I thought, from French Boulangist adventurers and journalist *arrivistes* of whom she had seen too much.

Yeats remembered Maud Gonne as the herald of the movement to revive Celtic culture. "I have seen the enchanted day/And heard the morning bugles blow," he wrote in his manuscript book. At the same time he regretted that her involvement in so much activity had kept her from studying the "spiritual philosophy" which seemed all-important to him. "What would I not have given," he wrote, "that she might think exactly right on all those great questions of the day?" But often his memory of their differences would vanish as he recalled Maud's appearance "when she passed before a window, dressed in white, and rearranged a spray of flowers in a vase." The impression is preserved in his poem "The Arrow," where he calls Maud's beauty something lodged like an arrow in his bones. "The Arrow" is one of hundreds of poems, stanzas, lines, and phrases, contained in ten volumes of Yeats's poetry, that refer to Maud Gonne. They do much more than laud her beauty. They celebrate Maud's nature and personality, and attempt to explain his obsession with her to himself and to others. The same subject appears in much of his prose. Here is an example of his musings which comes closer to the solution than most.

I felt in the presence of a great generosity and courage, and of a mind without peace, and when she and all her singing birds had gone my melancholy was not the mere melancholy of love. I had . . . an obvious deduction of an awaiting immediate disaster. . . . I was in love but had not spoken of love and never meant to speak, and as the months passed I grew master of myself again. "What wife could she make," I thought, "what share could she have in the life of a student?"

He did want her for his wife, of course, and the significant words here are Maud's "great generosity and courage," not his melancholy nor his premonition of disaster. From the beginning Yeats was deeply impressed by Maud's self-confidence, assurance, candor, and the conditions which produced them—inherited wealth and social position. They go far to explain her initial impact and lasting effect upon him. However fluent and confident Yeats was in his own world of literature, in every other kind of world he felt ill at ease, and inferior. He came of the same stock as Maud, the landed Anglican breed that had conquered Ireland several centuries earlier, and could thus claim social superiority over all Catholics. Among their own kind, however, the Yeatses were undistinguished, being mainly farmers, merchants, and rectors, and the current family fortunes were low indeed.

As Yeats's pursuit of Maud continued year after year, some of his friends and acquaintances criticized her for keeping him on a string when it was quite apparent that she did not intend to marry him. They found it distressing that, whenever he seemed interested in some other woman, he would get a note from Maud asking him to meet her in Dublin, London, or Paris—and the tentative affair would collapse. It seems evident that Maud did not act in this way from any "feminine" desire to keep him dangling; she acted carelessly and thoughtlessly, the way one might act toward a person one never expected to marry.

It is characteristic of their relationship that Maud could never remember when and where she first met Yeats. In her autobiography she never mentions her visit to Bedford Park, but gives the impression that she first met him at the O'Learys' in Dublin, that he read some of his poetry that day and helped her to carry away some of the books she borrowed.

She could not even remember the difference in their ages. Toward the very end, when she was eighty, she said on a BBC radio program that she was twenty and Yeats was twenty-one when they first met; "he was extremely proud of that one year's seniority." Actually, she had just turned twenty-three and Yeats was only six months older.

The simple fact is that Yeats was far from impressive at the time, and would have seemed inconsequential to almost anybody. He *was* inconsequential. Only a prophet could have guessed that some day he would amount to something.

In the first place, he looked odd. Maud saw him as "a tall lanky boy with deep-set dark eyes behind glasses, over which a lock of dark hair was constantly falling, to be pushed back impatiently by long sensitive fingers, often stained with paint—dressed in shabby clothes. . . ." To most people he seemed nothing more than a gangling, swarthy, painfully thin scarecrow, wearing a ridiculous pointed beard which he removed soon after meeting Maud.

His consuming passions were for poetry, of the kind written by William Morris, and the concepts of the three mystical B's—Blake the Englishman, Boehme the German, and Blavatsky the Russian. A former art student, he painted the signs of the zodiac on the ceiling of his room. Yeats talked about his career as a poet, but there was no indication that he would ever make a living from it. He almost didn't; he did not become self-supporting until he was forty-five.

In a flowing cloak and in all kinds of weather he went about the streets chanting poetry and gesticulating. Inordinately absent-minded, he consumed food in enormous gulps, without knowing what he was eating. He was the kind of person who, while waiting for a bus with Katharine Tynan in a drenching rain, held his umbrella over her "at an acute and absent-minded angle which could shelter nobody, pouring the while into my ears *The Sensitive Plant*. It was a moment to try any woman's temper. . . ."

Willie was raw, underdeveloped, uncertain and shy, a victim of repressed sexuality. He would listen with envy to Edward Ellis, his collaborator on a book about William Blake, telling about his sexual adventures, but could not rid himself of the ideal of poetic love garnered from the Romantics. He wrote in his journal, "Perhaps I should never marry in church, but I would love one woman all my life." It turned out to be a fair prediction.

Yeats's family was not one to foster self-confidence. The father was a struggling portrait painter, the mother was going mad. Ernest Rhys, a clever young Welshman who once visited the family at Bedford Park, wrote later that the two sisters were "delightful," that the father was "a vehement eloquent Irishman, hot on politics . . . but of all the household, it was the mother with her strange dark eyes who seemed nearest in mould to her unaccountable eldest son. . . . As he once said: 'I use all my great will power to keep me from reading the newspapers and spoiling my vocabulary.'"

In quoting these words, Rhys hit precisely on one of the principal reasons why Yeats eventually became a great poet; he believed that writing poetry was the most important thing a man could do, and worked at it unflaggingly.

Almost anybody must have seemed to Maud Gonne a more appropriate suitor and companion than Yeats—for instance, Douglas Hyde, the son of a Protestant minister with whom she was becoming acquainted at the same time. Five years older than Yeats, he was already a recognized expert on Gaelic language and literature, had won an astonishing assortment of Trinity College awards for both verse and prose, and in 1888, some months before meeting Maud, had taken first place in the doctor of laws examination.

Hyde's future fame, unlike Yeats's, was predictable. In 1893, with a few others, he would found the Gaelic League, which encouraged thousands to study ancient Irish, and was considered by Padraic Pearse, leader of the 1916 Easter Rising, "the most revolutionary influence that has ever come into Ireland." Hyde was president of the Gaelic League for twenty-two years; served for twenty years as professor of modern Irish at Dublin's University College, and in 1938 became first president of the independent Irish Republic.

When the young Hyde met Maud on the evening of December 16, 1888, he wrote in his diary: "To Sigersons in the evening where I saw the most dazzling woman I have ever seen: Miss Gonne, who drew every male in the room around her. . . . We stayed talking until 1:30 A.M. My head was spinning with her beauty!"

Six weeks later, just after she first met Yeats, Hyde began to give Maud lessons in Irish. "I stayed for lunch with her and we toasted cheese together by the fire. We talked about all sorts of things. . . . We did not do much Irish."

At the second lesson they lunched on omelets that they "had made together at the fire," and had a "long talk." The same program was followed on February 11 and 13. On the evening of the 13th Hyde also went with Maud to a meeting of the Theosophical Society and they drove home in a cab. On February 18, "I stayed for a couple of hours but we did not do much Irish." On March 13, "She was very cordial and made me a present of her portrait." On March 21 he saw Maud three times, the third at a meeting of the Pan-Celtic Society, a small, short-lived group of writers (Yeats was one) who were trying to produce literature that, though written in English, was inspired by the Irish past.

All of these meetings were unchaperoned and they pe-tered out within two months. Both circumstances were typical. Referring to the second, Katharine Tynan wrote: "At first every man on whom she looked was in love with her... the heads of all my male friends, young and old, were flustered by her beauty and grace. But they soon got over it. . . . Her aloofness must have chilled the most ardent lover." The reason, Miss Tynan thought, was Maud's consuming passion for Ireland, which led her to consider people only as "pawns in the revolutionary game," a treatment they would not long accept. The real reason has been indicated: in every way that counted, Maud was already married.

If Maud Gonne seemed to be absorbed by European events during her historic first meeting with Yeats at Bedford Park, she had every reason to be. Three days before, General Boulanger had won a seat in the House of Deputies. It had been a smashing victory; that evening thousands of monarchists, militarists, tradesmen, students, the discontented of all classes, had poured into the streets of Paris and waited for the signal to seize the key government buildings. But the man on the white horse would not spur his steed, preferring to dine at the Durand Restaurant with his intimate followers and his mistress, the Vicomtesse Marguerite Bonnemains. Finally having consulted her, he announced his decision: "Why should I seize power by illegal means when I can be sure of getting it six months from now by the unanimous vote of all France?"

The editor of a Boulangist propaganda organ looked at his watch, and said presciently, "It's five past midnight, gentlemen. For the past five minutes Boulangism has been declining."

The following week General Boulanger and Marguerite went away for a vacation—and his enemies, during the next two months, began to reassemble their forces. On March 29 the Senate authorized a High Court to try the general for plotting against the lawful government of France. On April 6, 1889, General Boulanger's most effective force, the League of Patriots, was dissolved. Three days later the Senate, sitting as a High Court, began its deliberations. Fearing imprisonment and even more the possibility that he would be separated from Marguerite, Boulanger fled with her to Brussels.

From there he issued countless manifestos but they were not convincing without his handsome presence. When on August 8 the High Court found him guilty of conspiring to overthrow the state, the verdict aroused little protest.

In the elections of October 6, 1889, only forty Boulangist candidates won seats in the House of Deputies. Six months later only two Boulangists were elected. On July 16, 1891, Marguerite died. On September 30, Boulanger went out to her grave, sat down with his legs stretched toward the lilacs that grew in front of it, and fired a bullet into his brain. He left instructions that on his tombstone there should be carved the words "How was I able to live 2 1/2 months without you?"

Only then did Lucien Millevoye give up hope that his country could be saved, or that he had reason to remain in politics. At the same time he ranted that he was too old—he was forty-one—to make a fresh start in anything else. Maud fought desperately to restore his spirits and to find ways in which he could still serve the "alliance." She came up with the idea that this could best be done by his accepting an offer to become political editor of *La Patrie*, a small, little-known evening newspaper owned by a merchandising tycoon. The move turned out to be a huge success both for the paper and Lucien's own reputation. His place in politics was assured, though the nation continued to go in a direction he deplored.

About this time Maud gave her first speech, the first of thousands. At the request of Tim Harrington, she had gone to Barrow in Furness, Lancashire, to help the Irish Parliamentary Party win a by-election that was being held there. Barrow was such a Conservative stronghold that the Liberal Party had not even fielded a candidate, a circumstance that made it seem possible that the Irish Party could win by stressing the issues of evictions and Home Rule in the same Irish community where the Michael Davitt family had once lived.

Maud had protested, "That's not the work I want. I know nothing and care less about English elections. It is in Ireland the work must be done. I am going back to Donegal to help O'Brien and Father McFadden build houses."

Harrington told her it would mean only one week's work; that she would not need to speak, only solicit votes house to house. Since she had just come from the evictions, her mere presence would be effective help.

The following morning she left for Liverpool with Harrington. They went directly from the railroad station to a meeting, where Maud was seated on the right hand of an elderly chairman, facing an audience of 1,500. He asked her if she was speaking next. Not knowing he was deaf, she told him that she was not speaking at all.

The next minute she heard the chairman introduce her,

and felt Harrington nudge her to get up. Maud herself tells the rest.

I got up: "Ladies and Gentlemen":—my voice, owing to my stage training, rang out alarmingly clear, then I stopped. "Tell them about the evictions you have seen," prompted Harrington, and I began. . . . I told of the old couple driven out of the house they had built fifty years ago; of the woman with her one-day-old baby left on the roadside, of the little children trying in vain to kindle a fire in the rain; of the desolation of the overcrowded workhouse and the separated families. I forgot where I was and then suddenly . . . I became aware of a dead silence, of thousands of eyes looking at me and my mind a complete blank. I stopped in the middle of a sentence, my knees began to shake and I sat down and began to cry. . . .

Mistaking her stage fright for intensity of emotion, the audience gave her an ovation. Soon there were demands on all sides for the presence of the beautiful "Irish" lady; eventually Maud was speaking at five meetings a day.

She also did some canvassing. Harrington told her that the Salvation Army was strong in the area, that its members generally voted Conservative, and that it would be helpful if she visited the local captain. He was not at home when Maud arrived, but she sat down comfortably at the kitchen table and talked with the mother about the children playing on the floor, about the work of the Salvation Army, and the delights of singing hymns. Maud's ability to converse easily with those who might be considered her social inferiors has often been noted and was unquestionably a strong element in her make-up.

When the Salvation Army captain arrived—"a tall, fair, soldierly man"—he questioned Maud about the causes of the evictions and then commented that there have been some terrible murders in Ireland.

"I wonder there have not been a great many more; crime begets crime," she answered.

"That doesn't justify it."

Looking at the golden-haired baby trying to pull itself up

by clutching its father's leg, Maud said: "If your home were knocked down and you and your wife put into separate wards in a workhouse; if the baby were taken from you and put in another part of the house and so neglected that it fell ill; if you and your wife were barred from seeing it or caring for it until it died, would you not feel like murdering somebody? Because cattle rearing is more profitable than raising children, the landlords of Ireland are destroying homes like yours all through the country."

As the captain's wife said goodbye to Maud on the doorstep, she whispered, "It's all right; they'll vote to stop the evictions."

When the election was over, Harrington told Maud, "You won it for us." Maud replied modestly, "The Salvation Army captain's baby won it."

The English newspapers devoted many columns to the role played in the Barrow elections by a woman of beauty and fashion. Pictures of Maud in court dress, taken by fashionable Dublin photographers, were dug up and published, but in the family only Aunt Mary was happy about the publicity.

Slowly Maud's life was developing an unusual geographical pattern. It consisted of living simultaneously in three different countries—France, where she maintained a home in Paris, England, and (a nation in embryo) Ireland. The pattern endured some twenty years. To it Maud added three lengthy tours of the United States. On the surface, the pattern seemed necessary if she were to be effective in her various causes; a deeper and more private reason was that after 1889 she had to spend time in France with her children.

In England, her center was London. Once, while there, she remembered her promise to some Donegal women that she would try to obtain the release of their husbands or sons who had been jailed for Land League activities or for other proscribed acts. When she brought the cases to the attention of government officials and members of Parliament, they displayed some sympathy for Land League offenders but little for the dynamitards who had tried to blow up the House of Commons and London Bridge. There was a typical "maudgonne" consequence. A graying Liberal, whom Maud tactfully calls Sir John in her autobiography, found her looks so much more interesting than what she said that he insisted on turning the conversation from prisons to romance.

Another Liberal, a young barrister named Morton, was more helpful. A remarkable speaker, he coupled a love of justice with an infatuation for Maud. When the Liberal government came into office, he was able to obtain the release of several Donegal men who had been sentenced to life, and to shorten the terms of some of the others. "His devotion to me lasted some years and I fear it was bad for his career, but I had to encourage it for the sake of the prisoners." This sentence is notable for being one of the few times when Maud confesses that she used her charms to further a political purpose.

In pursuit of her goal, Maud attended, with Yeats, a committee meeting of the Amnesty Association, which sought to liberate Irish political prisoners. The outfit was controlled by the Irish Republican Brotherhood, an organization founded by John O'Mahony in the United States in 1858, but with headquarters in London because in the United States another faction claimed the name. Yeats was already a member of the London IRB, controlled by Dr. Mark Ryan, and Maud Gonne joined it in 1895 or 1896.

At the committee meeting a rebel who had been released from Portland prison described horrible conditions and spoke of twenty-seven forgotten prisoners who had gone ten years without a single visitor. He urged Maud to apply for permits to visit them, and then to publicize their plight.

On Uncle William's best stationery Maud informed the home secretary that she had met the families of some eight prisoners incarcerated in Portland prison and, as a lady of benevolent intentions, desired to bring them news from home. After receiving the permits, she journeyed to Portland with an English journalist. On the way up the hill from the railroad station, they saw gangs of convicts dressed in yellow uniforms stamped with broad black arrows and harnessed like horses to great carts of stones. At the little office inside the prison gate, they were told to sign an official paper that asserted they would not use the visit for any ulterior purpose. (Later, when Maud wrote and spoke about the prison, she was accused of having broken this promise.) She was also told in the office that she would be able to see only seven prisoners, not eight. Later, she learned that the eighth man had gone insane.

Her conversations with the prisoners, conducted under the hostile eyes of armed wardens, went badly. The first prisoner was sullen and suspicious; the second had difficulty in speaking, perhaps because he had been in solitary so long; the third broke into complaints about the loss of his sight in one eye and his fear that the other was infected. When a warden roughly tried to silence him, Maud intervened, promising that she would arrange for an oculist to visit him, and that he would be freed in six months. She told others that they'd be released in two years, three years, or some other period of time.

Maud was stunned and depressed by the experience—the cold, black cells, the grim faces of the guards, the stern rules. As she sat wearily in the train on the return to London, her companion asked her if she hadn't done a dreadful thing by promising some of the men that they would be released within a specified period. "It's cruel," he said, "to raise hopes that can't be realized."

"Did I do that?" Maud said. "I don't remember, but if I did, they will be released. Something spoke through me, something stronger than myself."

Needless to say, the spirits did not play her false.

There were more relaxing moments in London when Maud would visit relatives, art museums, plays, and concerts.

She stayed now with her sister Kathleen, who had continued a family tradition by marrying an army officer—Captain Thomas David Pilcher. Maud approved of the marriage. Her dislike of the British military had not yet crystallized; she was genuinely fond of her younger sister, whose youthful battles she had often fought, and wanted her to be happy. In her autobiography, however, Maud does not mention the marriage and refers to Captain Pilcher only once—as a person whom she disliked that she once saw in a dream.

When Maud left London for Dublin or Paris, Yeats always insisted on accompanying her to the railroad station. (O'Leary, knowing this, wrote him a fatherly admonition, "I hope you are not paying for the hansoms." Yeats replied that his friend always insisted on paying her share.) They presented a curious sight—the tall, gangling poet with his long hair supervising the transport of Maud's paraphernalia beneath the high sooty arch of Victoria Station; and Maud, tall as he, wearing expensive Parisian clothes that swirled with her long strides and expansive gestures. The bird cages alone were enough to draw attention. Once Yeats carried a full-grown Donegal hawk into her compartment.

In Dublin, thanks to her many nationalist friends, Maud had various opportunities for relaxation. When Yeats was there, she often walked with him in the mountains while he talked about a book he was preparing that would contain translations from Gaelic works, call attention to the talents of Douglas Hyde, Ellen O'Leary, and Rose Kavanagh, predict the revival of Irish culture, and assert, "There is no fine literature without nationality." In a letter to a would-be poet, Yeats expressed the practical side to this involvement with the coming Celtic wave: "It helps originality—and makes one's verses sincere, and gives one less numerous competitors. . . ."

Maud used Dublin as her point of departure for the west of Ireland, where by this time, many persons considered her the reincarnation of a legendary Celtic goddess, mounted on a white horse and surrounded by birds, who had once ridden into a beleaguered Donegal and brought it victory. The local officials were also impressed, but more by her Protestant Ascendancy manner and clothes than by any mystical powers she possessed. Once she happened on a group of the emergency police who were waiting for a police car with four prisoners in tow. Maud high-handedly told the sergeant in charge that he had obviously made a stupid mistake; these were good honest lads, she said, and told them to take off. The prisoners did so without a finger being raised to stop them.

During this same visit, on the night before Maud left for Dublin, she sat upright in her little bedroom in a farmhouse fighting for breath and coughing up streaks of blood. She told no one, for it would not do for the Triumphant One to display human frailties. On the trip back, while staying overnight at another farmhouse she received an unexpected visitor—Sir John. The distinguished member of Parliament had considered everything carefully, weighed her awkward interest in political prisoners against his need for a wife that would do him justice, and tracked her down to this lonesome spot in order to insist that she marry him. Tempestuously he argued that Maud could do more for the Irish as hostess of a great Liberal salon in London than by wasting her time in the bogs of this impossible country. He clinched his argument by presenting her with a diamond pendant. When he learned that Maud turned it over to a woman who was facing eviction, Sir John went to the woman's cottage, purchased the pendant for the exact amount of her debts, and departed once and for all. Another legend was born—

about a woman who scattered jewels that prevented evictions.

There was another delay when a mail cart arrived with an urgent letter from Lucien Millevoye. He wrote that he had come to Ireland to see what she was up to and why she was delaying her return to France; he had landed in Belfast, had ridden through Londonderry and Donegal; had fallen ill in an obscure village with an unpronounceable name, and needed help. Maud was "surprised and rather annoyed. I didn't like being followed, even by a great friend, without being consulted. . . ." Yet he was ill and alone, so she left at once for Dunfanaghy.

It was dark when Maud arrived. She was relieved to find Father Kelly in Millevoye's room, acting as translator in that Gaelic-speaking area since both knew Latin. Lucien, propped up in a bed that was much too short for him, was running a high temperature; the doctor told Maud that he had just escaped pneumonia. During the week that she spent nursing him, they quarreled a great deal, Lucien arguing that her attempt to reinstate Donegal peasants in their homes was only a side issue in their alliance; that she would be far more useful to their great aims back in France, stirring up indignation and obtaining financial and political support for Irish rebellion. Maud counterargued that he was seeking to subordinate her plans to his. They went back to Dublin separately, he to take a boat to France, she to get medical attention.

Her cough was troublesome, and once her doctor stayed up all night with her. But when she heard that the emergency police had departed from Falcarragh, she returned there again, leaving a note to thank Dr. Sigerson and assure him that the joy of seeing people restored to their homes would cure her faster than anything else. And well it might have:

One by one, the priests and I reinstated the evicted and collected the neighbours to rebuild the gables and put in the broken window panes.

The honour of tearing down the wooden planks nailed across broken doors by the bailiffs was left to me. It was even more fun than building Land League huts. . . . The local police looked on helplessly . . . and, to be fair to them, they much preferred not being spoil-sports. Olpherts and his foxy agent . . . remained safely out of sight. Many of the short sentence prisoners had returned. We welcomed them with a torchlight procession. . . .

These rejoicings were interrupted by the arrival of Pat O'Brien with word that Dublin Castle thought Maud responsible for undoing the eviction campaign in the area and that a warrant for her arrest had been issued. Father McFadden joined Pat in urging her to flee the country, arguing that in her present state of ill-health six months in jail would kill her.

And though Maud disliked running away, she gave in. She too feared that "jail would be the end of everything, and before I died I wanted to get the prisoners released, I wanted to see Millevoye and I wanted to begin the fight against the British Empire in international affairs."

She had just time to pack her bags and get into O'Brien's carriage. In the darkening evening they drove to a lonely spot where the night train could be hailed on its way east to the port of Larne, north of Belfast.

Maud heard nothing further about this warrant for her arrest when she returned to Dublin at the year's end, perhaps because there were always people in Dublin Castle who felt queasy about charging members of the Ascendancy with the commission of a crime. This time Maud traveled southeast to participate in the formal opening of a town called New Tipperary, established near Limerick by tenants evicted from old Tipperary for withholding rent payments and then demanding 25 percent reduction. The struggle to oust them had been a bitter one, attended by bombings, riots, police brutality, and much publicity. During its course the persecuted tenants had displayed astonishing solidarity, offering to pay 10 percent of the valuation of their holdings to assist farmers engaged in a similar struggle on the Ponsonby estate near Youghal, a hundred miles away. Maud's heresy was coming near home; the Ponsonbys were related to the Cooks by marriage.

When John O'Leary heard that Maud had gone to attend the inauguration of New Tipperary, he made a historic comment. "She is no disciple of mine," he grumbled. "She went there to show off her new bonnet." This was consistent with O'Leary's belief that land reform should not be settled—or even discussed—until political freedom was won. But the charge is quite unjust; Maud did put national freedom first, but she always had great empathy with both rural and urban poor, and an instinctive readiness to assist them.

CHAPTER V

The Occultist

One of the better descriptions of Maud Gonne is that "she was larger than life." In her actions she felt free to travel alone (except for her dog and other fauna), smoke cigarettes openly, and talk with anybody. In her thoughts she could embrace many different religions, philosophies, and concepts, ignoring the fact that they often conflicted with each other.

After four decades of studying her largeness of spirit and independence of temperament, Yeats still wondered, "Which of her forms had shown her substance right?" But many declined to wonder; to them it seemed intolerable that, in addition to her beauty, wealth, and social position, she should possess such an untameable hawklike spirit. Their revenge was to spread fantastic slanders about her. Some of the mud stuck; but whenever an ugly rumor reached Maud's ears, she would remark, "They may say what they wish about me, but not *to* me."

Yeats was not able to brush off these stories as easily. Once he was told that she appeared at a meeting of a government commission dressed in a green frock ornamented with shamrocks, like some stupid English sympathizer; another time that she went on an otter hunt dressed in a muslin gown. He never forgave Sarah Purser, spinster, family friend, and portrait painter, for intimating to him that Maud was an intellectual dilettante. "Maud Gonne talks politics in Paris, and literature to you, and at the horse show she would talk of a clinking brood mare."

Yeats's maternal uncle, George Pollexfen, to whom all nationalists were socially impossible, reported that he had seen Maud talking politics in the Gresham Hotel in Dublin with a member of the Irish Parliamentary Party. "What will not women do for notoriety?" he wondered pointedly.

These opinions unquestionably dampened Yeats's ardor for a permanent relationship with her. But in July 1891, when he called on her at her little hotel in Dublin, he found her in such a state of melancholy that compassion swept away all qualms; it became one more element in the amalgam that kept him firmly attached to her side. In his *Memoirs* he wrote:

At the first sight of her as she came through the door, her great height seeming to fill it, I was overwhelmed with emotion, an intoxication of pity. She did not seem to have any beauty, her face was wasted, the form of her bones showing, and there was no life in her manner. As our talk became intimate, she hinted at some unhappiness, some disillusionment. The hard old resonance had gone, and she had become gentle and indolent. I was in love once more and no longer wished to fight against it. I no longer thought what kind of wife would this woman make, but of her need for protection and for peace.

Yeats may have magnified and dramatized Maud's condition. But it is true enough that she had reason to be despondent. Not only was it a hardship for someone so direct and outspoken to conceal her relationship with Lucien, but living with such a self-willed, pleasure-loving, somewhat arrogant man would have been difficult at best. In addition, she was burdened with the task of caring for a child, under the same equivocal conditions. It seems probable that this child was born on May 24, 1889 at Neuilly-sur-Seine and named Georgette Marie Louise "Gon." Such a birth is recorded in the Archives de la Seine, the central repository for French vital statistics. And if this Georgette was indeed Maud's child—French birth records do not give the full names of both parents—then we must accept the strange circumstance that she was five months pregnant when she first met W. B. Yeats.

The following day Yeats left Dublin to visit a friend in County Down. There he got a letter from Maud relating a sad dream in which, during a previous existence, they had been brother and sister, sold into slavery, and carried many miles into the Arabian desert. For some obscure reason, Yeats was deeply touched, and promptly returned to Dublin. He came into her hotel room determined to ask her to marry him, and sat beside her, holding her hand and speaking vehemently and confidently. When he had finished, he felt for a moment her nearness and her beauty, but an instant later she drew her hand away and told him that she could not marry him—there were reasons—she would never marry anyone—"but in words that had no conventional ring she asked for my friendship."

To propose marriage was an extremely reckless thing for Yeats to do. He and his family were living in, at best, genteel poverty. His father, the unsuccessful portrait painter, would often sit before the fire with his head in his hands, buried in gloom. Yeats felt the burden of his own poverty and indolence, yet he could not bring himself to accept an editorial job that would have given him a decent wage. At the age of twenty-six Yeats still had published very little of his own except a compilation of fairy tales and a few books of poetry.

Maud and Yeats spent the following day together on the cliff paths at Howth, which held so many childhood memories for Maud. As they watched two seagulls fly over their heads and out to sea, she remarked that if she were to have the choice of being any bird, she would prefer to be a seagull. Shortly afterward Yeats sent her a poem, "The White Birds," with its gentle theme: "I would that we were, my beloved, white birds on the foam of the sea." They dined at a little cottage near the Bailey Lighthouse where an old nurse of Maud's lived. Yeats overheard the woman ask Maud if they were engaged to be married. At the end of the day he found that he had spent ten shillings, to him a very great sum.

Before Maud was called back to France by some mysterious but urgent summons, Yeats had the opportunity to read to her part of *The Countess Cathleen*. He noticed that she seemed particularly moved when he read the passage, "there is a kind of joy / In casting hope away, in losing joy / In ceasing all resistance." The play was about a high-born woman who sold her soul to buy bread for her starving people. Yeats saw in this story "the symbolical song of my pity" for all people, like Maud, who lose their tranquillity for the sake of political achievement. Years later he restated this idea in the poem "The Circus Animals' Desertion":

> She, pity-crazed, had given her soul away,
> But masterful Heaven had intervened to save it.
> I thought my dear must her own soul destroy,
> So did fanaticism and hate enslave it.

Yeats was completing his play when he received from Maud in France "a letter of wild sorrow. She had adopted a little child, she told me, some three years ago, and now this child had died. Mixed into her incoherent grief were accounts of the death bird that had pecked at the nursery window the day when it was taken ill, and how at sight of the bird she had brought doctor after doctor."

The child, of course, was Maud's own daughter. Soon afterward, on October 11, 1891,—the one sure date that looms up in this chronological fog—the body of the disgraced leader, Charles Stewart Parnell, was brought to Ireland to be buried. Only two years before, in 1889, he had reached a peak of popularity when a special commission rendered a decision that the notorious letters sanctioning the

Phoenix Park murders that had been attributed to him were
out-and-out forgeries. Ironically, during the same year a
hitherto complaisant husband, Captain William O'Shea,
brought a divorce suit against his wife Kitty, naming Parnell as co-respondent. The adultery was proved. Though
Parnell married Kitty, priests and ministers denounced
him, the Irish nationalists split in bitterly divided factions,
and Parnell's efforts to remain in politics only shattered his
health. It took a decade for the Irish Parliamentary Party to
become an effective force again.

The overnight mail boat bearing Parnell's body arrived at
Kingstown shortly after six in the morning. On it, by coincidence only, was Maud, seeking solace for her personal
grief in the land she loved so much.

Yeats met her at the pier and breakfasted with her at her
hotel. She was wearing extravagantly deep mourning,
which everybody assumed to be a theatrical expression of
grief at the death of Parnell. Only Yeats knew that it was
for her daughter.

She told him that she had used some of her capital to
build a memorial chapel for the child, since money mattered not at all now. For days Maud went over the details of
Georgette's death, finding some sort of relief in speech. She
was very ill, Yeats confided to his journal. During her first
strong grief, she had lost her ability to speak French,
"which she knew almost as well as English, and she had
acquired the habit, unlearned afterwards with great difficulty, of taking chloroform to order to sleep."

Frequently they held long discussions about death. One
evening they were joined by George Russell, the painter
and poet, also known as AE (short for Aeon). He was then
the accountant at Pim's dry goods store on South Great
George's Street and a devout believer in a school of thought
called Theosophy. The name was new, invented in 1875 by
Yeats's Russian inspiration, Helena Petrovna Blavatsky,
but the philosophy dated back to the Neoplatonists, Gnos-

tics, and Cabalists; had included through the years such figures as Paracelsus and Swedenborg; and borrowed lavishly from doctrines found in Vedic, Buddhist, and Brahminist literature. Theosophists held that the universe was essentially spiritual and that man increased his latent spiritual powers by undergoing several consecutive existences. It was Russell's explanation of the transmigration of souls and reincarnation that particularly interested Maud. She asked him how soon a child might be reborn, and where. Could a child be reborn in the same family, for instance? Russell answered in the affirmative. Yeats saw that Maud was deeply impressed and was tempted to suggest that the doctrine of reincarnation, though plausible, was not entirely proved.

In November 1891, while Maud was in London, preparing to return to France, he took her to a meeting of the Rhymers' Club, a circle he had been active in forming and whose members were all poets. They met in the bare upper room of the Cheshire Cheese, off Fleet Street, where Maud may have joined them in drinking black coffee and smoking hashish—then, as now, symbols of revolt against the prosy world. Any Celtic blood a member had was glorified. A wit among them wrote, tongue-in-cheek,

John Todhunter, as you will gather from his name, was a Celt; and Plarr, whose father was an Alsatian, was a Celt; and Johnson, again the Celtic name, was a Celt—at one time he assumed a brogue and addressed me as "me dearr," and Mr. Symons, a Dravidian Welshman, was a Celt; and Dowson, who was probably of as pure Norman descent as you could find, was inclined to believe there was a Celtic strain in him; and Yeats, who was plainly a Firbolg, was the most Celtic of them all, and they all declared that there was a Celtic Renaissance.

Before the Rhymers' Club went out of existence in 1894, it had published two anthologies; one contained "The Lake Isle of Innisfree" by Yeats, the other, "Cynara" by Ernest Dowson.

Maud left for Paris, expecting to return to London in a

week or so. Yeats, continuing to worry about her, expressed their mutual sadness in a poem which ended with the lines, "Tread gently, treat most tenderly, / My life is under thy sad feet." He wrote John O'Leary, asking him to encourage Maud to work for the Young Ireland League as a form of therapy "for what she needs is some work of that kind in which she is, so far, enthusiastic about the League."

All these plans were changed when Maud fell ill and was told by her doctor that she had only six months to live unless she changed her habits completely. On his advice, she went to the little fishing village of St. Raphael, in southern France, where she could rest among the pine trees. She had good company, for Lucien Millevoye, whose family lived nearby, came to St. Raphael to see her; since he too needed to avoid the Paris winter, he stayed for the season. During the day they picnicked in the woods; in the evenings she read while he wrote pieces for the right-wing press; at his suggestion that she, too, should write, she wrote an article, her first, about the evictions in Ireland. It was accepted by *La Revue Internationale*.

Yeats got his first intimation of what was happening when he met Sarah Purser on the street and she jarred him with the news that "Maud Gonne is dying in the south of France." Sarah went on to tell him she had lunched with Maud in Paris, together with a very tall Frenchman (Yeats thought she dwelt on this in order to irk him) and a doctor who had told Sarah, in an aside, that they would both be dead in six months.

The next rumor he heard was that Maud had died. He expressed his sorrow in "A Dream of Death," which began "I dreamed that one had died in a strange place / Near no accustomed hand," and ended "She was more beautiful than thy first love / But now lies under boards." After the rumor was proved false, he sent Maud a copy of the poem. She was more amused than touched.

Maud Gonne's response to Theosophical doctrines after

her child's death derived directly from her unlimited and unqualified belief in psychic phenomená and the supernatural. She believed utterly. So did Yeats, with whom she experimented in extrasensory communication and studied the nature of mystic elements and objects. Though at times they questioned the integrity of this or that medium, this or that seer, they had precisely the same kind of faith George Russell expressed when he said that he had never painted an elf or fairy he had not seen.

Yeats stated the depth of his belief in a letter he wrote to John O'Leary in August 1892:

Now as to Magic. It is surely absurd to hold me "weak" or otherwise because I choose to persist in a study which I decided deliberately four or five years ago to make next to my poetry, the more important pursuit of my life. . . . If I had not made magic my constant study I could not have written a single word of my Blake book, nor would *The Countess Cathleen* ever have come to exist. The mystical life is the centre of all that I do and all that I think and all that I write.

Since Yeats and Maud Gonne had never had an hour of scientific education, they knew nothing about the need for documented experimentation and rigorous methodology before a concept can be considered a fact. They accepted without question mystical doctrines that had been obscurely conceived in the prescientific age. Yeats could spend hours, even days, weighing the value of one word in a poem as contrasted with another, but he could postulate, without a hint of skepticism, all-encompassing ideas about man and the universe that defy both belief and understanding.

Another reason why Yeats and Maud believed such rigmarole was that they could not accept the idea that industrial, Victorian England was the only world that existed. With William Morris, Walter Pater, Algernon Swinburne, Dante Gabriel Rossetti, and (later) Ezra Pound, they insisted that there must be other worlds. But it was not only aesthetes who shared their sympathies; millions of the educated, well-born, and rich, as well as the poor and ignorant, in France and England, accepted such concepts.

Yeats's ideas on magic first took form in the mold of Theosophy, about which he had read in a book by A. P. Sinnett, a wealthy English editor who had been overwhelmed by Madame Blavatsky's ability to produce rappings, bell ringings, and written messages that floated from the ceiling.

Like his fellow Theosophist, Russell, Yeats believed in the existence of an omnipresent and immutable principle, but not a personal God; in the fundamental union of all souls within a universal oversoul; in the teachings of all Eastern and Western mystics; and in the reincarnation of the individual soul, progressing in phases toward greater and greater illumination. Theosophy appealed to people like Yeats because it combined novelty and antiquity; opposed both atheism and clericalism; attacked science but fostered research, particularly in comparative religion; upheld fatalism but offered a hope of progress; denounced modern man and all his work, yet gave the Theosophist the possibility of becoming like a god.

In April 1886, two of Yeats's friends, Charles Johnston and Claude Falls Wright, established a Dublin lodge of the Theosophical Society of which he became a member. Later, he introduced Maud into the circle, but she was not made entirely welcome in those rooms that AE had decorated with wall paintings of fairies and ancient Irish gods; many members were unionists and disliked her nationalist activities.

On a different level, Maud had no difficulty in feeling at home in that atmosphere. It had been easy for her to believe that her friends C. H. Oldham and J. F. Taylor had seen her astral self, the supersensible body that was part of the oversoul, at a meeting in Dublin when she had actually been in bed in her small Paris flat; that others had seen her in Albert Hall or on a boat crossing to France when she had been somewhere else.

It was a natural progression for Maud and Yeats to conduct experiments in thought transference—Maud even gave him a vellum book in which to record the details. At a stated hour, he would try to send her an astral message or she would send him one; each would write down any thought received, and later they would compare the results. The attempts were not very successful, but once or twice Maud did manage to receive something vaguely resembling the idea Yeats had tried to send.

On one occasion, her use of hashish as a remedy for her insomnia elicited a different kind of astral message. Awakening one night with her legs feeling paralyzed and her heart beating irregularly, she saw a tall shadow at the foot of her bed who seemed to say to her: "You can now go out of your body and go anywhere you like, but you must always keep the thought of your body as a thread by which to return."

Maud made her wish and promptly found herself standing beside her sister Kathleen, who was sleeping with her little son Toby beside her. But the layout of the rooms and their appointments seemed different from those of Kathleen's house on Ely Place in Dublin. The reason, she learned later, was that her sister had taken Toby to Howth to convalesce from an illness in the very house where they had lived as children.

Maud tested this power with her skeptical friend Amilcare Cipriani, former companion of Guiseppe Garibaldi, and one of the many odd characters—émigrés, propagandists, former diplomats, homeless dukes—who moved in the strange world of international intrigue that Maud delighted in frequenting. She told him that she would visit him at midnight that evening—in the spirit. The next day she described minutely the room in which he lived and said he had been writing at a table.

"All these lodging rooms are the same," Cipriani said.

Then Maud told him something she had hesitated to mention because she had thought it might be merely a reflection of her own identification of Cipriani with Garibaldi's red-shirted army. When she visited him, she said, he seemed to have something resembling a big red scarf about his shoulders.

Astounded, Cipriani confessed that he had come home the night before with a cold and sore throat, that his kind landlady had brought out a large piece of red flannel which she said had great virtue and insisted that he wrap it around his neck. "No, that you could not have imagined," he acknowledged.

May Gonne, being a nurse, knew how dangerous the sleeping potions that her cousin was taking could be. During a visit to Maud in Paris, she hid the bottle of drops under the ashes in the hearth of the maid's room. That night Maud was wakeful as usual; when she found the bottle missing from its accustomed place, she said to May, "How stupid of you, May, to be hiding it again," and proceeded to the maid's room, where she found the bottle under the ashes without hesitation. On the following day, when she boasted about this uncanny feat to Millevoye over lunch at her flat, he commented sarcastically, "A wonderful feat, just as wonderful as a drunkard who in a strange town can always find the nearest pub." Disconcerted, Maud went into her bedroom, broke the bottle containing the sleeping mixture, and thereafter fought her insomnia without the use of drugs.

In the spring of 1887 Madame Blavatsky settled in London, as did the Yeats family. Yeats visited her and was easily persuaded to join the newly established London lodge of her Theosophical Society. She was then fifty-six, overweight, and ailing from the kidney disease which would kill her in four years. She smoked constantly, was given to emotional outbursts, and had a biting tongue. But her personality, which had enchanted such notables of the period as Sir William Crookes, Robert Browning, and Matthew Arnold, was still overwhelming. Yeats saw in this expansive Russian woman the model of a person fully her-self, free from self-doubt, living at ease with her "unfore-seen, illogical, incomprehensible" self, expounding with certainty and erudition many concepts that were simmering in his own mind.

When, not long before she died, he brought Maud to meet her, Maud saw "a strange, interesting figure, with big pale luminous eyes in a large yellow face. She sat in a big chair at the end of a long room in Kensington; a table in front of her and a pack of cards, with which she played continually and mechanically, even while she talked." When the light from the gas chandelier flickered, she said to Maud in a low tone, "They are all looking for a miracle." The gas flickered and went out. "Spooks," she said louder. "Now they think they have seen one. They are flapdoo-dles."

To Maud's satisfaction, Madame Blavatsky also called flapdoodles—it was her favorite term—those Dublin Theosophists who had objected to Maud's political activi-ties. "Politics has nothing to do with Theosophy," she told Maud. Referring to current stories about Land League felonies, she continued: "If a man cuts off a cow's tail, it will injure his own Karma, but it would not prevent him from being a member of the Theosophical Society."

After being a member of the London Theosophical Soci-ety for almost three years, Yeats left it because it would not go along with him in conducting an experiment he had read about in an astrology book. The experiment consisted of burning a flower and then trying to raise its ghost from the ashes.

But there was no vacuum. He had found a new guru, MacGregor Mathers, described by Virginia Moore as "a broad-shouldered athletic Scotchman of thirty-seven with a gaunt, resolute face and brown velvet jacket," who had just translated into English a Latin version of the cabala. This esoteric system of interpreting the Bible, which arose

among Jewish rabbis in the seventh century and reached
Christian mystics in the fifteenth, assumes that every word,
letter, and number has an occult meaning. Mather's pretty
wife, daughter of famed French philosopher Henri
Bergson, had mystic powers almost equal to his. Together,
Yeats felt, they could solve all mysteries. When George
Russell wrote to him about a vision that involved Maud
Gonne, Yeats was able to answer that his vision had been
"curiously corroborated in all the main points by the Kabal-
listic seership of Mrs. Mathers, helped out by Miss Gonne's
own clairvoyance."

Later, Maud herself told Yeats about the recurrent visits
she had from a dark woman with sorrowful eyes—Maud
had seen her so often she could have painted her portrait.
Yeats and Mathers, working together, decided that the figure was what in old Egyptian magic was called the Ka, a
part of Maud's personality that had survived death in a
former incarnation. One reason why priests used to preserve mummies, Mathers said, was to have the Kas of the
dead available for their magic performances.

As Maud came to feel more familiar with the mysterious
figure, she was emboldened to use its powers to perform
favors for friends. There were two consequences; some favors were rendered, and the woman in gray seemed to
develop a stronger, less grief-stricken, even contrary, personality.

Yeats, endlessly concerned for Maud, began to see the
woman as an evil spirit who stimulated Maud's desire for
power and excitement. Since he thought an attempt should
be made to evoke, and then to exorcize her, a séance was
held, during which the figure became visible (to some). The
conclusion arrived at this time was that she was a fragment
of Maud's personality, split off from the main soul because
Maud, while acting as a priestess in Tyre, had given a false
oracle.

Writing more than forty years later, Maud gave another

interpretation. She recalled that the figure in gray had appeared (though not to Yeats), confessed that she had killed her own child, "and wrung her hands in sorrow and remorse." Having decided that she must be evil and might become uncontrollable, Maud had resolutely put the apparition out of her mind and denied her existence. This had not been easy since the woman insisted on reappearing, particularly when someone with "mediumistic" powers was present.

In March of 1890 Yeats joined the Hermetic Order of the Golden Dawn, an organization founded in London in 1888 by MacGregor Mathers and two other high-ranking Masons. The Golden Dawn, which did not require its members to be Masons, was an offshoot of the Rosicrucian Society of England, itself a branch of a fraternity established in the Rhenish Palatinate by Christian alchemists early in the seventeenth century. Many of the groups then formed took their name from that of their leader, Christian Rosenkranz, whose surname means rose or rosy cross.

These alchemists believed that since the days of ancient Egypt a body of beneficent secret wisdom has been available to certain people in every era, who must use it to ease the sufferings of mankind. First discovered by an Egyptian priest whose name translated into Greek becomes Hermes Trismegistus, this occult knowledge is called the Hermetica, and the students thereof are enrolled in Hermetic Orders.

But the three founders of the Golden Dawn did not limit their claims to Hermetic wisdom. They also claimed a knowledge of Egyptology, the Mystery Schools, Orphism, Pythagoreanism, Gnosticism, Cabalism, and Rosicrucianism. That the order had some genuine intellectual stature is indicated by the fact that its members included the well-known writers Algernon Blackwood and Arthur Machen as well as John William Brodie Innes, Astronomer Royal of Scotland.

Following Yeats's example, Maud became a member of the Hermetic Order of the Golden Dawn on December 1, 1891. The date can be fixed from a letter Yeats wrote George Russell on November 30, a letter that gives some idea of how closely Yeats watched Maud's activities and of how much of himself was wrapped up in her.

I have seen Miss Gonne several times & have, I think, found an ally in the cousin with whom she is staying. An accidental word of the cousin's showed me that they had been discussing together and reading my poems in the vellum book, & yesterday the cousin gave me a hint to go to Paris next spring when Miss Gonne did—so you see I am pretty cheerful for the time until the next regiment of black devils come. Tomorrow Miss Gonne is to be initiated into GD—the next day she goes to Paris but I shall see her on her way through London a couple of weeks later—she promises to work at the Young Ireland League for me this winter. Go & see her when she gets to Dublin & keep her from forgetting me & occultism.

The ritual for inducting aspirants into the Golden Dawn was elaborate. All members wore gowns and hoods; each officer recited sentences in accordance with his title; the language was portentous. The ritual, described below in much-abbreviated form,* began with Maud Gonne's donning a black gown and red shoes. Three strands of rope were twisted around her chest. After a preliminary ode was recited to celebrate the rising of the sun, she was led blindfolded into the hall, and the officer called the Hierophant, resplendent in scarlet, began the round of symbolic words and actions.

The Stolistes: "The Mother of Darkness hath blinded her with Her hair."

The Dadouches: "The Father of Darkness hath hidden her under His wings."

The Kerus (bearing a lamp, symbol of hidden knowledge, and a wand, symbol of power) turned menacingly

---

*The full description is given in Virginia Moore, *The Unicorn: William Butler Yeats' Search for Reality.*

toward Maud: "Unpurified and unconsecrated, thou canst not enter our Sacred Hall."

The Stolistes, after making a cross on Maud's brow and sprinkling her three times: "I purify thee with water."

The Dadouches, making a cross over her with a censer: "I consecrate thee with fire."

The Hierophant ordered the candidate to the altar: "Inheritor of a Dying World, why seekest thou admission to our Order?"

The Hegemon answered for Maud: "My soul wanders in Darkness and seeks the light of the Hidden Knowledge."

Maud, speaking for herself: "I am willing to take the Solemn Obligation." Kneeling on both knees, with head bowed, she took the oath:

I, Maud Gonne, in the Presence of the Lord of the Universe . . . do, of my own free will . . . most solemnly promise to keep secret this Order. . . . I solemnly promise to persevere with courage and determination in the labours of the Divine Science . . . and I will not debase my mystical knowledge in the labour of Evil Magic . . . under the penalty of being expelled. . . . Furthermore, if I break this, my Magical Obligation, I submit myself, by my own consent, to a Stream of Power, set in motion by the Divine Guardians of this Order, Who live in the Light of their Perfect Justice, and before Whom my Soul now stands.

Then, after a good deal more of the grandiloquent ritual, during which she was told to be without fear, "for he who trembles at the Flame and the Flood and at the Shadows of the Air hath no part in God," and to eschew excessive power, excessive mercy, and excessive severity, Maud's blindfold was removed, she was summoned "to the Gentle Light," and welcomed into the Hermetic Order of the Golden Dawn.

At this same meeting Maud was told the meaning of certain symbols: the secret step, the salute, the answering sign, the Grand Word, the double cubical altar; and the significance of the Rose, Fire, Cup of Wine, and Bread and Salt placed at the corners of the altar. The rope around her chest, "the last remaining symbol of the Path of Darkness," was removed and she was invested with a sash over her left shoulder, badge of the Neophyte Grade.

All this was but the beginning of her education, which included studying "the signs of the Zodiac, the four triplicities, the planets, the vital twenty-two letters of the Hebrew alphabet . . . and the ten Emanations from God, forming the Tree of Life—its roots in Malkuth and its crown in Kether." She had to learn how to invoke higher beings and to study the deeper meaning of the Pillars of Hermes, between which she must walk in order to reconcile opposing forces. From that point on the lectures increased in difficulty.

Yeats was pleased when Maud Gonne took the first four degrees of the order and disappointed when she left it. Forty years after the event, she gave two reasons for her departure.

First, she had felt "oppressed by the drab appearance and mediocrity of my fellow-mystics," and by their fondness, typical of the English middle class, for cloaks, badges, titles—"Guardians of the Gates of the East and of the West," "Commanders of the Temple." The only persons of interest were Mathers himself, his wife, and Florence Farr, the actress. The more distinguished persons on the roster she never met because her visits to London were so short and hurried.

Second, she became convinced that the Hermetic Order of the Golden Dawn was simply another group of Freemasons. To Maud, English Masonry was basically an institution devoted to upholding the British Empire. Her suspicions were strengthened when during a visit to her friends, the Canes, she suddenly gave Claude Cane, a high-ranking Mason, a password she had learned at a Golden Dawn ceremony. He gave the correct reply and asked with astonishment, "Are you a Mason?" When she did not reply, he gave another password, to which Maud answered correctly. Cane then frankly admitted that these passwords belonged to the higher grades of Masonry. That evening Maud wrote her resignation from the order.

It seems likely that there was another cause: simply her feeling that the practical results of such intensive study were not worth the effort. Maud always found it difficult to study a subject—the Gaelic language, for instance—unless she saw quick and practical results.

Even while she was studying the mystic sciences, Maud began to consider joining the Catholic Church, a natural idea for a woman with a believing temperament who had been raised in Catholic France. Her first discussions were with Father Dissard, whom she met about 1891 at the little inn popular with Boulangists, La Belle Meuniere, located at Royat in the Auvergne mountains.

One day while they sat together watching the little black trout in a mountain stream, Dissard asked Maud, "Why aren't you a Catholic?"

She replied, "Because I believe in reincarnation," and she cited the case of Millevoye, whom she was certain she had met in an earlier existence.

The priest argued that these "memories" might be simply ancestral feelings transmitted in the blood. He himself had decided to become a priest not because he was the reincarnation of a druid who had died fighting against the Roman legionaries but because he was a descendant of that druid. He said he could not understand how she could refuse to accept Queen Victoria politically and yet recognize her as head of her religion. Maud answered that the only reason she was a member of the Church of England was that newborn babies are not consulted on such matters.

Father Dissard insisted that some day she would become a convert, that he had seen her praying at the cathedral in Clermont-Ferrand. Maud answered, "I cannot belong to any church because I wish to remain free. Nor can I confess my weaknesses and sins to any mortal man." The priest replied, "In the confessional you don't confess to a man but to God, who has chosen to work through man."

Maud reminded Dissard that the Pope and his bishops had often condemned Fenians and other champions of the nationalist cause. The priest answered that the Pope was infallible only on matters pertaining to the Faith.

Another influence was Father James A. Anderson, an Augustinian friar whom Maud first met in 1887 at the home of Dr. George Sigerson, whom she had known in France and who was also working for Irish independence.

Father Anderson frequently gave Maud advice and encouragement in her nationalist activities but never attempted to convert her. Perhaps piqued, she asked him why. He responded, "I don't have to speak to you about religion, because I am certain that my prayers for you will be answered and God will reward your work for Ireland by bringing you into his church."

On this subject, as on many others, Maud's autobiography conceals as much as it reveals. It does not tell us, for instance, the date when she was received into the Catholic Church. It does say that it was at the Carmelite convent in Laval, of which Dissard, by then Canon Dissard, was chaplain. Her avowed reason was highly appropriate for a servant of Ireland: "Every political movement on earth has its counterpart in the spirit world . . . and great leaders draw their often unexplained power from this."

Maud was faithful to the Church, even to becoming a member in 1910 of the Third (secular) Order of St. Francis, the saint whose teachings and love of animals were most attractive to her tastes. But part of her life-long devotion must be attributed to a desire to merge as closely as possible with the people whose nation she had accepted as her own. Maud's Catholic faith was always marked by a French flamboyance and refusal to accept clerical guidance in political matters; nor did it modify her belief in the existence of fairies and other extrasensory phenomena.

Many years later, William Butler Yeats told some non-Catholic companions how he had felt when "a female friend" was thinking of becoming a convert to Catholicism. He had tried to dissuade her, but she had left for another country still undecided. One night, while she was gone, he dreamt that he saw her entering a room full of beautiful people. As she walked through the room they all "smiled and smiled and smiled, but said nothing." Then Yeats realized that they were all dead. He woke up and said to himself, "She has joined the Catholic Church," and indeed she had. This anecdote tells us little about the reasons why Maud became a convert but much about the way some of Yeats's circle viewed the Church.

CHAPTER VI

Apostle of Irish Culture
(1892–1895)

THE EFFORT TO RESTORE Irish poetry, Irish history, and Irish legends to the Irish people intensified during the last decade of the century. Strangely enough, most of those involved in the movement were descendants of the English and Scottish settlers, Anglicans and Presbyterians, who had been crushing Irish culture for centuries.

Some of these felt that writing and publishing Gaelic grammars and translations of Irish folklore was not enough, that some degree of organized effort was required. The pioneer in this was Michael Cusack, who in 1884 founded the Gaelic Athletic Association, for the purpose of reviving ancient games and sports. In 1891 the Young Ireland League was formed to publicize the achievements and writings of Thomas Davis and other heroes of the 1848 Rising. In 1893 Douglas Hyde's Gaelic League and Willie Rooney's Celtic Literary Society were both established.

By 1892 Maud Gonne and W. B. Yeats were heading in the same direction. Each had private motives for deciding that an organizational underpinning was required to bring the cultural revival to fruition. Maud thought that public meetings and other events of the sort would be useful in strengthening the languid desire for Irish national independence. Because arousing Ireland must, of necessity, weaken

England, she would be fulfilling her pledge to Lucien Millevoye to injure France's traditional enemy with the Irish weapon. She could easily attach to her talks about Irish myths and ancient culture some cogent items from Irish history, such as the Great Famine and the number of tenant farmers being evicted annually—all leading to the conclusion that Ireland could be happy only if she freed herself from English rule.

In Yeats's decision there was "much patriotism, and more desire for a fair woman." He wanted to prove to Maud that he could be something more than a poet; that he could conduct public meetings, write reports and resolutions. He thought it was better to perform this work for cultural organizations than for political parties, which he detested.

Both had no trouble in agreeing that Maud Gonne, with her beauty, her background, her eloquence, and her exotic elegance, had excellent qualifications for the task of popularizing the concept of a Celtic Revival among both the Anglo-Irish and the Gaels. Besides (one must be practical), she had enough money to pay her own expenses. If she could find audiences in England and France, so much the better.

After several abortive ventures with Irish organizations in England, Yeats met a butter merchant in Dublin whose name had been given him by the Southwark Literary Society, and over a butter tub founded with him the National Literary Society of Ireland. Maud Gonne was one of the speakers at its formal inaugural meeting, held at the Rotunda, Parnell Square, Dublin, on May 24, 1892. When John O'Leary accepted the position of chairman, the society's success was assured. Numerous persons of distinction, including J. F. Taylor, Dr. Sigerson, the novelist Richard King, Dr. Douglas Hyde, and Professor Oldham, joined gladly.

Enthusiasm and activity abounded. Committees and

subcommittees proliferated. One subcommittee split off to become the Gaelic League; as Yeats wrote later, "We had dropped into the chemical solution the crystal that caused the whole mass to drop its crystals." Yeats was apparently not acquainted with the word "catalyst."

"This period of my life," Maud wrote in her autobiography, "was one of ceaseless activity and traveling. I rarely spent a month in the same place."

In January 1892 she was ten days in London working, probably with Yeats's help, on a series of lectures she intended to give in France. To publicize them, Yeats wrote an article called "The New 'Speranza',", which appeared in the January 16, 1892 issue of *United Ireland*. Speranza was the pseudonym of a woman who wrote a two-volume edition of Irish folk tales, published nationalist articles in the *Nation*, married a noted Dublin surgeon, Sir William Wilde, and became the mother of Oscar Wilde.

Yeats began his piece by pointing out the importance to Ireland of the Irish community in France.

Miss Maud Gonne has... founded an *"Association Irlandais"* to bring the Irish of Paris into touch with one another, and to keep France informed of the true state of the Irish Question. She began her work by presiding at a dinner given by French sympathizers... and made a great stir by her eloquent statement of the case for Ireland. The French papers are loud in her praise.... *L'Etendard Nationale* cannot find words strong enough to describe its effect. "Pathetic and persuasive, sweet and passionate, full of truth and indignation," it writes; "now dwelling on the past and now prophetic, she was soon absolute mistress of her audience.... Before her speech had closed the women were all in tears and the men seeking in vain to hide their emotions...."

"I have given all my heart to Ireland," she began, "and I will give her my life also if events permit me. If I could... pass into your hearts and consciences the indignation which fills my soul against the oppressors of my country, I shall have fulfilled my mission as a patriot and a woman.... Your great poet, Victor Hugo, has called hunger "a public crime," and that crime England has carried out against Ireland by cold premeditation and calculation....

"Do you ask us what we are seeking for? I will tell you. We are three things—a race, a country, and a democracy—and we wish to make of these three a nation."

What a singular scene—this young girl of twenty-five addressing that audience of politicians, and moving them more than all their famous speakers. . . . What does it mean for Ireland? Surely, that here is the new "Speranza" who shall do with the voice all, or more than all, the old "Speranza" did with her pen. . . .

In the issue of *United Ireland* that appeared two weeks later, Yeats took exception to an article in W. T. Stead's periodical, *Review of Reviews,* which termed Maud a Parnellite or separatist, said her mission in Paris was to obtain armed help for Ireland, and predicted that, though she was one of the most beautiful women in the world, she could not accomplish this task.

Yeats retorted that Maud was no separatist but was

succeeding beyond all expectations in her perfectly practical business-like, and unsensational project of organising the Irish People of Paris and the Parisians of Irish descent into a society which will be able to serve Ireland . . . by generally cultivating good relations between Ireland and her old ally, France.

Yeats included in his article a poem entitled "A Toast to Ireland," dedicated to Maud Gonne, and written by Clovis Hugues, poet, duellist, Boulangist. Yeats called the poem "the most charming of the many marks of sympathy" for Ireland that Maud's talks had inspired, but admitted it was rather slow in getting "into the full stream of inspiration." This was understandable, since the poem was composed at the dinner while Maud was speaking.

In the spring of 1892, Maud scored a signal success with a college audience. Her long speech before Le Cercle du Luxembourg de Paris was given verbatim in a twelve-column supplement to *La Revue Catholique.* In *The Pilot,* a Boston Catholic periodical, Yeats quoted from it her description of the famine of 1848.

Ireland was heroic in her suffering. Whole families, when they had eaten their last crust, and understood that they had to die, looked once upon the sun and then closed up the doors of their cabins with stones, that no one might look on their last agony. Weeks afterwards men would find their skeletons gathered round the extinguished hearth. . . . It has seemed to me at evening on those mountains of Ireland . . . that I heard an avenging voice calling down on our oppressors the execration of men and the justice of God.

It was not easy, he wrote, for anyone to give a clear picture of Irish history in three-quarters of an hour, yet Miss Gonne had done it.

She takes her audience . . . from the bloodless conversion of pagan Ireland . . . down to our own day and the death of Parnell, and every event is described as vividly and simply as if it were all in some famous ballad of "old, unhappy, far-off things, and battles long ago."

Yeats concluded:

Last week at Bordeaux, an audience of twelve hundred persons rose to its feet, when she had finished, to applaud her with wild enthusiasm. The papers of Russia, France, Germany, and even Egypt quote her speeches, and the tale of Irish wrongs has found its way hither and thither to lie stored up, perhaps, in many a memory against the day of need.

Shortly after Maud's lecture to the students of Le Cercle du Luxembourg, she received an invitation to a St. Patrick's Day banquet and ball from l'Association du Saint Patrice, a society founded by John O'Leary when he was in exile in France. Members were descendants of the Wild Geese, the Irish Brigade that had served in the French army. The banquet was small and select; among those present were le Comte O'Neill de Tyrone, the charming and courtly president; le Comte Marie-Henri d'Arbois de Joubainville, professor of Celtic literature at the College de France; le Comte Bonaparte Wyse, whose sister had published Maud's first article in the *Revue Internationale;* le Comte O'Kelly de Galway; and le Comte de Cremont. Their main interest was in their descent from Irish kings; when Maud later started *l'Irlande Libre,* she could have made it self-supporting had she consented to print genealogies.

Maud was the only woman at the banquet, for membership in the society was restricted, "in true Irish fashion," to
men. When she was called upon to speak, she tried to bring
reality into the rarefied atmosphere by reminding the
members that, while they were banqueting in honor of
Ireland, Irishmen were suffering unutterable horrors in
English jails and thousands of peasant families were being
evicted. Someone proposed, contrary to custom, that a collection be taken up for the tenants and 12 or 15 pounds
were given to Maud at the end of the evening.

She later claimed that she had seen at once that Irish
Brigade families were so reactionary, so hostile to the
French Republic, as to be embarrassing. She gave this as
the reason she and Yeats started l'Association Irlandaise,
the Paris branch of the Young Ireland Society, which drew
its members from homesick Irish governesses, a few young
Irish priests, including the future Irish playwright John
Millington Synge, and scattered litterateurs. Because of the
apathy of the Irish colony, Maud wrote later, "We never
did much effective work."

That was seldom the case with Maud. On her next trip to
London, her first visit was to the Amnesty Association
Committee in order to give it the proceeds of her talk before
Le Cercle du Luxembourg, and to tell the committee that
she was ready to speak at meetings concerned with liberating Treason Felony prisoners. She was delighted to learn
that the man with the injured eye had been taken to a
hospital and that her prediction that he would be freed
within six months was likely to be realized.

Maud next visited Pat O'Brien at the House of Commons, and obtained from him the gift of a set of slides
showing Irish huts being demolished by battering rams,
even while Mr. Balfour, chief secretary for Ireland, was
denying that any peasants were being evicted. When they
were joined, among others, by William Field, Irish member
of Parliament, she won his promise to speak at Amnesty

meetings scheduled for the next week at Manchester, Liverpool, Newcastle, Edinburgh, and Glasgow.

Soon back in France she spoke in dozens of university towns, at meetings sponsored by student clubs, chaired by scholars, and attended by town officials and the press. Whenever facilities were available Maud used the lantern slides O'Brien had given her, with the result that, at La Rochelle, people were so indignant after a lecture that they demonstrated outside the British consulate and had to be dispersed by the police.

A Dutch writer, Louise Stratenus, was so impressed by one of Maud's lectures that she arranged for her to speak before student groups in Holland and Belgium. At Amsterdam and Groningen mounted cavalcades of students met and accompanied her from the railroad station to her hotel as a guard of honor. Money collected at these meetings was sent to the Evicted Tenants' Committee and to Father McFadden.

As she went from town to town, reports of Maud's talks were written up in local and sometimes national newspapers. *Figaro,* the most distinguished of French newspapers, ran a front-page article headed, "Les Atrocites dans les Bagnes Anglais," and reported that "audiences of over a thousand were not uncommon."

The British government responded strongly to the *Figaro* article. Cabinet member Herbert Asquith showed it and others to John Redmond, leader of the Irish Parliamentary Party, and demanded that Maud's activities be stopped: "How can you expect us to make concessions to people who are doing their best to injure England?" Redmond answered that he was not involved at all in the publication of news stories or in Maud Gonne's travels, and that he was powerless to stop them. "No one can stop Miss Gonne," he said. "She consults no one and acts entirely on her own. Nothing will stop her but the release of the prisoners."

In January 1892, W. B. Yeats wrote John O'Leary that

Miss Gonne was expected to be back in Dublin in March in order to work for the Young Ireland League, that she was to concentrate on raising funds to start village libraries.

Despite her constant comings and goings, Yeats was ever hopeful of seeing more of Maud. By that summer, when Yeats had known Maud for more than three years, matters seemed to be going well with both his courtship and his movement. In July the National Literary Society received permission to hold its committee meetings in the Mansion House in Dublin. In reporting this to John O'Leary, Yeats added that Miss Gonne had refused to campaign for more than two days for her admirer Morton, who was running for Parliament, because she had work to do in Dublin. Morton, Yeats wrote, had replied "that if he was not returned he hoped he might never see her again. He must have quite lost his head over this election."

Yeats's hopes rose even higher when he learned that Maud had given up her lodgings in Paris; it was an indication, he thought, that she intended to spend more time in Ireland and devote herself to the work there.

In October he wrote to O'Leary to say that Maud

has indeed been better in the matter of letters and written at greater length and in a more cordial spirit. . . . I had a long letter yesterday and another the day before. She is to be in Dublin on the 1st of November and was to leave Royat for Paris yesterday (15th). She is very eager about the work. . . .

In November Yeats told O'Leary that Maud had returned to Paris to give some talks and had obtained a great many books for the library scheme. The unfortunate man did not yet understand the significance of Maud's visits to Royat.

For a time Maud's efforts to raise money for establishing village libraries continued to prosper. She founded three of the seven lending libraries that were started in Ireland, winning an accolade from Yeats: "the fiery hand of the intellectual movement." But beneath the surface political and personal differences began to simmer. Maud thought it was more important, and certainly more exciting, to participate in political elections than to preach the prospect of a Celtic literary revival to Galway and Donegal villagers. Yeats thought it was wasteful for Maud to devote her time to elections when the cultural forces he was setting in motion made all political maneuvers insignificant.

As yet, neither was wholehearted in his or her conviction. Once Maud failed to attend a political rally, preferring to spend the day playing with a hawk that Yeats had brought her from a Donegal admirer. When her candidate was defeated by a mere half-dozen votes, she reproached Yeats bitterly, saying the man would have won if he had not brought her the hawk. Yeats was unmoved in his belief that it was not worth foregoing one of their rare days together to add another Irish member to Parliament.

He was unhappy with Maud on other counts. She did not come to his defense when he was accused of thinking like any decadent English writer for criticizing the quality of Thomas Davis's poetry. He responded by saying that even patriotic poetry should be required to meet certain standards. Nor would Maud support him when he found fault with Charles Gavan Duffy, another veteran of the "Young Ireland" group, for his selection of books to be published and distributed by London and Dublin literary societies.

These differences were compounded by Yeats's subsurface but constant awareness that he was only peripheral to Maud's existence; that her life in France was fuller and more exciting than her days in Ireland and England. Had he been able to spend time at her bedside when she developed a serious lung congestion, it might have drawn the two closer together, but her doctor, George Sigerson, banned all visitors. Yeats thought Sigerson took special delight in doing this because he had quarreled with Yeats concerning the aforementioned selection of books. Yeats heard about Maud's condition only from her nurse, an unsavory woman who had got the position by chance; having seen an open door, she had climbed the stairs and found herself employed in the absence of other applicants. Yeats would meet this woman, with her "unhealthy clay-coloured complexion and moist, morbid hands," in a public garden each night and get news which became steadily more melodramatic.

I was to think no more of Maud Gonne—who was looking for some ground of quarrel—she loved another, indeed, perhaps two others, for ill as she was she had decided to hurry back to France to be present at a duel between them. Maud Gonne had even forbidden them to fight before her arrival, or anywhere but in her own drawing room.

On other occasions, the nurse would report that Maud was so sick that he would never be able to see her again.

When Maud's cousin, May Gonne, arrived in Dublin, Yeats received more reliable news. Maud, over her doctor's protest, was indeed leaving for France, but the rumors of the lovers and the duel were nonsense. Yet the old nurse was not finished. Soon Yeats discovered that she was circulating a story, more horrible than all the others, that he had been Maud Gonne's lover, and had been present when an illegal operation was performed upon her.

Maud later remembered one evening when she awakened to find the old woman's vague eyes fixed on her face. When Maud told her to leave the bedside, the woman refused, saying, "Dr. Sigerson says you may die at any time. I am waiting for the moment of death."

Yeats followed Maud to Paris for the first time in February 1894. Quite recovered from her illness, she was living in an apartment on l'Avenue de la Grande Armée that was hardly large enough for Dagda to move around in.

Together they went to see *Axel*, a play by Villiers de l'Isle-Adam, which Yeats, with Maud's help, followed well enough to review for the London *Bookman*. The play was having a tremendous impact on many intellectuals, and would be a signpost for Yeats in the writing of symbolic and allegorical drama.

He stayed in Paris with MacGregor Mathers. In the evenings, they played a curious form of chess; Yeats and Mrs. Mathers would be partners against MacGregor and his guiding spirit. The great mystagogue would shade his eyes with his hands, gaze at his partner's empty chair at the opposite corner of the board, and then move his partner's piece.

Upon his return to London, Yeats had the pleasure of seeing his own play, *The Land of Heart's Desire*, produced on March 29, 1894. The sybaritic novelist George Moore was less impressed by the "inoffensive trifle" than by Yeats's appearance "as he strode to and forth at the back of the dress circle, a long black cloak drooping from his shoulders, a soft black sombrero on his head, a voluminous black silk tie flowing from his collar, loose black trousers dragging untidily over his long, heavy feet. . . ."

Maud Gonne was much in Yeats's mind when he was writing this little fairy play that contrasts attachment for home and kin with "the maddening and bewildering light" from the old world of the Sidhe, the little people—banshees, elves, leprechauns—that had supposedly inhabited prehistoric Ireland. He felt that Maud's quarrels with him sprang from her vague desire "for some impossible life, for some unwearying land like that of the heroine of my play."

This could tire him. During the summer of 1894, he was introduced to the novelist Olivia Shakespear by her cousin, the poet Lionel Johnson. Married to an aging solicitor, she was about Yeats's age and he was impressed by the "perfect Greek" regularity of her features, her gift for sympathetic listening, and her willingness to be content with simple pleasures and attainable goals. Interested in Yeats from the start, she wrote to him frequently when he went to stay in Sligo with his uncle, George Pollexfen. During this winter of 1894–95 he was studying astrology, rewriting *The Countess Cathleen* from the knowledge he had gained from having a play produced, and adding some stories to a collection called *The Secret Rose*—not mere fantasies, he said, but "the signatures of things invisible and ideal."

During Yeats's stay at Sligo, he visited Lissadell, where Sir Henry Gore-Booth lived with his wife and daughters, Constance and Eva. Constance was two years younger than Maud, and resembled her, Yeats thought, in that both were tall and had low, soft voices. He told the two girls about his unfortunate passion for Maud and his interest in Irish folklore. Twelve years later, when she was forty and married to a Polish count named Casimir Markievicz, Constance became interested for the first time in Irish nationalism, and, acting in distant emulation of Maud Gonne, devoted the rest of her life to this cause.

On his return to London, Yeats invited Olivia Shakespear to come with a friend to have tea with him in his newly rented rooms in Fountain Court. While preparing for their arrival Yeats began to think of Maud Gonne and still was thinking of her when he went out to buy a cake. On his return he discovered with horror that he had forgotten his key, and so was unable to admit his guests until he had found a man who let himself in through a window and opened the door. A day or two later, Yeats received an urgent letter from Maud Gonne. Had he been ill? Had there been some accident? She was concerned because at the very moment he had been waiting for his guests in front of the closed door in London, his spirit had materialized, wan and distraught, in her Dublin living room. The spirit had apparently been unable to tell Maud his distress was caused by a forgotten door key.

Maud seems to have been little in England in 1895 but she did participate in a campaign to prevent the re-election to Parliament of John Morley, a prominent member of the Liberal Party who had reneged, it was charged, on his promise to work for the release of Irish political prisoners. Maud urged the Irish members of his constituency, in Newcastle-on-Tyne, to vote for the Labour Party candidate, even though Morley's Liberal Party had recently come out for Home Rule. The number of voters who deserted Morley was enough to throw the victory to the candidate of the Conservative Party.

During the same year, 1895, Maud Gonne gave birth to a child she named Iseult Gonne. And W. B. Yeats found, he thought, a way to bind Maud more closely to him. He would induce her to help him build a Castle of Heroes, where worshippers of beauty and ancient truths would celebrate rites similar to those conducted in ancient Greek times in honor of Demeter (Ceres) at Eleusis. The juxtaposition of these two facts about Maud Gonne and Yeats throws much light on the enormous differences in their ways of life.

CHAPTER VII

The Stirring of the Bones (1896–1897)

In April 1895, while on a visit to Douglas Hyde in Roscommon, Yeats rowed up a body of water called Lough Key, and saw a beautiful small island called Castle Rock, presumably because there was on it "a still habitable but empty castle." In his *Memoirs*, he wrote:

I believed that the castle could be hired for little money, and had long been dreaming of making it an Irish Eleusis or Samothrace. An obsession more constant than anything but my love itself was the need of mystical rites—a ritual system of evocation and meditation—to reunite the perception of the spirit, of the divine, with natural beauty.

He believed that, instead of thinking only of Palestine as sacred, the Irish should think of Ireland as holy, and most holy where it was most beautiful, untouched by the ugliness of commerce.

I was convinced that all lonely and lovely places were crowded with invisible beings and that it would be possible to communicate with them. I meant to initiate young men and women in this worship, which would unite the radical truths of Christianity to those of a more ancient world, and to use the Castle Rock for their occasional retirement from the world....

It was to be Maud Gonne's work and mine. Perhaps that was why we had been thrown together. Were there not strange harmonies amid discord? My outer nature was passive—but for her I should never perhaps have left my desk—but I knew my spiritual nature was passionate, even violent. In her all this was reversed, for it was her spirit only that was gentle and passive and full of charming fantasy, as though it touched the world only with the point of its finger.

Yeats also thought that he could use Maud's clairvoyant ability, stronger than his, to produce, from racial memories, mystical forms that were free of personal and material shackles. "I believed we were about to attain a revelation. Maud Gonne entirely shared these ideas, and I did not doubt that in carrying them out I should win her for myself."

For the next decade, Yeats devoted his "most impassioned thought" to the attempt to build at Lough Key this Castle of Heroes which would become a magnet for Celtic thought from all of Europe and to find for it an appropriate philosophy and ritual. He had "an unshakeable conviction, arising how or whence I cannot tell," that, if he pondered long enough, "invisible gates" would open to permit him to see the true meaning of the scriptures and of the universe, as they had frequently opened for Emanuel Swedenborg, the Swedish scientist and theologian, and for William Blake. An appropriate manual of devotion could easily be extracted from such works as the Chaldean Oracles and the Book of the Dead, and from the writings of Plotinus, Joachim of Floris, and Paracelsus. And there would have to be a special section containing Irish literature "which, though made by many minds, would seem the work of a single mind, and turn our places of beauty or legendary association into holy symbols."

Maud joined happily in Yeats's dreamings, seizing particularly on the idea that there was an inseparable link between a land and the people who lived on it. For the rest of her life she was convinced that the work of freeing Ireland included the unleashing of invisible mystic forces.

The land of Ireland, we both felt, was powerfully alive and invisibly peopled. . . . If only we could make contact with the hidden forces of the land it would give us strength for the freeing of Ireland. Most of our talk centred round this and it led us both into strange places. . . .

In her more political moments, Maud also thought that the new cult might work to separate Ireland from England in the same way that the Masonic lodges were working to maintain the connection. It would use Masonic methods to combat the Masons.

Maud and Yeats joined in collecting a long list of symbols, assisted in this task by George Pollexfen, Yeats's old uncle, who believed that ancient Irish mysteries formed part of a once existent body of beliefs "older than any Europen church" and could and should be rediscovered. Maud wrote later:

Various trees corresponded to cardinal points, and the old gods and heroes took their places gradually in a symbolic fabric that had for its centre the four talismans of the Tuatha de Danaan, the sword, the stone, the spear and the cauldron, which related themselves in my mind with the suits of the Tarot.

Maud and Yeats spent hours reconstructing the traits of the ancient divinities, who would occasionally materialize and enlighten them on some aspects of their world. From such works as John Rhŷs's *Celtic Heathendom*, the studious couple learned about life in pre-Christian Ireland and worked out parallels between the ideologies of the ancient Celts and the Graeco-Roman peoples.

MacGregor Mathers and his wife helped them frame the ritual. MacGregor told them that it could not be consciously developed; it had to be obtained through a system of his own which required "letting the will move of itself." Mrs. Mathers wrote on March 16, 1897 that the process could not be hurried; resurrecting the gods was serious business. Anything built "without the solid foundation of truth we will not have to do with, neither will you of course."

It is an irony of Irish history that, from such arcane

musings by Anglo-Irish, there developed a self-conscious separate culture which played an important role in strengthening the movement for political independence. Theosophy and other esoteric philosophies made the Celtic lore even more palatable. Madame Blavatsky's notions of a coming revolutionary epoch jibed nicely with Fenian hopes of a conflagration that would burn up the British Empire.

In his search for organizations that would help to restore Celtic culture, Yeats was open-minded. He did not hesitate to accept the suggestion of T. W. Rolleston, made in a Strand coffee shop, that he join the Irish Republican Brotherhood, the secret organization of direct-action revolutionaries which dated back to the Fenians of the 1860s. Rolleston, a Trinity graduate whose interests ranged from German literature to farming cooperatives, said that major changes were taking place within the IRB, making it less addicted to violence and more effective. Yeats was ready to listen, for he remembered that John O'Leary had said: "In this country a man must have upon his side the Church or the Fenians, and you will never have the Church." He was sworn in by Dr. Mark Ryan.

At this time the Fenian organization in the United States, the Clan na Gael, was split between two rival leaders: Alexander Sullivan in Chicago and John Devoy in New York. Rebel groups in England and Ireland were greatly affected, the Irish backing Devoy, Dr. Ryan siding with Sullivan, and in 1894 organizing an "Irish National Brotherhood" as a rival to the Irish Republican Brotherhood. All this was of small moment to W. B. Yeats. What he saw in Ryan's organization in London was a small group of Irish enthusiasts who were sensibly attempting to put some backbone into the constitutional Irish movement without engaging in foolhardy ventures which might put Maud Gonne in danger. He felt even more reassured when he found Dr. Ryan to be a man of "touching benevolence," with "a native and touching faith in men who were better educated." The members of the new secret society "were almost all doctors, peasant or half-peasant in origins, and none had any genuine culture. In Ireland it was just such men, though of a younger generation, who had understood our ideas."

In March 1896, W. B. Yeats, age thirty-one, rented an upstairs flat in the Woburn Buildings, located in a dilapidated courtyard behind St. Pancras Church. How Maud Gonne lit up this area when she visited it is vividly described by Ernest Rhys, an eyewitness, in an article published in *The Fortnightly Review*. Because the courtyard was so cluttered, her hansom could not enter it, and because it was raining, Yeats dashed out to the end of the court to receive "his Irish princess." When she emerged, "a gleaming figure, dressed as if for a state function... in emerald green, a gold toque round her neck," a dozen urchins who had gathered in the rain "were so astonished that they cried out in shrill admiration."

Other notables visited Yeats's low, dusky living room with its Blake drawings on the walls. Generally, they came to attend his weekly symposia, but such functions were not his principal reason for renting these rooms. It was to have a suitable place in which to lose his cursed virginity. His collaborator was Olivia Shakespear. She had gone with him when he had purchased the furnishings for his new lodgings in a shop on Tottenham Court Road where they had self-consciously discussed the proper width of the bed. The difficulty lay in the fact that every added inch of width increased its cost.

From all accounts, Olivia was everything a man could want in a woman. But Yeats's nervous excitement was so great during her first two visits that he was impotent, and "it seemed best but to sit over our tea and talk." Olivia's affection did not decrease; she "was only troubled by my trouble. My nervousness did not return again," he wrote in his *Memoirs*, "and we had many days of happiness."

His desire for Olivia ebbed after a year because "she was too near my soul, too salutary and wholesome to my inmost being." He also thought that his intense struggle to make a living often made him preoccupied when she arrived. But the main reason was that Olivia was not Maud. When Maud wrote to him saying that she was in London and asking him to dine with her, he had an intimation that his love still lingered. He was sure, however, that Maud "had no thought of the mischief she was doing."

Even while the affair was going on, Olivia knew how it would end. The break occurred one morning when Yeats failed to read love poetry prior to Olivia's arrival—this was his custom in order "to bring the right mood round"—and wrote some letters instead. Olivia, finding him unresponsive, burst into tears, and said, "There is someone else in your heart." With that she left, and they did not see each other for many years. Then a long and warm epistolary friendship began which gave them both much happiness; it lasted until her death in 1938.

Yeats described the break with Mrs. Shakespear in "The Lover Mourns for the Loss of Love," which appears in the 1899 collection called *The Wind Among the Reeds*.

> I had a beautiful friend
> And dreamed that the old despair
> Would end in love in the end:
> She looked in my heart one day
> And saw your image was there;
> She has gone weeping away.

Would Yeats have been better off if Olivia Shakespear had obtained a divorce and married him? Probably. The same can be said of several women of whom he became fond after meeting Maud. But none, he subconsciously knew, would have been as good for him as a poet. And his poetry meant everything.

One of these possibles was Isabella Augusta Gregory, born Persse in 1852 in Roxborough, County Galway, the widow of Sir William Gregory, a former Governor of Ceylon. She had married Sir William when she was twenty-eight and, though he was nearly forty years older, shared with him a love for books, pictures, architecture, and travel.

Yeats and Lady Gregory had their first long conversation in August 1896, when Edward Martyn, then active in the Irish Revival, brought Yeats to visit her at her luxurious estate, Coole Park. Martyn was a strange character, a slow-moving conservative bachelor deeply devoted to his faith—he came of ancient, upper-crust Catholic gentry— but open to any vital change in art, music, and literature. His friend Lady Gregory found Yeats to be "full of charm and the Celtic Revival." Thirteen years older than Yeats, she turned out to be a kind, practical woman with a high esteem for poets and an aptitude for writing comic plays that was to astonish everyone.

During the following winter, Yeats visited Lady Gregory at her flat in London, and talked with her about his unrequited love for Maud Gonne. On a visit he made to Paris in December 1896 in order to work with Mathers and Maud on the ritual for the Castle of Heroes, his infatuation, now eight years old, returned in all its fury.

I saw much of Maud Gonne and my hope renewed again. If I could go to her and prove by putting my hand in the fire till I had burnt it badly would not that make her understand that devotion like mine should [not] be thrown away lightly. Often as I went to see her I had this thought in mind and I do not think that it was fear of pain that prevented me but fear of being mad. I wonder at moments if I was not really mad.

Unconcerned, Maud was active during 1897 in France, England, Ireland, and the United States. In Paris she began to publish a monthly called *l'Irlande Libre*, which ran for eighteen issues, cost 10 centimes a copy, and consisted of four 9 by 12 pages. Billed as the organ of the Irish colony in Paris, the paper did a good job of publicizing nationalist views within its limits of size and money. Each issue carried articles on economic and political conditions in Ireland; on activities of the Amnesty Society; and on meetings of patriotic groups in Ireland, England, and the United States. Articles favorable to the Irish cause were reprinted from French periodicals and show that the monthly's aim of influencing French opinion was being achieved.

Maud was the dominant figure in *l'Irlande Libre*. She wrote many of the articles, including one that contrasted the plans for celebrating the sixtieth anniversary of Queen Victoria's reign with famine conditions in Belmullet. "Once more hunger and fever, auxiliaries of an inhumane government, are helping to exterminate a people who refuse, while their wounds are bleeding, to admire the oppressor's culture or take part in its Jubilee."

Poems dedicated to her, and laudatory references taken from other periodicals, appeared frequently. Every meeting that she spoke at or attended was listed—and during a six-month period beginning in April 1897 she spoke several times in Paris, four times in Dublin, and at least once in London, York, Glasgow, Manchester, and Cork. Almost every stop she made on her United States trip was covered.

Despite all this, the paper did more than magnify Maud's charms and abilities. It emphasized her message: the need to oppose England in every arena and to free Ireland from economic and political slavery. Maud had little idea of what a news story required in the way of accuracy, objectivity, and brevity. But she did have some of the attributes of a good editor. Besides being a fluent writer herself, she knew what the purpose of her publication was, and had a knack for selecting good assistants—Miss M. Barry Delany, a member of Maud's Association Irlandaise, was a reliable assistant editor.

For contributors Maud tapped friends, admirers, and members of organizations hostile to England in any degree. She printed contributions from Home Rule member of Parliament William Redmond as well as dynamitard John Daly. She published two articles by William Butler Yeats on the Celtic Revival. In the issue of May 1898, a radical named James Connolly described the famine in County Kerry, which he had visited at Maud's request.

Typical of the items published were poems by Clovis Hugues; an excerpt from *La Patrie* in which Millevoye paid tribute to a naval lieutenant who had revealed the nepotism existing in the war ministry; a statement from Connolly's Irish Socialist Republican Party concerning the Queen's diamond jubilee ("We owe no debt to this government of plunder and theft except that of hatred. Work, learn, and organize."); and a report on members of the Young Ireland Society who had left to fight for Greece in its struggle against Turkey.

On other levels of achievement, Maud became the first woman member of the St. Patrick Society, and successfully repulsed one more attempt to label her as a spy. Her strongest supporter in both cases was le Comte de Cremont, the new president of the society. His strong affection for Maud was based on the odd notion that, in a former incarnation, he had been a tiger and Maud had been his mother. Being something of a poet, he once shocked some of his fellow members by putting this notion into verse.

In March 1897 a man named Macarthy Teeling told Cremont, in the presence of Maud Gonne, that she was an English and German spy. Teeling was given a hearing because he was related to Bartholomew Teeling, who had been hanged for serving in 1798 with Humbert, the French general whose troops landed in Killala, County Mayo, that year and routed the English. In Ireland descent is taken seriously. Macarthy Teeling said he had been sent specifically by the Irish Parliamentary Party to repudiate Miss Gonne, who was known to be the daughter of an English colonel. Cremont ordered Teeling out. "Mademoiselle Gonne," he said, "requires no credentials from anybody";

but when a periodical printed the same charges, Cremont
wrote to John O'Leary, Timothy Harrington of the National League, and Michael Davitt, asking for the whole
story.

All three disclaimed any responsibility for Teeling's ac-
tion, and generously praised Maud's activities in France.
Yeats, who was given the task of transmitting the reply
from O'Leary to Cremont, added a note to the effect that he
himself knew that Teeling had once been expelled from the
Young Ireland Society for acting insolently toward
O'Leary, and that he had "for years been slandering Miss
Gonne in the most ignoble and infamous way."

The immediate reason for Teeling's extraordinary attack,
Maud later learned, was that he considered her responsible
for inviting Amilcare Cipriani, against whom he had fought
in Garibaldi's wars, to attend an event held by the newly
organized '98 Centenary Commemoration Committee.

On March 4, 1897 at a meeting held in Dublin with John
O'Leary in the chair, this committee had been selected to
insure that the 1798 rising was suitably remembered.
Branches were quickly established in Ireland, England, the
United States, Europe, Australia, and South Africa. In the
Dublin branch, which had as its principal aim the erection
of a memorial to Wolfe Tone, a subsidiary organization,
called the Wolfe Tone Memorial Association, was estab-
lished, with Yeats as president. He also became president
of the '98 Centennial Association of Great Britain and
France, of which Dr. Mark Ryan was named treasurer.
Yeats was also president that year of the Young Ireland
League.

Some '98 Centenary branches took on the additional task
of protesting attempts to celebrate Queen Victoria's
diamond jubilee. The most fervent was the Irish Socialist
Republican Party, founded in Dublin in 1896 by James
Connolly, the short, stubby, rather bowlegged emigrant
from Edinburgh who was contributing to Maud Gonne's

paper. Self-educated, poverty-stricken, twenty-nine years old, Connolly had the extraordinary notion that not only could an independent Irish nation be created but that its management could be put in the hands of the Irish working class. It was an idea guaranteed to infuriate all respectable elements, and its time has still not come; but it has shown so much vitality that almost every radical group and trade union in Ireland claims James Connolly as its ideological founder.

Connolly made elaborate preparations for the jubilee counterdemonstration. With Maud Gonne's aid he obtained the use of one of the National Club windows from which to throw lantern slides onto a huge screen in Parnell (then Rutland) Square. The slides were Pat O'Brien's photographs of eviction scenes and portraits of Irish martyrs and prisoners during Queen Victoria's reign. To dim the festive lights which might compete with the slides, he arranged with city workers to create electrical faults at the correct time. A large black coffin, inscribed with the words "British Empire," was to be paraded behind a workers' band whose battered instruments would be small loss if the police demolished them. Finally, Maud Gonne set to work turning out black flags embroidered with the fruits of Connolly's research—facts about famines and evictions during Victoria's reign. The demonstration was scheduled for the evening of the jubilee, June 22, 1897.

While these preparations were going on, Connolly asked Maud if she would speak at a meeting of his Socialist party on Jubilee Day. She accepted, thinking it would be a few Socialist faithful in a small hall. But some days later, when she and Yeats arrived in Dublin for a meeting of the '98 Centenary Committee, they found the streets placarded with huge announcements of an open-air gathering on Dame Street, with her name listed as principal speaker. Since Maud was not a Socialist, did not desire to appear as one, and had never spoken at an open-air rally, she sent a note to Connolly withdrawing her acceptance. He promptly visited her and pleaded with her to keep her promise. If she did not, he said, his reputation would be ruined, for no one would believe that she had once consented. She was firm and Connolly left, but W. B. Yeats, who was present, was so touched by Connolly's despair that he succeeded in softening her heart. She called on Connolly and came back "with a pathetic account of his wife and his four children and their one room."

On the appointed day, a huge crowd appeared on Dame Street. While Maud was speaking, an old woman kept waving before her face a miniature of a famous patriot and kept calling out, "I was in it before she was born." Maud, unperturbed, told how she had attempted to decorate the graves of the Manchester Martyrs and had been refused permission because of the jubilee. "In a low voice that yet seemed to go through the whole crowd, she demanded, must the graves of our dead go undecorated because Victoria has her Jubilee?" The whole crowd went wild. Yeats reports that Maud wanted to join in the ensuing riot, but he prevented her from doing so, to her great irritation.

At eight o'clock that evening, while the executive committee of the '98 Commemoration Organization was meeting at City Hall in contempt of Jubilee Day, the first sounds of a band were heard. At Maud's suggestion, chairman John O'Leary suspended the meeting so that all those present could go out to witness the parade. Maud and Yeats were among those who joined it, distributing black flags as it moved down Dame Street to the tune of a funeral dirge.

By the time the procession reached O'Connell Bridge, the police were clubbing heads to disperse the crowds and it was clear that the parade could advance no further. Just before he was arrested Connolly ordered the coffin to be thrown in the Liffey, crying out, in a flash of inspiration, "Here goes the coffin of the British Empire!"

Maud and Yeats continued along O'Connell Street to see how the magic lantern show at Parnell Square was faring. The city electricians had effectively done their jobs, for the pictures were vivid and were being shown over and over again to a group consisting mostly of older people and children.

The two companions then went into the National Club to order a cup of tea for Maud, then hearing a tumult outside, rushed to the window, saw police wielding batons, and a woman lying prone on the ground. Someone called out, "The police killed her."

What took place next is told so differently by each of them that they do not appear to be describing the same incident, further evidence of the great divergence in concerns and temperament that existed between them. According to Maud's autobiography, she went downstairs to the outside door. It was locked, and the key was in the club secretary's pocket.

Willie was saying, "Don't let her out." "I must get out," I called, and was making for the back door when Lorcan Sherlock consented to unlock the front door and Willie followed me out. A crowd was gathering again and the police were in an ugly mood, but somewhat frightened at having killed a woman absolutely without provocation. . . .

On all sides I heard people saying: "They have killed an old woman, the cowards!" I pushed my way into the group round the prostrate figure. Someone said: "This is your work, Miss Gonne, I hope you are satisfied."

The girl kneeling beside the old woman said: "Mother wanted to see the pictures so I brought her when the crowd had gone and they have killed her."

An ambulance arrived and the men lifted the dead woman, and her daughter followed. A man whispered to me: "We will avenge her, Miss Gonne." . . .

Slowly, Yeats and I walked down O'Connell Street. Suddenly we heard a crash of glass and a big plate glass window on the opposite side of the street was shattered. The news of the killing of the poor old woman had spread like wild fire and the people were avenging her death. £2,000 worth of plate glass in shops with Jubilee decorations was smashed that night.

In Yeats's *Memoirs,* the incident begins with a man rushing into the club and crying out, "The police are batoning the people outside. It's awful, awful."

Maud Gonne got up and said she was going out and somebody else said she would be hurt. I told them to lock the door and keep her in. . . . She was perhaps right to be angry when I refused to let her out unless she explained what she meant to do. "How do I know till I get out?" she said. I offered to go out myself if she would not try to get out when the door was opened, though what I could have done with my whisper I do not know, but she would make no promise. Later on she told me that I had made her do the only cowardly thing of her life.

Early the next morning, Maud went to the Bridewell,* sent in a breakfast for Connolly, and spoke with him before he went into the dock. He was cold, hungry, suffering from lack of sleep, worried about his family's support if he were to be long detained. He asked her to tell his wife about his arrest and Maud gives two different accounts of what Mrs. Lilly Connolly said when she received the news. One version reads: "I was sure something like that had happened when James didn't come home." The other: "He cares for nothing but the cause, and I would not have him otherwise."

Maud went back to court, arranged bail for all those who had been arrested, and later got Tim Harrington to defend them. The nationalist leader, famed for his advocacy of land reform, proved that the glass breaking and other damage attributed to the defendants were provoked by the brutal murder of an old woman, and everybody was released.

*British term for any local house of correction, after a famous prison that formerly existed at St. Bride's Well in London.

During those same crowded hours, Maud sent Connolly a brief note:

Bravo! all my congratulations to you! You were right and I was wrong about this evening. You may have the satisfaction of knowing that you saved Dublin from the humiliation of an English jubilee without a public meeting of protestation. You were the only man who had the courage to . . . carry through in spite of all discouragement—even from friends!

Connolly so treasured this letter that he preserved it through many years of wandering. It was found among his papers after he died.

To stimulate celebrations of the '98 Centenary, Maud Gonne and W. B. Yeats traveled together throughout England and Scotland and it was then that it occurred to Yeats that the nationalists might form an alliance with certain unionists who were indignant about the overtaxation of their property in Ireland. Maud seemed to support the idea, but, whenever he heard her mention it to others, it came out as a proposal that Ireland should replace its present members in Parliament with "eighty ragged and drunken Dublin beggars or eighty pugilists 'to be paid by results.'"

What she meant was that Irish representation at the Parliament in Westminster should cease. It was, Yeats thought, a historic suggestion. In his autobiographical work, *The Stirring of the Bones*, he wrote that Maud Gonne "was the first who spoke publicly or semi-publicly of the withdrawal of the Irish Members as a practical policy for our time, so far as I know." This is worth remembering in an assessment of Maud's contributions to Irish history.

Yeats concluded that the alliance he had planned was premature and impossible because of his own sedentary and thoughtful disposition; "but Maud Gonne was not sedentary, and I noticed that before some great event she did not think but became exceedingly superstitious. . . . Once upon the eve of some demonstration, I found her with many caged larks and finches which she was about to set free for luck's sake."

His description of Maud at this time deserves to be given at length.

Her power over crowds was at its height, and some portion of the power came because she could still, even when pushing an abstract principle to what seemed to me an absurdity, keep her own mind free, and so when men and women did her bidding they did it not only because she was beautiful, but because that beauty suggested joy and freedom. Besides, there was an element in her beauty that moved minds full of old Gaelic stories and poems, for she looked as though she lived in an ancient civilisation where all superiorities whether of the mind or the body were a part of public ceremonial, were in some way the crowd's creation. . . . Her beauty, backed by her great stature, could instantly affect an assembly . . . for it was incredibly distinguished, and . . . her whole body seemed a master-work of long labouring thought. . . .

A more casual description is contained in a letter Yeats wrote to Lady Gregory, to whom he owed a debt of gratitude for two summer months at Coole Park obtaining much-needed sustenance for his body and spirit. The letter was written from Manchester, where he and Maud had endured a long and exhausting political meeting in the morning, and were scheduled for another that evening.

After the meeting this morning Miss Gonne and myself went to the picture gallery to see a Rossetti that is there. She is very kind and friendly, but whether more than that I cannot tell. I have been explaining the Celtic movement and she is enthusiastic over it in its more mystical development, and tells me that her cousin Miss May Gonne, who is clever I think, will be anxious to help. . . . She and Miss Gonne are going to some place in the West, if Miss Gonne can make time, to see visions. I told Miss Gonne what Lady Mayo said about her losing a lot of money at Aix les Bains and she says it is quite accurate except that she won £100 instead of losing. . . . I have been chairman of a noisy meeting for three hours and am very done up. . . . Everything went smoothly this morning in spite of anonymous letters warning us to keep a bodyguard at the door. Perhaps the disturbance waits for tonight. I find the infinite triviality of politics more trying than ever. We tear each other's character in pieces for things that don't matter to anybody.

Maud tells the story of her big gambling win in *A Servant of the Queen*. Accompanied by May Gonne, she had gone to Aix-les-Bains for a three-week stay because she was tired and suffering from "a bad attack of rheumatism." Advised by a fortune-teller "to play boldly," she piled up a fortune in one afternoon and evening, more than she needed for the defense of all the Jubilee prisoners. She returned to Aix-les-Bains a few years later, took the advice of the same fortune-teller, and lost. "But I was merely playing for myself at that time and I never have luck when I try to do anything for myself."

Encouraged by the success of her speaking engagements, Maud Gonne thought that it was time for her to make a tour of the United States. She proposed to encourage Irish-Americans to attend the '98 Centenary events being held in Ireland, to raise funds for the Wolfe Tone monument and the Amnesty Association, and perhaps reduce antagonism between the rival Devoy and Sullivan factions of the Irish Republican Brotherhood in the United States.

The Dublin IRB, followers of Devoy, refused to give her permission, knowing she would be sponsored in America by the Sullivanites. Yeats, beginning to display his aptitude for organizational work, countered this move by calling a meeting in his rooms of the London Fenians and obtaining their approval for the trip. He based his argument on Maud's recent induction into Dr. Ryan's organization.

Maud left on Sunday, October 17, 1897, on the Cunard liner *Lucania*. A few weeks later, the Devoy faction began circulating, with many new details, the old story that Maud was a British spy.

CHAPTER VIII

Ireland's Joan of Arc

🌿 MAUD GONNE SPENT two and a half months in the United States, traveling west as far as Denver, north as far as Chicago, south as far as Fort Worth, and east as far as Boston. The newspapers gave her journey ample coverage, although the *New York Times* was less likely to print her speeches verbatim that the *Irish World*. The latter was a weekly founded in 1870 by Patrick Ford, a native of Galway, that printed news from all thirty-two Irish counties; fanned the flames of Irish wrath against the English; and fought rampant prejudice against the Catholic Church and the Irish, campaigning against the prevalent image of the grotesque stage Irishman with his pig and shillelagh.

Maud's trip started badly. The tender on which she left Cork harbor was small and she was thoroughly wet with spray by the time she boarded the steamer. She retired miserably to her cabin, further oppressed because the only pet she could have with her was her tame canary.

Maud told the steward that all she was having for lunch and dinner were some of her own chloral drops. She had intended to have the same menu the next day, and to stay in her stateroom, but changed her mind when Fridtjof Nansen, the famed Norwegian explorer, sent her a message insisting that she join him on deck. Maud was not sorry, for

Nansen turned out to be a handsome man only four years older than she and an excellent storyteller.

Nansen and Maud were curious about the quarters in which the emigrants lived, but were not permitted to examine them because of a strict rule barring all other passengers from any communication with the steerage. Indignant at this rejection, Maud became even more so when she discovered that the first-class passengers were served seven lavish meals a day.

Maud was met at New York harbor on October 23, 1897 by a band playing Irish music in a boat bedecked with Irish and American flags. She was greeted by William Lyman, president of the Irish National Alliance that was sponsoring some of her meetings, and by a little red-haired man named James F. Egan, one of the first prisoners to have been released from Portland jail. No one seems to have worried about customs inspection. Amid cheers and handshakes Maud, Lyman, and Egan were driven off to a magnificent suite that the reception committee had engaged at the Hotel Savoy.

Maud had insisted that Egan come along because he was the only person she had met before. Later she asked him to accompany her on her tour and, when he answered that William Lyman would not permit it, brushed his objection aside. "He'll have to, if I say that I need you as a first-hand witness about the horrors of Portland." Needless to say, she won her point.

She wanted to relinquish the expensive suite at the Savoy for a single room in a cheaper hotel. "The prisoners' families need all the money we can raise," she said. "I am not going to allow it to be wasted on me." But when Lyman argued that in America if you didn't appear to have lots of money you wouldn't get any, Maud compromised. She would stay in the suite to sleep that night and for press interviews the next morning but then she would move to a single room.

In reporting the arrival of the "Irish Joan of Arc" (probably the first use of the term), the *New York Times* described Maud as "tall and lithe, with a typical Irish face and voice," aged twenty-nine, born in Dublin, the daughter of a colonel in the British army. It stated that she expected fully a million Irish Americans to attend the '98 celebrations, that she had "a comfortable income" and would pay her own expenses on the tour.

In her first talk in the U.S., given at the Grand Opera House, 23rd Street and 8th Avenue, and in all her subsequent talks, Maud told her audience that the population of Ireland since the beginning of the century had shrunk from 8½ million to 4½ million; she herself had witnessed in County Donegal a thousand families "turned out in the fields to die." The jubilee of Queen Victoria, she told her audience, "marked sixty years of plunder, rapine, and piracy. Ireland's jubilee will reflect the noblest struggle for independence the world has ever seen."

Other details in the *Irish World* account were that Maud had spent a large part of her inherited fortune in Ireland's cause; and that she had become an Irish patriot because, while driving on the west coast of Ireland, she had witnessed the eviction of an old man who had died from exposure to wind and rain "forced to seek shelter with his family in a boat.... In his death was the birth of Miss Gonne's determination to devote her life to the cause of Ireland." The *New York Times* story was equally sympathetic, giving the full text of the introductory speech by William McAdoo, assistant secretary of the navy under Cleveland (not to be confused with William Gibbs McAdoo, Woodrow Wilson's secretary of the treasury). McAdoo called Maud a woman who "has foregone her rank and station to serve her native country," and spoke of the charm of person and of mind that had won her admission "to the exclusive courts of Europe, where she has eloquently pleaded the cause of Ireland."

When Miss Gonne first rose to speak, the *Times* continued,

Every motion she made betrayed the deep nervous strain under which she was laboring, but her voice was clear and strong, and she made her points with telling effect. Several times her remarks were greeted with ringing cheers, while at the tragic parts of her narrative sobs and moans were distinctly audible. Many a handkerchief was held to the eyes while she recited the story of privation and destitution which her countrymen had undergone during the last century.

Maud ended her talk by asserting that England's boasted civilization was only a blind for a policy of exterminating women and children of other races; and by urging her audience to "rise up and tear the veil of hypocrisy from England's face and show the baseness and horrors of English rule."

She arrived in Washington, D.C., on November 9, ready to confer with many prominent people to whom she had letters of introduction, and eager to see places of public interest. Toward the end of the week she visited a number of New England cities, and a few days later received a tremendous ovation in Youngstown, Ohio, at a meeting held in honor of the Manchester Martyrs.

In Chicago, a much larger meeting to honor the Manchester Martyrs was held on November 23 with the mayor in the chair. The audience, which occupied "every seat and every inch of standing room in Central Music Hall," passed a resolution disapproving passage of a bill, then under consideration, that would compel the United States and England to submit to arbitration any future disagreements. The Irish-American assemblage believed, with Miss Gonne, that England wanted this "not to preserve peace, but to guarantee her a position in which she can make war." Maud proclaimed that England was "never more to be dreaded than when she holds out her hand in friendship, when she professes honor and justice."

On the front page of its issue of December 25, the *Irish World* published a two-column article by Maud Gonne in which she cited to good effect the words of Jefferson and Adams against ever signing a treaty with England, and asked, "If England is so enamored with the principle of arbitration, why is she unwilling to consent to submit the Irish question to arbitration?" England, she argued, wanted the treaty for strategic reasons only—so that she could withdraw from the Western Hemisphere the forces maintained there for fear of complications with America.

Speaking in Brooklyn on the day after Christmas, she said, among other things: "England has claimed that the Irish are incapable of government. Look at the number of our race who are holding positions of trust in politics, professions, and among the brilliant writers of the day. Is not this sufficient evidence that we have men who can govern? Gladstone was a hypocrite."

On Monday, December 27, 1897, Maud Gonne was given a farewell reception at the Cooper Institute in New York City. An official of the United Irish Societies and their women's auxiliaries, sponsors of the meeting, presented her with a purse of $250. James F. Egan, now billed as a delegate from the Amnesty Association of Ireland and Great Britain, delivered an address, and many patriotic songs were sung: "Who Fears to Speak of Ninety-eight?," "The Green Old Flag," and "O'Donnell Aboo."

In her final address, as reported in the *Irish World*, Maud praised the contributions made to America by Irish immigrants, urged them to visit the old country for the '98 Centenary celebration, and said that the road to Ireland's freedom must be the same one that the American colonies had taken in 1776. Obviously reflecting the anti-Semitic sentiments of her reactionary French friends, she called Britain "the fortress and stronghold of the cosmopolitan financiers and monopolists and money-lenders" who had brought "ruin and misery" on the working classes in Europe.

As a parting gift Maud Gonne was presented with a

handsomely embossed and framed resolution of gratitude
from the Irish-American women of Brooklyn, hailed by
their spokeswoman as "Ireland's Joan of Arc," and thanked
for abandoning "a charming home . . . devoted friends," and
"high social position" in order to "disseminate the doctrine
of union and independence among the scattered children of
Erin."

Maud did not forget her resolve to try and mend the
differences between the Irish factions in America. Though
her tour was "severely boycotted" by the Devoy section of
the IRB, she managed, with the aid of James F. Egan, to
locate and talk persuasively with its leaders in almost every
city she visited. To each she said, "I ask you, in the name of
Ireland, not to waste time on past regrets. Dr. Cronin is
dead. . . . Alexander O'Sullivan is dead, more is the pity,
for he seems to have been a great man. . . . Why are you
wasting the strength of this great organization on dead
men's quarrels? The British Empire is not dead yet, and
you are pledged to fight it. Get on with the work. Ireland is
waiting in slavery."

Maud spoke on an average of four evenings a week, and
raised $3,500, half of which went to the Amnesty Society,
the other half to the '98 Centenary Committee. She left
the United States with her mind full of confused memories
of crowded auditoriums, trains, hotels, reception committees, and hospitable people whom she wanted to know better
but couldn't. It seems that, with true maudgonne unpredictability, her happiest days were spent in some mining
villages in the west.

Owing to an error in scheduling, she and James Egan had
a free day in Denver, Colorado. Maud was delighted, for
she was tired and getting "unbecomingly thin." But her
plans for a day of rest were shattered when three boisterous
miners, speaking with an Irish brogue, invaded her hotel,
insisted on piling her and Egan into a waiting carriage, and
taking them to the towns where they worked. It was a

wonderful trip in the moonlight through the mountains, "through gorges and roads edging dark precipices." A woman from County Mayo, who lived in a wooden frame house in Cripple Creek, welcomed Maud and Egan with an early-morning breakfast of bacon, eggs, and tea, sent them off to sleep, and told them they would be called for at noon. At that time Maud went down into the mines and gave the men from two shifts the latest news from Ireland. That evening she gave another talk in a hall at Victor. Let Maud Gonne finish the story in her own words.

I spent the happiest days of my whole American tour in those mining villages. In their hard, exciting lives, these people never forgot Ireland, and Egan and I were both sad to leave the following day. . . . We were laden with all sorts and sizes of rocks, with little bits of shining gold glistening on them, given us as souvenirs, and three hundred dollars for the prisoners and messages innumerable for folk at home and promises that when the fight was on for Irish freedom, the men would be back with us.

The veteran Fenian, O'Donovan Rossa (originally Jeremiah O'Donovan), came to the boat to see her off. Now in his late sixties, he had been a red-haired giant from Bantry in his twenties, when, as a grass-roots organizer for the Irish Republican Brotherhood, he had taken on the task of overturning the British Empire. A lengthy term of imprisonment in Dartmoor had shrunken his stature, but his spirit was unbroken and his faith in the eventual freedom of Ireland was unshaken.

CHAPTER IX

The End of an Affair (1898)

Maud landed in England the first week of January 1898; spoke on January 9 at a Centenary meeting; and had a conversation with W. B. Yeats that raised his spirits considerably. He wrote George Russell on January 27 that Maud and he were "going for a week or two perhaps to some country place in Ireland to get as you do the forms and gods and spirits and to get some sacred earth for our evocation. . . . MG has seen the vision of a little temple of the elements which she proposes to build somewhere in Ireland when '98 is over and to make it the centre of our mystical and literary movements."

Maud's immediate interest in rural Ireland arose from famine conditions in counties Mayo and Kerry. With James Connolly she wrote a two-page leaflet proving that it was moral for starving men to seize food that did not belong to them; that the right to life countermanded the right to hold property. The leaflet was headed by appropriate quotations from Pope Clement I: "The use of all things is to be common to all"; Pope Gregory the Great: "The fruits which the earth brings forth must belong without distinction to all"; Cardinal Manning: "In case of extreme need of food, all goods become common property"; and St. Thomas Aquinas: "If . . . urgent necessity has to be relieved . . . man may lawfully relieve his distress out of the property of another, taking it—either openly or secretly."

The body of the text tried to teach the Irish a lesson from history:

In 1847 our people died by thousands of starvation though every ship leaving an Irish port was laden with food in abundance. The Irish people might have seized that food . . . but did not do so, believing such action to be sinful and dreading to peril their souls to save their bodies. In this belief, we know now they were entirely mistaken. The very highest authorities on the Doctrine of the Church agree that no *human* law can stand between starving people and their RIGHT TO FOOD including the right to take that food whenever they find it, openly or secretly, with or without the owner's permission.

Irishmen were urged to

. . . take with the strong hand, if need be, that which rightfully be-longs to you . . . and show the world that you are resolved never again to let the sun shine upon the spectacle of Irish men and women dying as dogs would die—of hunger in the sight of food.

The pamphlet was signed Maud Gonne, but most of the writing, and certainly all of the research, was Connolly's. She gave him £25 to have the leaflet printed and to cover his expenses while he toured County Kerry distributing it. It is not likely that Connolly, with his strange Edinburgh accent and obvious city ways, made many converts.

Maud soon headed for the west herself, seeking to publicize the '98 Centenary observances, gather further material for articles on the famine (she had already published one in the *Freeman's Journal*), and inspire the farmers to take militant action to improve their situation.

Maud arrived on March 12, 1898 in Ballina, northern Mayo, accompanied by various dignitaries of the centennial movement. After she got off the train, the local newspaper reported,

a bright and handsome lad of tender years . . . nicely attired, and hold-ing a banner in one hand bearing the words in green and gold, "Who fears to speak of '98?" and an elaborate bunch of flowers in the other, presented the latter to Miss Gonne who received the gift very gracefully and imprinted a kiss on the youth's cheek.

Miss Gonne was seated in a waiting "wagonnette,"

the horse was withdrawn, and the wagonnette was drawn by willing hands to the residence of Mr. T. B. Kelly, Arthur-st., the band proceeding and playing, and the crowd cheering, Miss Gonne all smiles, and greatly appreciating the attention she received. In the evening... at eight o'clock a procession was formed, a number of men carrying lighted torches, lighted tar barrels, and the band playing....

When Miss Gonne and her party mounted the platform, they were greeted by an outburst of applause, to which "the popular and fascinating lady bowed her acknowledgments." Maud wore a green costume but no hat. To the reporter, obviously a believer in phrenology, she appeared "tall and graceful . . . evidently a strong person—the formation of the head denoting both physical and mental strength." He detected in her expression and movements tenderness, womanly grace, and "a kind and sympathetic disposition. . . . Her sweet voice, clear enunciation, and graceful action" were "pleasing beyond description." Toward the end of her lecture, when she appealed to the patriotism of the audience, "in a subdued, and even plaintive tone of voice, the effect was almost electrical. Having seen and heard Miss Gonne, one is not surprised at the influence she wields, whether in private circles, going about on errands of charity, or on the public platform."

The gist of Maud's talk was that Ireland's opportunity was close at hand. England was in difficulties with both Russia and Germany, while France had its eye on England's possession Egypt. "When these several powers closed in on England," she was quoted as saying, "then Ireland would be prepared, and go in for her share."

Maud went on to other towns in County Mayo. In one village she heard a tale about children's graves being left unfinished because the people were too weak to dig any more; in another village, of people begging for scraps of food from the coast guard station near Belderrig. The man there told her, "They would do far better to go to the workhouse, even though the fever is there too; but they won't go because they would then lose their title to the land and they prefer to starve."

Maud stayed up all night, wrapped in the fur coat that Uncle Charlie had given her when she came of age, writing to Ellen Ford, wife of the editor of the *Irish World*, to ask for money with which to feed school children and nurse fever patients. Ellen promptly opened a subscription list in the paper, and money began to come in.

In the morning, with the help of a local woman named Peggy Hegarty, Maud cooked oatmeal over a turf fire for a group of women from homes where someone had already died of the fever. Since they had no fear of infection, they joined in a rough-and-ready scheme for nursing sick inhabitants of the village. Maud wrote in her autobiography: "All the credit for the nursing scheme was due to Peggy who was far more knowledgeable and helpful than myself, but my cheerful confidence was more infectious than the fever."

That evening Maud held a meeting on the quay where the fishing boats came in. She spoke to the men about the need for a fish-curing plant, so that no fish from a big catch would be wasted, and each home would have some herring when the weather was too bad for the currachs to go out. She promised that if they put up a demand for a plant, she would see that they got it, and told them they would get better pay while building it than they did on relief. The men seemed to like this point, but the ideas in the leaflet that she distributed were harder to swallow.

One man said, "What is there for us to take? There is nothing except Kelly's store and it is Mrs. Kelly who is keeping us all alive."

When Maud suggested that there were sheep on the mountains belonging to the landlords, one man said, "We are not sheep-stealers"; another, "We don't like mutton."

Maud answered, "You are worse than sheep-stealers if you allow one of your children to die of hunger when there is food to be taken—food which will keep your wives and children alive. If you go to jail for it, you will go as honourable men, for a decent cause, but if you are clever, no one will go to jail. Who is to stop you on these lonely mountains? Be men. Go out hunting." Few took her advice.

When two boys were arrested for distributing her leaflets around Ballycastle, Maud ordered more leaflets, this time with her name printed on them, so that if the distributors were arrested she would have to be prosecuted also.

Monsignor Hewson, the parish priest of Belmullet, received her kindly, somewhat to her surprise, for some Mayo clergy were denouncing her and the '98 Centenary Committee for stirring up old hatreds. He said her article in the *Freeman's Journal* had understated the famine. "You have not said the worst, which is that they have been forced to eat seed potato. It is now time for spring sowing and there is nothing being put into the ground, so famine next year is inevitable."

When Maud asked the Monsignor what she should write about the work relief projects, he said, "Say they are only organising famine. Sixpence a day for useless work, making roads leading nowhere, or moving hillocks from one side of the road to the other. Sixpence a day to feed a family often of twelve or thirteen people!"

The following day Maud visited several relief stations and, with a curate acting as interpreter, told the men that the famine must be stopped, that she knew how to stop it, that it would be worth their while to come to Belmullet the following morning at eleven. To an overseer who announced that any man absent from work the following day would be discharged, Maud replied that any such person would be employed by her at double wages.

As they drove off, the curate asked Maud, "How will you keep that promise?"

"I don't know," Maud replied. "But I must have them all

in Belmullet for the board meeting if we are to stop the famine."

Showing her usual facility in mastering new fields, Maud drafted a list of minimum demands; the pay for relief work should be raised from sixpence to one shilling a day; no woman should work on the roads if she could get a man to replace her; lodging money should be given anyone who had to walk over a mile to get to the relief works; seed potatoes should be distributed free to prevent recurrence of famine; men preparing the ground and planting seed on their own holdings should be considered as doing relief work and be paid accordingly.

On the way back to her hotel Maud noticed that the country people were looking at her with mixed feelings of awe, affection, and fright. The curate told her that they still believed in the prophecies of Brian Ruadh, a great scholar who, on the day before his death, predicted that some day news would be carried into Belmullet on the top of sticks (the telegraph), that carriages without horses would drive through the mountains (the railroads), that there would be a famine, that a woman dressed in green would come and preach revolt, and that the English would be driven out. The superstitious natives thought that Maud was fulfilling part of the prophecy.

The next day people from the entire countryside abandoned their relief jobs and crowded into Belmullet. Standing before them, Maud read out her list of demands, then said that she was going into the courthouse to present them. She asked that no one leave until she had returned with an answer. The audience waited.

Two vice-guardians from Dublin Castle, a representative from the Congested Districts' Board, two representatives from the government relief works, and the town clerk were sitting in the courthouse. All of them refused to consider her demands, or even to read them, until she threatened to tell the people outside to take by force whatever food or anything else they saw in the town, and neither you nor your policemen can prevent it. It will mean bloodshed, perhaps death for some, as your twenty policemen are armed. But ten thousand people will soon take the guns from twenty policemen and it will be at least two, perhaps three days before you can get reinforcements of either police or military. . . . You may make some arrests, but in jail the prisoners will be fed. You may arrest me and much good it will do England in America and France to arrest a woman trying to save life.

The officials took her document and Maud worried while they deliberated. She realized that "starving people are not the best material for a fight; that the prejudice against stealing was inbred. The prophecy of Brian Ruadh was my best hope. Some of the men, I knew, would obey me and people would certainly get killed."

To her joy, the board capitulated, promising that the relief workers would get double pay from the following day and wiring Dublin that day for seed to be shipped in from Scotland for free distribution. The scene that followed outside the courthouse was "indescribable," with people kissing Maud's hands and her dress and urging her to stay, because "If you go, they won't keep their promises."

However, Maud was eager to get back to Dublin to try to get a fish-curing plant for Belderrig. With the assistance of Sir Joseph Robinson, an official of the Congested Districts' Board, she succeeded, then returned to County Mayo, and spent nearly two months in the villages arranging nursing schemes and promoting the Centenary. Before leaving she gave Peggy Hegarty two lambs so that the next year she would have wool enough for a dress.

When Maud got back to her comfortable Paris flat, she did nothing for two weeks except stay in bed and read novels, warmed by the conviction that "I had stopped the famine in Mayo, and, I think, saved many lives. Talking in the British House of Commons would never have done it."

Maud fails to mention in her autobiography that she was more than weary; she was suffering from bronchitis. Yeats visited her in Paris and wrote Lady Gregory on April 25,

1899, "One of her lungs is affected a little so that she had to rest. She is unable to do any politics for the time and looks ill and tired."

During the month of May, however, Maud was able to attend a meeting of the Paris '98 Centenary Committee and to speak about the Centenary at Amiens. Previously, she sent the Lord Mayor of Dublin £20 collected by *l'Irlande Libre* "for supplying bread to the school children, whose sufferings are terrible." She had been shocked, she said, by "the sight of those poor little pinched starved faces" in the west of Ireland. She thought it was "a disgrace to our country . . . for which the English government is alone responsible." This was probably the inception of her concern for feeding school children.

Back in Dublin in June, Maud suffered an accident during a demonstration. Yeats learned about it the following day and immediately wrote Lady Gregory:

Miss Gonne was thrown from a car yesterday by a horse falling. Her arm is broken and her face scratched and bruised. . . . I did not know until a few minutes to nine to-day when a messenger came to tell me. . . . She is so self-reliant that she would probably ask no one to nurse her, if she could get on at all without. . . . The doctor tells me that the break is not a bad one . . . I am most anxious about the shock for she has been very ill this spring with her old trouble in her lungs, and she was looking pale and ill as it was.

After seeing Maud, who was recovering at the home of the artist Sarah Purser, Yeats added a postscript saying that she was much better than he had. feared. He found her "cheerful and talkative," but he intended to remain for two or three days to see if he could be of any use in helping her handle her political correspondence and the like.

In a few months Maud's hectic round resumed. On August 9 Lionel Johnson sat next to her at a banquet held in London by the '98 Centennial Association of Great Britain and France. Afterward he said to Yeats, "I had thought she did her work, perhaps, from love of notoriety, but no, it is a sense of duty. I saw while she was speaking that her hand was trembling. I think she has to force herself to speak."

As time went on, Maud became increasingly impatient with the "senseless bickerings and intrigues" going on in the central Centenary Committee; and felt that chairman John O'Leary, however beloved, was too old to grasp and control the situation. She considered the bishops consistently hostile—"perhaps because they put interests of the Church first and judge that a Catholic Ireland is of greater missionary value than a small separate Catholic nation would be." This was a common belief among nationalists.

Maud shocked an audience in Kerry by saying that she approved the bishops' action in forbidding priests to participate in plans for the Centenary. It was unfair, she felt, to put men in a position where their duties could conflict. "Freedom could be won only by free men with one allegiance, Ireland," she wrote later.

Nor was Maud pleased by the artistic quality of the memorials to the '98 heroes that were being erected. She had supported autonomy for local committees in selecting monuments, but the results were disastrous. To make matters worse, Yeats charged her with encouraging the production of bad art. She answered that she would have been delighted if the committees had merely inscribed the names of Irish patriots on great hilltop rocks or copied Celtic crosses. But what could you expect, she asked, when Irish art schools refused to allow their students to use nude models?

Despite all this, Maud laid the foundation stone of a creditable memorial in Tralee, and saw a good Celtic cross unveiled in Mount Mellick. She considered the monument erected in Ballina as a tribute to French General Humber quite unsatisfactory, but was pleased that its unveiling gave two French groups the opportunity to come to Ireland. According to *United Ireland*, Maud's denunciation of England on this occasion "roused the dormant spirit of a military race, and a wild, defiant cheer rang through the Mayo town."

The most important of the Centenary meetings was held in Dublin on August 15, 1898, when the foundation stone of a monument to Wolfe Tone was laid at an entrance to St. Stephen's Green. For Maud the significant feature was the tight control of the Irish Parliamentary Party over the proceedings; the principal speakers were its leaders, John Redmond and John Dillon. Yeats was allowed to speak, she believed, only as a minor concession to the Irish Republican Brotherhood. She herself preferred not to be on the platform "while Parliamentarians were eulogising Wolfe Tone and trying to keep the people from following his teaching," so in company with the president of the Amnesty Association, she descended to explore the cavity that had been dug for the foundation stone. When it appeared that her movements were causing a disturbance, she climbed back up the ladder and walked down Grafton Street to her hotel. She felt depressed and dispirited, but might have felt better if she had at least been *asked* to speak.

The Centenary celebrations continued to the end of 1898. In November John O'Leary unveiled in his native Tipperary a statue of Charles Joseph Kickham, author of *Knocknagow*, a classic of rural Irish life, and in Manchester, Maud addressed 100,000 cheering Irishmen.

Even Dublin Castle seemed to be swept into the movement for eulogizing and restoring Irish culture. Lady Betty Balfour, wife of the chief secretary, made plans to stage in the Viceregal Lodge some *tableaux vivants* based on the text of *The Countess Cathleen* by William Butler Yeats. Someone suggested that Miss Gonne might play the principal role. "Imagine Miss Gonne at the Chief Secretary's Lodge!" commented Yeats in a letter to Lady Gregory.

Two significant events took place in October 1898. Arthur Griffith returned to Ireland after a stay of two years in South Africa, and a Fenian named Tom Clarke was released after fifteen years in English jails. Maud Gonne might have paid more attention to these events had she not been in the process of ending her long liaison with Lucien Millevoye. This took place in November or December 1898, a date deduced from the only existing accounts of the break-up: Maud's autobiography, Yeats's recently published *Memoirs*, and some of Yeats's letters to Lady Gregory.

It appears from *A Servant of the Queen* that some time after the Wolfe Tone ceremonies in Dublin Maud felt ready for a rest and accepted an invitation from her sister, Kathleen Pilcher, to join her and her family at Vevey, Switzerland. Shortly before her departure from Paris, she invited a friend, Ghenia de Sainte Croix, and Lucien Millevoye to go with her to a performance of a Wagner opera, in which one of her favorite singers, Breval, was taking the principal role. During the intermission, Millevoye remarked that he knew someone who, though she sang in a coffee house, performed the Valkyrie music much better than Breval. Only because this woman would not give herself to the managers, he said, did she not sing at the Opera.

Ghenia said acidly, "The Opera generally doesn't select its singers from coffee houses," whereupon Millevoye offered to bring his songstress to Maud's next party.

On the way home, Ghenia said significantly, "You are away from Paris too much, Maud *chérie*." Maud did not take this seriously, especially after she received a letter from Millevoye, asking her to meet him at Chamonix in the French Alps.

When they met, Maud was irate. She had just read in *La Patrie* an article over his signature which she considered nothing more than a sentimental, exaggerated appeal for liberating the people of Alsace-Lorraine. It pointed to Germany as the one and only enemy of France.

She asked Millevoye, "How could you have written this article which is so bad and which contradicts all we have been working for? It is entirely unlike your style."

Millevoye admitted that he had not written the article

but only signed it. "A woman who loves Alsace-Lorraine as you love Ireland wrote it."

Maud continues the story in a style reminiscent of Elinor Glynn or Marie Corelli:

For a long while I did not speak. I gazed at those cruel snow mountains which were turning my heart into stone in spite of the scent of the flowers and the hum of the wild bees around us, whispering of life.

Millevoye was talking a great deal; I hardly heard what he said. I think it was about the change which he said had come over me since I had taken up with those absurd Irish revolutionists who would never do anything. . . .

"I have seen them and judged them. Go back and work with the Home Rule party. Outside parliament you won't be able to do anything for Ireland. Take my advice."

My voice sounded strange and toneless to myself as I replied to these last words: "I would be foolish to do that, now our alliance is at an end. It has lasted for thirteen years, a long time in human life."

"Don't talk nonsense. You know I will always help you."

"You can't now, for we have different friends, different enemies and our roads lead different ways. You need not tell me the name of the writer of that article. It is the singer you wanted to bring to see me in Paris, a friend of Clemenceau. He has triumphed at last through her and has broken our alliance. Good-bye, old friend, I go on my way alone and carry on the fight."

She told Yeats the story of her liaison with Millevoye a month or two later.

It was her custom to inform him when they could meet and in December 1898 or January 1899 he received a letter from her saying she was coming to Dublin and would be staying at her usual hotel. Yeats left England and, following his own custom, checked into a different Dublin hotel. He feared that if he stayed in the same one, it might compromise her, a scruple Maud found amusing.

On this occasion, Yeats joined Maud for breakfast. During it she asked him, "Did you have a strange dream last night?" He replied, "I dreamed this morning for the first time in my life that you kissed me." She spoke of the matter no further, but that evening, after they had dined together,

Maud told him about her own dream of the night before. "A great spirit" had appeared at her bedside and had taken her to a great throng of other spirits, among whom was Yeats, had placed her hand in his, and told her they were married. Then Maud, for the first time, kissed him.

The following day Yeats found her sitting gloomily beside the fire. She said she should not have spoken to him in that way for she could never be his real wife. When Yeats asked, "Do you love someone else?" she said no, but admitted that there had been another person in her life.

Then bit by bit came out the story of her life, things I had heard all twisted awry by scandal, and disbelieved.

She had met in the South of France the French Boulangist deputy, Millevoye, while staying with a relative in her nineteenth year, and had at once and without any urging on his part fallen in love with him. She then returned to Dublin where her father had a military command.

One day, while sitting in her father's study looking at a book on magic that he owned, she had prayed to the devil that he might "give her control of her own life and offered in return her soul." Within two weeks her father was dead, and she was stricken with remorse.

She had control of her life now, and when she was of age settled in Paris, and after some months became Millevoye's mistress. She was often away from him, for sexual love soon began to repel her, but was for all that very much in love.

Maud went on to relate, not very coherently, that Millevoye had failed her in many ways. Once he had urged her to become the mistress of someone who could help him in his political projects. She had refused. After a daughter was born (Maud believed that sexual love was justified only by children), she had been on the verge of removing with her to Ireland and breaking with Millevoye when the child died.

As it was, after its death she had thought of breaking with him, and had engaged herself for a week to someone else—I thought, I may have had that poor betrothal for my reward—but had broken it off. The idea came to her that the lost child might be reborn, and she had gone back to Millevoye, in the vault under the memorial chapel. A girl child was born, now two years old. Since the child's birth, I understood her to say amid so much broken speech, she and Millevoye had lived apart.

After this confession, Maud returned to Paris, where Yeats shortly joined her and heard further details about her past life. Deeply perturbed, he wrote to Lady Gregory, who was in Venice, on February 4, 1899: "If you knew all . . . you would understand why this love has been so bitter a thing to me, and why things I have known lately have made it, in a certain sense, the bitterer, and the harder." The following week he wrote her in a second letter:

I have had rather a depressing time here. During the last months, and most of all while I have been here, she has told the story of her life, telling gradually, in more detail, all except a few things which I can see are too painful for her to talk of and about which I do not ask her.

But it was apparent to Yeats that Maud still felt necessary to her French lover ("She did not know what would happen to him if her influence was not there") and he was careful not to try to arouse any "temporary passionate impulse" on her part.

A few days later, while he was sitting quietly with Maud, she told him she heard a voice saying that they were about to receive the initiation of the spear.

We became silent; a double vision unfolded itself, neither speaking till all was finished. She thought herself a great stone statue through which passed flame, and I felt myself becoming flame and mounting up through and looking out of the eyes of a great stone Minerva. Were the beings which stand behind human life trying to unite us, or had we brought it by our own dreams? She was now always very emotional, and would kiss me very tenderly, but when I spoke of marriage on the eve of her leaving said "No, it seems to me impossible." And then, with clenched hands, "I have a horror and terror of physical love."

Yeats proceeded to tell, in the next paragraph, an incident that illuminates the kind of world in which he and Maud Gonne lived. He had just recovered from

a cold of an astonishing violence that kept me in bed without eating anything for a day and then went completely. MG is quite convinced that it is the work of a certain rival mystic, or of one of his attendant spirits. She points out that I went to see him without it and came back with it, which is circumstantial evidence at any rate....

Lady Gregory responded to Yeats's distraught letters with her usual solicitude. She immediately left Venice for home, offered him money to travel with Maud, and told him not to leave her side until he had obtained her promise of marriage. He refused; "No, I am too exhausted; I can do no more."

From this material, so short on fact, so long on international intrigue, occult phenomena, self-dramatization, and genuine torment, one clear conclusion emerges: the end of this love affair (like any other part of it) cannot possibly be told in a way that meets the standards of modern biography. No contemporary letters by Maud Gonne are available; her only account of it is in a section of a political autobiography written almost four decades after the death of the affair. From Yeats we get a few contemporary letters to Lady Gregory and a memoir describing events that had happened almost two decades earlier and written by a man whose mind was steeped in love and mysticism. From nowhere, of course, do we get Millevoye's side of things.

Almost any conclusion can be drawn from this untrustworthy, albeit enchanting, material. It is quite possible to believe that Maud first met Lucien as early as mid-1884, when she was nineteen and her father still alive; that she once wished for her father's death (a not extraordinary circumstance among angry children); and that Iseult was conceived in a vault under a memorial chapel. It seems doubtful that Maud was frigid, for Millevoye would not have remained so long with her if she had been. But that he wanted her to become the mistress of a man who might be politically useful to him is preposterous. At bottom Maud must have known that she was not really needed to keep Millevoye on the correct political path or provide a "moral nature" for him.

CHAPTER X

Up the Boers (1899)

THE FIRST ISSUE of the *United Irishman*, with Arthur Griffith as editor, appeared on March 4, 1899. It revived the name of an earlier periodical issued by the intransigent rebel John Mitchel, in 1848, and, like its predecessor, it preached Dean Swift's doctrine that "by the law of God, of nature and of nations," the Irish "had a right to be as free a people as the people of England." Though he was a member of the Irish Republican Brotherhood, Griffith was convinced that the policy of armed uprising would not be feasible until his fellow countrymen had recovered their self-respect. This required, first, that they become familiar with their own language, literature, and history; second, that they rely on their own efforts and cease looking to England with slavish gratitude for every improvement in their lot—which could come about only if the Irish representatives at Westminster left England and established a native parliament on Irish soil. A third stipulation was that Ireland must become a manufacturing nation, for otherwise it could never stem emigration, increase in population, or improve the quality of its political, intellectual, and social life. Arthur Griffith even fought against higher wages for factory workers because it hindered the growth of Irish industry. For that reason he and James Connolly never became friends.

Griffith's followers were abstemious, sober, puritanical men who tried, on principle, to use only Irish products. Even when they smoked or drank, it was Gallaher's tobacco, Guinness beer, and Jameson whiskey.

Griffith was a reserved, harsh, intellectual man six years younger than Maud Gonne. Sean O'Casey once jeeringly charged him with posing deliberately as Ireland's "strong, silent man," adding that his "great protruding jaws" were considered by his admirers "the God-given sign of a great man." In *Drums Under the Windows*, O'Casey portrays him listening skeptically to a speech by James Connolly, "hunched close inside his thick dark Irish coat, a dark-green velour on his head, a thick slice of leather nailed to his heels to lift the lowness of his stature." O'Casey did not know that these lifts were necessary because both his feet were deformed, which caused the rolling, sailor's walk that many people noted.

Early in the life of the *United Irishman*, Maud Gonne made a practice of paying Griffith's salary as editor. It was 25 shillings a week, the exact amount he needed to pay his mother for his room and board; he would take no more. In view of the weekly's role in strengthening the Irish desire for separation, this subsidy must be considered one of the most important ways in which Maud influenced Irish history. Typically enough, she mentions it only once, and very briefly, in her autobiography.

Griffith was grateful for the stipend; he had, moreover, a genuine admiration for Maud's abilities and almost certainly a sentimental, if hopeless, affection for her. For all these reasons he opened wide the pages of the *United Irishman* to articles by and about her. During the first ten months of the weekly's existence every other issue, on the average, contained a Gonne item. Griffith also showed his concern for Maud in another way. When her friend's play, *The Countess*

Cathleen, was produced on May 8 by the New Irish Literary Theatre, he refused to join other nationalists in calling it an insult to faith and Christian doctrine because of its theme of a willingly sacrificed soul.

Yeats had asked Maud to play the title role, but she had refused, fearing it might divert her from her other activities. She was like "a horse that has to wear blinkers to prevent being sidetracked—I must not look to the right or left," she wrote later. But her refusal did not indicate any lack of support and enthusiasm for the Irish Literary Theatre. When Lady Gregory asked her to become one of its "guarantors," she consented "with great pleasure." She also said, in the same undated letter from Paris, that she was sorry to hear that Willie Yeats had been ill and hoped he had already recovered.

From the invaluable columns of the *United Irishman*, one can see how Maud's interests in 1899 alternated between two major issues: the condition of the peasantry and the Boer war.

On the eve of St. Patrick's Day, she was in Ireland, discussing peasant evictions at a meeting held in Belfast. In April she twice discussed Ireland's agricultural problems with George Russell, who had left Pim's drapery shop to become an employee of Sir Horace Plunkett's Irish Agricultural Organisation Society, which sponsored farm cooperatives.

By the fall of 1899, however, the dispute between the British government and the Boers of South Africa had become a flaming issue for Maud. On September 2, at a meeting of the Irish Socialist Republican Party, founded by James Connolly, a letter from her was read praising the minuscule organization for opposing British aggression in South Africa. The *United Irishman* reported enthusiastic cheers for the Boers, the social revolution, and Maud Gonne.

In its issue of September 23 the same paper published a

long article by Maud protesting the shipment of regiments
with Irish names to South Africa to participate "in one of the
most unjust and iniquitous wars that ever disgraced the
world. . . ."

The Dublin and the Munster Fusiliers are not entirely composed of
Irishmen . . . recruiting in Ireland I am glad to say (and I have this from
the lips of an English general) is falling off very considerably; the
so-called Irish regiments have to be made up by a large mixture of
English Cockneys. England jealously conserves the Irish names of her
regiments in order to show the world that there are still Irishmen so
devoid of dignity that they will wear the uniform of their oppressors. . . .

She ticked off the reasons why some Irishmen persisted
in joining the British army: essentially a military people,
they had no army of their own to join; they joined to avoid
starvation; they got drunk and didn't know what they were
doing; they were gulled by the English, and most of the
Irish, press into considering "Irish" regiments as their own.
England needed Irish soldiers, Maud continued, because
she

knows that sooner or later she will have to fight a coalition of Europe.
Her able diplomatists and, above all, her Jewish allies, who foment
quarrels and internal strife among the different countries whom her
policy of grab has exasperated, may be able to stave off the day of
reckoning for a time, but sooner or later it will come, and she knows
that it is not with the puny, diseased refuse of the slums of her great
manufacturing towns that she will be able to meet the armed nations of
Europe.

In the same issue, the *United Irishman* admitted that
Alfred Dreyfus and Christ were both Jews, as asserted in a
Dublin newspaper, but pointed out that the Bible also mentions one Iscariot who "more fittingly compares with the
'martyr' who has just accepted a pardon . . . an innocent
man would have scorned to accept."

On October 7, 1899, the *United Irishman* carried another

long article by Maud Gonne, in which she attacked Dublin officials who invariably spoke "with a weak and quavering voice when faced with a Nationalist issue." This discrepancy, she wrote,

> was never more strikingly manifest than on the question of an expression of sympathy with the Transvaal. On this question all Nationalists of Ireland are agreed, and messages of sympathy and encouragement to the Boers have been sent from most of the towns and corporate bodies in Ireland. . . .
>
> Throughout Ireland people were asking, why was Dublin silent? The Lord Mayor was urged to call a meeting, but refused. Then it was that the people of Dublin took the National flag from the shaking and timid hands of their representatives and held it aloft in the name of Ireland and of liberty. At a meeting called on three days' notice by a few earnest men, 20,000 Dublin citizens came together, led by Mr. John O'Leary to proclaim their sympathy with the Boers. . . .

Maud modestly did not mention that she had spoken at this meeting and been wildly cheered.

In the same issue the *United Irishman* reported that Irish nationalists in South Africa had met in Johannesburg, and had resolved to offer their services, one thousand strong, to the Boer government. John MacBride, the chairman of the meeting, was a thirty-year-old assayer, who had learned his political lessons well at the feet of Willie Rooney, John O'Leary, and Dr. Mark Ryan. The Boers accepted the offer; an Irish Brigade was formed, and a manifesto was issued calling on Irishmen everywhere to seize this opportunity to strike hard at England.

On October 10, with Maud Gonne presiding, an Irish Transvaal Committee was formed in the offices of the Celtic Literary Society, the organization founded in 1893, and still run, by Griffith and Willie Rooney. Since the prime purpose of the new committee was to discourage recruitment in the British forces, posters were authorized informing all true Irishmen that enlistment in the English army was treason to Ireland, and reminding them of past abuses.

The meeting voted congratulations to John MacBride on the formation of the Irish Brigade, and ordered a flag for it, to be made of gold-fringed Irish-green poplin with a harp in the center, the inscription "Transvaal Irish Brigade," and the motto in Gaelic, "our land, our people, our language." Arthur Griffith later described this flag in a poem to be sung to the tune of "The Wearing of the Green." Here are a few lines:

> In far-off Africa today the English fly dismayed
> Before the flag of green and gold borne by MacBride's brigade...
> "Revenge! Remember '98! and how our fathers died!
> We'll pay the English back today," cried fearless John MacBride.

When Maud presided at a second meeting of the Irish Transvaal Committee, Yeats wrote his sister Lily that Maud Gonne was "working with extraordinary energy" to discourage Irishmen from joining the British forces to fight in South Africa, and, conversely, to recruit men for the Irish Brigade.

Two pieces by Maud Gonne appeared in the November 11, 1899 issue of the *United Irishman*. In one, she rebutted a claim made in the previous issue that an Irishman had the right to serve in the British army to keep from starving to death. In the other, she reaffirmed the wisdom of holding demonstrations outside courthouses when peasants were being tried for agrarian offenses.

The occasion was the trial of two men in a Ballina court for performing acts encouraged by the United Irish League. Formed a few years earlier by William O'Brien, the League's policy had rapidly developed from advocating simple land redistribution to a vigorous and articulate demand for buying out the landlords by compulsory methods.

It was wrong, Maud wrote, for the learned defense counsel to stop the planned demonstrations in Ballina. Disappointment had been clear to read in the faces of the poor country people who had trudged long distances to be present. The result had been to strengthen the "superstitious fear of the law" already so prevalent among the masses, and to obstruct the objective of teaching them to look on English law and justice with contempt and defiance.

Until mid-November, Maud was in Ireland active in the Irish Transvaal Committee. When the committee started an ambulance fund, she gave five pounds, the top contribution, then spoke for it at Balinteer and Cork. At Cork, where she arrived with Arthur Griffith, a crowd removed the horses from the carriage and dragged it in triumph from the railway station to the Victoria Hotel. Shortly thereafter she left for Paris, disconcertingly enough in the same boat as a group of soldiers on the first step of their way to South Africa. About a hundred relatives and friends were present at the North Wall of Dublin to say goodbye to them,

and as the vessel steamed out into the river they raised a cheer for the soldiers, and I heard insulting reference made to President Kruger.

I thought that all such indecent displays of English feeling had been effectually stopped in Dublin.... It is imperative on us to make our protest clear and to guard against the lying misrepresentation of the English and Unionist Press, which would make us appear loyal and contented slaves of that Empire whose blood-guiltiness and crimes are a horror to us. The Irish people are full of tolerance, and this virtue has often been exploited.... If the English friends and relations of the soldiers are allowed unchallenged to cheer for England and England's army we shall soon see articles appearing in the *Irish Times* and the English papers describing "the loyalty of Dublin as demonstrated by the magnificent send-off given to the troops bound for South Africa."

Maud seems to have been back in the British Isles two weeks later. It may have been on this occasion that Yeats saw her, travel-stained and weary, at the London home of her sister, Mrs. Kathleen Pilcher. Turning away from a critical look at Maud, he complimented Mrs. Pilcher on her dress and appearance. Kathleen replied, "It's hard work being beautiful," lines which inspired Yeats a few years later to write one of his best poems.

The following day Yeats again brought up the subject of Maud's weariness and her failure to take care of herself. If she gave up politics and married him, he said, she could lead a peaceful life surrounded by artists and writers who appreciated her beauty and charm. At this moment they were standing in Westminster Abbey near the Coronation chair, to which is attached the Irish Stone of Destiny. According to tradition, Ireland will be free when the Stone is returned to Irish soil, and now Maud wondered out loud how the Stone could be removed from the Abbey and sent home. "Have you no magic, Willie," she asked, "to get it to the Island of Heroes, in triumph, ceremony and rejoicing?"

This sort of diversionary tactic was one of her ways of turning Yeats down. On another occasion, she told him, more directly, that he had no reason to marry, for he was making poetry out of what he considered his unhappiness, that the world would some day thank her for not marrying him, that poets should never marry. Besides, she mused in secret, marriage would be such a dull affair, and especially for herself.

For whatever reason, the quality of Yeats's poetry was indeed improving. Arthur Symons and many other critics agreed that the poems in *The Wind Among the Reeds*, published in 1899, marked an increase in directness and technical accomplishment. In one of them Yeats asserted that his work, though "made out of a mouthful of air," would endure long enough to convince the grandchildren of Maud Gonne's maligners that their ancestors had lied. The assertion was beginning to seem credible.

When both were in Dublin again Yeats took Maud to the Contemporary Club, where she had first encountered John O'Leary. It was then that the popular journalist Henry W. Nevinson saw her for the first time. He describes in *Changes and Chances* how he was "overwhelmed by her beauty. . . . I held my breath in adoration. Tall she was, and exquisitely formed; the loveliest hair and face that ever the sun shone on. Exquisitely dressed besides."

At this first meeting Maud was silent until the war in Greece was discussed. Then he realized "the meaning of that strong and beautiful chin. I knew that her longing was for action in place of all the theorising and talk, so general in Dublin."

In later meetings he decided that she was "not over-whelmingly clever" nor "smart"—meaning witty or apt at repartee—but felt that no one could regret the absence of these qualities in such an "indignant and passionately sym-pathetic heart."

Nevinson and his friends would frequently wait for Maud at the railway station when she was due to arrive in Dublin on the morning train that met the London boat. All night they sat up conversing in order to "see her home with the milk."

Shortly before Christmas, the most famous protest meet-ing sponsored by the Irish Transvaal Committee took place at Beresford Place and College Green in Dublin on the day that Joseph Chamberlain, British colonial secretary, was given an honorary degree by Trinity College. The police had banned the rally—Maud, who was to speak, was awakened at 1 A.M. by an inspector who insisted on reading the notice to her. It was decided to go ahead anyway even though several of the listed speakers failed to appear on the scheduled day. The others, including James Connolly, John O'Leary, Maud Gonne, and Patrick O'Brien, M.P., got on the "brake," the cart which served as both a means of transportation and speaker's platform. As it turned the corner of Abbey Street, a line of policemen stopped it, ordered the driver to turn back, and when he hesitated, pulled him off the driver's seat and arrested him. Connolly, who was sitting alongside, seized the reins, whipped up the horses, and drove through the cordon, scattering police and spectators before him. His years of driving a rubbish cart in Edinburgh had proved their worth.

At Beresford Place, "a seething mass of people" was shouting "Up the Boers! Up the Republic." O'Leary, his gray beard waving in the wind, urged support of the Boers, and called on Maud Gonne to read the resolutions. They were being passed by acclamation when the police forced their way through the crowd, surrounded the brake, and drove it and its riders into the yard of the Store Street police station. The station sergeant, nonplussed by a captured O'Leary, Maud Gonne, and a Home Rule M.P., consulted with his subordinates, and finally told Connolly, still in the driver's seat, "You can't stay here." "We don't want to," Connolly answered with praiseworthy accuracy.

Since they had been warned that any attempt to return to Beresford Place would mean a repeated arrest, Connolly drove across O'Connell Bridge to resume the meeting at College Green. There the crowd that reassembled gave a cheer for the Boers and was dispersed by mounted police. Connolly drove the brake down Dame Street and here Maud Gonne takes up the story:

"There are only two sentries at the gates of Dublin Castle," whispered Connolly to me. "Shall I drive in and seize the Castle?"

"There are soldiers inside. It will mean shooting and the people are unarmed," I said, hesitatingly, and Connolly turned down Parliament Street and over Chapel Street Bridge.

I sometimes wonder if I was wrong to hesitate. It would certainly have caused a great sensation, but I doubt if that unarmed crowd could have taken the Castle. John MacBride, to whom I told the incident later, said I was wrong not to have tried.

The year ended with Maud wondering, in a *United Irishman* article published December 9, 1899, why evicted Irish peasants did not adopt the policy of forcibly retaking their land, lighting the fire in the old hearth, and accepting the resultant imprisonment rather than settling down to years of idle, hopeless watching. Maud thought that, for herself, she would prefer going to jail

but I have not suffered as those poor over-patient tenants have suffered. . . .

To succeed, this policy would . . . need self-reliance, it would need energy. Could desperation supply the needful strength which hope once gave till hope revived again? How can I tell—how can I advise them? Is it not mockery for the well-fed to judge the starving?

CHAPTER XI

The Famine Queen (1900)

To Maud Gonne matters seemed to be going well at the turn of the century. The Afrikaners were still beating back the British effort to combine Natal, Orange Free State, and the Transvaal with the previously conquered Cape Province. The nations of the world were learning, she thought, that England's vaunted might was mere pretense, and were beginning to demonstrate their sympathy with the Boers: France and Germany by refusing to sell cannon and ammunition to England, and by investigating ways of increasing their Transvaal trade; and Russia by massing her troops on the Afghan frontier.

Maud wrote in the *United Irishman* issue of January 13, 1900: "The Boers have forever destroyed England's prestige.... Does the Irish nation realise that her tyrant is being beaten to the dust by a nation much smaller than herself? Do the children of the 'Mother of Exiles' realise that the hour of destiny, which, if wasted, can never be recalled, is perhaps passing?"

A week later Maud set out on the French liner *La Normandie* for her second tour of the United States. She arrived in New York on January 29, 1900 and clapped her hands with joy when the reception committee, all wearing Kruger buttons, told her about the Boer victories that had taken place during her journey.

The purpose of her visit, Maud told the *New York Times*, was

to arouse American sentiment in favour of the Boers and particularly to cement the unity of sentiment existing between the Irishmen of America and Irishmen in Ireland. I have been in France, Germany and Holland, and everywhere I have heard expressions of surprise that America has not been foremost in championing the cause of the Boers. The sentiment in favor of the Boers is now so strong in Ireland that they do not dare march troops down the main streets of Dublin for fear of having them hissed and assaulted.

She added that this was the best opportunity Ireland ever had to strike a blow for freedom, since there were barely 6,000 soldiers on the island whereas there were usually 20,000.

Maud gave her first speech on February 4 at the Academy of Music in New York City. She declared that no matter what nation England was fighting it was Ireland's duty "to oppose, thwart, and hinder her at every step," that only a coward could stand by and watch the English invaders destroy the Boer people as the Irish had been destroyed.

In contrast to President Kruger's humane treatment of sick and wounded British prisoners, she said, the English treated their ailing captives with callous brutality. To prove her point, she read extracts from letters written by captured British soldiers. The climax of her speech was reached when she asserted that any Irishmen found fighting on the side of the Boers were immediately put to death.

The account given by the *Irish World and American Industrial Liberator* was less restrained. It said that "the walls of the Academy rang with hisses and cheers as Miss Gonne vehemently denounced the British conduct of the war in the Transvaal," charging that "England's methods of warfare have not changed since she turned loose the red savages

armed with scalping knife and tomahawk to make savage
war on the American colonists." An unexpected member of
the audience was the famous Irish actor and singer,
Chauncy Olcott, who had written "My Wild Irish Rose"
two years earlier, and who when recognized consented to
sing a few numbers.

On February 20, 1900 Maud spoke on the same theme in
Baltimore, Maryland, where she was escorted to the Central YMCA by members of the ladies' auxiliary of the Ancient Order of Hibernians, and appeared on the stage behind an escort of three little girls carrying the Irish, Boer,
and American flags.

Maud sailed to Havre on March 8, on the French steamer
La Champagne, first telling the reporters at the pier that her
trip had been successful in arousing pro-Boer sentiment and
in raising funds for Boer widows and orphans. She said that
on arriving home she would contradict the assertions of the
press that the Americans were on the side of the English.

Concerning the rumored visit of Queen Victoria to Ireland, Maud was expansive, announcing that if the Queen
came as a private citizen she would not be disturbed, since
she was a feeble old woman, but that if the unionists attempted to whip up a favorable demonstration for her the
nationalists would respond appropriately. She told the reporters that Victoria was mistaken in the stated purpose of
her trip, which was to thank her Irish troops for their loyalty. Many troops had thrown their rifles overboard at
Waterford in preference to taking them aboard; men on a
boat leaving Cork harbor had pulled Boer flags out of their
pockets and cheered for the Afrikaners. She personally had
been told by some Irish soldiers "that they were going to let
the Queen pay for their journey out and then fight for the
Boers." These statements were as reckless and unfounded
as any Maud ever made. She was taken to task for them by
a former resident of County Fermagh, who wrote indignantly to the *New York Times* to say that the story about

troops throwing their rifles into the water at Waterford had been completely discredited and that the "Irish Joan of Arc" knew it. The correspondent may have been right; accuracy was never Maud's strong point. In her autobiography she dated this second American trip 1896 instead of 1901.

A few days after her return to Paris, the St. Patrick Society held its usual St. Patrick's Day observances, consisting of mass at Notre Dame, a grand banquet, and a ball. Many of those present expressed regret at the absence of Miss Maud Gonne, whose work for the Irish cause in America was the subject of many eulogies.

Maud was absent because on March 17 she was seriously ill with enteritis. In its April 7 issue, the *United Irishman* reported that she was still ill with "la grippe" but expected to be better soon. Two weeks later it reported that she looked "a bit worn" when she participated in a meeting commemorating James Napper Tandy, an advocate of Irish independence; but that "her face was aglow with patriotic enthusiasm" and she was heartily cheered.

No doubt the same patriotic glow was on Yeats's face when he wrote an open letter to the editor of the Dublin *Daily Express* protesting the elaborate plans that were being made for Queen Victoria's visit. She was the head of an empire, he said, "that is robbing the South African Republics of their liberty, as it robbed Ireland of hers. Whoever stands by the roadway cheering for Queen Victoria cheers for that Empire, dishonours Ireland, and condones a crime." A year later, Yeats was still being barred from admission to the Sligo Constitutional Club on account of this letter. "Between my politics and my mysticism I shall hardly have my head turned with popularity," he observed wryly to Lady Gregory.

On April 9 Yeats had the good fortune to catch up with Maud as she was passing through London on her way to Dublin. She was delighted, he wrote to Lady Gregory, that an issue of "her newspaper," meaning the *United Irishman*, had been suppressed "as it will give a lift to the circulation." But she was not at all happy to learn that the editor had been imprisoned "for a month for horsewhipping the editor of the Dublin *Figaro*, who wrote something against her, but what she does not know. The *Figaro* is a kind of society paper and very loyal as you may imagine."

This act of violence by the reserved and scholarly Arthur Griffith reflected the extent of his affection and respect for Maud Gonne. It must be considered one of the greatest tributes she ever received, though, in a single, slur-filled paragraph in *Drums Under the Windows*, Sean O'Casey trivializes the episode and distorts the relationship between Griffith, Maud, and Yeats. He begins with a description of Griffith

tormenting himself with the fading vision of a most lovely lady whose golden hair was hanging down her back, so full of fire that a tress of it would give light to a group threshing corn in a black barn on a dark night. Maybe stroking the right hand, oh! worthy right hand, that had laid a whip on the back of a little tittle-tattle Dublin editor of a gossip journal when he whispered *spy* about the Helen of Eireann who had the loveliness to launch a battle and go through it with the walk of a queen. He hid his hatred of a rival in the wrapping of Erin's noble emblem, boys, the green flag, around him; he composed gnarled remarks in his weekly paper against him who . . . sang songs that made a flame of her fair ear and sent a swell into her bosom with the pride of what a singer can say out of a purple-and-white love.

The dispute itself started when the *Irish Figaro*, a paper popular in Dublin Castle circles, became so irritated by Maud Gonne's drumfire of criticism against Queen Victoria in the *United Irishman* that on April 7, 1900 it maintained in an editorial that

Herodotus was a lover of the plain, unvarnished truth when compared with his unblushing modern rival, Miss Maud Gonne. This lady—if a liar can be considered a lady—lately communicated falsehoods to the French gutter press to the effect that the Irish soldiers now serving in South Africa were put on board the transports with "manacled wrists," and she added that the majority laid down their arms and refused to fight the Boers.

The article said that the only difference between Maud Gonne and Margaret Nicholson, a crazed washerwoman in the news, was that Miss Gonne did not have

the plea of madness to condone her absurd and despicable conduct. Women of this stamp have no sense of the ludicrous, or I would ask Miss Gonne to cease to thus throw discredit on her sex. Her conduct is all the more to be regretted when it is remembered that she is related by marriage with that most gallant officer, Colonel Pilcher....

Ramsay Colles, managing editor of the *Irish Figaro*, it must be said, was an able and respected journalist. On the same page containing these paragraphs, he reproached Queen Victoria for failing to display any interest in higher education for women. She had "never uttered a syllable of sympathy with the efforts made by women to improve their education during the last fifty years," and had failed "to realise the pressing needs of the large number of women left to provide for themselves...."

In his reminiscences, Colles turns Griffith's assault into farce. He had spent Saturday, March 7, 1900, acting as a steward in Phoenix Park when Queen Victoria inspected the children assembled to celebrate her arrival. On the following Monday he was watching the royal procession from a window of his Grafton Street office when a gentleman wearing a frock coat entered the room, asked if he were Ramsay Colles, and, on receiving an affirmative answer, struck his silk hat from his head, saying, "Then take that." Once recovered from his surprise, Colles placed his own frock coat and silk hat in a safe place, took two short swords off the wall of his office, and offered one of them to Griffith, saying, "Defend yourself, or you will not leave this place alive!"

When Griffith refused the challenge, Colles "assumed the airs of a maniac," chased him around the table in the center of the room, and when Griffith tripped and fell, said, "If Her Majesty were not passing through this street under these very windows, I would throw you out of them." He wound up the matter "by taking him by the back of the neck and handing him over to the constable on duty at the corner of the street."

At the police station, Griffith explained the reason for his assault to a magistrate who fined him one pound or fourteen days' imprisonment. In addition, he was ordered to give "two sureties of five pounds each" to guarantee that he would not again attack Colles. When Griffith refused to make such a promise, he was sentenced to an additional fourteen days of imprisonment.

In the April 21 issue of his paper, Colles "apologized" for his statements about Maud. He said they were so "utterly outside the pale of respectable journalism" that her friend Griffith "could take no other steps than that of giving the editor a sound thrashing." It should make all good nationalists happy to learn that "the scurrilous Editor of *Figaro* did not get off scot free."

Colles then went much further than before. Using information he had received from an assistant commissioner of police, he argued that it was unconscionable that Miss Gonne should be receiving a British government pension of £300 in recognition of her father's services in the very army which she was trying so hard to discredit. He wrote that she should be ashamed of living "in idleness on gold from England's treasure while she traduces Irish soldiers for accepting the same for services rendered on the field of battle."

Now it was Maud's turn to be wroth. She promptly had Colles hauled into court on a charge of slander. A suitable and serious apology was made her in court by Colles's counsel, who appeared in City Sessions to term "entirely incorrect" the statement in *Figaro* that Maud Gonne, as the daughter of a deceased officer, was receiving a pension from

Her Majesty's Government. "We unreservedly withdraw the statement, and apologise for the mistake and for any misconception as to Miss Gonne's position."

Counsel for Miss Gonne responded by saying that she had no desire whatever "of acting in any severe manner towards Mr. Colles," and had instituted the court proceedings only for the purpose of making it quite clear that her character in public was "consistent" with everything in her private life.

These proceedings were printed in the May 19 issue of the *Irish Figaro*, but in the next paragraph Colles ungenerously asserted that his feelings about Maud Gonne's political views remained the same. Though he had never considered her a spy, he said, he regretted that she troubled herself so much about Ireland. It was not, after all, her country. Because she did not seem to know the birthplace of her father, he had taken the trouble to ascertain from the war office that Colonel Gonne had been born at 19 Gloucester Place, London. Since Maud was born at Aldershot, and her mother was entirely English, he failed to see where her claim to be Irish came in.

The next item was equally waspish. Colles wished his readers to know that his inability to appreciate the verse of Yeats and AE did not mean that he was blind to the merits of good Irish writers such as Katharine Tynan.

When he first attacked Maud, Colles may already have known why police raided the office of the *United Irishman* on the evening of April 6, 1900 and seized the entire issue dated April 7. That issue contained the first section of an article called "The Famine Queen," the remainder of which appeared in the issues of April 21 and 28. Because it is the most famous piece Maud Gonne wrote, a large section of it is quoted here.

And in truth, for Victoria, in the decrepitude of her 81 years, to have decided, after an absence of half a century, to revisit the country she hates, whose inhabitants are the victims of the criminal policy of her reign and the survivors of 60 years of organised famine, the political necessity must have been terribly strong.

For, after all, she is a woman, and however vile, selfish and pitiless her soul, she must sometimes tremble as death approaches, when she thinks of the countless Irish mothers who... watching their starving little ones, have cursed her before they died.

Every eviction during 63 years has been carried out in Victoria's name, and if there is a justice in Heaven the shame of those poor Irish emigrant girls, whose very innocence rendered them easy prey, and who have been overcome in the terrible struggle for existence on a foreign shore, will fall on this woman, whose bourgeois virtue is so boasted. . . .

England is in decadence. The men who formerly made her greatness, the men from the country districts, have disappeared, they have been swallowed up by the great black manufacturing cities; they have been flung into the crucible where gold is made. Today the giants of England are the giants of finance and of the Stock Exchange, who have risen to power on the backs of a struggling mass of pale, exhausted slaves.

The storm approaches, the gold which the English have made out of the blood and tears of millions of human beings attracts the covetousness of the world. Who will aid the pirates to keep their spoil? In their terror they turn to Victoria, their Queen. She has succeeded in amassing more gold than any of her subjects, she has always been ready to cover with her royal mantle the crimes and turpitude of her Empire, and now, trembling on the brink of the grave, she rises once more at their call. . . . Taking the Shamrock in her withered hand, she dares to ask Ireland for soldiers—for soldiers to fight for the exterminators of their race!

And the reply of Ireland comes sadly but proudly, not through the lips of the miserable little politicians who are touched by the English canker, but through the lips of the Irish people.

Queen, return to your own land; you will find no more Irishmen ready to wear the red shame of your livery. In the past they have done so from ignorance, and because it is hard to die of hunger when one is young and strong and the sun shines, but they shall do so no longer. See! Your recruiting agents return alone and unsuccessful from my green hills and plains, because once more hope has revived, and it will be in the ranks of your enemies that my children will find employment and honour.

When the old Queen visited Dublin on April 4, 1900, she was greeted with the usual addresses of loyalty from unionist organizations and institutions. She probably failed to notice that, owing to the steady growth of nationalist sentiment, fewer government officials were present than was usual.

One feature of the attendant festivities which particularly irked Maud Gonne was the "treat" or picnic for children in Phoenix Park. Instead of protesting in words—words were never as satisfactory as action—she decided, with Father James A. Anderson, to organize a counter-treat, and from such groups as the Ladies' Wolfe Tone Committee formed the Ladies' Committee of the Patriotic Children's Treat, Maud Gonne president. With funds collected by committee members, she paid for newspaper advertisements asking for gifts of food for the picnic. Donations poured in, not only from Dublin bakeries but also from John Daly's bakery in Limerick, and soon a vacant store on Talbot Street was full of hams, rolls, butter, cakes, buns, candy, oranges, and casks of lemonade and ginger beer.

According to the *United Irishman*'s estimate, 30,000 children attended the outing held in Clontarf Park on that July Sunday. Of this event, one of her most cherished memories, Maud wrote in her autobiography:

Headed by beflagged lorries, piled with casks of ginger beer and twenty-thousand paper bags containing sandwiches, buns and sweets, that wonderful procession of children carrying green branches moved off from Beresford Place, marshalled by the young men of the Celtic Literary Society and the Gaelic Athletic Association, on the march to Clontarf Park. Mary Quinn and I on an outside car, drove up and down the line, for the safety of such a huge concourse of children was a fearful responsibility; but there was no hitch. . . .

The Patriotic Children's treat became legendary in Dublin and, even now, middle-aged men and women come up to me in the streets and say: "I was one of the Patriotic Children at your party, when Queen Victoria was over."

The effectiveness of the *ad hoc* committee convinced Maud that, without the participation of her women, Mother Ireland was going into battle with one arm tied behind her back. At a meeting of the Celtic Literary Society, she asked all members to persuade their sisters and sweethearts to come to the Society's office on Abbey Street to discuss with her the possibility of founding a women's separatist organization.

Fifteen girls appeared for the first meeting, held in early October 1900. In presiding, Maud referred to a list, which W. B. Yeats had helped to frame, of things that must be done to achieve Ireland's independence. The girls decided to establish free classes for children in Irish history, the Gaelic tongue, Irish music, and Irish dancing; to combat recruiting in the British army by distributing leaflets in the wake of recruiting sergeants and by urging Irish girls not to consort with soldiers; to popularize the purchase of Irish-made goods; to discourage the reading and circulation of English newspapers, the singing of English songs, and attendance at English entertainments.

When all this became known, enemies of the organization spread the story that its real purpose was to teach children a new catechism beginning with the question, "What is the origin of evil?" The answer: "England."

Maud Gonne was elected first president of Inghinidhe na hEireann (Daughters of Erin). Vice-presidents were Mrs. James F. Egan, wife of the former Treason Felony prisoner; Jennie Wyse Power, who had done work as a member of the Ladies' Land League; Anna Johnson, the Belfast poet better known as Ethna Carberry; and Alice Furlong. There were three "Hon. Secs," one of them Maire T. Quinn, who later married the noted actor J. Dudley Digges, and two "Hon. Treasurers." Another member of the organization was Sinead Nic O'Flanagan, who later married Eamon de Valera. To prevent those members who worked for Unionist firms from being identified and persecuted, the girls all took Gaelic names for use in the organization. For the same reason, the idea of wearing distinctive uniforms was rejected.

Late in October 1900 the Daughters of Erin held their first Ceilidh (a party where only Irish traditional set pieces are performed) at the Derrybawn Hotel in Dublin. The *United Irishman* reported that among those invited were John O'Leary, James F. Egan, and W. B. Yeats, and that refreshments "were of a first-class and substantial character."

As a feature of the evening President Gonne read a paper on the ancient Celtic goddess Brigid (or Bride) and the festival held on her sacred day, February 1, the beginning of spring. She thanked such men as Kuno Meyer, the German philologist, for their work in bringing these legends to light—legends which the Irish should consider more beautiful than those of ancient Greece because they were more fully in accordance with the needs of their own race.

Ella Young, the poet and scholar of Celtic, wrote in her memoir, *Flowering Dusk*, that the Daughters paid much attention to the four ancient festivals which marked the Celtic year and which Yeats was eager to revive. At one time Ella herself composed a ceremonial for each of the four festivals. Part of one was written by Maud Gonne.

Ever resourceful in obtaining laborers for the Lord's work, Maud persuaded William Butler Yeats, George Russell, Arthur Griffith, the founder of the Ladies' Land League, Anna Parnell, and a playwright and poet still in his teens, Padraic Colum, to give talks to the Daughters of Erin. Through her friend Father Anderson, she met a shy young schoolmaster, Padraic Pearse, who agreed to test periodically the children's knowledge of Gaelic.

Ella Young describes in her memoirs her experience as a teacher for the organization. Her task was to tell sagas about Irish heroes to

eighty denizens of untamed Dublin: newsboys, children who can scarcely write their own names. Outside there is a continuous din of street cries and rumbling carts. It is almost impossible to shout against it if the windows are open, and more impossible to speak in the smother of dust if the windows are shut. Everyone is standing, closely packed—no room for chairs!

During its second year, the Daughters of Erin fostered a hurling club for boys, and received a generous donation from the Ancient Order of Hibernians in the United States to establish brigades of boys pledged never to join the British army. This idea did not come to full fruition until, nine years later, Constance Markievicz started Fianna hEireann, the so-called Irish boy scouts.

To keep the children interested in their singing, dancing, and language lessons, they were taken to concerts, parties, and magic lantern shows, while the forty who did best in Irish history and Gaelic were given outings to Wolfe Tone's grave in Bodenstown. To pay for refreshments and transportation, the Daughters began to give "entertainments"— *tableaux vivants*—taken from the history of Ireland. The most popular one had a great Celtic cross designed by George Russell in the background and showed first "Erin Fettered," then "Erin Free."

Soon the "Ninnies," as they were sometimes called, formed a full-fledged dramatic troupe under the tutelage of Dudley Digges and Maud Gonne. Out of it emerged a number of distinguished actresses and actors. Sean Connolly, the first man to die in the Dublin 1916 Rising, was a member of both this dramatic group and the boys' hurling team.

Maud Gonne herself appeared in *The Deliverance of Red Hugh*, the second of two plays by Alice L. Milligan that were produced late in 1901 or early in 1902. Maud's part was to read the legend upon which the play was based. When the curtain rose, Ella Young wrote, Maud appeared sitting

in an ancient carved chair, with an illuminated parchment book on her knee. She had a splendid robe of brocaded white poplin with wide sleeves, and two little pages in medieval dress of black velvet held tall

wax candles on either side of her. The stage was strewn with green
rushes and branchlets of blossomed heather.

Maud Gonne has a sun-radiance about her. The quality of her beauty
dulled the candle-flames.

The Daughters of Erin flourished. Soon it added the
rooms of the Workers Club on York Street and a loft in
Strand Street to its available space. In 1901 Maud Gonne
was invited to form a branch in Limerick. The following
year she performed the same task in Cork. Margaret Gould-
ing, the teenaged girl who was elected its first president,
later became prominent in the labor movement and, as Mrs.
Buckley, was eventually elected president of Sinn Fein.

Another organization begun at the same time, Cumann
na nGaedheal, was remarkably similar in ideology, being
the first phase in Arthur Griffith's search for a political
instrument that would implement his cultural and economic protest. The Cumann was the outcome of discussions led by Willie Rooney and Griffith in John O'Leary's
home and in Maud Gonne's hotel rooms. Its first annual
convention was held on November 23, 1900 in the offices of
the Celtic Literary Society.

About this time Maud's penchant for international intrigue led her to make two serious errors in that shadowy
world. First, she persuaded a French intelligence agent that
he should visit Dr. Mark Ryan for information. The agent
did so, passing as a half-blind invalid, and was promptly
betrayed by a man assigned to him as a secretary by the
London IRB.

Maud's second idea was to place bombs disguised as
lumps of coal in British troopships, for even the loss of a
single ship, she thought, would materially deter enlist-
ments. With Dr. Ryan's approval, she went to Brussels and
presented the scheme to Dr. Leyds, the Transvaal representative in Europe. When he rejected the offer, she returned to Paris. The next morning, however, his secretary
appeared in her drawing room to say that Dr. Leyds had

reconsidered the proposition and was sending her £2,000 to finance it. When the secretary called the following day, he was surprised to learn that Maud had not received the money. A gentleman who said he was a colleague of Maud's had visited Dr. Leyds, declared that Maud was too valuable to the Irish movement to be risked as a courier, and kindly accepted the task himself. The man and the money both disappeared.

Maud hastened back to England to discuss the matter with Dr. Ryan, W. B. Yeats, and Arthur Griffith. She decided that a writer and former member of Parliament named F. H. O'Donnell had pulled the trick. But she was told that the case would be difficult to prove, and that it would be even more difficult to punish him.

At this juncture, Maud received a note from Lucien Millevoye, whom she had not met since their parting "under the snowy whiteness of Mont Blanc." He asked her to see him on a matter of extreme importance, something that, under the circumstances, no woman could refuse. Her speedy return to Paris astonished her ménage, which consisted at the time of a housekeeper; five-year-old Iseult; and Daphne Robbins, Maud's unacknowledged half-sister, whom she had brought to Paris so that she could learn French.

It was then she was told by Millevoye and an officer in French intelligence about the betrayal of the agent who had visited Dr. Ryan. Millevoye said the agent's career had been ruined, and his group would never trust the Irish revolutionaries again. After Maud told him about the swindle played upon Dr. Leyds, he became doubly angry. The Irish Parliamentarians might indeed be nothing but opportunists, but they were better than the so-called Irish revolutionaries, who were simply buffoons and idiots.

On her next visit to London, Maud told her colleagues in Dr. Ryan's secret organization that she was leaving it. "It's impossible," she said, "to stay in an organization where such things can happen; where, even after a spy has wrecked the chance of a lifetime, excuses are found to do nothing about him."

Actually some members did reconsider, and decided that perhaps O'Donnell should be executed. It took a long time for Yeats and Maud to persuade them not to go to such lengths. Maud, in an untypical retrospective and chastened mood, began to think that she lacked a sense of proportion in her work; that she was losing sight of the main objective, which was to liberate Ireland from British rule. Instead of dreaming up bombing schemes, she might be better employed influencing French public opinion against Clemenceau's proposed Entente Cordiale. But it was certainly less fun.

Yeats, for his part, was relieved to turn from spy plots to the writing and production of poetic dramas. And once again he asked Maud to marry him. He had known her now for more than a decade, but the answer was still the same. Lady Gregory wondered why. The two women met when Maud found Lady Gregory occupying the rooms that she herself usually had in the Nassau Hotel in Dublin. In a brief conversation, Lady Gregory mentioned her pleasure at being able, at Coole Park, to provide Yeats with the comforts that were helpful to his art. "I'm doing for him," she said, "what I would do for my son. I feel for him as if he were my son." Maud may have looked a bit quizzical, whereupon Lady Gregory asked her what her intentions were regarding Yeats. Maud's answer was brusque: "I have more important things to think about than marriage, and so has he."

Maud wrote in her autobiography many years later that she was greatly amused by the rivalry for Yeats's affections between Lady Gregory and Annie E. F. Horniman, the Theosophist who financed the purchase of the Abbey Theatre's first permanent home. "Miss Horniman had the money and was willing to spend it, but Lady Gregory had the brains. They should have been allies, for both stood for art for art's sake and deprecated the intrusion of politics, which meant Irish freedom."

Maud pictured Lady Gregory at their first meeting as "a queer little old lady, rather like Queen Victoria." Elizabeth Coxhead, Lady Gregory's biographer, points out, "Not even the widow's weeds can make that an accurate picture of a woman still under fifty, by one who would not herself see thirty again."

Maud had indeed important things to think about in 1900. While still on the battlefield in South Africa, John MacBride had announced his candidacy for Parliament from South Mayo, and the *United Irishman* had rushed to support him. "If today Ireland ranks higher in the world than she has ranked for many years," its editor wrote, "it is largely due to John MacBride and his Brigadiers." In the next issue it published his biography.

John MacBride was born on May 7, 1869, in the village of Westport, County Mayo, as poverty-ridden and parochial a place as most Irish communities of the time. The only whiff of fresh air came from the family's nationalist tradition, whose principal exponent at the time was John's brother Anthony, a London doctor who was active in several nationalist groups.

John himself found employment as a chemist's assistant in Dublin, where he joined the Celtic Literary Society and became friendly with William Rooney and Arthur Griffith. In 1896, shortly before going to South Africa as an assayer in one of the Rand mines, he entered Dr. Ryan's secret revolutionary organization. He was described at the time by Arthur Lynch as "an active and determined young man, ruddy of countenance and with reddish hair."

The formation of the Irish Brigade in September 1899 is credited chiefly to his exertions. It numbered over 250 men, and suffered about 80 casualties, including 17 deaths. There is no question about MacBride's valor, patriotism, and general decency. Michael Davitt wrote that he was "very reticent about his own doings in his conversations, but I have heard several Boer officers speak in the highest terms of his pluck in the fighting round Ladysmith, at Modderspruit, and at Colenso."

Maud Gonne, still in the United States at the time, was as enthusiastic as the *United Irishman* about the hero's candidacy. She sent a wire to the paper saying that an immense assembly in Boston's Tremont Theater had acclaimed MacBride's nomination. Then she sent another wire to report that a Baltimore meeting had done the same. Both cables were published in the February 24 issue of the *United Irishman*. Yeats put in his oar, suggesting that Harrington, the rival candidate, leave the race in favor of MacBride.

MacBride ended up with less than 20 percent of the votes. The *United Irishman* blamed the result on intimidation and continued to publicize his activities and virtues in issue after issue. The one of August 25 recorded a meeting of the John MacBride Athletic Club, which after receiving a "magnificent donation" from Maud Gonne had elected her and Arthur Griffith honorary members. When MacBride left South Africa and arrived in France, the *United Irishman* carried the story and printed interviews with him in its next two issues.

He was met at the railway station in Paris by Maud Gonne, Arthur Griffith, Stephen McKenna, and other members of the Paris branch of the Young Ireland Society. After the others left, MacBride and Maud had dinner together and talked all night, discussing plans for his projected tour of the United States. "America is the only chance," she told him. "Now that the Clan na Gael is reunited, you may be able to get it moving again."

The following morning MacBride and Griffith came to Maud's flat, and drafted appropriate remarks for MacBride to make on his tour, and stories for publication in the *United Irishman*. Maud sat in an armchair smoking cigarettes and listening with delight to accounts of Irishmen actually firing cannonballs at English soldiers.

Toward the end of November President Paul Kruger arrived in Paris. Maud Gonne, John MacBride, John O'Leary, and hundreds of other Boer sympathizers were on hand to greet him. With difficulty members of the Young Ireland Society pushed their way through so that Maud could read an address to him from the women of Ireland. Kruger, a weary, tragic figure, took the scroll and kept Maud near him, telling her that the Irish had done fine work but that henceforth all soldiers must know the country and speak the native language. He was sure then that the Boers would eventually wear the English down but was proved wrong a year later when the peace of Vereeniging was signed.

In December Maud Gonne tore herself away from France and from a man who had risked death in a war against the enemy, and sailed to England to fill a speaking engagement.

She had been invited to speak there on December 10, on the subject of "Irishmen in the English Army," and during the week before the meeting, the Liverpool papers were full of letters from English loyalists threatening to break it up. Her sponsor, a new branch of the Celtic Literary Society, responded by issuing a leaflet headed "Miss Maud Gonne's Meeting, Monday Night."

An organised attack on this patriotic Irish Lady is threatened by the Orange rowdies of Liverpool. They boast they will subject her to brutal violence to-morrow night. Irishmen of Liverpool and Bottle, rally in your manhood to defend our noble young countrywoman from the gang whose fathers ran away from the Women of Limerick! God save Ireland.

At noontime on the 10th, the owner of Albert Hall informed the society that the police had banned its use. It was promptly decided to hold the meeting in the open air. At 7

P.M. Maud, the Irish-born Vicar of Plumpton, Reverend Mr. Kennedy, and three society members took a train to Edgehill; they were driven in a hansom cab through the streets of Liverpool, surrounded by a "howling mob of Orange rowdies, who, bubbling over with loyalty and arsenicated beer . . . relieved their feelings by brutally beating and partially maiming an isolated woman whom they pretended to mistake for Miss Gonne." Toward the end of their trip Maud and her companions walked through the Irish section of the city accompanied by nationalists singing patriotic Irish songs. At Saltney Street they mounted a wagon that lacked both sides and a horse. Maud opened her remarks from this platform by saying three times, "Irishmen and sons of Irishmen, never enlist in the English army." Each time the audience responded by roaring, "Never!" The police thereupon broke up the assemblage, and ordered the people on the platform to descend.

This they refused to do, and a horse having been procured, the police attempted to remove the vehicle, but the horse declined to stir. Then the police, jumping on the lorry, threw off all the occupants, except Rev. Mr. Kennedy, whom they assisted to alight, and Miss Gonne, who was carried to her cab on the shoulders of the people.

When Maud left the following day for Limerick, "A great crowd of Irishmen thronged the platform, singing 'God Save Ireland,' and the train left the station amidst prolonged and enthusiastic cheering for Miss Gonne and the Transvaal Irish Brigade."

On December 13 Maud addressed the Limerick branch of the Young Ireland Society on the subject of "Ireland and Her Foreign Relations," and was presented with a key to the city. Thanks to a full report carried in the *Limerick Leader*, we have a good picture of Maud Gonne's message as she reached her thirty-fifth year. She began by speaking against England and emigration, which she said was destroying Ireland, and then stressed the need for Ireland to cultivate good relations with other countries.

It was against England's interest that Ireland should be prosperous.... But, in spite of England, by a little initiative and energy on the part of our manufacturers much could be done to find markets for Irish goods abroad. An enormous amount of Irish lace is sold in France, and at very high prices.... Miss Gonne asked the head of a lace department where he bought the Irish lace, and he said it was got in London, and that he had to pay such a price for it there that but little profit could be made on it in France. She told him the price that would be paid for the article under discussion (an Irish crochet lace collar) in Dublin, and he seemed surprised, and asked her for an address to write to so that, if possible, the next order, which was over £1,000 for crochet lace, could be placed directly in Ireland, and so do away with the English middleman....

I consider that John MacBride has done more for Ireland by organising the Irish Brigade in the Transvaal than any living man. It saved Ireland's honour at a time when there was great need.... The Editor of *Le Petit Parisien*, a well-known French paper, which has generally been friendly to the Irish, told me plainly.... "Keep your countrymen out of the English army if you wish us in France to believe in your sincerity."

One year I counted that I had got two thousand notices on Ireland in the French Press. Far more might be done in this direction if the leaders of the Irish people would only turn their attention to it....

Let us look away from England and turn our eyes to France, and strengthen by every means in our power the relations, commercial, social, and political, which exist between us and that great Republic.... Let us cultivate such friendships more than we have done in the past....

While Maud was still speaking in Ireland, Major John MacBride arrived in New York to begin his lecture tour. His main purpose, he told waiting reporters, was to inform Irish-American organizations about the progress of the Boer War; he vigorously denied the assertion of Winston Churchill, who was also in the United States, that the war was over. "He doesn't know what he's talking about,"

MacBride declared. "The war will last as long as there is a man, woman, or child left in the Transvaal."

The tour started badly, for MacBride lacked the experience or poise to hold an audience. Before long he wrote to Maud Gonne asking her to join him in America, saying that he could not make an effective appearance without her and that the Clan na Gael was ready and willing to handle a joint tour. It did not take Maud long to decide.

CHAPTER XII

Maud as "Cathleen"
(1901–1902)

ON JANUARY 22, 1901, Queen Victoria died. In an article in *La Patrie*, Lucien Millevoye proved his fidelity to the Irish cause, if not to Maud Gonne, by calling Victoria's death "retribution for fifty years of infamy in Ireland."

Maud's opinion was similar. When she debarked from the French liner *La Champagne* in New York on February 10, for her third tour of the U.S., she told a *New York Times* reporter that Irishmen had little reason to mourn the queen. "She was an avaricious woman. As for King Edward— well, his dissipation and his life are known . . . he will be a sort of discredited reigning sovereign."

She also said that her object in coming to America was to discourage the enlistment of Irishmen in the British army; since beginning that task three years earlier, the number of Irish mercenaries had shrunk from 35,000 to about 20,000. She predicted that the Boers would hold out for another two years, and denied she had been implicated in an attempt to blow up the Welland Canal. Whereupon, she left for the Fifth Avenue Hotel, escorted by the "Miss Gonne Ladies Reception Committee."

At Maud's first meeting, held on February 17 at the Academy of Music in New York City, she shared the limelight with MacBride, who "modestly refrained from telling of his own exploits, but gave much praise to the men who fought under him."

Maud spoke on her usual subjects and in her usual vein. When she applauded Boer military successes, the *Irish World* reported, "The cheering and applause were deafening, and were interspersed with highly complimentary remarks not only about Miss Gonne's personal appearance, but her courage in coming out so openly against England."

But in the same issue of the *Irish World* there were ominous signs that Maud's censure of Irish members of Parliament for trying to remedy the Irish problem constitutionally was not acceptable to most Irish-Americans. An editorial, bluntly titled "Evil Work," began by noting the small size of the audience, and hoped that, with more practice, Major MacBride would be able to tell his story without needing to read it, which "takes away very much from its interest." It reported that Miss Gonne was cheered on rising and that a large harp of roses was presented to her. Then it swung into a condemnation of her views.

But her audience was evidently puzzled and disappointed when she switched off from the Boer war to make a bitter attack on the United Irish League that was most unfortunate. It was unexpected and unnecessary. People were present to hear about the Boer war, not to listen to Miss Gonne's political squabbles. That sort of thing will not do....

On another page, in a letter to the editor, P. A. Moynahan of New York City protested Miss Gonne's "defamation" of the United Irish League. He named its distinguished leaders; asserted that the League's principles were accepted by the Irish people at home and abroad; and denounced "the screechy abuse" of it by the visitors.

The conflict, it should be noted, was not between those who advocated freeing Ireland by the violent and immediate overthrow of the British Empire and those who did not (an interpretation of this squabble that Maud favored in later years). Rather, it was between those who wished Irishmen to bury their differences and present a united front that would speed the coming of self-government within the empire, i.e., Home Rule; and those who believed that more militant steps (short of insurrection) would hasten attainment of the same goal.

The storm broke out in earnest in the March 9, 1901 issue of *Irish World*. It contained a letter from Maud Gonne stating that she agreed with the principles of the United Irish League concerning the restoration of Irish land to the people of Ireland. It was only when the League tried to prove that it was stronger than the Fenians, when it opposed Major MacBride's candidacy for South Mayo and John Daly's for the mayoralty of Limerick, that the Cumann na nGaedheal found it necessary to oppose it. The League, she wrote, had supported as candidates for municipal office in Cork and Dublin men who had signed pledges of loyalty to Queen Victoria; only after it explained this adequately would persons who believed in the principles of Wolfe Tone and the United Irishmen give it their backing. It was a temperate and rational defense worthy of Arthur Griffith and James Connolly.

But now the letters from readers of the *Irish World* were pouring in. P. A. Moynahan repeated at greater length his argument that there had never been a time when the will of the Irish people was so thoroughly represented as it was now by the United Irish League.

John Sullivan inquired of Miss Gonne whether the "James Eagan" who had joined in singing "God Save the King" at Dublin Castle when the new king was proclaimed was the same Egan who had accompanied her on her previous tour of the United States. Maud Gonne replied, evasively, that she did not know since she had not been in Dublin at the time.

Jeremiah B. Murphy called the United Irish League "a proud monument to the perseverance and genius of Irish patriotism."

Standish J. Reidy of Boston said he did not have much confidence "in any individual or organization that calumniates others for their own aggrandizement."

Michael Fox corrected Maud's errors. MacBride, he said, had entered the Mayo campaign late, after a nominating convention had unanimously selected as candidate a man who was in a British jail.

The average local newspapers gave favorable notices to Maud and Major MacBride, if only because they dared not offend their local Irish communities. During their wide-ranging itinerary, one reporter called Miss Gonne "the very embodiment of grace and culture—tall, stately, and slender . . . a magnificent type of the patriotism, devotion and brilliancy of Irish womanhood." MacBride was modest, unassuming, "rather small in stature, but possesses nervous energy, keen intellect, quiet humor, and all the characteristic physical vigor of the race."

In St. Louis, another reporter described MacBride as soldierly, not oratorical. "His language was honest and plain, but forceful." He spoke from notes, and made few gestures, keeping his hands in his trouser pockets. "He had just enough of a brogue to make his words pleasing."

During the course of the tour, MacBride became sufficiently influenced by Maud's ideas to add general support of the doctrine of physical force to his history of the Irish Brigade. A second development was the increasing amount of attention given to Maud. She was certainly the star in Kansas City, Kansas, where the *Journal* reported that Turner Hall was sold out despite an admission charge of 50 cents. Here she denounced the idea that Irish representation at Westminster was at all useful.

We had eighty Irishmen in Parliament at a time when thousands of the homes of our people were burned over their heads. . . . Since we commenced Parliamentary agitation we have spent 10,000,000 dollars in talk. . . . But, some say, we cannot hope to gain anything by revolutionary methods. Why can we not? Irish soldiers have fought and won freedom for so many other countries that they certainly can win it for themselves.

After the meeting, a reporter from the *Kansas City Star* asked Maud how she had become what she was. Maud let her head droop—"the head with the great mass of short, curling brown hair that falls over her temples"—and told how, as a motherless child running free, and her father away to the wars, she had played with poor Irish children and seen the condition of their thatched cabins. In France she had studied with a wise woman who also sympathized with the poor, until at the age of sixteen she had returned to Ireland where she had seen the disdain with which her own social class treated the peasants. And then one day she had seen—her voice becoming deep and almost tragic—

a village burned for debt, yes, yes, it is true! An Irish village of poor people who were unable to pay certain taxes levied upon them by the English. The village was burned to the ground and—and a baby died in the flames. Yes, a baby! I saw it. I never can forget what I saw that day!

After that I changed a great deal. I began to ask questions, to wonder why things were as I found them. . . . Then I wanted to do something to help. And so I busied myself with my poor, caring for those who were evicted, finding new homes for them or putting them back in their old homes. . . . Then at nineteen my father died, and a year after that I began public life.

Maud added that her family was now arrayed against her and that she had lost her aristocratic friends, but she never longed for a return to her old life.

"In one word, what would you have the Irish people do?" the reporter asked.

She smiled and said, "Fight."

The interview ended with Maud quoted as saying: "Some day the great war will break out, and then all the preparation and all the toil and hardship, and all the fine spirit of Ireland will come into service and win battles for her. That is what I am waiting for. It will come before long. I am thirty-four now. I will see it."

Maud wrote in *A Servant of the Queen* that John MacBride proposed to her during this American trip. It is hard to believe. His letters to his mother show that he regarded Maud with such awe and deference that it is unlikely that he could have brought himself to do it. In one letter he wrote, "I felt very nervous at first and could not keep my eyes of [sic] my manuscript, but now I can get along in fine style. Miss Gonne, of course, is a practised speaker and being a good looking lady captures her audience at once." Again, writing from Marquette, Michigan, he told his mother, "Miss Gonne astonishes me. The way in which she can stand the knocking about. For a woman it's wonderful."

In Boston Maud received a cable from Griffith telling her of the death of his best friend, Willie Rooney. She answered that the only consolation she had ever found for sorrow was redoubled work. Then, in St. Louis, a letter arrived from Griffith asking her not to stay too long in America since she was badly needed in Dublin.

On that day she and MacBride were visiting the stockyards where most of the mules for British army transports were bought. They were discussing ways to stop the shipments, when Maud broke off to tell John that she had decided to leave him to finish the tour alone. She said she did not feel she was really needed, since it was *his* lecture on the Irish Brigade that the people wanted to hear; and it was *his* work in visiting the Clan na Gael branches that was really useful. A desire to see her five-year-old daughter, Iseult, probably played a part in her decision to return.

She wrote in her autobiography:

He tried to keep me but I was resolute, and after a big meeting in Chicago we separated, he to go on to San Francisco and I to return to Europe. Except for the money our tour had ensured for the *United Irishman*, I didn't feel I had accomplished much, but I still hoped Mac-

Bride might succeed in setting the match to the inflammable fighting forces of the Clan-na-Gael, in spite of the politicians.

Six months after Maud returned, she intervened to save some alleged Irish terrorists from being imprisoned in English jails. She awoke one morning, in her rooms over Morrow's Library in Dublin, to read a newspaper account of an "Irish and Nihilist Plot to Assassinate the Czar." The story said that some Fenians had been arrested in France, Holland, and England for plotting to murder the czar during an impending visit to France. Maud sensed that the arrests were part of a British secret service frame-up. Leaving untouched the breakfast tray on her bed (members of the Cook family did not lightly abandon such small luxuries), she dressed hastily and, with her faithful Great Dane, in tow, walked to the Ely Place lodgings of barrister J. F. Taylor. He was inclined at first to discount the sensational story, but Maud convinced him that the Irish cause in France would be ruined if the Irishmen were convicted, and reminded him that he had once promised to defend any prisoners in whom she was interested. At the moment she was curious about the identity of the man called Bell, who had been arrested in England. He might be honest or he might be a knave, but through him she thought they might get to the bottom of the mystery.

Taylor put aside his own work (W. B. Yeats had good reason to be jealous of him), left Ireland, and went with Maud to see Dr. Mark Ryan in London. At first Ryan would have nothing to do with the matter, but became more amenable when Taylor said he would defend the mysterious Bell without charge, and Maud said she would supply the funds for a solicitor. In that case, Ryan promised, he would get the Clan na Gael to refund the money. Maud was thankful, for her bank account

was always overdrawn, but I never let want of money prevent me from doing anything I really wanted and I felt the bank, who held my trust securities, and where many of my family had accounts, would not refuse me an extra overdraft of £100. If they did, I reflected, I still had some jewellery to pawn, but I said nothing of this and only asked who was the best solicitor to engage.

It turned out to be Charles Russell, whom she quickly visited with a draft of £100 from Cox's Bank. Before accepting the case, he wanted to know, "Who is behind you? For whom are you acting?"

"I'm acting for myself as a member of the Amnesty Association," Maud answered. "We find it easier to keep a man out of prison than try to get him out after he's been convicted."

After a brief stop at her sister's home, Maud hastened to meet Taylor at the Grosvenor Hotel. He had been provided with IRB credentials by Dr. Ryan, had shown them to the imprisoned man, and "Bell" had confessed that he was an American citizen named Ivory who had come to England to take part in a dynamite plot, but knew nothing about a scheme to kill the czar.

The following morning Maud met Lucien Millevoye and Arthur Lynch in Paris at Lynch's home on rue Chaptal. Here her purpose was to get Millevoye's help in keeping Patrick Tynan, the alleged conspirator seized in France, from being extradited to England. But the respected deputy from the staid 16th Arrondissement, the maker of important speeches on foreign policy, fine arts, and social problems, was even less inclined than before to assist Irish bomb throwers. Maud pleaded that Tynan, who was reputedly "number one" of the terrorist group called "Invincibles," should not be extradited unless it could be proved that he was plotting against the czar, not England. He had probably walked into a trap, she said, and deserved a prison term for having been so stupid, but his extradition to England would make it more difficult to get at the truth and would encourage the English to continue inventing plots.

Millevoye was hard to convince; he felt that the French police must have acted with sufficient evidence. But old friendships die hard and eventually he promised to use his influence to save Tynan from being extradited. He went further. Knowing that Maud's opinions as a leader of the Irish nationalists in France would be asked for, he drafted a statement for the French press for her to sign, in which she stressed the point that there must be "no repudiation of my friends the Irish revolutionaries."

By this time she was exhausted. She had not slept for two nights. Rejecting an offer of a bed in the Lynch home, she staggered to her own flat and slept eighteen hours straight.

Tynan was not extradited. Two months later Arthur Lynch brought him to Maud's flat so that he could thank her personally. Until he died in 1936, he sent Maud Gonne every Christmas a greeting card and a small sum of money to assist her in providing comforts for political prisoners and their families.

Taylor put up a good fight for Ivory, going himself to Holland in order to search for the third man, the leader in the plot, who had vanished. Taylor became convinced that this man had been an *agent provocateur*, and that Ivory had acted simply as a patriot. He raised enough of a defense on these grounds to win a *nolle prosequi*. The judge gave Ivory a stern lecture about the dangers of keeping bad company, and ordered him to be shipped back to his own land.

More than three decades later, Maud was still regretting that this British plot was never aired in the House of Parliament. The reason was that Taylor had given his notes to Tim Healy, who was more intent on his own advancement than on the cause of Irish freedom. Maud wrote in her autobiography: "This case, which might have had real diplomatic reactions against the British Empire, was quietly interred by Tim Healy, as many other things damaging to the British Empire were interred. He certainly earned his Governor-generalship of the Free State!"

During the second half of 1901, Maud used the columns of the *United Irishman* to air her views on a wide variety of subjects. In the issue of June 22 she stressed the fact that the English controlled the news agencies that provided the American press with what little Irish news it received, which was primarily news about the Irish Parliamentary Party.

This would not matter if it were news of the Irish Parliamentary Party as they are, but it is news of the Irish Parliamentary Party as they wish to appear in Irish-America; . . . our Parliamentarians at home are revolutionists in America!

She recommended that the *United Irishman* be circulated more widely in the United States, and that Irish-American papers be distributed in Ireland. Above all, she wished that the great American newspapers would station correspondents in Dublin.

On July 6, Maud described the appalling conditions under which Boer women and children were living in refugee camps set up in South Africa by the British. Her information was taken from a report prepared in Parliament by Emily Hobhouse, a Quaker who was seeking conciliation with the Boers. After reading the report, Maud happened to meet an Englishman on the street and allowed him to shake her hand. This led her to express some thoughts about the way Irishmen act toward the English.

The Irish people know this murder is being done. They murmur a prayer . . . and where an Englishman comes among them they take his hand as I, may God forgive me, took the hand of that Englishman yesterday.

We have learned toleration! Toleration of evil!

In the issue of September 21, 1901, Maud told of meeting a seven-year-old lad who asked her, "When will the fight be with the English?" She went on to describe the hovel in which he and his mother lived; how rents for this and similar lodgings supported people living in luxury in England.

Local Boards of Guardians, she continued, were making insufficient use of the Labourers' Dwellings Act, under which they could erect "decent and wholesome cottages" and rent them at a low price. "We say we want to check emigration; what are we doing to check it?" Emigration could not be entirely stopped until the English were thrown out of the country, but meanwhile much could be done to improve present homes and find employment for workers. It was dreadful to see the few measures available for combating emigration being neglected.

On November 2, Maud discussed "the vile hypocrisy" of the English legal system. She conceded that, in England, trial by jury was "as near as human law can attain to justice." The same system was ostensibly practiced in Ireland, but there the Crown could say to every nationalist and Catholic juror, "Stand by," until only unionists and Protestants filled the jury box.

She did not think the proper remedy was for Catholics to abstain from serving on jury panels. The enemy would then say that Catholics didn't choose to serve as jurors. Instead, whenever a jury was obviously packed, the counsel for the defense, with the consent of his client, should declare that he would not go on participating in this legal farce. "The prisoner would be convicted, but he would be convicted anyhow with a packed jury. At all events he would not be assisting England to keep up the hypocritical majesty of her law."

During these early 1900s, Maud's interest in the Irish drama burgeoned through her association with two brothers named Fay. Frank, by profession an accountant, was a serious student of the new theater; he knew about the Ibsen plays in Oslo, the Théâtre Libre in Paris, the Free Stage Society in Berlin, and the Independent Theatre of London; and had a feel for significant acting. William Fay was an experienced, professional actor and a comedian of genius.

Maud Gonne knew Frank particularly well because he contributed dramatic criticism to the *United Irishman*. With her knack for finding assistants who would work without charge, she asked the brothers to help coach the Daughters of Erin in their dramatic presentations. Yeats, coming in to watch rehearsals, was impressed by the brothers' knowledge of stage technique and ability to get results from untried actors. He decided that the time had come for the incipient Irish drama to renounce its reliance on the English actors of F. R. Benson's Shakespearean Company and use this native talent. He therefore offered his new one-act play, his first in prose, to the Daughters of Erin. Maud Gonne, who had inspired the play, *Cathleen ni Houlihan*, liked it immensely and was eager to play the name role. Yeats was willing to have her, for he knew that she would "certainly be a draw."

George Russell's play *Deirdre* was to form the other half of the bill. He wrote Sarah Purser that "The Daughters of Erin have flung their Aegis over us, and Yeats and I are being produced under their auspices."

In a letter postmarked February 3, 1902, Maud wrote to W. B. Yeats that she was:

delighted to hear that you have given Kathleen ni Houlihan to Fay. Did you write him that I would act the part of Kathleen? Have you got another copy that you could let me have, as I would like to learn the words here and then go over them with you in London . . . and I would not be in Dublin long enough to do all that with them. I have a lot of work here, a lecture on the 4th on the 14th and on the 20th of February, and another one on the 4th March, besides a lot of other work.

During rehearsals of the two one-act plays, a new producing outfit was formed, called "Mr. W. G. Fay's Irish National Dramatic Society." The distinctive features were that the Fay brothers were in charge, and that an amorphous new ideal was being shaped—to present only Irish plays performed by Irish actors. In December 1902 the name of the group became the Irish National Theatre Society. Officers were W. B. Yeats, president; Maud Gonne, Douglas Hyde, and George Russell, vice-presidents; W. G. Fay, stage manager; and Fred Ryan, secretary.

The plays were given on three evenings—April 2, 3, and 4, 1902—in St. Teresa's Hall, a tiny place, seating only 300. There were no dressing rooms, and very little space backstage for anything. Maud Gonne, arriving late, swept through the auditorium in lordly disregard of previous instructions and commotion in the audience.

It was a famous first night. Inoffensive as *Cathleen ni Houlihan* may appear today, it seemed at the time a revolutionary declaration that Irish drama would henceforth be based on native tradition. It was written in "country speech" (thanks perhaps to the assistance of Lady Gregory) and was played by Irish actors in a new way that stressed voice rather than gesture and movement, in contrast to the flamboyant style then prevalent among English actors. When Maud Gonne flung off the trappings of a bent crone, and drew herself up to her magnificent height to become "a young girl with the walk of a queen," she became the image of a free and independent nation.

One viewer emerged from the theater wondering whether such inflammatory plays should be permitted, and how audiences could be restrained from attacking Dublin Castle forthwith. It was this play Yeats was referring to when he wrote, after the 1916 Rising, "Did that play of mine send out/Certain men the English shot?"

The scene of *Cathleen ni Houlihan* is a cottage close to Killala in 1798, at the time the French troops were landing. The synopsis below comes from the diary of an extraordinary Dubliner of the period: Joseph Holloway, bachelor, architect, inveterate playgoer, and incorrigibly mediocre reviewer.

To the cottage comes a mysterious old lady—"Cathleen ni Houlihan"—who so plays on the feelings of the coming bridegroom that he gives up his bride and follows her to strike a blow for ould

Ireland, whom she symbolises. The matter-of-fact ways of the household and the weird, uncanny conduct of the strange visitor make a very agreeable concoction. . . . Most of the sayings of the mysterious "Cathleen" (a part realised with creepy realism by the tall and willowy Miss Maud Gonne, who chanted her lines with rare musical effect, and crooned fascinatingly, if somewhat indistinctly, some lyrics) found ready and apt interpretation from the audience who understood that Erin spoke in "Cathleen," and they applauded each red-hot patriotic sentiment right heartily. . . .

However effective Maud may have appeared as Cathleen ni Houlihan, there can be some question about the quality of her acting. Many years later, William G. Fay wrote that Maud did not have "Miss Farr's technical skill nor her experience in playing before an audience, but she had a natural gift for reading poetry, and combined a fine voice with a magnetic personality. To Yeats' verse she gave a vitality that has not been equalled since. . . ."

A contemporary criticism by the *All-Ireland Review* may be used to support any opinion of Maud's acting. It said, "The well-known Nationalist orator did not address the other actors as is usual in drama, but spoke directly to the audience, as if she was addressing them in Beresford Place. . . . She can scarcely be said to act the part, she lived it. When she entered the little firelit room there came with her a sense of tragedy and the passion of deathless endeavour."

Yeats was delighted. After the first performance he wrote Lady Gregory that the only defect "was that the mild humour of the part before Kathleen came in kept the house in such delighted laughter, that it took them some little while to realize the tragic meaning of Kathleen's part, though Maud Gonne played it magnificently, and with weird power." After the last performance, he wrote, "Crowds have been turned away from the doors every night. . . . The audience now understands Kathleen ni Hoolihan and there is no difficulty in getting from humour to tragedy."

Maud Gonne, too, was pleased with the success of the play, and often said that this was the kind of play Yeats should have continued to write. She remained interested in the Irish theater in any case; whenever she was in Dublin, she made a point of seeing whatever was playing. And on November 1, 1902 she attended a lecture by W. B. Yeats on his theory of chanting in the theater. Miss Florence Farr, using a sort of lyre, demonstrated what he meant.

After the triumph of *Cathleen ni Houlihan*, an attempt was made to extend the run, but the leading lady felt that she had more important things to do, both public and private. The most pressing was the explosive situation on the De-freyne estate, where the tenants had refused to pay their rent. They had written to her to go to Roscommon to help arrange a settlement, for they had got to the point where they were willing to settle for even the smallest concession. The treatment of Roscommon peasants had been a controversial matter since the eighties, and Maud had often protested the bailiffs' practice of setting fire to the thatched roofs of evicted tenants' huts to insure that no one else could live in them. Now she was torn, but eventually decided that she could not interfere, since the United Land League was directing the peasants' campaign. She had no desire to receive further criticism for reckless behavior from that organization.

All this agitation induced a unionist landlord, Captain John Shawe-Taylor, who happened to be Lady Gregory's nephew, to suggest, in a letter to the newspapers, that a meeting be held of tenants and landlords in order to arrange for a final settlement of the land controversy. A consequent conference, held in December 1902, led to the passage in 1903 of the Wyndham Land Act, which greatly stimulated the transfer of estates from the great landlords to the small farmers. Between 1903 and 1920 nearly nine million acres changed hands, and two million more were in the process of being sold.

Many hands and much hard work went into the framing and passage of the Wyndham Act. Maud Gonne deserves some small share of the credit because of her frequent efforts to publicize peasant wrongs and demand a fairer distribution of the land. Maud herself never claimed any credit, since she considered the Act too little and too late, but this fact should not obscure our perception of what her strong voice accomplished in obtaining this reform.

Maud's private problems consisted of the ordinary ones of raising a little girl and the more unusual ones of helping John MacBride readjust from war hero to unemployed foreigner in Paris. The money he had saved in the Transvaal before entering the war was nearly exhausted, and there were few jobs in France for someone who did not know the language. He longed for Ireland, but, as a traitor, he could not return there.

At last, in May 1902, he arrived at Maud's flat in high spirits—he had been hired as secretary to the correspondent of the *American Sun* and Laffan's News Bureau at a salary of £2 a week. Maud, seeing conspiracy everywhere, pointed out that his new employer was sympathetic to England.

MacBride admitted that the man had formerly been a member of the English Liberal Party, but contended that he was Irish in origin and was beginning to accept nationalist ideas about an Irish Republic. Overriding Maud's further objections, he kept the job, but it never led to much.

Maud and MacBride were constantly in each other's company during this period. One day, after they had attended a lecture in the Latin Quarter, MacBride suggested that they go to a café. "Why don't we have tea in your room instead," Maud asked. "It will be so much quieter, and we can talk there much better." What she was really thinking was that it would be much cheaper. She knew that the money spent at the café would mean no dinner for him the following day. When she saw that he was shocked at the idea, she told him that he must get rid of the notion that a man's bed-sitting room was an improper place for talking. She realized, not for the first time, that MacBride was full of conventional ideas, the result of a background that was narrow in both its English and Irish Catholic aspects. Unfortunately, she did not realize how deep-seated those ideas were.

MacBride lived in a tiny, bare attic in the rue Gay de Lussac, but it was tidy and he was adept at making tea. In that little room and in her more comfortable drawing room they spent many hours discussing ways, many wildly impractical, of speeding up the overthrow of the British Empire.

It was Maud's belief at the time, and one she never repudiated, that it was actually the attempt of dynamitards to blow up the Houses of Parliament and London Bridge that had been instrumental in converting some Liberals to Home Rule and in obtaining the few concessions the Parliamentary Party boasted of. She held that if such acts were performed continuously, like Moses administering the plagues to Pharaoh, Ireland would soon be free, with small sacrifice of life. Specifically, if every Irish chief secretary, lord lieutenant, or even English king, were assassinated one after the other . . . she did not need to finish the thought. It was only the lack of continuity that made individual acts of violence futile.

MacBride did not agree. It was impossible, he said, to obtain that continuity. Men could face certain death in battle but could never be counted on to keep their nerve in such a solitary and personal kind of war.

It is an odd but well-known fact that such discussions of terrorist tactics do not seem to disturb the growth of love.

CHAPTER XIII

Marriage (1903)

 THE POSITION THAT Maud Gonne occupied in France at the turn of the century is described in a book called *Confessions of a Journalist*, published in London in 1904. It was written by Chris Healy, a reporter from Liverpool who was moving about Paris at the time recording his impressions of such figures as Zola, Anatole France, Oscar Wilde, James MacNeill Whistler, and Rodin. The dozen pages he devotes to Maud Gonne establish that her importance in building anti-English sentiment was not merely the product of her own superheated imagination.

Maud enters the narrative during Healy's description of Arthur Lynch, a handsome man, with an "athletic figure," and a "cordial smile in his dark blue eyes," who had turned from writing unsuccessful novels to reporting French news for a London daily. It was Healy's opinion that Lynch had acquired his violent hatred of England because of

the influence of "the most beautiful woman in Europe," the latter being the verdict of no less a judge of beauty than the late Benjamin Constant. Since then the pitiless finger of Time has scored her face with lines which dim its charm; but when Arthur Lynch first met Maud Gonne, she was in possession of unequalled beauty and fascination of manner. . . . Lynch revered her in her character of an impulsive patriot who had sacrificed a brilliant career for Ireland. . . .

Healy wrote that Maud had been able to embitter French
feeling against England

thoroughly and effectively. Not only has she guided the pens of MM.
Millevoye and Drumont, the editors of *La Patrie* and *La Libre Parole*, but
in many cases the articles denunciatory of Great Britain which have
enlivened the columns of those papers have been written wholly by her,
although they have appeared above the name of some member of the
staff. Her own journal, *l'Irlande Libre* (Free Ireland), is a sub-editor's
paper, printed so that any Continental paper may quote specimens of
England's misdoings, and it figures very largely in most of those French
newspapers which have distinguished themselves by their furious attacks of Anglophobia.

At her handsome apartment in the Avenue d'Eylau are to be seen
deputies, journalists, and irreconcilables—men who have great power
in the moulding of French opinion . . . it would be ill to under-estimate
her ability. She is shrewd, witty, and has the rare ability of uniting
opponents to act against a common enemy.

For some reason, Healy wrote, Maud was *persona non
grata* in certain upper-class circles which did not normally
object to receiving Anglophobes or Bohemians. The
Princess Karageorgevitch, for instance, told him frigidly
that "We used to receive Mlle. Gonne at one time, but we
do not know her now." It is possible that there existed in
these circles an element of puritanism that looked with dis-
favor on Maud's liaison with Millevoye, which she seems to
have made little attempt to conceal. In his memoirs, published in 1924, Arthur Lynch speaks of lunching at Maud's
home with them both when a message, delivered by hand,
was brought to Maud. She read it, and casually informed
Lucien that it was a proposal of marriage. Lucien responded gravely that she must send back a correct and
polite reply. Later Lynch discovered that the offer had been
from a "Marquis of one of the most famous and wealthiest
families in France."

Maud was also under attack from some Irish patriots who
thought that, as the daughter of an English colonel, she

must be a secret English agent. To Healy this theory was "in such extraordinary contradiction to the active part she undoubtedly plays in outwardly organising an anti-British sentiment on the Continent that it scarcely seems credible."

He said that Maud had given Irish malcontents on the Continent "a policy and a purpose which, some day, might shatter the proud bulwarks of the British Empire. This is not an empty phrase when one studies the plan." Its elements consisted of the manipulation of public opinion in the royal courts and cabinets of many nations by Irish extremists; a union of France and Russia (with America and Germany benevolently neutral) to crush the British army and navy; the submarine, a new and powerful French weapon; superior French artillery, and the superbly trained Russian and French armies; the mess and muddle apparent in the British military. "And then—the hidden fires of Irish discontent leap into flame all over Ireland, the French make a sudden dash on the Irish coast, and land men in the same skillful way that they did in 1798, and up would go the flag of a Green Republic." This was indeed Maud's dream, and, unlike many other Irish nationalists in France, she could express it in a French of "remarkable purity of phrase and accent."

Maud's decision to marry John MacBride proved a shock to everyone and dismayed those who knew the couple best. Her seven-year-old daughter, whom she visited with the news two days before her marriage, burst into tears. Iseult, "a beautiful . . . strangely wise child," Maud thought, was then a boarding student at a Carmelite convent in Laval, a historic town in northwestern France. Maud had placed her there because her friend Father Dissard was chaplain of the convent, and perhaps because Laval's distance from Paris—more than 200 miles—insured that her activities would be hindered minimally by the existence of her child.

Iseult liked neither the idea nor John MacBride. She refused to be consoled even when her mother enumerated the lovely things she would bring back to her from her honeymoon in Spain. Canon Dissard, brought in to appease the child, promised that she would be dressed like a queen at a banquet he would give when the couple returned, but she only cried harder. Eventually a nun had to take her away.

Maud spent the next day packing and closing her apartment at 7 Avenue d'Eylau, for she and MacBride were to take new lodgings when they returned. She also wrote out her will, making May Gonne guardian of Iseult in case of her death.

When everything had been done and Maud was resting on her bed she heard her father's voice, warning her distinctly, "Lambkin, don't do it. You must not get married."

The doorbell rang, John MacBride entered the dismantled drawing room, and commented on how tired she looked. He asked if she were ill.

"No, but I've just had a warning. Tommy says we must not get married."

"My mother says the same thing." MacBride showed her a letter he had received from Westport. His mother had written, "I have seen Maud Gonne. She is very beautiful; she is a great woman and has done much for Ireland, but she will not make you happy."

He had received the same opinion from his brother Joseph: "I think it most unwise. Maud Gonne is older than you. She is accustomed to money and you have none; she is used to going her own way and listens to no one. These are not good qualities for a wife. A man should not marry unless he can keep his wife. . . ."

Maud could match these with a letter from Arthur Griffith: "Queen, forgive me. John MacBride, after Willie Rooney, is the best friend I ever had; you are the only woman friend I have. I only think of both your happiness. For your own sakes and for the sake of Ireland to whom you both belong, don't get married. I know you both, you are so unconventional, a law to yourself; John so full of conventions. You will not be happy for long. Forgive me, but think, while there is still time."

Like most good advice, it went unheeded. On the morning of February 21, 1903, Maud Gonne and John MacBride were married in Paris in the Roman Catholic Church of St. Honore d'Eylau—it is quite possible that Maud had at last become a Catholic in preparation for this marriage. Only a few persons were present. The bride wore a costume of "electric blue"; the best man carried the flag of the Irish Brigade; another flag sent by the Daughters of Erin was also in evidence; shamrocks and violets had been shipped from Ireland to decorate the church. Father Van Hecke, former chaplain of the Irish Brigade, who had come especially from Belgium to perform the ceremony, spoke of the bride as "one of those women who rise scarcely once in a century to sacrifice themselves for their country;" the bridegroom he had seen "enduring the hardships and dangers of the battlefield with all that courage and gaiety which has long been traditional with the Irishman in whatever clime he has had to fight."

Why did Maud Gonne marry John MacBride? The reason usually given is that, as the daughter of a colonel and as a militant Irish patriot, she had a fondness for the military and for men of action, not poets. But Maud knew as well as anyone that MacBride had not received any military training to speak of; that his title, "major," was largely honorary; that he was not "a tall, soldierly man" as sometimes described. He was still little more than a Westport Irishman of unimpressive size who had been a chemist's assistant and assayer.

Was she "in love" with him? Elizabeth Coxhead, author of a profile of Maud Gonne in *Daughters of Erin*, speculates as follows:

She does not seem to have been in love or to have had any illusions about him, though doubtless there was a physical attraction, over and above the womanly pity she felt for an unemployed hero, flung on the scrap-heap almost overnight. She knew that he was really nothing but a fighting machine, that his upbringing had been narrow, that his views on women were the Irish peasant ones, and that he was only likely to settle down with a woman who knew her subordinate place.

Aside from the description of MacBride as "a fighting machine," there is much to commend in this point of view. But what really carried her away was doubtless the overwhelming appropriateness of the union from the patriotic point of view. It was incredibly right that Ireland's Joan of Arc should marry the outstanding hero of the Boer War. That she got married on a wave of patriotic sentiment is borne out by a letter Maud wrote during her honeymoon to Octave Montorgeuil, editor of *l'Eclair*. She told him that people who believed that with marriage she would abandon her patriotic tasks were entirely wrong. "On the contrary I expect that with the husband I have chosen I shall be able more effectively to serve the cause of independence." She ended by thanking Montorgeuil for reporting the marriage so accurately in his periodical, and for giving such a good description of MacBride's characteristics, including his longing to return to Ireland.

The possibility of danger might have been another attraction. In a letter written to thank Lady Gregory for her wedding congratulations, Maud wrote:

I was married at the English Consulate, as well as at my parish church, so I think it is quite legal.

We had heard that there was a possibility of the English trying to arrest Major MacBride at the consulate—but I do not think it would have been really possible, as even if the consulate is English territory, which is doubtful, they could not have imprisoned him there for long, and once outside he would have been free. No such attempt was made. The Consul was rather rude and began asking irrelevant questions, but when Major MacBride refused to answer, and told him it was no business of his, he went through the ceremony without further trouble. . . .

W. B. Yeats was just about to give a lecture when he received Maud's letter telling him that she had just married

John MacBride in Paris. Yeats told his wife many years later that he could never remember what he had said in his talk and that afterward he had walked the streets in a daze. He never forgot that day when, at the age of thirty-seven, his fourteen-year-old pursuit of Maud came crashing down about his head, that day

> When, the ears being deafened, the sight of the eyes blind
> With lightning, you went from me, and I could find
> Nothing to make a song about but kings,
> Helmets, and swords, and half-forgotten things
> That were like memories of you. . . .

During the next few years Yeats drew from this cauldron of his torment some of the best love poems he ever wrote, poems telling in spare, unadorned language the story of his ill-fated devotion to Maud Gonne.

Another, less important, consequence of Maud's marriage is that it gave James Joyce, that most famous of Irish novelists, reason for not visiting her after his arrival in Paris. He had tried once, early in December 1902, but then Maud's "niece" had been ill, and Maud had been quarantined. She had invited him to call again, but the young, obscure, would-be writer never did, despite the urgings of his mother, who considered Maud's "marriage and love making naturally kept her from looking after more serious business and you will make a big mistake by not keeping as yr Pappie says 'in touch with her.' *You cannot get on in your line without friends.*" However, when the time came for Joyce to write *Ulysses*, Maud Gonne did not escape his attention. He imbedded in the mind of a fictitious dynamitard, Kevin Egan, a sequence of historical and sexual fantasies: "Maud Gonne, beautiful woman, La Patrie, M. Millevoye, Felix Faure, know how he died? Licentious men." Faure, a French president, had died in his office in the arms of his mistress. An astonishing rumor that persists in Dublin to this day is that the name of the mistress was Maud Gonne.

Maud's marriage went well at first. The fact that she left

France three months after her marriage indicates no rift, but only that she had important things to do elsewhere. The prime one was to attend the wedding in London on May 15, 1903 of May Gonne to "Bertie" Clay. Her second task was to insure that when King Edward VII visited Dublin the city officials would not present him with the keys to the city. She hints that she cut her honeymoon short for this purpose.

Yeats met Maud at Victoria Station and accompanied her across the city to Euston Station. It was their first meeting after her marriage, but there are no emotional overtones in Maud's account of it that appeared, almost fifty years later, in an issue of *Our Nation*, a short-lived monthly established to further her son's political ambitions.

In her own words, Maud's meeting with Yeats resembled a conference of nationalist politicians in Dublin's city hall. Yeats told her that the death of Willie Rooney had depressed the separatists, while the unionists, in order to insure that King Edward would receive a warm welcome when he came to Dublin, were trying to create a romantic aura about him. Many people, tired of Victoria's virtuous court, were enjoying stories about Edward's love affairs. Then she quotes Yeats as saying: "To placate Ireland, it is being industriously whispered that he is secretly a convert to the Catholic religion and has deep affection for his Catholic subjects. I hear he is to be received at Maynooth by the bishops."

Maud replies in the same style, "The oath he took at coronation should dispel that rumor. I will get it printed and circulated. I don't believe that Edward will be given the keys of the city as they were given to Victoria. After all, Tim Harrington is Lord Mayor now, and I can't see Tim going on his knees to an English king."

The coronation oath, which was being well publicized in nationalist periodicals, required the monarch to declare his solemn belief that there could be no "transubstantiation of

the Elements of Bread and Wine into the Body and Blood of
Christ," and that the "adoration of the Virgin Mary or
other saint, and the Sacrifice of the Mass, as they are now
used in the Church of Rome, are superstitious and idola-
trous."

"The keys will be presented all right," Yeats said—and
he showed Maud a copy of the *United Irishman*, which asserted that a unionist plot was afoot to insure Harrington's
absence when Edward arrived, and that his *locum tenens*, a
unionist alderman named Cotton, would receive the king.
"Harrington is dreadfully in debt and they can bring pressure to bear on him. You won't be able to stop it."

As the train moved off, Maud retorted, "Yes, I will," but
had no plan in mind until, outside the Harcourt Street
station in Dublin, she saw a poster that announced a public
meeting of the Parliamentary Party for the following evening, Monday, May 18, 1903, at the Rotunda assembly
rooms, Parnell Square. Tim Harrington was to preside and
Maud's idea was to ask him publicly to deny or verify the
truth of the story in the *United Irishman* and to pledge that
he would not receive the royal visitor.

On the way to her Coulson Avenue home, she stopped
her hansom at the Rathmines Post Office in order to send
telegrams to Arthur Griffith, Edward Martyn, Father
James A. Anderson, Seamus MacManus, George Moore,
Alderman Tom Kelly, Henry Dixon, and Maire Quinn,
secretary of the Daughters of Erin. She asked them to as-
semble at her home that afternoon.

After most of the recipients of the telegrams had arrived,
Arthur Griffith told them that the story in the *United
Irishman* was true, whereupon Maud suggested that they
form a "People's Protection Committee" (which she later
remembered as a "Citizen's Watch Committee"), so that
delegates from it could attend the Rotunda meeting and put
the question publicly to Timothy Harrington.

Tom Kelly, arriving late, was nearly knocked over by

George Moore as he rushed out, aghast at the thought of
joining a delegation that might seem disloyal to the English
king.

Father Anderson, Irish patriot and strong supporter of
the Daughters of Erin, said he, too, could not be a member
of the delegation, since the rules of his order forbade it.

Edward Martyn, named as spokesman, set to work with
Arthur Griffith to compose the question to be asked, and a
brief speech to accompany it. Maire Quinn left to inform
the Daughters of Erin that they should attend the Rotunda
meeting with their sweethearts, the brawnier the better, in
order to quell any disorder that might arise.

When Maud and her friends arrived at the Rotunda the
next evening they were given seats on the platform. It was a
fund-raising function and the ushers figured from their
clothes that they might be generous contributors. Maud
promptly told Tim Harrington that she wanted him to
pledge at once not to recognize the English king when he
arrived in July.

Tim, who had led the fight against the reception for
Queen Victoria, answered laconically, "You know me well
enough to know that we shall not receive him."

"We do, Tim," Maud, said, "but have you read the
United Irishman?"

The time for questions would be after the meeting, the
lord mayor retorted, and opened the session. Maud feared
that Tim, as an old parliamentarian, might keep the meeting running so long that there would be no time for awkward questions. Hence, when he was introducing the principal speaker, John Redmond, she raised herself to her full
height and said in a resonant voice, "Mr. Martyn wishes to
put a question about the proposed visit of the King of England and we will go only when it is answered.

As Redmond started his talk, a din arose in the audience.
Harrington thundered, "Sit down, Miss Gonne." He had
forgotten that she had married.

"Only when our delegation from the Citizen's Watch Committee has been answered," Maud replied. "Put the question now, Mr. Martyn."

Unfortunately, the uproar went far beyond anything that Martyn, litterateur, bachelor, and devotee of the Gregorian chant, could cope with. He told Maud helplessly, "I can't. My voice won't be heard."

Maud took the paper from his faltering hand and began to read it amid shouts of "Sit down" and countershouts of "Quiet, we want to hear." Partisans on the floor started to throw chairs at each other. The fighting spread to the platform. Someone tall and strong seized Maud around the waist, lifted her off her feet, and carried her off. She stopped struggling when she saw that it was Seamus Mac-Manus protecting her from harm. Her last sight of the audience was Mickey Quinn, Maire Quinn's brother, fighting with blood flowing from a cut on his forehead.

The newspapers covered the incident with gratifying fullness. The *Irish Times* of May 19, 1903 identified the People's Protection Committee as responsible for "one of the most sensational incidents in the recent history of Irish politics." It reported that Mrs. MacBride and Edward Martyn were greeted with cheers when they entered; that a parley between them and the lord mayor seemed friendly at first but "smiles turned to frowns" when Mrs. MacBride insisted on addressing the audience; and that she remained "calmly imperturbable" even while the lord mayor was shaking his fist in her face.

But on another page the *Times* condemned the hooliganism of the nationalist group, and called Mrs. Mac-Bride "whom we had hoped had permanently retired to Paris . . . the most picturesque but impracticable of lady politicians." It said that when the audience heard her request—did the lord mayor intend to arrange for an address to His Majesty?—"the great majority called on her to sit down."

On May 23 the *Times* published a letter from John Mac-
Bride in Paris, saying that he was ready to "afford satisfaction" to anyone who felt aggrieved by his wife's actions.

The *Freeman's Journal,* spokesman for the Irish Parliamentary Party, deplored the fact that the incident would
be "magnified by the enemies of Irish Nationality as evidence of dissention," and printed a repudiation of the event
by the "Nationalist Party." Maud Gonne promptly wrote
to the editor asking who had composed this last item, since
no one she talked to had ever heard of such an organization.

The *Daily Express* considered it unfortunate that the instigators of the demonstration included a "number of individuals who pose as nationalists of exceptional refinement
and culture." It published a letter from the People's Protection Committee stating that the refusal of the lord mayor to
listen to a respected committee of nationalists was the reason for the audience's turbulence; it had desired to "protect
the deputation from personal violence."

Maud and her colleagues felt that part of their objective
had been reached since the Irish Parliamentary Party's
fund-raising efforts in Dublin would henceforth encounter
great difficulty. Years later, she philosophized in *Our Nation* that she had felt no fear during the Rotunda Riot, as it
came to be called, because she was working to free Ireland.
Whenever she did that, she felt so protected that she never
"raised a finger or spoke a word against any enemies who
tried to injure me." On the other hand, she was often
"frightened to see how misfortune always fell on them."

But not enough had been done, she felt after the riot, to
show how deeply Dublin disapproved of Edward's forth-
coming visit. She set about remedying that deficiency. In a
tea shop near Parnell Square that was run by Maire Quinn's
sister, Maud Gonne and other Daughters of Erin assembled
one noon hour to plan more anti-reception demonstrations.

They started with the idea of displaying the black flags
that had been used during Victoria's jubilee to counteract

the unionists' planned show of Union Jacks. But Maud
thought there were too few of the black flags to make it
worthwhile. She suggested that instead the Daughters seize
some of the unionist flags and burn them at a public meeting. Edward Martyn could act as chairman of the meeting;
he had not got cold feet at the Rotunda meeting, she said,
only stage fright, which was quite a different thing and
entirely pardonable. Maud never considered that Martyn
was hostile to women, even though he could not stomach
the thought of women's voices in church choirs. She once
wrote that she had "never met a man more ready to work as
a comrade with women or one on whom one could rely
more thoroughly."

Her second idea was that thousands of copies of the royal
oath should be printed and pasted up everywhere. When
someone pointed out that the treasury was empty, Maud
said that St. Brigid, patron saint of their organization,
would provide. If not, the People's Protection Committee
would. Everyone laughed at that because they knew its
total membership was five.

Almost as if they knew what was brewing on the
nationalist side, the unionists assembled on June 16, 1903 in
the Antient Concert Rooms on Brunswick (now Pearse)
Street near Trinity College, and made plans for a lavish
reception for the royal couple. The chairman was Reginald,
12th Earl of Meath, K.P., who told about this and other
festivities in his *Memories of the Twentieth Century*, published
in 1924.

On July 20, 1903, the day before the royal couple ar-
rived, there occurred the Battle of Coulson Avenue, named
after a quiet suburban street in the Dublin suburb of
Rathmines where Maud was living at the time, next door to
George and Violet Russell. It made a suitable sequel to the
Rotunda Riot, and is described in great detail in one of
Maud's articles in *Our Nation*.

That day the Irish newspapers appeared with black bor-

ders to mark the death of Pope Leo XIII. Many people
expected that the banquet the Catholic bishops were giving
in Edward's honor would be cancelled. Maud, who had
been disappointed when Archbishop Walsh had agreed to
attend it—he had subscribed to the Wolfe Tone Memorial—was shocked when it was announced that it would
be held nonetheless.

With these disappointments, and with the Dublin streets
well covered with bunting, Maud Gonne and Maire Quinn
were feeling discouraged when they took the last Rathmines
bus that evening. They were tired as well, for they and
their comrades had spent the entire day posting 10,000
copies of the coronation oath on every available wall, lamp-
post, and billboard. Many had been torn down by the
police, forcing the Daughters to redo the job.

Maud had a special worry with regard to some street
corner meetings, scheduled for the following evening,
when many captured Union Jacks were to be burned. The
participants might be sent to jail; what was worse, they
might be dismissed from their jobs by their unionist employers. Arthur Griffith and Charles Oldham had often
mentioned this dangerous possibility. Oldham had told her
quite sharply, "It's all very well for you who are independent to carry out your wildcat schemes but you should
think of what arrest might mean to girls earning their living." Maud felt the caution was unjustified. She had taught
the members that an injury to one was an injury to all; and
that so long as any one of them had means, no member
would be allowed to suffer want. Moreover, her organization was sufficiently popular and influential, she felt, to
obtain jobs for any victimized members.

As Maud turned into Coulson Avenue, she saw the house
opposite hers plastered with red, white, and blue bunting
and British flags. Once indoors, she put on the tea kettle,
sat down for a minute, and then noticed a broom in the
corner. It would make a good flagpole, she thought. She

went upstairs, found an old black petticoat, tore it in half, nailed one half to the broom stick, and hung it out the living room window on the first floor, as a contemptuous, if somewhat childish, answer to her neighbors' Union Jacks.

She was awakened the following morning by her house-keeper with word that the police had seized both the black flag and the broom stick. "Never mind, Mrs. Fitz," Maud said sleepily, "Just find the other half of the petticoat and if you haven't another broom borrow one from Mrs. Russell."

When she came downstairs, another black flag hung out the living room window. But while writing at her desk, she heard Mrs. Fitz arguing with the police. Maud, always peace-loving, pulled in the flag, went upstairs, and hung it out of the bedroom window over the tiny garden. But since the folds of the black petticoat hung dangerously low, she put a padlock on the small entrance gate.

A bit later she heard two detectives telling Mrs. Fitz to open the gate, and Mrs. Fitz saying, "I can't. Madame has the key."

"Then take down the black flag yourself."

"I can't. Madame put it there and said it was to stay."

When one of the agents stepped over the little garden railing, Maud thought it was time for her to go out to intervene.

"What do you mean by trespassing in my garden?" she asked with dignity. "Leave at once."

"We will have to get that black flag first."

"Who are you?" Maud asked.

"The police."

"You'll have to prove it."

An identification card was produced. After carefully reading it, Maud demanded to see a warrant for forcibly entering upon her property.

Instead of answering, the detective tried to get past her, but she got in front of him. The man laughed, tried to push her aside, and a tussle followed, with Mrs. Fitz supporting her mistress by hanging onto the assailant's arm. Conscious of neighbors gathering to watch, Maud inwardly reproached herself for the childish impulse that had got her into such an undignified situation. Then she heard Mrs. Fitz say, "You dirty scoundrel, daring to lay hands on a lady. You double-murderer, daring to touch a lady in her condition."

Maud was too excited to grasp her meaning, but suddenly the government agent loosened his hold. "Come on, we'll have to get a search warrant," he told his companion, and both disappeared around the corner.

Mrs. George Russell, in a blue apron that matched her eyes, came out of her house. "Whatever is the matter?" she asked. "Why, your blouse is torn."

"Only the police breaking the law, and trespassing without a warrant," Maud replied, still breathing hard.

"Disgraceful!" Violet commented loudly. "As an Englishwoman I care nothing for politics but if those people opposite may put out flags, why shouldn't you?" Coming closer, she whispered to Maud, "The neighbors are all unionists. They may try to attack you."

The small crowd which had gathered in the road did look hostile. Maud was relieved when she saw Maire Quinn approaching. Taking in the situation at a glance, Maire asked, "What weapons do we have?"

"Only our respectability," Maud answered, "and in my torn blouse I'm not sure of that. Mrs. Fitz might prepare a kettle of boiling water; I saw many houses defended that way during the Land War. You and Violet hold the fort while I change my dress and find a weapon."

The weapon turned out to be a perfume atomizer which had a convincing resemblance to a pistol. When she returned with it a small errand boy in the growing crowd cried out, "Up the rebels!"

As Violet left to prepare a meal for her family, she caught

sight of the weapon in Maud's hand and said, "For God's sake, don't use that."

Not wishing to leave the flag unprotected, Maud and Maire were having lunch in the open air when a sergeant and a dozen stalwart Dublin Metropolitan Police marched into Coulson Avenue, elbowed the crowd away, and formed a double line in front of Maud's tiny house.

The sergeant, a big red-faced man, pleaded good-naturedly with Maud Gonne not to cause any further trouble.

Maud left her coffee, assured him that she sought trouble as little as he did, and thanked him for removing "those rude people" from the front of her house. "Apparently they've never seen anyone having lunch in the garden on a fine May day."

Coaxingly, the sergeant said, "You know it's against the rules to show a black flag today. You've had your little demonstration, now please take it down."

Maud explained that she had the right to express her sentiments, that it was a matter of principle, and that anyone who tried to enter her property would get hurt. She conceded that it was excessive to take a man's life for trespassing, but since she was a good shot, it was likely that he would only be wounded. The black flag would fly as long as did the Union Jack on the opposite side of the street.

Then, raising her resonant voice, Maud launched into that peculiar mixture of personal and political appeal that is characteristic of many Irish speakers, past and present.

"I'm sure, sergeant, you're an Irishman and a Catholic. So, probably, are all your men. Now don't you think that all of you would be acting more like Irishmen and Catholics if you insisted that those flags across the street were hauled down instead of bothering me? Don't you know that right now our Holy Father is lying in state in Rome, and that in every Catholic country in the world—except here in

Ireland—flags are flying at half-mast in mourning for him?
While here, just because an English king who has taken a
blasphemous oath against our religion is arriving, Catholic
Dublin is being disgraced with these unseemly decorations."

The constables, dazed by this appeal to their faith and
patriotism, were speechless. But the sergeant, gifted with
mental agility and a readiness to compromise that had
earned him his rank, saw a way out.

"Miss Gonne," he said, "if you will but tell me that this
black flag is flying because you are mourning the death of
His Holiness the Pope, I shall not interfere."

Maud responded, "I shall tell you nothing of the sort. As
an Irishman and Catholic you know as well as I do the
meaning of this flag." She was returning to her coffee when
a small boy yelled shrilly that there was a man on the roof
trying to reach the flag.

Indeed there was. A neighbor had climbed onto the roof
at the back end of the house and was now trying to lower a
noose to capture the flag. Maud raised her "revolver," and
Maire, who knew what it was, caught her hand, saying,
"Don't fire, let me take care of it." Country-bred and used
to throwing stones, she picked up a bottle from the table
and fired it with such force and accuracy that the man on
the roof promptly tumbled off.

After the unionist neighbor was taken off to the hospital,
Mrs. Fitz investigated the situation and reported that he
was not much injured; he had only a bump on the head and
perhaps a broken arm. Since the man had no right to be on
her roof, Maud was sure that he had no legal case against
her. She now remembered, too late, that she was supposed
to meet with the Ninnies in Dublin that afternoon, and was
relieved to learn that Maire had long since dispatched a note
saying that the president's home on Coulson Avenue was
under attack and that all members should rally at once.

A subtle change was coming over the police and spectators. The police seemed to be guarding the house instead of attacking it; the number of patriots in the audience had increased, while most of the unionists had vanished.

Victory was assured when, to the unmistakable sound of marching feet, a great procession swung into Coulson Avenue. The marchers were Ninnies, and members of the Cumann na nGaedheal, of the Celtic Literary Society, and of a National Council formed that summer for the purpose of protesting the visit of Edward VII.

Arthur Griffith approached the sergeant with his peculiar walk, and assured him that there was no longer any possibility of disorder. The sergeant recalled that it was past his tea time, and marched his men off "to the cheers of the crowd."

Maud Gonne, who believed that Irish girls were natural hostesses, was proved right by the speed and efficiency with which the Daughters of Erin set about serving tea to the scores of people present. A few Ninnies went off to forage in little shops for bread and pats of butter, while others brought in hot water and cups from Violet Russell's kitchen. Maud herself went into the garden, and, before starting to help serve, made a little speech thanking the visitors for their timely arrival. "This is what solidarity means," she said. "By our own strength, numbers, and courage, and by standing together in this way, we can free our country."

One of the most efficient servers was a shy young girl named Helena Molony, who had gone that day to the office of the Inghinidhe na hEireann in order to join, and there found a notice telling members to go to Coulson Avenue. She became one of Maud's closest aides and succeeded Maire Quinn as secretary of the Daughters when Maire and Dudley Digges left Dublin to act in an Irish play at the World's Fair in St. Louis.

Others present at Maud's tea party were some foreign correspondents who had come to Dublin to cover the king's visit, and having seen an unpublicized procession passing through town, had followed it to Coulson Avenue. Taking advantage of the opportunity, Arthur Griffith and George Russell explained to them the republican position with regard to Edward's visit. As a result, the Battle of Coulson Avenue received attention not only in Irish newspapers but in those of many foreign countries as well. There was no mention made, however, of a black petticoat or an atomizer masquerading as a pistol.

The following morning, after reading a congratulatory telegram from her husband in Paris, and a similar letter from Yeats, Maud remembered Mrs. Fitz's words about a "lady in her condition."

"What did you mean?" she asked her housekeeper.

"Don't you know, Madame?" Mrs. Fitz asked. "I saw him in the tea cup clear as day—a little boy in a pram."

Mrs. Fitz must have had the gift of prevision. Mrs. MacBride's son Sean was born the following January.

The National Council remained in being after the king had departed in order to serve as a forum for representatives of the various nationalist societies. Its membership was appropriately broad. Edward Martyn was chairman, Maud Gonne was an honorary secretary; other members were W. B. Yeats, John Daly of Limerick, Dr. Mark Ryan of London, Seamus MacManus, George Russell, and Tom Kelly.

The National Council has been called an outgrowth of the People's Protection Committee, but its aims were wider, for it sought to include everyone who accepted in any degree the policies of Griffith's *United Irishman*. One more stone in the building of Sinn Fein, it was open to all who believed in the absolute independence of their country . . . in stamping out flunkyism and toadyism in the land.

But though the nationalists took heart from their own increasing activity, the unionists had no reason to be depressed. The Dublin Corporation voted against presenting a loyal address to the king by three votes only; and the reception Ireland gave the royal couple was as impressive as any in the past. More than eighty Irish bodies gave Edward addresses of welcome in St. Patrick's Hall in Dublin on July 22, 1903. The *Daily Express* said: "Ecclesiastical organisations and learned professions, scientific associations and mercantile bodies, vied with one another in assuring King Edward and Queen Alexandra of the fervent attachment of their members to the dynasty." The king's gracious thanks would never have been spoken, the paper declared, if Dublin citizens had "tamely acquiesced in the stigma which the Lord Mayor and Corporation of Dublin"—and Maud Gonne, it might have added—"sought to affix to the fair name of the city."

The gratification of the Earl of Meath was unbounded. When he dined a few days later with his sovereign, he was further pleased by the change in atmosphere that had taken place since the death of Victoria. In those days no one spoke above a whisper; "on this occasion," he wrote in his memoirs, "the conversation was general and the laughter unrestrained. The guests seemed to be thoroughly enjoying themselves." There was only one flaw. After dinner, he was taken to task by his wife for laughing so loudly.

On October 8, 9, and 10, 1903, the Irish National Theatre Society produced a set of three one-act plays: *The King's Threshold*, by W. B. Yeats, with settings and costumes designed by Miss Horniman; *Cathleen ni Houlihan*, also by Yeats; and *In the Shadow of the Glen* by J. M. Synge. The last concerns a young wife married to an old man and condemned to a life of loneliness, frustration, and monotony in a remote Wicklow cottage. She escapes by eloping with a "travelling man," that is, a tramp.

In three issues of the *United Irishman*, Griffith denounced the play as a travesty on Irish womanhood. He declared that everyone knew that "in no country are women so faithful to the marriage bond as in Ireland"; he called the plot a reworking of the old Greek tale, "The Widow of Ephesus"; and he asserted that "cosmopolitanism never produced a great artist nor a good man and never will. . . . If the Irish theater ceases to reflect Irish life and embody Irish aspiration the world will wag its head away from it."

Griffith, to his credit, gave Yeats, spokesman for the movement, plenty of room to reply in his weekly. Yeats chastised "the chimeras" of the pulpit and press. He blasted three kinds of ignorance: that of the Gaelic propagandist who would accept nothing that had not been conceived of in "country Gaelic"; that of the priest who would ban all ideas that might perplex the ignorant faithful; and that of the nationalist politician who would reject every idea that was not of immediate service to the cause.

Maud Gonne had no trouble deciding what side she was on. When she first saw Synge's play, she left the hall with Maire Quinn and Dudley Digges as a protest against the intrusion of decadence when "the inspiration of idealism rather than the down pull of realism was needed." In an article in the *United Irishman* entitled "A National Theatre," she declared that:

> It is for the many, for the people, that Irish writers must write, and if the Irish people do not understand or care for an Irish play, I should feel very doubtful of its right to rank as national literature, though all the critics in England were loud in its praise and though I myself might see beauty in it.
>
> Mr. Yeats asks for freedom for the theater, freedom even from patriotic captivity. I would ask for freedom for it from one thing more deadly than all else—freedom from the insidious and destructive tyranny of foreign influence.

Maud had two simple tests for the play. One: could a play which mocked Irish peasants for making loveless marriages and applauded wives for escaping with young lovers be helpful in convincing the outside world that the Irish people were mature, moral, ready for political freedom and self-rule? Two: could any play that pleased Dublin Castle reflect the true life of Ireland? She once broadened that concept to the extent of stating: "The centre of the national life is still among the poor and the workers, they alone have been true to Ireland, they alone are worthy and they alone are capable of fostering a national literature and a national dream."

The split between the nationalists grew wider when an anti-recruiting play called *The Saxon Shilling*, written by the young poet Padraic Colum, was rejected by the Fay brothers. Because Maud Gonne and Arthur Griffith thought that the reason was craven fear of bringing down the wrath of Dublin Castle on the fledgling theatrical enterprise, they withdrew from the theatrical society.

The controversy between Maud and Yeats spilled over into their correspondence. When Maud accused him of giving up his conviction that "our literature should be national," he complained to Lady Gregory: "One doesn't mind the misunderstandings of the indifferent world but one is hurt by the misunderstandings of friends." There was no doubt, however, that Yeats had gone fast and far from his belief of only a few years earlier that, if the intellectual is to avoid becoming a lackey for the imperialists, he must join in the cry of the Russian radical, "To the People."

Historian F. S. L. Lyons calls 1903 a critical year in the life of W. B. Yeats. From this time on, writes Lyons, "he began that withdrawal into aristrocratic contempt for what he saw as the base and squalid elements in Irish life which was to become so central to his late attitudes." The precipitating elements were the loss of Maud Gonne by marriage to a man he could not respect; and the sighting, because of the furor over the Synge play, of his predestined enemy—the rising Catholic, nationalist middle class, reunited after the Parnellite split, which aimed, among other goals, to put the creative mind into prison.

However, Yeats's distress was ameliorated to some extent by the success of an American lecture tour upon which he entered in November 1903 and which lasted over four months. Now thirty-eight, he was beginning to acquire a distinguished appearance. Though still "gaunt of body," the *Irish World* reported, he had "a classical, finely chiseled face and a heavy shock of black hair, finely sprinkled with silver."

And since the Irish-Americans found his lectures on the Celtic literary revival more comfortable than Maud Gonne's against the United Irish League, he had the novel and pleasant sensation of feeling a substantial amount of money jingling in his pockets.

Soon after arriving in America, while he was staying in New York City with John Quinn, the Irish-American art patron, he heard some distressing news. In a letter postmarked November 16, 1903, he wrote Lady Gregory: "I have just heard a very painful rumour—Major MacBride is said to be drinking. It is the last touch of tragedy if it is true. Mrs. MacBride said in one of her last letters that he has been ill all summer."

The marriage was less than a year old but the news was unfortunately true.

CHAPTER XIV

Collapse of a Marriage (1904–1906)

THE YEAR 1904 WAS a creative one for both Maud Gonne and W. B. Yeats. She gave birth to a child and a one-act play while Yeats, in collaboration with Anne Horniman and Lady Gregory, founded the Abbey Theatre, and continued to write poems immortalizing his disastrous love for Maud. In one of his best, "Old Memory," he reminded his beloved that "her strength . . . so lofty and fierce and kind" was only half hers, for he had "kneaded in the dough / Through the long years of youth, and who would have thought / It all . . . would come to naught, / And that dear words meant nothing?"

Sean MacBride was born on January 26, 1904. He was baptized on May 1 at St. Joseph's Church in Terenure, a part of Dublin. The occasion was not entirely peaceful since the parish priest refused to perform the ceremony when Maud told him that John O'Leary, the notorious Fenian, was to be godfather. Maud left the church in anger, but returned when a young curate caught up with her and offered to do the christening on her own conditions. (On the official baptismal record the space for the name of the godfather is still blank.) The entire MacBride family came up from Westport for the affair. Since they were all notorious nationalists, the police wrote down every detail.

While in London, en route to Paris, Maud found time to write a letter to the newspapers endorsing an official Dublin complaint about the patronizing of the Tyrone and O'Connell streets prostitutes by five thousand British soldiers. She agreed with the city fathers that the scenes of degradation resembled those of Port Said, Cairo, and Bombay, and called upon the army to remedy the condition. When the protest was rejected, Arthur Griffith wrote in the *United Irishman*, "This is what we expected . . . in no city in Great Britain . . . is such latitude permitted to the soldiery as in Dublin." The protagonist of James Joyce's *Ulysses*, Leopold Bloom, remembered all this when he ran into a grenadier in a bearskin cap. "Red coats. Too showy. . . . Maud Gonne's letter about taking them off O'Connell Street at night: disgrace to our Irish capital. Griffith's paper is on the same tack now: an army rotten with venereal disease."

Late in October 1904 Maud was in Dublin again, where she had the pleasure of seeing the Irish-American Celtic enthusiast John Quinn. It was the third successive year he had come to Europe and he already knew almost all the participants in the Celtic Revival, including Maud. On this occasion they met at a large party held at the George Russells'. Quinn, four years younger than Maud, wrote in his travel diary that she entered before midnight, "looking very charming."

Quinn was a successful corporation attorney, rare in those days for an Irish-American. Even rarer, he was willing to contribute both time and money to any project concerned with the new Irish literature and drama. Eventually, he became a collector of manuscripts by James Joyce, Joseph Conrad, and T. S. Eliot, and purchaser of graphic works by dozens of artists unknown at the time—Picasso, Matisse, Brancusi, Dufy, Braque, Derain, Roualt, Villon, and Laurencin. When he died in 1924, he was, in the opinion of Aline B. Saarinen, "the twentieth century's most important patron of living literature and art." He was also by then one of Maud Gonne's staunchest props and most constant correspondents.

Quinn may still have been in Dublin on October 29, 1904, when the *United Irishman* published the text of a one-act play by Maud MacBride entitled *Dawn*. Stage rights were reserved for the Daughters of Erin, but it has never been produced.

The time of the play is the Great Famine of the forties. The principal character is Bride (for Bridget) an old woman who is brooding over the loss of her home. Her husband has been killed defending it against the tax collectors; her son, sent to jail for the same reason, has died there; another son is in the British army; and her daughter Brideen, whose husband has gone to America, is raising a son called Eoin and is worried about feeding him.

The symbolism is embarrassingly simple: each day Bride "wanders round the fields that was hers—it's that which angers the Stranger against her." The Stranger, personified by the landlord, is the English government. The final blow comes when Brideen is told she will no longer be allowed to work on relief projects because of the Stranger's implacable hostility toward her mother.

Other characters in the play are neighbors who are wandering along the road because they have been evicted from their farms. Their conversation about their suffering takes up much time. Whatever plot there is begins when Brideen dies at the end of scene two, a victim of hunger, overwork, and possibly a surfeit of poetic imagery. When Eoin refuses to leave the body of his dead mother, the peasants are moved to action. One says, "The child has spoken. He has told us what to do. Bride, we will fight for you." Another peasant says, "No more starving on the Relief Works." A third pledges, "Bride, you shall have your land again. We will drive the Stranger out." Meanwhile Bride is saying in her usual misty fashion, "Brideen is with the mighty dead. They are driving back the clouds."

Seamus, the son in the British army, enters. He rises

from his dead sister's side to vow vengeance on the Stranger. All characters swear that they will turn Bride of the Sorrows into Bride of the Victories.

As the curtain falls, Bride sings,

> They have bright swords with them that clash the battle welcome,
> A welcome to the red sun, that rises with our luck.

The music came to Maud Gonne "in a dream—music out of the faery world." This is reported by Ella Young, who contributed two poems to the play; the appalling lines above are quoted from one of them.

The text of *Dawn* is available in a book called *Lost Plays of the Irish Renaissance*. The editors, Robert Hogan and James Kilroy, say that "it still evokes some real intensity of feeling . . . it is not baldly simple and it may well stand as a better than usual example of the new patriotic drama that flourished in Dublin."

They are charitable. *Dawn* is a dreadful play; the wretchedness of its thin and visionary concept is exceeded only by dialogue which, even to an American ear, sounds incredibly false. In this passage two evicted peasants discuss the Stranger's hostility toward the old woman Bride.

> "It was angered he was that she would not notice him, for he went off muttering to himself."
> "Mary Ryan that has the shop at the crossroads is after telling me that she was to give no credit to yourself or Brideen . . . or it would go hard with herself; he says Bride is mad, and he won't have her wandering over the fields that he took from her any longer."
> "It's the hard man he is."

The play illustrates again Maud's readiness, regardless of lack of experience, training, or talent, to engage in any project that would increase national fervor and publicize the plight of the tenant farmer.

John MacBride was also in Ireland in October 1904 but not in Dublin. He had slipped into Westport, heart in mouth, to visit his mother. Maud Gonne wrote Lady Gregory, "I hope the English Court will leave him in peace—but I feel a little anxious." Her principal reason for writing was to ask Lady Gregory if she would autograph one of her books and donate it for an auction, with the proceeds going to finance the classes in Gaelic sponsored by the Daughters of Erin.

By November 15, MacBride was back in France and writing John Devoy that his wife had returned from Ireland a few weeks earlier and "gives a very encouraging account of the state of affairs there. She finds fault with our friends for not being as active as they might be, but women are never satisfied." It will be observed that both were pretending to outsiders that their marriage was a successful one.

It seemed impossible for a year to pass without Maud and Yeats coming into conflict. This time the occasion was the announcement that, after the new national drama group had been established in a building of its own, the old Mechanics Institute on Abbey Street, there would no longer be any sixpenny seats. Patriotic groups set up a cry of outrage. Maud joined the protest, informing Yeats that the absence of sixpenny seats seemed further proof that he was "lost to Nationalism." Yeats was adamant. The Abbey Theatre opened its doors for the first time on December 27, 1904, with productions of two plays by W. B. Yeats, *On Baile's Strand* and *Cathleen ni Houlihan*, and one by Lady Gregory, *Spreading the News.* All three plays were smashing successes. Joseph Holloway was right for once when he called the opening "the most momentous event of the year in Dublin. . . . History may come of it!"

This controversy did not keep Yeats from feeling deep compassion when he started getting letters from Maud, a month before the news became public, about the collapse of her marriage. It was exactly sixteen years since he had met and fallen in love with her; it was only two years since Ireland's Joan of Arc and the hero of the Boer War had married.

Irish communities in many countries were shocked at

word from France that the Civil Tribunal of the Seine had heard Maud's plea for a preliminary divorce decree on February 24, 1905. The efforts of the court to effect a reconciliation were unavailing; and the court granted Mrs. MacBride custody of their infant son, pending final adjudication.

The letters Yeats received from Maud—now unavailable—seem to have described in detail her suffering and MacBride's brutality and drunkenness. Yeats, greatly shaken, wrote John Quinn on January 14, 1905 that the event was "the most painful affair of my life." He rushed to Paris to console Maud but all she would say was, "You must keep out of this. I brought this trouble on myself, and must fight it alone." From Paris he wrote Lady Gregory, "I turn to you in every trouble. I cannot bear the burden of this terrible case alone—I know nothing about lawyers and so on. When you know the story you will feel that if she were the uttermost stranger, or one's bitterest enemy, one would have, even to the putting aside of all else, to help her. . . ."

Maud was inevitably affected by Yeats's reaction. Only now did she begin to appreciate his readiness to assist her in every emergency, value him as a friend, appreciate the depth of his devotion.

We cannot know with precision why the marriage foundered. Elizabeth Coxhead believes that MacBride found Maud's "brilliance, her leadership, even her money exacerbating his sense of being on the scrap-heap. He drank, he knocked her about. It is possible to feel profoundly sorry for them both."

One cause, certainly, must have been the divergence in their basic beliefs on the position of women. Every time Maud lit a cigarette, drank a glass of sherry, or bought a painting without consulting him, it affronted the standards he had learned at home concerning the behavior of a wife and mother. It was all right for her to take their son to Dublin to be baptized, but there was no reason why she should spend two months in London on the way back to Paris, and then leave for Dublin four months later, leaving behind a baby less than a year old.

There is another possible reason. It cannot be documented but it seems reasonable to suppose that not many months of marriage could have passed without MacBride realizing that the child Iseult was more than a "kinswoman." If so, the effect on him must have been shattering. The fact that he and his family never made the charge, in public or in private, that Iseult was Maud's illegitimate daughter only serves to corroborate how shocking Maud's past must have appeared to those good Irish Catholics from Westport.

Maud's petition for a final divorce decree was heard by the Civil Tribunal of the Seine on July 26, 1905. Maud's attorney, a man with the Dickensian name of Cruppe, recited the tale of a woman who married because her imagination and patriotism were fired by a man's heroism in the Boer War, and then discovered he was a roisterer and rake. For their child's sake she bore with him until she could do so no longer.

MacBride's attorney, a man named Labori who had been one of the legal defenders of Captain Dreyfus, responded: "Major MacBride admires feminine beauty as do all brave men, but he is no rake. His wife is insanely jealous, but without just cause. Nor is he a drunkard. He is what we call here in Paris a *rude buveur*—he can drink heavily without getting tipsy. He was known in the army as a heavy drinker. But his brain is always clear—nay, brilliant. He has collaborated with his wife in her literary work; indeed, he wrote some of the most striking passages in her lectures and books."

Attorney Cruppe retorted that Major MacBride had no literary ability whatsoever. He could write only the roughest of drafts for an article.

The attorneys then squabbled about the validity of Maud's reputation as Ireland's Joan of Arc. Labori contended that she was born in England of English parents and had not a drop of Irish blood. Cruppe responded that Maud was born in Ireland, and had dedicated her life to Ireland's cause. Labori retorted, "Let her produce her birth certificate. It will show she was born in England. Nor was she a Roman Catholic until she became one for love of MacBride, that she might marry him."

No one raised the question as to what MacBride's literary talent or Maud's birthplace had to do with the merits of her petition for a divorce. This illogical and irrelevant debate was reported in the *New York Evening World* of August 10, 1905.

On August 9, 1905 the judges granted Maud a separation but not a divorce, on the ground that international law prevented them from granting a divorce when both parties were not French nationals. The mother was given custody of the child. The father was given the right to see his son twice a week, for two hours at a time, until the child turned six. Then the father could, in addition, have complete possession of the boy during the entire month of August each year.

The Paris correspondent of the *New York Evening World* interviewed Maud "in the pretty glass-walled drawing-room of her home at Passy." To his question, "Is marriage a failure?" she answered, "If a woman really has something worth while doing in the world, I say unhesitatingly that marriage is a deplorable step, or is likely to prove so until after she has accomplished her work. If she is an ordinary, commonplace woman, then she might as well marry as not."

Man is so inherently selfish, she continued, that, "no matter how loving he is when he first marries, he is sure to become jealous or sarcastic about his wife's career. In the end, he is likely to make his wife's life a hell. . . . In these days the woman is likely to be better educated than her husband. It is a fatal error for such a woman to take on such a man. Then, he makes another kind of hell by misunderstanding her and ridiculing her from the standpoint of his hopeless inferiority." She thought the worst obstacle to marital happiness was "man's inborn conceit, his tremendous half-hidden egotism. Biologically, marriage may be an undoubted necessity... from the viewpoint of woman's best happiness, I deny that marriage is the best arrangement possible."

Maud said that if one questioned 100 husbands on her street, 75 would be quite happy, whereas at least 95 of the wives would be unhappy or feel their lives were incomplete owing to their husband's "congenital conviction that the main thing in the world is his content and comfort." He thinks he is the worthiest person in the world, she continued, simply because he keeps a roof over his wife's head; he concentrates only on his own career and personal development, unless, indeed, he is too sluggish to think about mental improvement. His poor bewildered wife takes his point of view on every matter until she forgets that she ever had a different idea about anything.

The *World* correspondent interrupted Maud Gonne's flow of indignant eloquence to ask, "Is it not true that the family responsibilities common to most marriages are more to blame for marital unhappiness than the husband's deficiencies?" Maud replied:

I do not see why, just because a woman is a wife and mother she must be a housekeeper. ... If she has capacity to follow a profession and to help to earn money, why should she not give over domestic drudgery to well-chosen and well-trained servants? Why should a man feel that other men fault him if his wife makes money, follows her profession for love of it. No, no! To my mind the whole situation can be summed up thus. Marriage could be the greatest success in the sociological history of humanity if the man would or could play fair. But, I believe any woman with independent instincts, with the dream of making her individual personality count for something in the world, might just as well shun marriage.

It is easy to understand how such talk about "well-trained servants" and women who follow a profession "for love of it" must have baffled a Westport man who had never moved

in this kind of society. Soon after the divorce suit was
heard, John MacBride went back to Ireland to stay.

Maud had expressed her ideas frankly and courageously
to the *New York World* reporter, but in print they seemed
more radical than she had anticipated. She decided that the
reporting had been "unfair and dishonourable," and wrote
John Quinn to ask if he could do something about it. Quinn
wrote a letter of protest to the editor, a man named
McLaughlin, but received no reply. He sent this word to
Maud but she too did not answer.

Those who knew the MacBrides were split badly on the
wisdom of the divorce. John O'Leary, now aging and frail,
said, "John has his weaknesses but I know him to be a good
man." Anne Horniman hoped that the number of Maud's
critics would increase. She warned Yeats that "the greatest
poet is always helpless beside a beautiful woman screaming
from a cart." Canon Dissard, Maud's French confessor,
who was aware of all the circumstances, justified her action
in a letter to the bishops and priests of Ireland.

The blow Maud had given to the religious and hero-
worshipping sentiments of the Irish nationalists was strong
and lasting. She was booed at a performance at the Abbey
Theatre on October 20, 1906. A Dublin schoolgirl named
Mary Catherine Maguire, who later married Padraic Colum
and became a distinguished literary critic in the United
States, was present and has given us a description of what
happened when W. B. Yeats entered the Abbey in the
company of a tall woman dressed in black. As soon as they
entered, a small group in the pit began to hiss loudly,
and some shouted, "Up John McBride!"

The woman stood and faced the hissers, her whole figure showing a
lively emotion, and I saw the most beautiful, the most heroic-looking
human being I have ever seen before or since. She was about six feet tall
and of both romantic and commanding presence. Her height would
have drawn attention anywhere, but it was her beauty that produced
the most startling effect. It was startling in its greatness, its dignity, its
strangeness.... Yeats, standing beside her, looked bewildered as the

hissing went on... but she was smiling and unperturbed. Soon a counter-hissing set up, the first hissers being downed by another group, and then I realized who she was....

Mary Colum relates in her autobiography, *Life and the Dream*, that a few days later she saw Maud on the street and noticed that

in spite of her tallness there was nothing oversized or Amazonian about her. She looked very feminine in her Paris clothes, and with what Yeats called her "delicate high head"—that was it—for all her height there was something exquisitely delicate in all the lines of her, she was perfectly proportioned, and not only that, there was a physical delicacy about her—she did not look very robust. And yet she was full of an electric psychic life; she was alive to the last hair of her head....

During the next dozen years, Maud continued to make frequent visits to Ireland, but they were extremely brief. She could not take her son with her, for fear—justified or not—that his father might snatch him away; and she could not leave him alone in France for any length of time because he was prone to so many ailments. The brevity of her stays in Ireland had important consequences. These were fateful years, comprehending the establishment of Griffith's separatist political party known as Sinn Fein, the recruiting of an armed force in the North to resist Home Rule, and one in the South to hasten it, the beginning of the modern labor movement, and the 1916 Easter Rising. Because she could not make a sustained contribution to these developments, and perhaps because of her divorce, she could never again play a key role in Irish politics.

The same held true even on cultural matters. A case in point is the controversy over J. M. Synge's *The Playboy of the Western World*, which opened at the Abbey Theatre a year and a half after Maud's separation. The play concerned a young man who was lionized by the women of a village in County Mayo because he claimed that he had murdered his father.

It was roundly condemned by the nationalists. *Sinn Fein*,

the new name for the suppressed *United Irishman*, called it a story of "unnatural murder and unnatural lust, told in foul language . . . under the protection of a body of police, and concluded to the strains of 'God Save the King.'" The *Freeman's Journal* said it was an "unmitigated protracted libel upon Irish peasant girlhood." Joseph Holloway termed it "the outpouring of a morbid, unhealthy mind ever seeking on the dunghill of life for the nastiness that lies concealed there." Even the *Irish Times* could not find praiseworthy a humorous extravaganza based on a "grimly realistic treatment of a distinctly unpleasant theme."

This verdict has, of course, been overturned by history. Final ratification occurred in 1968 when a group of Abbey Theatre players visited Rome and presented the Pope with a copy of the play bound in white leather. However, it is possible to excuse the initial nationalist reaction. The purity of Irishwomen was one of the few bastions they could rally around; the play still reflects rather unduly the Ascendancy attitude toward a picturesque but inferior peasant class; Synge, himself irreligious, suppressed or ignored the large part that faith played in his characters' lives; and it can hardly be expected that fanatics will ever appreciate broad comedy, which *The Playboy* essentially is.

The significance for us is that, while the controversy was raging, Maud had no good platform from which to deliver her opinion. She agreed heartily with those who condemned the play; she had an enduring argument with Yeats about it; and she conveyed her stand to John Quinn. Her public silence at the time was the first installment of the heavy price she was to pay for her extended absence from Ireland.

On May 24, 1906 John Quinn wrote Maud Gonne a second time to say that he had never received an answer from McLaughlin concerning the *New York World* interview and had been advised to drop the whole matter. Quinn said that McLaughlin had been in Ireland, where he had met MacBride, and was now back in the United States full of MacBride's side of the story. The same slanders were being spread by a man named Concannon who had come to America to help organize a tour for Douglas Hyde.

I said nothing to Concannon and I said nothing to any of the Irishmen here except that McBride was a liar and a libertine and a drunkard and that I felt sorry for any lady that had anything to do with a middle-class Irish drunkard. . . . I shall be glad to know what the status of the case is at present.

The last rumor he had heard was that Maud had gone back on her nationalist principles and allied herself with the English. He had been sure it was only slander and had denied it, but, to tell the truth, he often felt like washing his hands of the whole business.

Quinn had every right to ask about the progress of Maud's divorce suit, for he had tried to help her win it by hiring detectives to investigate MacBride's conduct during his United States tour. Maud failed again to answer Quinn's letter, more because she was busy than because she was depressed.

CHAPTER XV

A Spiritual Marriage
(1907–1908)

🦋 MAUD GONNE'S ABSENCE from Ireland did not indicate any flagging of her interest in things Irish. She wrote every week to the new secretary of the Daughters of Erin, Helena Molony, and often lodged Helena in her Paris flat to facilitate discussion. She corresponded with W. B. Yeats and many others about Irish politics and literature. She read every Irish publication she could get. At the same time she took good care of her children, often preparing special dishes for them and for frequent guests. Maud was a good cook, in the way that she was good at anything that required manual dexterity from gardening to converting seashells into flowers.

When the St. Patrick Society held its annual celebration, Maud dressed three-year-old Sean in a white suit, put around his neck her own cross signifying membership in the society, and sent him around distributing shamrocks to members attending mass at the church of Notre Dame des Victoires. The shamrocks had been sent from Ireland by the Daughters of Erin. After the mass Father Gaffrie met Maud Gonne and complimented "the great Irishwoman on her noble work for Ireland." All this was reported in a new nationalist periodical called *The Republic*. The same issue of March 28, 1907 regretted the death of John O'Leary.

He died on March 16, shortly before his seventy-seventh birthday. During his later years he resembled, James Joyce wrote, "a figure from a world which had disappeared. He would often be seen walking along the river, an old man dressed in light-coloured clothes with a shock of very white hair hanging down to his shoulders, almost bent in two...." But his mind remained alert. "Are you one of those dreadful people called teetotallers?" he asked scornfully of Joseph Holloway, chronicler of drama in Ireland. John MacBride was a coffin bearer at the burial. Arthur Griffith and other prominent nationalists were present. Both men were again present when, two years later, a Celtic cross was unveiled over O'Leary's grave in Glasnevin cemetery.

The Republic had been started in 1906 by two young Ulstermen, Denis McCullough and Bulmer Hobson. They were also organizing Dungannon Clubs, whose slogan was "National independence is our right; we ask no more and we will accept no less."

It was inevitable that Maud Gonne and *The Republic* should join forces. It printed a long article in which Maud once more expounded Arthur Griffith's ideas on Ireland's need for industrial independence as a means of stopping emigration and creating prosperity. Since England would never allow industrial competition, Maud wrote, the Sinn Fein policy—"by ourselves alone"—was the only recourse. Ireland could protect her infant industries only by boycotting English goods and buying things of Irish manufacture. "Under this system of popular protection, numbers of small industries have started, and those already in existence have doubled and trebled their output, and, naturally, are able to employ more labour, which is the great, the all-important point."

One of the great advantages to the movement, in Maud's eyes, was that it was injuring Britain's trade. She scoffed at the idea that Ireland would be wise to participate in a great international exhibition that was being planned in England. She thought that Irish infant industries "would be swamped by English traders who, with goods far inferior in quality and sincerity to Irish ones, would be able to spend much more in gaudy display."

John MacBride felt the same way. Taking time off from a foredoomed attempt to write a definitive history of the Irish Brigade, he told a Sinn Fein audience at Castlebar that the way for Irishmen to injure England was "by boycotting her manufacturers, by supporting the Irish industrial and language revivals, and by working might and main to prevent young Irishmen from joining any branch of the British service."

Two years later, at a meeting in Kilkenny to commemorate the Manchester Martyrs, MacBride predicted that if war broke out between England and Germany, any Germans that landed on Irish soil would be received "with willing hearts and strong hands . . . twelve months later this land will be as free as the Lord God meant it should be."

Early in 1908 a driving force emanating from Paris encouraged the Daughters of Erin to establish a monthly magazine. Letters appealing for funds and literary contributions were written and circulated. Each Daughter was asked to canvass her friends for contributions of one shilling a month to pay the printer. The first issue of *Bean na hEireann* (Woman of Ireland) appeared in November 1908 at a penny a copy. It was the first Irish women's magazine to preach the doctrine of complete national independence. In the process it advanced some truly feminist notions, ridiculing, for instance, the idea so strong in popular fiction that happiness for a servant girl consisted of marrying her rich and titled employer and living in luxury for the rest of her life.

During its existence of more than two years, the monthly printed a wide range of pieces: historical articles, poems, book reviews, cooking recipes, gardening advice, fashion notes, correspondence, editorials, and paid advertisements. In Number 6 there was a quotation from "our bright little contemporary *The Harp*," whose editor, James Connolly, wrote that, until women made their influence felt more effectively, politicians would continue to "rave about the beauties of the Daughters of Erin and continue telling those same daughters to stay at home and mend socks, or plant potatoes, whilst their lords and masters are settling the fate of Ireland over a pint of Guinness' or suffering for their country in a tall silk hat and white waistcoat 'on the flure of the House of Commons.'"

The same issue contained the magazine's slogan, "Freedom for our Nation and the complete removal of all disabilities to our sex"; and an editorial advising Sinn Feiners not to use the Parliamentary Party to seek any goal, for that would be a tacit indication of Sinn Fein weakness. In Number 18, readers were reminded that "that which was wrested from us at the point of the sword must be won back by the power of the sword . . . such doctrine is not unbecoming to a woman, and an Irishwoman." A long editorial, no doubt written by Maud Gonne, fumed about the ascension to the English throne of "King George the Bigamist."

Number 19 contained an article on the art of street fighting—it should be conducted at night; first business was to break streetlamps; next was to stretch ropes and wires across the street, etc.

In Number 21, Maud Gonne pleaded for the installation in Dublin of an in-school system of feeding children similar to that existing in France.

To defray the expenses of the free meals . . . an appeal to public charity would have to be made, and, as in France, house to house collections taken up, and I think that if the managers of schools brought the matter before the Dublin Corporation that body would not refuse to provide kitchens and perhaps make a grant in aid of the scheme.

Another article in this issue reported that the Daughters of Erin, at their tenth annual meeting held October 21, 1910, unanimously re-elected Maud Gonne as president. It will be observed that she was using her maiden name on all occasions.

Number 25 reported a meeting in Paris of the St. Patrick Society, during which Maud Gonne described "the pitiable state" of the children of the poor in Ireland because they were often insufficiently fed although forced by law to attend school.

During the course of the evening her little seven-year-old son, Seaghan, went among the members with his collecting card for the benefit of the poor Irish children. He wore his mother's cross of the Knights of Saint Patrick, and his collecting card was almost filled in a few moments.

The garden notes in the magazine were written by a member, Countess Markievicz, whom Yeats had met years before in Sligo as Constance Gore-Booth, and who shared Maud Gonne's interest in art, drama, and gardening. Not long before, she had come directly to her first meeting of the Daughters of Erin from some Dublin Castle function, wearing a satin dress with a train, diamonds in her hair, and carrying a long blue velvet cloak on her arm. Naturally the members had looked upon her with suspicion, almost hostility. This refreshing change from being "kowtowed to as a countess" made Constance all the more eager to become a member.

She proved to be as single-minded and militant in her patriotic fervor as Maud Gonne. The following passage illustrates Constance's brand of horticultural instruction: "It is very unpleasant work killing slugs and snails, but let us not be daunted. A good Nationalist should look upon slugs in the garden much in the same way she looks on the English in Ireland, and only regret that she cannot crush the Nation's enemies with the same ease that she can the garden's, with just one tread of her fairy foot."

In the spring of 1908, Maud Gonne finally got around to answering John Quinn's communications. Her letter was the first of fifty, many long and informative, that she sent him during the next dozen years. She began by thanking him, belatedly, for the help he had given her in her divorce petition, and told him that as a result of a request she had recently filed the judges had reduced her husband's visiting rights to once a week and cancelled the provision that he could have the boy during the entire month of August. All this was *pro forma* since MacBride was in Ireland and gave no sign of returning to France. The judges still refused to grant the absolute divorce she had asked for, but said she could renew her request in three years if she wished. At the moment, she felt that, so long as the Major did not interfere with her life or that of her son, she would not bother to enter court again.

In reference to a mention by Quinn that his companion Dorothy Coates was making a trip to France, Maud said that she would be glad to see her. Miss Coates, a former school teacher, was a tall handsome brunette, whose relationship with Quinn lasted twenty years. Maud mentioned her frequently in her letters to him as a way of indicating that she was not shocked by it.

Having dabbled in watercolors, woodcuts, and pencil drawings (eventually it would be gold leaf on parchment), Maud was now trying oils. In answer to Quinn's offer to buy one of her paintings, she said that she wanted to wait until her work had improved. She applauded the efforts of Hugh Lane and others to establish in Dublin a gallery of modern art. Lane was Lady Gregory's nephew, an energetic art dealer and a sponsor of Irish artists. Maud could not understand why Arthur Griffith did not share her admiration of Hugh Lane. She thought Griffith was "too suspicious" of people's motives, the result of living in a conquered country.

One grows suspicious and narrow and often intriguing because life is so hard and treason and meanness so well paid. I don't at all put Arthur Griffith, though I see his faults, on the same line with the Fays and those others you criticise. He has done and is doing a very big work for Ireland. . . . I am not in the least surprised the Fays have been giving you trouble. . . .

In mentioning their mutual friend, W. B. Yeats, Maud made a point that she was often to repeat to Quinn. She regretted that Yeats was still involved with the Abbey Theatre, for his poems were of more value to Ireland than managing a theater.

This letter, and all succeeding ones to John Quinn, was signed Maud Gonne, not Maud Gonne MacBride.

Maud's address, when she next wrote Quinn in July 1908, was Les Mouettes (the Sea Gulls), at Colleville-sur-mer, in Calvados, Normandy. There is no way of knowing how many summers she had spent there previously, but the story that it was given to her by Lucien Millevoye, to be held in trust for their daughter Iseult, is apparently correct. Maud wrote Quinn that Yeats had been in Paris for a short time. She thought he was weary of the theater but was reluctant to leave it because of his sense of responsibility to those connected with it.

She said she was working very hard at her painting and had just sent off three pictures to an exhibition being held at the Albert Hall in London. She had been told that Roualt was sending some of his work there.

On August 14, 1908 she thanked Quinn for sending her a copy of *The Golden Helmet* by W. B. Yeats. Quinn had printed it in an edition of fifty copies in order to establish a U.S. copyright. He performed the same service for Yeats and other Irish writers several times, and was chagrined when he got little gratitude for it.

In these letters Maud had no reason to disclose to Quinn, who was only a new acquaintance, the fact that her association of almost twenty years with W. B. Yeats had suddenly entered a new phase. On June 20, 1908, when Yeats and Maud were in their early forties, Maud said something that "blotted away the recent past" for Yeats "and brought all back to the spiritual marriage of 1898." On the following day, she talked more plainly. "She believes that this bond is to be recreative and to be the means of spiritual illumination between us. It is to be a bond of the spirit only and she lives from now on . . . for that and for her children." The purpose of the new bond, it became clear as time went on, was to exchange descriptions of their meetings on the "astral plane" while their material bodies were sleeping.

Yeats promptly produced a dream of being in a painted boat, and of seeing people running beside the shore while pointing to a shrouded figure at his feet. Maud said she had dreamed of being with him. When he asked her for a blank book in which they could record such visions, she brought one forth "triumphantly," saying "I have already planned to give you that."

This large notebook covered with white calfskin contains the story of a spiritual marriage that lasted from June 1908 to January 1909. The entries, in both handwritings, have never been published in full, but Virginia Moore printed extracts in *The Unicorn*.

Pasted in the book is a long and intimate letter that Maud wrote to Yeats on June 26, 1908 in which she regretted his having had to leave Paris so soon; there was so much that they had not had time for. She said she did not think he should give up his life in London since it held elements that he still needed. The theater was the millstone around his neck. "For the sake of Ireland you must keep your writing before all else."

She scolded him gently for taking up "old class prejudices," and for speaking slightingly of George Russell's play *Deirdre*. "Of course Russell cannot write as you do, but all the same Russell is an artist and has a very noble mind."

She apologized for these remarks should they anger him;

she had not had time to make them before. "Everything else seemed too unimportant to waste the short time we had together.... Even in little things I don't want there to be the least jar between us."

She felt that "a most wonderful thing has happened—the most wonderful thing I have met with in life. If we are strong enough to hold the door open, I think we shall obtain knowledge of life we have never dreamed of."

Throughout the summer both strained to achieve evocations and dreams of a spiritual union. After Yeats had used the mingling of colors in a red and green globe to arouse "meditation for communion with P.I.A.L.," he decided that it "caused too painful absorption in her during the day." These were the initials of her name in Hermetic circles.

But on July 25, after an evocation, he experienced "a great union" with P.I.A.L. The next day he felt extraordinarily well and "for the first time in weeks physical desire was arrested."

By no coincidence (according to mystic lore), Maud had had a similar experience at the same time. She wrote Yeats on July 26,

> I had such a wonderful experience last night that I must know at once if it affected you and how?... Last night... I thought I would go to you astrally. (It was not working hours for you and I thought by going to you I might even be able to share with you some of my vitality and energy....)
>
> We met somewhere in space, I don't know where—I was conscious of starlight and of hearing the sea below us. You had taken the form, I think, of a great serpent.... As I looked into your eyes... your lips touched mine. We melted into one another till we formed only *one being, a being greater than ourselves*, who felt all and knew all with double intensity.

As they separated she "felt as if life was being drawn away" from her through her chest "with almost physical pain," and twice she found her way back to him. Then she dreamed they were in Italy together talking happily of this "wonderful spiritual union," of which Yeats said—in the dream—that it would tend to increase physical desire. But she had assured him that by comparison material union was but a pale shadow. She ended her letter, "Write to me quickly. . . . My thought with you always."

Yeats's dreams continued. He too imagined himself a great serpent, "we became one," then they were folded into a mouse-gray veil; he "looked into her being," and found himself in a "dazzling dark" of green and red.

Two weeks later he dreamed that he saw Maud with an emerald crown on her head, reproaching him because she could not break down the barrier. On another occasion when he and Maud "became one," he thought he was "fluid and she hard."

The entry for October 20 is in Maud's handwriting. She noted that Yeats, who was then in Liverpool, "came to me and we became one being with an ecstasy which I cannot describe." In her vision she saw Yeats looking "very beautiful and happy and triumphant," felt "a great gust of wind blowing through the room"; she heard voices saying that, since she had not understood "it"—the closeness with Yeats?—it had been taken away from her. Since she had now been purified by suffering, "it" was returned. "See that you guard it, holy, for from it great beauty may be born." Then Maud saw a globe of light that she and Yeats had previously seen "from the cave in Paris." They stood with clasped hands in a white radiance, a bird flew up, and a voice said, "It is the magic of Forgael's harp which nothing can destroy."

In this fashion, with visions being seen and recorded, the fall passed. Yeats was both happy and tortured, for the spiritual union was always taking place where desire in the ordinary sense was unthinkable. In December, hoping to put an end to his suspense, he went to Paris, where he stayed at the Hotel de Passy, conveniently near to Maud's

flat at 13 rue de Passy. He did many things—worked on
The Player Queen (a play intended for Mrs. Patrick
Campbell), attended French language classes, read Balzac
in English—but principally discussed with Maud the mystic significance of such objects as the spear and sword, such
elements as fire and air, and planetary conjunctions.

One day they quarreled about a Dublin girl they both
knew. Yeats became greatly upset, and lost "all social presence of mind through the very ordinary folly of a very
ordinary person." The discussion, he thought, brought out
Maud's old propensity to judge people and things "by an
exclusively political measure, which I cannot accept as
complete."

He reproached himself as well. He considered his "petu-
lant combativeness" his worst fault, rooted in his stars but
arising also from impatience and fear of strangers. He
dreaded, in addition, "representatives of the collective opinion, and so rage stupidly and rudely, exaggerating what I
feel and think."

The turmoil in his breast found expression in one of the
most magnificent poems ever indited to (and indictment of)
fair lady. Called "No Second Troy," it was written in December 1908.

> Why should I blame her that she filled my days
> With misery, or that she would of late
> Have taught to ignorant men most violent ways,
> Or hurled the little streets upon the great
> Had they but courage equal to desire?
> What could have made her peaceful with a mind
> That nobleness made simple as fire,
> With beauty like a tightened bow, a kind
> That is not natural in an age like this,
> Being high and solitary and most stern?
> Why, what could she have done being what she is?
> Was there another Troy for her to burn?

But worse was yet to come. On January 21, 1909, he
recorded with grief Maud's decision that they must always
live apart.

We are divided by her religious ideas, a Catholicism which has grown on her—she will not divorce her husband and marry because of her church. Since she said this, she has not been further from me but is always very near. She too seems to love more than of old. In addition to this the old dread of physical love has (re) awakened in her.

This dread has probably spoiled all her life, checking natural and instinctive selection, and leaving fantastic duties free to take its place. It is what philosophy is to me, a daily rooter-out of instinct and guiding joy—and all the while her heart grows nobler under the touch of sorrow and denial.

Yeats felt that, no matter how the thing might end, "she has all myself." He had never felt more deeply in love, but his physical desires, "always strong, must go elsewhere if I would escape their poison." He was thinking of the fact that he had recently become involved with a mistress in London, and feared that this might part him from Maud, since "all the while I know that she made me and I her. She is my innocence and I her wisdom." Once he had considered her a sort of phoenix and feared her, but lately he thought her more his child than his sweetheart. If she seemed cruel at times, it was only because she was like a child who might tell one, "You will not suffer because I will pray."

His torment took various forms. On January 22, 1909, Yeats wrote in his *Memoirs:*

Today the thought came to me that P.I.A.L. never really understands my plans, or nature, or ideas. Then came the thought, what matter? How much of the best I have done and still do is but the attempt to explain myself to her? If she understood, I should lack a reason for writing, and one never can have too many reasons for doing what is so laborious.

He put this thought into poetry on the same day. "My darling cannot understand / What I have done, or what would do / In this blind bitter land."

The lines he wrote on the following day were less tolerant.

> My dear is angry that of late
> I cry all base blood down

> As though she had not taught me hate
> By kisses to a clown.

It is the second line that is important. Yeats was beginning to glorify the stock from which he had sprung (or thought he had sprung): courtiers, soldiers, landowners, huntsmen, such men as Grattan, Swift, Emmet, Parnell, Goldsmith, Berkeley, Burke.

CHAPTER XVI

Dual Residence
(1909–1910)

THE COMPLEX RELATIONSHIP between Maud Gonne and W. B. Yeats did not prevent each from pursuing his own goals. A chronology of their activities and thoughts during 1909 and 1910 makes this clear.

In January 1909 Maud wrote John Quinn to thank him for the gift of an Indian pipe. She told him she was busy with her painting; and that their mutual friend, W. B. Yeats, after spending Christmas in Paris, had gone back to Ireland to look after "the terrible theatre...."

Soon after this, a seer told Yeats that the prominence of Uranus in his horoscope showed that he embodied "abstract intellect," and he promptly began to worry about the position of Maud's Sun opposite his Uranus. "This would mean," he wrote anxiously in his diary, "that her active being could be repelled by my intellectual side."

On March 24, 1909, J. M. Synge died at the age of thirty-seven. For the rest of his days, Yeats bemoaned the loss to Ireland of a great dramatic talent. He was marginally consoled when his own *Collected Works* appeared the following month in eight gray volumes with gold lettering and were well received. Even the *Freeman's Journal* was laudatory. The best the Irish press had come up with previously was to hail him as the Celtic equivalent of Maurice Maeterlinck, whose characters also moved in a misty world and were threatened by unseen forces.

Maud Gonne was in England and Ireland during the spring of 1909. While in London in May she visited an ailing Arthur Symons, at Yeats's request, and at his bedside met a young American writer named Agnes Tobin. Yeats had known her in San Francisco, and liked her; Symons considered her "bright, warm-hearted, very talkative, very amusing," with "a passion for meeting famous writers." The two women, Yeats wrote Lady Gregory, struck up "the most surprising friendship." Maud felt Miss Tobin was "so good—it flows from her," while Agnes found Maud "the most glorious of human creatures," and sent her a string of pearls. They spent a morning together in Westminster Abbey before Maud left for Dublin.

A year later Agnes Tobin demonstrated much tact in helping the British government find out that Yeats was willing to accept a Civil List pension—provided he could participate in any kind of political activity he wished. The award was announced in August 1910.

Back in Paris, Maud wrote Quinn on June 22, 1909 that she had enjoyed her time in Ireland, where "everything seemed much more beautiful and much more alive than in France. But for the sake of a peaceful life I find it better to live with my son in France." In response to Quinn's inquiry about the possibility of buying something by Augustus John, Maud wrote that it should not be difficult, "but do you really like his work?"

She returned to an old subject. "When you see Willie Yeats do try to make him see how he is wasting his time with the theatre. It has kept him from doing any good work for years. He is tired of it himself, but doesn't seem to know how to drop it.... They still seem able to keep Willie unsettled in his own work settling their rather unimportant difficulties."

Yeats was actually being unsettled by other matters. In

early summer Olivia Shakespear brought to the Woburn Buildings a brash American poet named Ezra Pound. Though twenty years younger than Yeats, he had odd but convincing ideas about the nature and purpose of poetry that could not help but influence the older man.

Maud, too, was a disturbance. In June 1909 Yeats had a dream in which he asked a spirit if there was any possibility that he and Maud would ever become closer. There was no clear answer. Again, on a soft July night in Dublin when he was talking with a friend about ancient sacrifices at the Druidic mount called New Grange, he had a sudden and piercing vision of Maud as one of the victims.

During that month he visited Maud in Paris. He found Sarah Purser there, he wrote his father on July 17, 1909. "Maud Gonne had a cage full of canaries and the birds were all singing. Sarah Purser began lunch by saying, 'What a noise! I'd like to have my lunch in the kitchen.'"

Hardly had Yeats left when Maud received a letter from John Quinn in which he wrote that in his opinion William Butler Yeats had "shot his bolt." He went on harshly:

He is too likely for the good of his art to be obsessed by theories. His theories of the small stage and of mean scenery and of no properties were of course absurd. . . . His theory that poetry should be as near like prose as possible is of course absurd. . . . As a lyric poet you could make ten like him out of the mind of Swinburne. . . . I don't allude to Yeats' selfishness, for he is selfish, or to his lack of appreciation of what people do for him. . . . What we expect from an artist is art and not philanthropy or political dogmas or doctrines or propaganda. . . . He has been trying for years to become a dramatist. He has not the dramatic sense or instinct.

What lay behind these critical judgments were some perjorative remarks Yeats had made about Quinn that had been transmitted by a "friend," Yeats's lack of gratitude for Quinn's efficient management of his first American tour, and Yeats's lack of respect for Quinn's ability as a literary critic.

On August 5, 1909, Maud Gonne, who was then staying at Aix-les-Bains, wrote Quinn that the more she thought about it, the more sure she became that "you ought to see Willie and hear his explanation . . . what he said may have been twisted and exaggerated. I know he is incapable of deliberately making mischief. I hope you will write to him to meet you in Dublin."

On August 9 Maud wrote Quinn that she had painted a small picture of St. Bridget and he could have it if he wanted it. She invited him to visit her in Normandy for a few days provided he would be satisfied to "live on potatoes and such fish as the sea sends us." Again she urged him to make his peace with Yeats.

On September 18, 1909, Maud wrote that she, her son Sean, and Ella Young, who was visiting her at Les Mouettes, had just returned from nearby Mont Saint Michel, "the most magical and wonderful place in France"—a "perfect example of 13th century architecture" that the English had failed several times to capture. In the same letter, she said:

> I am really very pleased that you saw Willie Yeats and spoke quite straightly and frankly to him. It was necessary and right. . . . I do hope very much that now, as you say in your letter, you will "let it go" and your friendship on both sides be the same as before.
>
> You say I being a woman could easily forgive if he had done a thing like that to me. I do not know for though Willie Yeats and I have been friends in the truest sense of the word for 23 years and though we have differences often on things and even said hard things to each other I have always found him a very loyal friend who I could trust and capable of great unselfishness.

She said that Yeats had written her about *The Showing-Up of Blanco Posnet*, a one-act play by George Bernard Shaw which had just been successfully produced by the Abbey Theatre. It had been banned in England and Dublin Castle had tried to prevent its appearance in Ireland. Yeats's letter, nevertheless, seemed "rather sad and not as triumphant as I expected. . . ."

Earlier that month Maud had written Yeats that she had seen him in a past incarnation in India, when their complexions were dark and they were lovers. In Yeats the old passion flared up again. Age had not tempered it. In 1909 Maud turned forty-four, and she no longer resembled the lush young woman whom Sarah Purser had painted in 1896. She was thin and her face was becoming lined.

Yeats also was changing. There were white strands in his hair and he was putting on weight. He was becoming important—and beginning to look it. In April 1910 he was invited to become a member of the Royal Society of Literature, then just being formed. A new book, *The Green Helmet and Other Poems*, had good notices. Several poems in it, beginning with "A Woman Homer Sung," were about Maud Gonne, and critics were beginning to realize that this was "love poetry" of a special and lasting kind. Yeats was fitting Maud into a "heroic dream," painting her portrait for all "coming time," constructing another Helen of Troy.

This was one activity of Yeats's that never aroused gratitude in Maud's soul. She knew what he was trying to do but her heart was not softened. For one thing, she suspected that his poetry would not endure. She had been warmed by his sympathy when her marriage to MacBride foundered; and she had taken seriously the spiritual marriage they had contracted in 1908. Now, in her mid-forties, after knowing Yeats for more than twenty years, she was still unable to return his devotion. Was it because she lacked emotional depth, sensitivity to another's woes? Was it because he did not seem to her masculine enough?

In many women there seems to be a mechanism that converts pity into love. Why was there none in Maud? Like Candida in Shaw's play, did she sense in her bones that Yeats was not truly bereft without her, that he was ultimately self-sufficient, that the muse of poetry was the only wife he needed? Or was Yeats right in thinking that she was too wrapped up in her political and philanthropic causes to pay attention to him?

There is a little truth in all of these guesses. But the major cause was a bone-deep incompatibility. Maud's essential temperament would not let her marry Yeats. In later years she scoffed at the idea that she had ever considered it. Once one of her friends asked her, why not? She turned her deep-set, reddish-brown eyes upon the questioner and said, "Why should *anyone* want to marry Willie?" This was a game. She knew that people were puzzled, but felt that if they couldn't see the obvious answer—the incompatibility of her nature and Yeats's—*tant pis*, so much the worse for them.

Yeats was beginning to forge a new aesthetic for himself, one touched with savagery and a love-hate attitude toward his nation. He wrote a friend, "What Dublin wants is some man who knows his own mind and has an intolerable tongue and a delight in enemies." When Miss Horniman, who had left the Abbey and was starting a repertory theater in Manchester, asked if she could produce his plays in England, he answered that his interest was in writing for his own people, "whether in love or hate of them matters little. . . ."

On January 19, 1910, Maud Gonne wrote John Quinn to thank him for some books he had sent to her children, and to ask if he had received Ella Young's *The Coming of Lugh*, which she had illustrated. The real news was that a flood had hit Paris

and since then all my time is taken up working with the relief to feed, clothe, house the unfortunate families who are homeless. . . . It is all a horrid nightmare. Beautiful Paris is a wrecked city. I have sent the children away to Normandy for it is thought that the flood will be followed by an epidemic. . . . I shall go away when I feel I have done all I can for the victims of the disaster. The all is but very little but still I feel I must do it.

The flood, the worst Paris had experienced in 170 years, was caused by the fact that the rivers Yvonne, Marne, and Seine overflowed their banks simultaneously. The American novelist Edith Wharton, then in Paris, wrote to one of her friends, "If it could only have happened to Omaha."

In response to Maud's letter, Quinn said he had been sorry to learn from Agnes Tobin that Maud had gone somewhere to look after her sister who was ill. He thought her illustrations for *The Coming of Lugh* were splendid and would make good designs for tapestries.

In the same letter Quinn spoke about William Bulfin, a friend of Arthur Griffith. "Bulfin came on a wild-goose errand in December to raise money to keep the daily *Sinn Fein* on its legs. Of course he failed. They seem to think in Ireland that dollars grow on trees over here instead of leaves. . . ."

Bulfin was an energetic man who had left Ireland at nineteen to settle in Argentina, where he eventually owned a successful Buenos Aires newspaper. After his return, he published numerous popular articles in American magazines, and his book, *Rambles in Ireland*, became so popular that a Dublin street was named after him. His daughter Catalina (Spanish for Kathleen) was destined to marry Maud's son Sean.

In May 1910 Yeats paid a long visit to Maud at Les Mouettes. On a rainy afternoon, they resumed their old argument about *The Playboy of the Western World*, after which Yeats wrote in his journal that Maud still felt strongly on the subject. Thinking of her, as he did, as "a summing up . . . of what is best in the romantic political Ireland of my youth," he decided that the future of the literary revival and his own integrity as a man of letters depended on a proper solution of the quarrel. He determined to close the introduction he was writing for an edition of Synge's works with a definitive statement about the purpose of national literature as he wanted to re-create it.

But there were quieter moments. Once he visited many churches, including Mont Saint Michel, with Maud and observed that she prayed in every one of them. When he asked her what she was praying for, she said that it was for the success of the two-year-old National University of Ireland. On the following day, as they crossed a stream, she told him a strange incident. In 1903 she had picnicked at that very spot. After Sean was born, when she passed the place with him for the first time, he said,

"That is where we lit the fire." He could not have known the fact in any ordinary way, Iseult... too heard the words. Both also tell how one day in a place they have never been before he said, "There's a stream up there," and it was true though it was too far off for him to have heard the sound of water. They say he has now lost these faculties.

Maud spent half the summer of 1910 in Ireland, much of it in the "wonderful wild sad" western part. Her children were with her. Apparently, for reasons unknown, she did not fear at the time that John MacBride would seize custody of their son.

On this visit to Ireland she was determined to introduce into the Dublin schools, "of course in a very modest way at first," the French system of providing lunches for school children. To accomplish this purpose she spent another two months in Ireland in the fall.

During one or both of these visits, Maud Gonne saw James Connolly, who had returned to Ireland in July of 1910 after spending seven years of fruitless propagandizing in the United States. Remembering her contribution to the lord mayor in 1898 to provide food for school children, he suggested a campaign to extend to Ireland the provisions of an act that permitted the use of tax money to feed school children in England, Wales, and Scotland. Connolly thought the Daughters of Ireland and the Irish Women's Franchise League should be asked to help. The League, which sought to win the vote for women, had been founded in 1908 by a group of suffragists that included Hanna Sheehy-Skeffington, a dozen years younger than Maud, and Margaret Cousins, of whom we shall hear later.

On November 10, 1910, Maud Gonne and Connolly attended a meeting of the executive committee of the Irish Trades Council to solicit its aid in obtaining passage of the amendment. In consequence, a special meeting of the full Trades Council was called for the following week, during which it agreed to ask the lord mayor to summon a conference to discuss the matter. When he failed to reply, a group of labor leaders, socialists, and feminists called upon him without ceremony, and won his consent to a public meeting. It was held on December 12 at the Mansion House, the lord mayor's offices, where arrangements were made for a deputation to go to London and present the matter to the home secretary.

On December 31, Maud wrote Quinn from France:

> I worked very hard in Ireland and succeeded in getting one school canteen started in one of the poorest parts of Dublin and enough money to ensure the feeding of 250 children for a year so I feel I can take a holiday with my own family with a clear conscience. I shall leave to go back in February to organise a second school canteen and above all to shake up our M.P.'s to get a law passed enabling the school children to get fed in all the schools in Ireland.
>
> It is horrible to think that Ireland is the only country where education is compulsory where nothing is done to provide food for the bodies as well as the minds of the children. I am sure this school day starvation is the real cause of the overcrowding of lunatic asylums.
>
> The number of deaths from consumption in Ireland—the more I looked into the question—the more shocking I found this neglect of the children. It is one of the most vital national questions if we are to get free or . . . keep up the strength of the race.

Her comment on Irish politics was brief. What the unionists feared most was "a sham home rule bill which would make the Irish government tax collector for England and end in bankruptcy and ruin." She thought that, if a Home Rule bill was passed that provided for proper financial arrangements and for an Irish Parliament with real power to govern the country, the unionists would accept it.

She ended by saying that she was sending him another book by Ella Young which she had illustrated. George Roberts, of Maunsel and Company, had done a much better job on her previous book, but "he is in love and going to get married on January 7 so we must excuse him a good deal. Lady Gregory and Willie Yeats are on the war path against him, for which I am sorry, for though he is terribly aggravating and unbusinesslike he is clever and is the best publisher we have in Ireland. . . ."*

Ella Young was a true believer. She wrote poetry (*The Rose in Heaven*, with black and white decorations by Maud); two books of Irish legends (with illustrations by Maud); and her aforementioned memoir, *Flowering Dusk*, which gives a variety of valuable first-hand impressions of Maud. Ella came of Presbyterian stock in County Antrim, but accepted the authority of the Pope. In her social attitudes she was anti-democratic, holding that it was best for the common man to conform with elitist views.

But her passion was for Irish mythology, reincarnation, psychic phenomena, and worship of the power of the Irish soil. She became part of a circle whose members, because they all held similar beliefs, could communicate with each other in a kind of shorthand. A note† from W. B. Yeats to Ella illustrates this point:

Thank you many times for your stories. Both are interesting and the one about the fight for the harvest is really of great importance. It completes a link in my argument. These . . . "Seven Sanctuaries" are the "Seven Lights" of Celtic Religion. 1st Custom. 2nd Myth. 3rd Dancing. 4th Modes of Obeisance. 5th The Hidden Meaning of vegetable things. 6th The meaning of Germs. 7th The "Dim Shapes of the Blue Wood."

Ella Young and George Russell became friends when both were members of the Dublin Theosophical Society.

---

*Of numerous others who suffered from the Dublin publisher's deviousness, the most famous was James Joyce in connection with *The Dubliners*.
†In U.S. Library of Congress.

He edited her first book of poetry, but she broke with him in 1900 because she felt that Eastern mysticism was unsuitable for Ireland. She formed a rival group called Fine, whose object (Maud wrote in her autobiography) was "to draw together for the freeing of Ireland the wills of the living and of the dead in association with the earth," as well as the natural elements, which seemed to her living entities. In 1926 Ella went to the United States, refusing to live any longer in the Irish Free State, taught Celtic mythology for ten years at the University of California, and found a friend in a poet named W. W. Lyman, who remembers well the frail but determined woman with the Northern Ireland accent, silver-gray hair, gray-blue eyes, and aquiline nose. She told him that Yeats was frequently annoyed because Maud would leave him to go on country weekends with her in order to discuss book illustrations. Ella Young died in 1956, at the age of eighty-eight. Here are some of her memories, as recounted in *Flowering Dusk*.

She recalls seeing Iseult Gonne and Brian Russell, AE's son, sitting on top of the dividing wall that separated the Russell and Gonne houses on Coulson Avenue. Between them is a pile of snails in their brown shells. The children are arguing whether snails are good for agriculture; Iseult maintains with her strong French accent that they must be or the French farmers would not sell them, and Brian disagrees.

Ella remembers a Theosophical center consisting of two rooms on the second floor of a deserted house located in a blind alley. The walls of one are covered with sonnets and lyrics handwritten by the authors—Seamus O'Sullivan, Padraic Colum, AE. The other room, the so-called library, has a few books and pamphlets and a great deal of dust. Both rooms are weakly lit by tallow candles. AE lectures on occultism every Thursday evening. After the lecture, he discusses poetry and criticizes the work of his young protégés.

Ella Young and her sister visit Maud Gonne on Nassau

Street and invite her to join them on a mountain walk to see a friend who lives on the holy mountain known as Slieve Cullen Mor. They find Dagda, the lion-colored Great Dane, lying beside Maud in his accustomed place. Yeats is seated in a distant corner holding a volume of Keats's poems in his lap. He is happy to join the expedition. Maud suggests inviting Arthur Griffith, who "loves mountains and works too hard—we must persuade him."

It turns out to be an overnight affair, but Griffith, over-fond neither of the country nor of W. B. Yeats, does not stay for the second day. He is replaced by Phyllis Mac-Murdo, who is well qualified to discuss the question of whether a holy mountain has a symbol and a color. Yeats says it has both. Phyllis tells of a time when she invoked a mountain as she was lying sleepless in bed. "The strong power of the Mountain invaded the room and took such whirlwind possession of mind and body that she feared exceedingly and could scarcely endure the anguish." Maud Gonne comments sagely, "Sacred Mountains are too strong for mortals. It is like inviting a lion to play with you."

Maud remembers that she has to get back to address a political meeting that evening, and they wander down the hillside—"a loitering, straggling, happy-hearted procession in the waning light." Yeats, abandoning himself to the magic of the moment, "would swoop down on a stray twig and toss it in the air; he would gather a stone from the roadway, make it skip from one hand to the other, then fling it skyward." When the Dublin housetops form a pattern in the sky, Yeats says, "In an old ballad this town is called Dublin of the Curses."

Ella Young remembers seeing Maud Gonne and W. B. Yeats in a Dublin art gallery viewing a painting by Whistler.

They are almost of equal height. Yeats has a dark, romantic cloak about him; Maud Gonne has a dress that changes colour as she moves. They pay no attention to the stir they are creating; they stand there discussing the picture.

I catch sight of them again in the reading room of the National Library . . . a pile of books between them . . . consulting the books and each other. No one else is consulting a book. Everyone is conscious of those two. . . .

Once Ella Young rented a dilapidated old house on Temple Hill in Dublin. She furnished it with discards from friends, including some carved oak pieces Maud had given her when she relinquished her house in Coulson Avenue. Soon afterward Maud stayed overnight at Ella's new home. At breakfast the following morning, she said, "You never told me you had a ghost here," and she described her experience:

After the lights were out in my room, I felt a cold wind on my face. I thought that a window was open, but both were shut. Then I became aware of the ghost. He said that he wanted to show me a secret passage, and immediately I found myself outside the house. We went round one wing and came to a place with high green banks and a large pine tree. The secret passage was there, but I refused to explore it, and immediately I was back in my room. The ghost was there too. He wanted to explain something that I could not understand. I told him that he was wasting time here: he should go forward in the spirit world.

The advice apparently had some effect, for the ghost was quiet during the rest of Maud's stay.

About 1908 Ella Young visits Maud's home in Passy. The house sits

green-shuttered and demure beyond a stone-flagged courtyard and a clipped lawn. A stout oaken door, flanked by a high wall, shuts all view of it from the street. It is a house with a plentitude of beautiful things: carved wood, Russian embroidery, Oriental rugs—all thrown together carelessly. There are mirrors everywhere reaching from floor to ceiling. Maud Gonne likes the effect of light and space that they can give. There are many dogs, large and small; Great Danes, Toy Pomeranians, haughty court-bred Pekinese, and one Persian cat. There is a parrot that curses in Spanish and a comrade that yells in a language of its own. There are many servants. Everyone speaks French.

The centre of delight in the household is Maud Gonne's son, Shaun McBride, a golden-haired boy of four, gracious and fascinating. . . .

The other child in the household, Maud's "adopted daughter," is being instructed in art and literature by William

Butler Yeats, a daily visitor. Iseult Gonne, "a beautiful dark-eyed dark-haired girl of twelve or thirteen . . . has a lovely voice, and the Poet is teaching her to chant verse to the sound of a plangent string, a note now and then for accompaniment or emphasis. . . . Maud Gonne is rather in favour of the voice alone."

Another frequent visitor is Miss Barry O'Delany, the former assistant editor of *l'Irlande Libre*, who is devoted to both Maud and her son. She has built a toy theater for Sean. Barry acts as secretary for Yeats when he is in Paris. Privately she thinks that she can turn a verse as skillfully as he can and with more of an Irish twist to it. She has a poor opinion of Yeats as a mystic, remembering how he once hypnotized her and was unable to bring her out of the trance. Luckily, Maud Gonne stepped in and brought her to. Nothing daunted, Yeats continues to believe that only MacGregor Mathers outdistances him as a master of the occult. Maud Gonne thinks Mathers is by far the greater.

The days are spent in talking about the fairy world, magic, and astrology. These conversations between Maud, Ella, Iseult, and Yeats are interrupted by frequent excursions to the Louvre—all of them are particularly fond of Leonardo da Vinci's paintings—and less frequent visits to friends. Once Maud Gonne takes Ella Young and Yeats to Rodin's studio. They find Rodin, a "broad-shouldered, bronzed, bearded" man, chiseling a block of marble. He shows them a second room, where his sketches are on display. While Yeats examines them "reverently," Ella whispers to Maud, "He is mad, brutally and sensually mad. Perhaps it will never break out, but it shows in those sketches." "It does break out," Maud retorts. "At times he has to be shut away. He is dangerous." Maud is conversant with all the stories told in Paris about artists.

On another occasion Ella Young goes with Maud Gonne and May Gonne Clay to call on MacGregor Mathers. Maud and Yeats regard "Count" Mathers "with respect and, at times, with astonishment." To Iseult, with her romantic turn of mind, he seems "a righter of wrongs, a chastiser of evil-doers, a champion of the oppressed." But Ella too is enraptured by this "tall square-shouldered man with a strong clean-cut face, dark hair, and strange steel-blue eyes." The mantelpiece in the living room "displays the richest collection of Egyptian treasures I have ever seen outside of a museum."

Ella Young describes her visit to Les Mouettes, a large, rather dreary-looking building, in a rolling countryside, though the water is only fifty yards away. This Normandy beach is one of those on which American troops landed in 1944. Here Ella saw "Iseult dancing at twilight on the long flat Normandy sands at Calvados—the flat sands and the flat sea-bitten meadows deserted save for a little stir of wind from the sea. Iseult, with hair outblown, dancing a fantasy of her own composition. Minnelouse, her black Persian cat, dancing opposite with plumy tail erect and serious-minded orange eyes."

A more detailed picture of life at Les Mouettes is given by James Henry Cousins and his wife Margaret (called Gretta) in their joint autobiography, *We Two Together*. They were an extraordinary pair. James, born in 1873, turned from teaching stenography in Belfast to writing a play for the Abbey and a narrative poem in the style of the Celtic bards. He went to Dublin in 1897 to meet the tall Irish poet who wore a velvet jacket with braided edges, remained thin no matter how much he ate, and consorted with "a lady said to be equally tall, with hair as golden as his was raven, handsome as Venus, and enthusiastically Irish." Maud and Yeats once attended a séance at his home where a visiting medium managed to invoke the notorious Richard Pigott, who had forged the letters that had brought Charles Stewart Parnell to trial.

Gretta Cousins was a skilled pianist (she used to accompany James Joyce, local tenor, in her drawing room); a strict vegetarian; a militant suffragette (jailed both in London and Dublin for smashing windows); a follower of Madame Blavatsky; and a practicing medium. The Cousinses went to India in 1915, where James became principal of Besant Theosophical College and Gretta instituted all-women conferences, fought against forced marriages and premature motherhood, protested bills curbing Indian rights to free speech, and was elected first woman magistrate in India. Her sturdy personality forms part of the magnetic Gretta Conroy who appears in James Joyce's story "The Dead."

In August 1912, when the Cousinses were staying at the French village of Balleroy during a very wet summer, they received a note from Maud Gonne suggesting that it was better to be "drowned with friends" than "alone in a strange village hotel. So come over here." In the left-hand lower corner there was scribbled as an obvious afterthought, "Mr. Yeats is here." To get to Les Mouettes, James and Gretta Cousins went by rail to Bayeux.

> When we alighted I saw Yeats standing like an elongated rook... near a donkey cart in which Madame Gonne was apparently trying to pack things. She greeted us warmly. A young lad, thin, pale and dreamy, was introduced as Shawn. This was Madame's son by her marriage with Major MacBride. He disposed of us quickly ... we being only human beings, and busied himself over the important matter of the safe transit of a pet bantam cock home in the cart. . . . [When] we reached the house . . . I was received with much friendliness and natural freedom by a tall, slender girl of great beauty of countenance and grace of form. This was Madame's niece, Iseult. She was accompanied by a dog and two cats. There were cooings in the background mixed with chirpings in different keys, and a sharp parrot-like exclamation. . . .
>
> "Les Mouettes" was situated on the edge of the English Channel just above high-water-mark. There was no road to the house, and no inducement to usual seaside futilities. . . . At the dinner table the bantam roosted on Madame Gonne's shoulders.

Yeats, engrossed in talking about Oscar Wilde, Lionel Johnson, and William Morris, kept piling up in front of him the dishes that were supposed to be passed to others, until finally Madame had to remind him

that there were others at the table and that their interest was not solely conversational. . . . After dinner we gathered around a large open fire. Yeats got on astrology with Mrs. Cousins, and this and mediumship kept us awake till after midnight.

The next day, August 15, being Lady Day, Madame went to church and asked Gretta, though a Protestant, to accompany her, with Iseult and Shawn. She was to present a new embroidered cloth for the altar. . . .

That evening, after dinner, W. B. Yeats read some pieces of lyrical prose that he had translated from the Bengali poems of Rabindranath Tagore. According to "Madame Gonne," Yeats had an extraordinarily high opinion of the Indian poet.

The next day Maud invited James and Gretta Cousins to visit Bayeux, traveling "in a *voiture*, a large Normany farm-cart with hooped canvas covering." Iseult and Yeats also went along. The party had lunch in Bayeux, and it is typical of Maud's interests that they were joined by two young French people who were publishing a poetry magazine and helping to form a Celtic League.

CHAPTER XVII

Feeding Irish School Children (1911–1913)

MAUD GONNE SAW her husband once more. It was not by choice. During the first of two visits she made to Dublin in 1911, she attended a meeting of which he was chairman, held March 4 at the Rotunda on Parnell Square to commemorate Robert Emmet's birthday. Emmet was a deist and democrat who tried in 1803 to raise an insurrection in Dublin. It ended as little more than a street brawl, but his speech at the prisoner's dock has inspired many generations of Irishmen. Maud described the meeting in a letter to John Quinn, but she did not mention that John MacBride had participated. She did not say whether their eyes met, whether she nodded to him, spoke to him, or ignored him. As often happens whenever question arises about Maud's personal life, the sources run dry.

MacBride had earned his place on the platform. The meeting was sponsored by the Wolfe Tone Committee, a front organization for the Irish Republican Brotherhood, of which MacBride was official representative from the ancient province of Connacht. As such, he had commented authoritatively in *Irish Freedom*, the IRB organ, on a recent incident when two armed men in East London had held at bay for twelve hours some 1,500 soldiers armed with automatic rifles. "The whole business," he wrote, "should put heart into the young generation of Irishmen," and proved again the lesson of the Boer War, that "the English army is of very little account as a fighting force."

At an IRB demonstration on June 22, 1911, the day of George V's Coronation, when more than thirty thousand people crowded Beresford Place and overflowed far up Lower Gardner Street, MacBride was one of the orators. Other speakers included Madame Markievicz, John Devoy, Arthur Griffith, James Connolly, and Alderman Kelly.

Such public manifestations of his anti-British sympathies did not prevent MacBride from being appointed the same year as a water inspector for the city of Dublin; the city government occasionally made such appointments in order to assert its independence of Dublin Castle. Furthermore, MacBride had useful family and County Mayo connections, which would, incidentally, have been just as useful in getting a city job in Boston, New York, or Chicago during the same period.

For a time MacBride's participation in rebel activities seemed to lessen, but by 1914 he was again speaking out. When World War I broke out, he addressed a meeting in Cork, where he termed the Irish members of Parliament "recruiting sergeants for the British Empire." He showed no discomfiture, the *Freeman's Journal* reported, when the bulk of his audience arose in protest, gave three cheers for John Redmond, head of the Irish Parliamentary Party, and marched out of the hall leaving only a dozen people behind.

In a letter to the *Mayo News*, he urged Irishmen not to join the British army. England wanted to send Irishmen away to die on foreign soil, he said, so that none would be left to defend Ireland. A member of the House of Commons rose to ask when the solicitor general intended to take action to prevent the publication of such seditious letters but received no answer.

MacBride was considered one of the new breed of rebels that was taking over the Supreme Council of the Irish Re-

publican Brotherhood, but he was not made privy to all its
deliberations because of his "well known predilection for
drink." This judgment by Robert Kee in *The Green Flag*
reflects the opinion given earlier by journalist H. W. Nevinson: "Unlike the usual Sinn Feiner, he was something of . . .
a swashbuckler, dissipated, devoid of character." It was not
Yeats alone who considered MacBride a "drunken vainglorious lout."

Maud agreed with all of her husband's sentiments but her
pro-Irish activities were increasingly taking the single form
of feeding Irish children in school. As she was preparing for
her first trip to Ireland in 1911, she received a long letter
from John Quinn offering to contribute £25 to her project
and an equal amount in three months. He said that he had
bought ten copies of Yeats's most recent book; found three
or four of the personal poems as good as, or even better than
earlier ones of the same sort; but it was all "tears, idle
tears." He asked Maud if she was acquainted with Picasso's
work. Augustus John liked it "immensely."

Maud answered gratefully that nothing warmed her
heart so much as getting money for the school children; she
has turned "into a real jew when feeding the children is
concerned." She was leaving for Ireland the next day, February 14, 1911, but would spend four days in London in
order to induce Irish members of Parliament to vote for the
extension to Ireland of the law that provided free meals for
British school children. It was all part of England's policy
of oppression that this action had not been taken long since.
Since England could not prevent the Irish from having
large families,

she succeeded by school starvation in destroying the health of a very
large proportion. . . .
We are just starting dinners at a new and very big school at
Ringsend, a terribly poor district of Dublin, and it is always a little
nervous work. The ensuring of sufficient money to keep the dinners

going till we get the free meal act extended. Getting the children used to dinners and then stopping would be worse than never having begun at all.

She reported that Iseult and Sean were rather angry with her for leaving them again so soon, but "the hungry school children have got on my nerves so I must go."

She wished fervently that a man with his energy, love of life, and love of beauty lived in Ireland today. What wonderful things might then be accomplished! She sometimes thought that most Irish dreamed too much, even though the poet O'Shaughnessy said that the dreamers were "the movers and shakers" of the world. But she still held the belief that the immense spiritual forces which had been accumulating in Ireland for centuries would some day reach a successful culmination and Cher Ireland would emerge as "the Candle, the Light, the Grail Maiden before the World."

Upon her return to Paris, Maud wrote Quinn: "We are meeting secret but very troublesome and dangerous opposition from some of the school managers who are so jealous of their exclusive control of the schools that they don't want the free meal school children act to be extended to Ireland." The managers feared, she said, that the act might bring some measure of public control, and they would rather let the children starve than permit that to happen. They had secretly approached Irish members of Parliament and asked them not to support the bill.

As for herself, she was determined not to stop "until all the schools in Ireland have canteens for children who need them." She quoted figures from the inspector of public health. Strangely enough, "the class of children who escape the high death rate of Dublin are the little waifs and strays and street traders who don't go to school at all, they succeed in collecting pennies for food when they are hungry and they are not forced to work their brains when they are in a starving condition." They grow up "demoralized, perhaps, but healthy."

In April 1911 Maud was in Rome, where her son had the distinction of being given his first communion by Pope Pius X in his private chapel. At an audience for perhaps fifty persons on the previous day, the Holy Father had noticed the seven-year-old boy in a velvet suit (which Sean detested) and asked him in French whether he had received his first communion as yet. When the boy answered in the negative, the Pope asked him and his mother to come to his chapel the following morning, at which time, attended by some high Vatican officials, he performed the ceremony.

Maud discussed a wide variety of subjects, but not this one, in a letter she wrote John Quinn from Colleville on June 17. She felt that her stay in Rome had been helpful to the cause of feeding school children, because she had met "the sisters of the Holy Father, who took a great fancy to my little Sean, and I profited of this to try and enlist their sympathies in the cause of the Irish children and get their Brother to say a word to the Irish Bishops in the matter." Since there is no record of a religious order called Sisters of the Holy Father, these women must have been the Pope's biological sisters.

Maud had enjoyed her stay in Italy even though much Roman pagan art "had been spoiled by the Renaissance and by 16th and 17th century architecture"; and she preferred smaller cities such as Siena, Perugia, and Assisi, to Rome. She would not be happy until she could spend an entire month in Assisi, whose Church of San Francesco was, she thought, the ultimate in art. Its frescoes by Giotto and others reminded her of Chinese paintings.

On her return to Paris, the heat seemed so oppressive, especially to Sean, that she had felt it necessary to pack up her children and pets and hasten to Colleville. It was a difficult decision to make, for she had been attending a "wonderful" congress on liturgical music that was taking place in Paris.

During the summer of 1911, the Daughters of Erin became increasingly inactive, and publication of its organ ceased. These circumstances reflected both Maud's concentration on school feeding, and the absence of anyone else to take her place. Her chief lieutenant in Dublin, Helena Molony, was too young, and was attracted more by violence than editorial work. On July 4, 1911 she participated in the public burning of the English flag. Then while walking through College Green, still in a mood of patriotic fervor, she took a pebble out of her handbag and heaved it at an optician's sign. The following morning she was sentenced to jail, thereby becoming the first woman of her generation to win this distinction. Her only worry—that she might have disgraced the Daughters of Erin by her rash act—vanished when she received a telegram from Maud Gonne telling her she had acted splendidly.

Helena served only a few days in Mountjoy Jail. On a hot Sunday afternoon, the Daughters of Erin and the Socialist Party of Ireland sponsored a demonstration to celebrate her release. In her remarks, Helena described King George as not only "the descendant of a scoundrel, but himself one of the worst scoundrels in Europe." She was promptly taken back into custody, this time with the chairman of the meeting, Constance Markievicz. After the two women had spent a dull hot afternoon in the police station, they were released on bail, and Dublin Castle tactfully dropped the matter.

But Maud Gonne, writing John Quinn on August 3, 1911, was still wrathful. The arrest was "quite illegal and the magistrate had to release them at once. Indeed if there was any sort of fair justice in Ireland they have a good case for damages against the police for illegal arrest; but it is no use looking for justice from English trial judges."

Mixing personalities and patriotism in the way she loved, Maud said that the real reason for their arrest was as follows:

The English like to find sentimental names for their Kings and Queens. There is Victoria the Beloved, and Edward the Peacemaker; and they are puzzled for a name for the almost imbecilic George, so they want to call him George the Virtuous, but the story of his first marriage spoils this and at all costs they want it forgotten and contradicted. You remember some months ago a wretched rag called the Liberator, published . . . the story of George's first marriage only giving a wrong name of the lady and thus providing the occasion to the police to prosecute for libel. . . . Countess Markievicz happens to know the true story and the name of the real lady to whom George was married . . . she does not think it would be honourable to tell the story, also we none of us care about attacking the king of England because of his private character; if he were a saint we should object just as strongly to his receiving loyal addresses from Ireland. . . .

The police, who have had orders to prevent at all costs any word of the bigamy story coming out, heard the word "ruffian" and fearing it was coming rushed in and arrested Helena Molony and Countess Markievicz. . . . I hope when you are next in Ireland you will meet Madame de Markievicz who is so charming and so brave. I know you would like her.

Maud regretted that Quinn's work in Washington to prevent passage of a new Anglo-American arbitration treaty then being considered was delaying his visit to Europe, but felt that this task was "so all important that I don't wonder that you are looking after that first."

Amused by a comment he had made about convents, she told him that he didn't realize "how charming and beautiful and how intense life can be within the walls."

Maud got to Dublin in mid-October, and from the Nassau Hotel wrote John Quinn:

When I returned after 5 months absence I found a really marked improvement in the appearance of the children in the school where we are giving dinners; and . . . during two epidemics of scarletina and diarrhea this school had exceptionally few cases of illness, I think because the children were better able to resist infection.

We are extending our work to another very poor school in John's Lane.... The Dublin corporation has passed a resolution calling on the Irish M.P.'s to obtain an act of parliament to enable them to strike a ½ penny rate to feed the school children, but we can't get the M.P.'s to move....

Have you seen Moore's book *Ave?* What do you think of it? It is certainly clever and amusing reading but it is yellow journalism turned into a novel and all pleasant social intercourse would come to an end if many people were like George Moore. He called to see me in Paris several years ago and after drinking his tea, he began in quite a businesslike way "Now I want you to tell me all about it, just why did you get married? I can understand the separation but I want to hear all about that too." I asked him if it was for his book, and then I talked about the weather... for I felt the only way to escape Moore books was not to interest him in the least.

I have been in Dublin for the last three weeks and am beginning to want to get back to Paris and the children, but I can't stir till the second school is in good working order—and in the meantime it is very pleasant seeing all my old friends. I love Dublin. People are all so keen on things here, they have time to be interested in them.

An enclosed balance sheet of the "Ladies School Dinner Committee" listed total disbursements of £193 during the period from November 1910 to October 1911. Among those named as contributors were John Quinn, £50; Arthur Griffith, £1; W. B. Yeats, 10s; Transport Workers' Union, £5.

Maud succinctly summarized the need for school canteens in an article entitled "Responsibility" that appeared in the *Irish Review* issue of December 1911. When bad marks are issued to Maud Gonne for superficiality, fickleness, and self-dramatization, this sober and sensible document, and the achievement it describes, should be remembered.

Under pain of imprisonment Irish parents are by English law obliged to send their children to school, and from 9:30 to 3 o'clock the children are obliged to remain in school.

No provision is made for feeding the children thus taken into custody.

Growing children need more frequent food than adults... and in all free countries where education is compulsory, for the sake of the future of the race, arrangements are made to ensure school children being fed. . . .

In the poor districts in Dublin one half of the children bring no lunch with them to school, and many have actually left home without breakfast; most of them have only had an inadequate breakfast of bread and tea. When they return home at 3:30 the family dinner is over, the breadwinner, whose strength must be maintained, has eaten whatever of nourishing food there was; and in poor households, or rather poor roomholds, little is left for the children after their long cruel school fast but bread and tea again.

The result of this school starvation is a terribly high rate of child mortality and an enormous increase of consumption and insanity. Doctor Gogarty, in his address at the Meath Hospital, said of the three thousand children he had examined . . . "The greater parts of their suffering and ailments could be traced to the continued strain of long hungry school hours on their childish systems." And Doctor Donelan, Medical Superintendent of the Richmond Insane Asylum, states that "many instances of mental breakdown are due to excessive strain on the young of long hours of restraint coupled with insufficient physical nourishment." . . .

True, in the actual political condition of Ireland public money may not be used to save the health and the efficiency and the lives of Irish children, though it may be, and is, used to support the weak and broken victims of the schools later on in the workhouses and in the asylums. Revolutions have been made for less valid causes, and I do not think we can entirely shift the responsibility for our supine indifference.

A committee to which I belong has written to, or interviewed, all the Irish M.P.s with the object of getting the Free Meal for School Children Act which obtains in England altered and extended to Ireland, but our M.P.s remain uninterested, and some tell us we must wait for Home Rule. In the meantime the children are starving.

A body of women, a small uninfluential body to which I belong, composed mostly of working women, are attempting in desperation to do what the State ought to do—we are providing 450 dinners daily during the half hour's recreation at 12 o'clock in two of the poorest schools in the city. . . . Irish stew or rice and jam can be given on the five school days at the cost of 4d. a week per child. . . .

Some French friends of mine want to arrange some lectures for me in France to raise money to help our work. I cannot bring myself to accept, though I long for the money for the children; but how can I say in a foreign country: "We in Ireland are letting the children of our Nation starve?"

Maud Gonne described the progress of this school feeding movement in the course of some radio talks she gave in
1949–50. It was an impressive job of recollection for a
woman of eighty-four.

One day in 1912, as I was crossing Stephen's Green on my way to meet
my dear friend Hanna Sheehy-Skeffington at the offices of the Woman's Franchise League, I saw a little girl who was retrieving crusts
from the duck pond. I stopped to question her. She said, "When we get
back from school and when mother says there is no dinner for us, I
bring my little brothers to the Green to get bits off the ducks." She
added defensively, "That's not stealing." I repeated the child's words to
Hanna. Typical of the way women work without formality... Hanna
asked Mrs. Conroy, the secretary of the Woman's Franchise League, to
write to the Dublin Corporation and ask it to receive a delegation of
women to discuss the necessity of providing dinners in the schools.
Hanna names as spokeswomen herself, the president of the League,
and me, as president of the Daughters of Erin.
  A few days later, our delegation... was received by the Dublin
Corporation, and the Councillors promised us to strike a penny rate for
the purpose of providing school dinners.

Soon afterward, the group was told that the Dublin Corporation could not levy this kind of tax without a special act of
the British Parliament. Hanna drafted such an act, Maud
took it to London and presented it to Stephen Gwynn,
M.P. In his reminiscences Gwynn describes her visit to
him on the terrace of the House of Commons. He found the
bill so well prepared that he had nothing to do but present
it.

  Meanwhile, the Daughters of Erin decided that starving
Irish children could not wait until a British Parliament gave
Ireland permission to feed her own children. They started

a school feeding committee to do the work until Irish municipalities
were empowered to strike the rate.... The Irish Trade Unions and
Woman's Franchise League gave us great help.
  I regret to say that most of the reverend managers of the schools
chose to call our school feeding effort "outside interference." But the
saintly parish priest of St. Audeon's, the Reverend Canon Kavanagh,
invited us to come and feed the starving children... in St. Audeon's

schools. A couple of months after, two Augustinian friars, one of whom was manager of schools in John's Lane, asked us to feed the hungry children in his school also, and at last we were feeding two thousand children every day, a tremendous effort for a small voluntary committee.

It was a great relief when at last the Dublin Corporation was empowered to strike the rate and set up its own school feeding committee. But during those two years everyone in the Daughters of Erin who was free in the daytime took turns at the work. I did whenever I was in Dublin.

One of the people Maud recalled "ladling out stew and washing greasy dishes and spoons in the open playground in all sorts of weather" was Constance Markievicz.

These activities took their toll. In February 1912 John Quinn received a letter from Iseult Gonne, now sixteen, thanking him for a barrel of pippin apples he had sent the family for Christmas, and explaining that her "cousin" had overworked herself in Ireland and fallen ill of influenza.

In Quinn's next letter, he described his successful legal action to prevent John Devoy and the Clan na Gael from sabotaging the Abbey Theatre's American production of *The Playboy of the Western World*, and said the Abbey Players had presented him with a loving cup. He also reported that the attempt to pass the Anglo-American arbitration treaty had been defeated, not because of the influence of the Irish-American societies, but because of the Senate's jealousy of its treaty-writing prerogatives.

In April, writing from a new address in Passy, 17 rue de l'Annonciation, Maud gave a somewhat different reason for her illness:

About three months ago my little boy was taken suddenly ill, very ill, of appendicitis. For two months I hoped—in spite of what the doctor said—to avoid an operation but it had to come. After it was all over and the child quite well again, I fell ill, chiefly from the anxiety and strain, and am still rather "patraque" (the worse for wear) as the French say.

I am glad to read about the presentation of the cup by the Abbey Company . . . and I must say you were right to help them. As a play I dislike the Playboy though after the idiotic conduct of the Clan-na-Gael I shall never be able to say so. I also can never quite forgive Lady Gregory and Yeats for having had it played under police protection in Dublin when the opposition to it was entirely spontaneous and when we know what police protection in Ireland stands for.

Maud spent the summer of 1912 in Normandy, where she was visited briefly by John Quinn and Willie Yeats. Yeats saw Iseult dancing on the shore and his increasing *Weltschmerz* came out in the poem he wrote:

> What need have you to care
> For wind or water's roar? . . .
> Being young you have not known
> The fool's triumph, nor yet
> Love lost as soon as won,
> Nor the best labourer dead
> And all the sheaves to bind.

In his diary for this year we find Yeats condemning the students at the new National University for joining with the Ancient Order of Hibernians in a campaign against immoral literature; and describing with contempt the urge of many contemporaries "to toil and grow rich."

In October 1912 Maud returned to Dublin to work on the school meals project. While there she saw an exhibition by a young Irish-American painter named Power O'Malley, and thought his work "as clever and far more sincere than most of the paintings I have seen in France." She gave O'Malley a letter of introduction to Quinn, and sent Quinn a clipping from *The Leader* that compared O'Malley to Manet.

As usual, she worked so hard in Dublin that she had to go to bed when she returned to Paris. In December her children went without her to Florence, where they stayed at a cousin's "lovely villa." Sean MacBride remembers it as a lavish place that Maud rented with a full staff of servants. She arrived there in time for Christmas, just after celebrating her forty-seventh birthday.

During these years of Maud's school canteen activities, Ireland was being rent by three controversies. She had strong convictions about each.

The most important one concerned a proposed Home Rule bill that would give Ireland some degree of self-government but not separate her from the Empire. While Parliament deliberated, a newly formed Ulster Volunteer Force in the North swore to use arms if the government tried to impose Home Rule upon them. At the Curragh camp, the officers, almost all Protestant, threatened to resign if they were ordered to enforce the act. Former Solicitor General Sir Edward Carson, M.P., warmly supported their stand. In Southern Ireland a force known as the Irish Volunteers was established to counteract these pressures.

About the so-called Curragh mutiny, Maud wrote Quinn on November 20, 1913: "The Ulster affair would be only funny if one were sure the Liberal government would not get excited and lose their heads. They are doing so, I fear. Talk of concessions, which will mean lots of trouble later on, is in the air. The English are so panicky always."

The second controversy was a labor struggle in Dublin. James Larkin, head of the Transport Workers' Union, led one side (with James Connolly assisting), and William Martin Murphy, wealthy businessman and publisher of the *Irish Daily Independent*, led the other. Maud Gonne, who was in Ireland in October 1913, gave her views in an article that appeared in the November 1 issue of Jim Larkin's paper, the *Irish Worker*. The workers "have shown that, poor and downtrodden as they are, their souls are not enslaved and they are worthy of Ireland." The same issue contained articles of similar import by W. B. Yeats, George Russell, Susan Mitchell, and Constance Markievicz. It was during this struggle that Constance learned from James Connolly that national freedom would be worthless without the overthrow of the exploiting class.

Having seen what was going on, Maud wrote an account of it to Quinn on her return to Passy in November:

I have just got back from Dublin. The situation there is terrible. It proves over again how utterly incapable the English are of government and how urgent it is for us to have Home Rule. . . . Last August the tramway conductors with Larkin to back them up struck for shorter hours (they think 14 hours a day too long for any man to be expected to guide a team). Murphy, the head of the tram company, . . . got the employers of Dublin . . . to draw up a fool paper which they were to force all their workmen and women to sign, undertaking that they never would join or if already joined would immediately leave the Irish Transport Union. To the credit of the men they all refused.

This has been going on over ten months and the employers refuse all arbitration. In any free country after they had refused arbitration, the government would simply have withdrawn the police and military from the guard of their houses and factories, and the strike would have ended in a few days. . . . It is all folly and confusion. Fat English Socialists talking all sorts of nonsense that the men listen to without enthusiasm but dare not resent because they are living on the food sent by the trade unions. . . .

The labor struggle, however, benefited Maud's school canteens. Every school was providing meals; the Archbishop of Dublin sponsored collections for the project in all the churches; and the Lourdes Pilgrimage Committee donated £2,000 to the cause. For the present, she wrote Quinn, the children were safe from starvation but their parents were pawning everything they owned. Maud was trying to think of a way to get their possessions back when Sean fell sick and she had to return to take care of him.

A month later she told Quinn of her hope that the British Empire would eventually disappear and be replaced by "a great Celtic Federation, with Ireland as the moving active force." She advised him to hoard some of his energies and power for that time. Meanwhile

we are going through a bad time. . . . Larkin is a *painful* necessity, but a *necessity* and has done great good in many ways. It was necessary to wake people up in Ireland to the condition of the working people. As you say, those 21,000 one-room tenements are a disgrace to any community. The sleepy indifference of comfortable people to the sufferings of the poor is very bad in Ireland, but most of it comes from the fact that we do not govern ourselves. . . .

I am glad George Russell is taking up these matters, for he has a constructive mind. He has shown wonderful courage in his letter to the employers. Larkin has a wonderful magnetic influence on the crowd, but I fear he is too vain and too jealous and too untruthful to make a really *great* leader.

Maud's opinion of James Larkin was precisely the same as James Connolly's.

The third controversy then raging in Ireland was between those who wished to accept Sir Hugh Percy Lane's gift to Dublin of his famous collection of modern French paintings, and those who did not. Lane's offer was contingent on the city's building a gallery to house the paintings on a bridge across the Liffey according to the specifications of the English architect Edwin Landseer Lutyens.

As Lady Gregory's nephew, Lane could command much Ascendancy support, but the opposition, again headed by William Martin Murphy, was stronger. The result was that Lane lent his pictures to the National Gallery in London, and Yeats vented his wrath on Lane's opponents in such magnificent poems as "To a Shade" and "September 1913." Few can forget Yeats's description of those middle-class, money-grubbing Irishmen who

> ... fumble in a greasy till
> and add the halfpence to the pence
> and prayer to shivering prayer...
>
> Romantic Ireland's dead and gone,
> It's with O'Leary in the grave.

Maud took the opposite side. She wrote Quinn on September 4, 1914, from a primitive mountain village in the Hautes-Pyrénées where she was staying for part of the summer:

Have you followed the story of *Sir* Hugh Lane's transactions with the Dublin Corporation about the picture collection he pretended to give to Dublin? He has behaved like a *cur*. He got his knighthood by this *supposed gift* and now probably he wants to get some other advantage by giving it elsewhere, so he makes impossible conditions.... I believe some of the pictures, like the one *presented* by Cottet, a great Breton painter, were *given* by the artists out of enthusiasm *for Ireland*. As soon as I get back to Paris I am going to see these painters and if possible get them to insist on their gifts being left in Dublin. Lane has practically made all his money by picture dealing, in other words by swindling unfortunate artists. I cannot remember the exact details which Willie Yeats once told me of the origin of Lane's fortune, but I know it was a piece of swindling called by the Jew dealers a *knock out*. If I could only remember the exact details I would send them to Sinn Fein for Lane certainly deserves to be shown up.

During Maud's stay in Dublin in the fall of 1913, she had brief contacts with two memorable persons, Oliver St. John Gogarty and Padraic Pearse. Dr. Gogarty is recalled for many reasons—one is that he was the "stately, plump Buck Mulligan" of James Joyce's *Ulysses*—but generally forgotten are his efforts to combat the hunger, venereal disease, and tuberculosis running rampant in the crumbling Georgian houses on Dublin's north side. In November 1914 he gave a talk before the Academy of Medicine in which he ex-coriated the evils of slum life. Maud sent him a letter con-gratulating him for being "almost the first who has had the courage to speak publicly and frankly on the subject," and described the work and frustrations of her committee in running school canteens. "Medical inspection," she con-cluded, "is just as necessary as school dinners, but one re-quires the other—for food is the medicine most of those children need."

Maud's meeting with Padraic Pearse, orator and Gaelic scholar, concerned his hope of making a trip to the United States in order to give talks about Irish heroic literature and Gaelic education and—not incidentally—obtain contribu-tions for St. Enda's School, of which he was headmaster. Maud sought the assistance of John Quinn and John Devoy in lining up Irish-American societies to welcome him, but her efforts were unsuccessful.

This attempt was typical for, despite her "blinker" vi-sion, Maud could never manage to restrict her list of good causes as much as she wished. For instance, she became indignant when Parliament passed a bill, unofficially called "the Cat-and-Mouse Act," which permitted prisoners who went on a hunger strike to be released but, after they had recovered their health, forced them to return to finish their sentences. A letter from Maud Gonne protesting the provisions of this Act was read at a meeting held in Dublin in June 1913.

In various letters Maud sent John Quinn in 1913, she revealed some interesting autobiographical tidbits.

> I am so sorry to hear of Miss Coates illness. . . . If she gets over it, she will be as strong as ever. I was *very ill* once with consumption. . . . Willie Yeats had written my epitaph, which he showed me after. I got quite cured by living an open air life, one month in the mountains of Donegal, and when the weather got too cold and wet, three months in the hills in the south of France. Once cured I was much stronger than before, and yet my family are very consumptive. My mother and both my grandmothers died before 30 of consumption. . . .
>
> My sister had nearly the same thing and was operated on twice and had a great quantity of water taken from the lung. She was of course very delicate for a long time after, but got quite well and is keeping well.
>
> I quite agree with you in theory about the folly of taking unnecessary risks in nursing, though in practice I am afraid I do much as Miss Coates does. When Sean got the measles I had a bad cold and if only I had let a nurse or my cousin do the night work, which they could have done quite as well as I did, I should probably not have got pneumonia and had to spend over six months in enforced idleness—but one never thinks of these things in time.

Maud Gonne and W. B. Yeats were slowly drifting apart. It no longer mattered much whether they agreed or disagreed about Hugh Lane's proposed gift of a municipal art gallery. They were beginning to live in different worlds. The essential change was that Yeats had no interest in an independent Ireland, the plight of political prisoners, or the hunger of Dublin school children. He was all taken up by Ezra Pound's unrelenting effort to inject into the despised art of poetry such elements as "hardness," objectivity, concreteness, "edge," brevity. The influence of the young American, who had graduated from assistant host of Yeats's Monday evenings to secretary, was modified only by the teachings of a poet of the older school, T. Sturge Moore. "The criticism I got from them has given me new life," Yeats wrote Lady Gregory. He never grew too old to investigate and adopt new poetic ideas and techniques.

In 1911 Yeats had visited Olivia Shakespear, now a good and loyal friend, at the Devonshire home of her brother H. T. Tucker and his wife. There he met Mrs. Tucker's daughter by a previous marriage, George Hyde-Lees. George was a wealthy, charming, cultivated English girl not half Yeats's age, but still able to recognize the reservoir of warmth and feeling that lay beneath his stiffness. She was glad to see him again in 1914 at the wedding (or shortly after it) of Ezra Pound to Olivia Shakespear's daughter Dorothy. Since George was a friend of both newlyweds, it was natural that she should meet Yeats there, and later at the various places that the Pounds and W. B. Yeats lived in or frequented.

CHAPTER XVIII

A Terrible War, a Terrible Beauty (1914–1916)

"THE PLAYBOY OF THE WESTERN WORLD" seemed to dog Maud Gonne's footsteps. On December 13, 1913 she saw it in a French version, as did the American critic Barrett H. Clark, who was amused by the setting: a "highly ornamental and romantic Irish interior," with geraniums on the windowsills, bric-a-brac in every corner, and a large Celtic inscription in the background. "Belasco could hardly have collected so many and so unnecessary a roomful of accessories."

Maud gave her opinion of the play in the January 1914 issue of *Les Entretien Idealistes*. In the course of a hastily written article, she said that the translation by Mr. Bourgeois was a remarkable *tour de force*, but regretted "that the first Irish play performed in France has been *The Playboy of the Western World*," which was so inferior to others by Synge, "whose dramatic work, moreover, seems to me quite inferior to that of W. B. Yeats." She admitted that the play "probably has certain qualities of savage power," but considered it a vulgar and sinister caricature of the life of the Irish peasant, "in which one of our national virtues is ridiculed, the solidarity of race which induces all Irishmen to give asylum to every fugitive from the army or the English police. . . . With us, the prisoner's clothes have lost their infamous character; they wear well. . . ." "Synge," she ended by saying, managed to imitate the peasants' dialect, but "never understood their soul."

Five months later in a letter to John Quinn, she commented further on the play: "In translation it lost all the vividness of Synge's language and only kept the sordidness. I heard French people say, 'If the Irish peasants are such drunken besotted creatures as that, England does well to oppress them.' From a theatrical point of view, it was a dead failure and . . . the manager told me 'after that experience it will be a long time before I put on another Irish play!'"

On March 8, 1914, two days after returning from Ireland, Maud wrote John Quinn that the Archbishop's fund for the strikers' children had been "so extravagantly spent that none remains of it. . . ."

People who . . . said I was destroying the sense of parental responsibility because I urged . . . *one* meal costing 1d a day in the schools, once they looked the matter up went mad on it and insisted on giving *three* meals a day. . . . It might have been very good if they could have kept it up, but as they could not and have stopped feeding altogether, it is rather hard on the children. Our committee are still giving 650 free meals every school day, and dinners on Saturdays as well, to any children whose parents are out of work, and as we have not yet succeeded in getting the Free Meal Act passed we were obliged to make another appeal for funds . . . your second cheque of £10 was a very good lead to encourage subscribers.

I also did a good deal in getting clothes and bedding out of the pawn shops for the people when they returned to work. Just a few of us took up this work privately. It was terrible the misery it brought us in contact with—whole families living in one room without a stick of furniture or bedding was no uncommon thing to find. And they are so brave and so uncomplaining. . . . The employers are triumphing horridly . . . mercilessly refusing to take back men who are getting on in life and whose years of service would soon entitle them to pensions. . . . My only hope is in Home Rule . . . bad as that bill is, it will cheer us all up a bit, put us in a better position to get more.

She had seen in Douglas Hyde's home a reproduction of the Augustus John portrait of Quinn and thought it was a wonderful job. "It has all the strength and determination, which makes me feel wild that you do not belong to Ireland *entirely*, for you would have led the people and made history as Parnell did. With the Irish people, in the Isle of Destiny, that would be possible. In America . . . people do not sacrifice all for an ideal and incarnate that ideal in a leader as our people at home do."

She wrote that men from all walks of life were joining the Irish Volunteer movement. She was right. It had very soon numbered four battalions in Dublin alone. On April 2, 1914, a women's auxiliary was formed called Cumann na mBan (meaning league of the women or Irishwomen's council; pronounced cummon-na-mon). It was pledged "to work for the establishment of an Irish Republic, by organising and training the women of Ireland to take their places by the side of those who are working and fighting for free Ireland." The following month Constance Markievicz described the purposes of the new organization to an assembly of Daughters of Erin and they voted to convert their group into a branch of the Cumann na mBan. Although the new branch elected Maud Gonne and Padraic Pearse's mother honorary presidents (meaning they were excused from drilling or wearing uniforms), there was no disguising the fact that the Daughters of Erin had been swallowed up. Maud realized that the move was inevitable and accepted it amiably. But in later years she never wearied of lauding the Daughters for their work in arousing nationalist sentiment among the women of Ireland. The Cumann itself became the spearhead of republican sentiment among women, flourishing throughout Ireland, and later solidified feeling against the treaty with England that established the Free State. That Maud Gonne played little part in the organization is one reason her name appears so rarely in histories of the Irish independence movement.

In March of 1914 Maud was delighted to hear that during Yeats's current American tour, the breach between him and John Quinn had been completely healed. Yeats stayed with

Quinn in New York for about ten days and Quinn found him "not a bit changed, but some gray in hair." He gave a dinner party in Yeats's honor with an impressive array of guests that included former President Theodore Roosevelt, James Huneker, Charles Dana Gibson, Amos Pinchot, and Richard Le Gallienne. Only three or four of those present were of Irish descent. One of them asked Quinn, "Does Yeats really believe what he says?" "Certainly." "Why, he must be a regular pagan." "And it is that kind of Irishman," Quinn wrote, "who feels perfectly competent to sit in judgment on poetry and the drama."

Maud answered that she could see from Yeats's letters to her that "it has been a real joy to him meeting you again in the old friendly way."

The poet's father, John Butler Yeats, was also pleased. He had gone to the U.S. in 1907 and liked it so much that he could not bear to return. He thought his son had acquired "a quiet importance," and acted toward Quinn like a brother. "They seemed to have the same thoughts and interests," he wrote his daughter Lily. "What one said was echoed by the other. The time spent by Willie in art school was, as it turns out, well spent. Quinn's collection of pictures gave him great delight. . . ."

Meanwhile, Maud had become involved in another matter. On April 1, 1914 she asked Quinn for his help in preventing a Hindu nationalist named Har Dyal, whom she had met in Paris, from being extradited to England from the United States. "He is a most intelligent cultivated man. . . ." she wrote. "It would be terrible if he were handed over to the English who have got up some sort of conspiracy charge against him saying he advocated assassination in India. I know how terribly busy and overworked you are, but if you could do anything to prevent Har Dyal being given up, I would be so grateful."

Maud spent the Easter holidays at her cousins' home, the Villa Castiglione in Florence. From there she wrote Quinn on May 6 to thank him for getting Har Dyal out on bail. Because Sean got the chicken pox, she was still in Florence when she wrote again to thank him for concluding the Dyal case so successfully. She had heard that Dyal was now settled safely in a part of Europe where he was free from any danger of extradition.

In the same letter Maud expressed the opinion that John Redmond's action in consenting to exclude Northern Ireland from the provisions of the proposed Home Rule bill was a mistake "for which we shall, I fear, have to pay heavily in the future."

No sooner had Maud returned to Paris than she was visited by W. B. Yeats and the Hon. Everard Feilding, who had come to Paris to see a "most sensational materializing medium." For Feilding, member of a prominent English Catholic family, the trip was in the line of duty, for he was president of the British Society for Psychical Research. For Yeats, it was because he could never resist an opportunity to attend a séance.

Maud accompanied the two men to their next destination, the little town of Mirabeau, where they wished to investigate a color lithograph of the Sacred Heart that was said to be dripping blood. The parish priest, Father Vacher, who had been censured for his credulity by his bishop, showed them some fresh drops of blood, but since they failed to see new ones actually form they would not authenticate the miracle. They were impressed, nevertheless, by the sincerity and piety of the old priest and of the old women attending mass in his private chapel.

On the following day, as the researchers prepared to leave, the priest told Yeats that, while at prayer that morning, he had received a message for him. A voice had said, "He is to become an apostle; he must use his intelligence. If he does not, our Lord will take away his intelligence and leave him at the mercy of his heart."

This is what Yeats heard Father Vacher say. Maud, who

knew French and Catholic thought much better, heard him say: "He will have to become an Apostle of the Sacred Heart. He will have to use his intelligence for the service of the Sacred Heart. Our Lord will help him." It can be taken for granted that she was right. Yeats was hearing the expression of his own feeling that it was time to fill in his piecemeal education, perhaps time to begin the study of philosophy. In any case, the thought that he might become an apostle of any kind was wildly exciting.

The priest had a message for the lady, too, a warning that she must leave France before certain "terrible events" occurred. This disturbed Yeats deeply. Though Maud was approaching fifty, his desire to protect her was still strong. The same feeling was beginning to extend to Iseult. In his poem "Two Years Later," in 1912 or 1913, he had hoped that Iseult would learn from her mother's experience "how despairing / The moth feels when it's burned"; that she would never "take the enemy for the friend," suffer as her mother had suffered, and "Be as broken in the end. / I could warn you but you are young / And I speak a barbarous tongue."

The "Guns of August" spectacularly bore out Father Vacher's second prediction. From the first, World War I seemed to Maud Gonne a bloody, wasteful mess, caused by the detested Entente Cordiale between England, France, and Russia, and ruinous for everyone except England, who was "grabbing everyone's trade." For Maud the only war worth fighting would be the one for Irish independence. But the same impulse that had caused her to feed school children impelled her to work with the Red Cross for the French wounded. Her letters to John Quinn were frequent now. On January 7, 1915 she wrote:

It was good to get your kind Xmas wishes in this land where war has put Christmas out of everybody's thoughts and indeed made Christmas seem a mockery.

For three months I have been doing Red Cross nursing in a hospital at [illegible] patching up poor mangled, wounded creatures in order that they may be sent back again to the slaughter. It is all terribly depressing. I feel I would be better employed in feeding my children in Ireland, but I can't make up my mind to leave Sean . . . when German submarine activities may possibly render return difficult, and Mac-Bride and the English law make it impossible for me to have him in Ireland until he is old enough to defy both.

On April 22, 1915, Maud apologized for not thanking Quinn earlier for his gift of apples

but we were all rather upset by the death of a dear nephew killed at Neuve Chapelle and I had to go to take care of my sister as we were afraid the shock would kill her. He was such a beautiful boy only 21. All the best, all the strongest are being killed. It is race suicide. . . . Poor France, she did not want this war. She is paying terribly for her un-natural alliances. England is losing heavily in men especially in Irish and Scotch men. She is spending money like water but she is gathering the trade of the whole of Europe so she can afford it.

Will your country be able to make them stop before France and Germany have quite destroyed each other? . . .

Again thank you so much for the wonder apples. James Stephens and his children enjoyed some of them with us. . . . I always feel jealous for Ireland when her writers live away from her though personally I am very glad to have Stephens here.

I don't know what I would give to be able to live in Ireland and have my boy educated there at Pearse's School. . . .

By July 15 she was nursing French wounded full-time at a military hospital in Paris-Plage, Pas-de-Calais, about 140 miles from Paris.

Iseult, and I and my sister were all working at hospital No. 35 (1100 beds) but I have lately been transferred to a new hospital No. 72 (400 beds) which was only opened three weeks ago and where they are very short of nurses.

It is a strange absorbing life which brings one very near to the suffer-ing and horror and waste of war. The long hours and the routine tire one physically so much, one has little time for thought. Iseult says it is an "abrutisement life and leaves no room for the intellect," but she makes a very good nurse all the same and the soldiers love her. . . .

The English-made Ulster revolt is quite triumphant in the Coalition

Government, and Home Rule is again far away. Once again Ireland has been deceived and cheated. . . .

On October 7 Maud wrote Quinn to thank him for his check of 250 francs, the second he had sent her. She had spent some of it, as she had the first, to eke out the inadequate rations given to the wounded French soldiers. "The food we serve at the French hospitals is very bad" though "different hospitals vary very much in this respect." She promised to send a full accounting when the money was exhausted.

The rest of her news was equally dismal. A few years earlier, her sister Kathleen, following family tradition, had obtained a divorce from General Thomas David Pilcher, who had soon married again. Now, under the additional blow of her son's death at Neuve Chapelle, Kathleen Picher's health had finally given way, and she had been forced to give up nursing. Maud herself had asked for a rest and had returned to Paris

> but the new French offensive has crowded the hospitals, and nurses are in great demand, so Iseult and I are both at work at the hospital which is established in the big Lycee Jansen. . . .
>
> Entre nous, I am utterly hopeless about the war, as the young art and intellect of France is being killed in the trenches. . . .
>
> Hatred of our enemies and fulsome admiration for our own side is the only expression of opinion allowed; and, granted the war, this is wise and necessary, but it makes all intellectual life impossible.

She told Quinn that Sir Edward Carson's army of Orange Protestants was finally being shipped out of Ireland because their distance from the front was discouraging Catholics from enlisting. But the regiment had got only as far as safe and easy Sussex, while most Catholic ones had been sent to the trenches in Flanders from which few men would ever return. "England is calmly continuing this policy of destroying the Nationalist majority in Ireland," and is being greatly helped by the war and the Irish Parliamentary Party.

In December 1915, Maud Gonne turned fifty. Her hair was now gray. Yeats wrote, "Young men no longer suddenly catch their breath / When you are passing," but his own obsession showed no signs of lessening. Three poems he wrote about Maud in January 1915 are among his best. In "Her Praise," he asserted that "Though she had young men's praise and old men's blame, / Among the poor both old and young gave her praise." In "The People," Yeats told of being abashed when Maud reminded him that, when she was booed by the masses, she never complained about their fickleness as he was now doing. In "His Phoenix," he conceded that some day "that barbarous crowd" might indeed consider some new beauty Maud's equal, but that to him she would never have Maud's "exact likeness, the simplicity of a child / And that proud look as though she had gazed into the burning sun.../I knew a phoenix in my youth, so let them have their day."

The war ground on. The hospital was packed all Christmas with men wounded in an attempted advance on Champagne. In January 1916 the wards began to empty in preparation for the victims of spring fighting. "The horror of it all!" Maud exclaimed to Quinn on February 4, 1916. "Then my boy, as usual when he works hard at school, got ill, and now I am in turn laid up with influenza, but the boy is all right again and back at school and my illnesses are never long or severe and I expect to get back to work in a few days."

Kathleen Pilcher was worse off. One son was dead, another badly wounded, and a third, at the tender age of seventeen, was a lieutenant in the army. When her doctor recommended that she move to Switzerland to avert consumption, she had great difficulty in obtaining a passport and in getting permission for her daughter to accompany her.

I don't suppose United States citizens are treated in the same way! I believe after this war I shall come to America with Iseult and the boy and get naturalised, for Europe won't be a place to live in for generations. If the allies win, only England and Russia will be strong and the vilest jingoism and imperialism à la Rudyard Kipling will prevail. . . . As for Ireland, God help her after the war!

I suppose you have seen Lady Gregory? What has she been doing in America? Have you seen Willie's "Reveries in Childhood"?

Maud thanked Quinn warmly for sending another barrel of apples; the wounded soldiers and her son had greatly appreciated them. Sean now wanted to go to the land where the apples came from, for there was nothing like them in all of France.

Two weeks later she had a favor to ask; that he receive kindly the French dramatist and novelist Jules Blois, who was going to America on a quasi-diplomatic mission and wanted to call on him.*

Apples, books, and Blois became trivia when first word of the Easter Rising reached her. This term describes the week of fierce fighting that started in Dublin on Monday, April 24, 1916. It marks the beginning of the modern struggle for an independent Irish Republic; it is the Irish equivalent, all in one, of those events that took place in the American colonies between 1775 and 1783: the Declaration of Independence, Paul Revere's ride, Lexington and Concord, Valley Forge and Yorktown.

The roots go back to the start of World War I, when the

---

*Blois was an extraordinary man. Though filled with a passion for French Catholic tradition, he became president of the French Society for Psychical Research; wrote a study of underground religions, particularly those that practiced the black mass; and was censured by the Church. "Religion and sex were to him the great experiences," Mary Colum writes in *Life and the Dream*, but neither was connected in his mind with morals or ethics. Blois's friendships with Maud Gonne and W. B. Yeats did nothing to disabuse him of a common French belief that Ireland was a land inhabited by mysterious Celts with magical powers. He spent his last days in dire poverty in New York City, but after his burial, it was discovered that he had savings of nine thousand dollars.

leaders of the Irish Volunteers decided that, the moment there was a reasonable prospect of success, they would strike a blow for freedom. As the war continued, a group in their midst from the Irish Republican Brotherhood— Padraic Pearse, Thomas MacDonagh, Joseph Mary Plunkett, Sean MacDermott—were resolved to take action even if defeat was well-nigh certain. Early in 1916 Pearse came to terms with James Connolly, commander of a small group of armed trade unionists called the Irish Citizen Army, and together they decided to strike on Easter Sunday. At the last minute the elected leaders of the Irish Volunteers became aware of the conspiracy, and cancelled the "maneuvers" scheduled for that day—a change that meant that no rebellion took place at all in the countryside, and that even in Dublin no more than a thousand men would be reached. To make things worse, a German ship bearing arms for the insurgents had to be sunk by its captain after an unfortunate error in communications prevented it from reaching its destination.

The day after Easter was a bank holiday, and the weather was unseasonably fine. Many Dubliners slept late; officers and gentry thronged out to the Fairyhouses Races; middle-class families carried picnic baskets to Phoenix Park, whole cycling parties picnicked at the Dargle, Killiney Beach, or the Scalp. Less fortunate families went by foot or bus to Sandymount Strand. By mid-morning the city was almost deserted.

It was at that time that groups of rebels fanned out from several assemblage centers in Dublin and began seizing strong points according to plan. Some were in the dark green uniform and cocked hat of the Citizen Army, others wore the heather green of the Irish Volunteers; the rest wore trench coats, sport jackets, suits. They carried rifles of mixed and antiquated origin, as well as pikes and pick-axes.

The men may have been doubtful about their aims and

purposes, but there was no question about the determination of the leaders. Pearse and Connolly seized the General Post Office on O'Connell Street and made it rebel headquarters. A mathematics teacher named Eamon de Valera took over Westland Row railway station and other points on the southern approaches to Dublin. Eamonn Kent seized some hospital and poorhouse buildings close to the Richmond barracks. Edward Daly occupied the area around the Four Courts. Michael Mallin, with the assistance of another devoted Connolly lieutenant, Countess Markievicz, began to dig trenches in St. Stephen's Green.

Thomas MacDonagh with a small group of Irish Volunteers occupied Jacob's biscuit factory, an enormously large and well-situated building overlooking Portobello Bridge, the Ship Street barracks and Dublin Castle. John MacBride, on the way to his civil service job, saw them moving in and politely asked if he could join them. He was in civilian clothes, of course, and knew nothing of what was taking place. For MacBride it was like old times. According to Desmond Ryan's *The Rising*, he "threw himself enthusiastically into the fray as MacDonagh's ablest auxiliary, and led in addition several dangerous raiding parties...." His habit during the week was to drop quietly from one of the windows in the great building and lead Volunteers to positions where the sniping was most productive.

It took the British forces six days to crush the Rising. The General Post Office, together with many neighboring buildings, went up in flames. Liberty Hall, the home of Connolly's nest of radicals, was demolished by a British gunboat on the Liffey. Total losses consisted of about 450 killed (60 Irish Volunteers and Citizen Army men, 130 British military and police, 260 civilians); 3,000 wounded; 179 buildings wrecked. Estimated damages amounted to £2,000,000.

At first the Irish populace showed no sympathy for the insurgents. Their attitude changed only after British, convinced that the rebels were hirelings of Germany, put six-teen leaders before a firing squad within two weeks. Among them were Padraic Pearse, his brother William, Tom Clarke, James Connolly, and Major John MacBride. When MacBride faced the firing squad, he told the priest who attended him "I've often looked down the barrels of their rifles before." The British sentenced another hundred to death (including Countess Markievicz and Eamon de Valera) but the sentences were commuted to life imprison-ment. About 1,500 more were sent with them to prisons in England.

That the news of the Easter Rising took Maud com-pletely by surprise is not to be wondered at. Almost all prominent nationalists were equally astonished.

Maud was spending the Easter holidays with her chil-dren in her Normandy home when she received the first fragmentary and garbled accounts (Connolly killed in the fighting, Markievicz arrested, Pearse wounded). Shaking with deep emotion, she sent off long and frantic letters to John Quinn and W. B. Yeats before a single execution had taken place. Her immediate reaction was a resolve to get back to Ireland. If she could not obtain a passport to go directly, she would try to get one to England and reach Ireland from there.

She wrote Quinn that the Rising was caused by the weakness of the Irish Parliamentarians "in allowing the En-glish government to play fast and loose with Home Rule." Petty and large provocations, arrests without trial, were continually taking place. There was no end to the crimes of the British government.

She felt that Connolly, Markievicz, and Pearse were "the best in Irish politics. . . . I feel so wretched and powerless," brought to the edge of madness "by the tragedy and the greatness of the sacrifice our friends have made." Neverthe-less, practically and politically their sacrifice will avail. They have raised Ireland to tragic dignity, and in the conference at the end of the war where the rights of small nations will be talked of it will be impossible to ignore Ireland or to go on saying what I am hearing every day said, "Ireland is quite satisfied. England has done justice to her, and by her liberal measures has won her loyalty." England has given us nothing but promises and barely even taken the trouble to hide her intentions of breaking them.

I hope American opinion outside the Irish American organizations will sympathise and understand. . . . I am very sad when I think of the friends I have lost, but very proud to belong to the Irish Nation which has produced them.

What Maud wrote to Yeats can be gleaned from a letter he sent to Lady Gregory on May 11, 1916:

I had no idea that any public event could so deeply move me—and I am very despondent about the future. At the moment I feel that all the work of years has been overturned, all the bringing together of classes, all the freeing of Irish literature and criticism from politics. Maud Gonne reminds me that she saw the ruined houses about O'Connell Street and the wounded and dying lying about the streets, in the first days of the war. I perfectly remember the vision and my making light of it and saying that if a true vision at all it could only have a symbolised meaning. This is the only letter I have had from her since she knew of the Rebellion. I have sent the papers every day. I do not yet know what she feels about her husband's death. Her letter was written before she heard of it. Her main thought seems to be "tragic dignity has returned to Ireland". . . . She is coming to London if she can get a passport, but I doubt her getting one. Indeed I shall be glad if she does not come yet—it is better for her to go on nursing the French wounded till the trials are over.

Maud wrote Quinn the same day that, having seen the English papers, she now knew "the ghastly extent of the tragedy." Dublin, an open town, was "recklessly shelled from the surrounding hills and from the river." No one would ever know the number of people buried in the fallen buildings. The dead were buried without coffins, often without identification. She quoted Augustine Birrell, secretary of state for Ireland, as admitting that the insurgents were armed only with *"a job lot of old rifles and shotguns. Most of my best friends have been executed in cold blood."*

Constance Markievicz was like a sister to me. I feel so stunned at the savage brutality of it all. I cannot think clearly. Only I know I must try to keep down impotent rage and despair, for Ireland still exists, and more than ever claims our service.

My husband is among those executed. He and McDonough gave themselves up from Jacobs biscuit factory to save the civil population of that crowded district from indiscriminate shelling by the English. He has died for Ireland and his son will bear an honoured name. I remember nothing else.

Early in June 1916 Maud was alerted by the Franciscan Capuchin Friary in Dublin that she could soon expect some information about her husband's last moments from Father Augustine, who had attended him. Immediately afterward, she heard from W. B. Yeats that a story was being spread that Major MacBride had refused the assistance of a priest. Father Augustine, writing on June 22, categorically denied the rumor.

He prepared for the end like a good Catholic and met his fate with a most admirable fortitude. . . . He was quite calm, gave me some money for bread for the poor and felt very glad when I told him I would be by his side when he fell to anoint him. . . . I am the only one who can say how beautifully and how bravely he died and it is a shame and a crime for anyone to write anything which is not true in connection with such a thing as death.

MacBride's body was buried in lime at Arbour Hill. Maud tried to have it exhumed and buried at the Glasnevin cemetery in Dublin, to rest with patriots of earlier days, but the authorities refused. "I do not mind," she wrote on copies of the clerical correspondence she sent to John Quinn, "for he is with his comrades and England is powerless to dishonor their memories."

Yeats spent much of June and July 1916 trying to obtain a passport so that he could visit Maud Gonne in Normandy. While thus occupied, he received a messenger from

Maud who was eminently qualified to give him the latest news: Iseult Gonne, now a twenty-one-year-old, brown-eyed, pre-Raphaelite beauty. Her mother, Iseult said, seemed sad and lonely; was sleeping badly; and wanted Yeats to find a lawyer for Helena Molony, who had been swept up with the others after the Rising. After that, she hoped he would accompany Iseult back to Normandy.

Yeats introduced the young girl to his fashionable friends. Lady Cunard said, "Never in my life have I seen such a complexion." Yeats wrote Lady Gregory,

She looks very distinguished and is now full of self-possession. She is beautifully dressed, though very plainly. I said, "Why are you so pale?" and she said, "Too much responsibility." She makes me sad, for I think that if my life had been normal I might have had a daughter of her age. That means, I suppose, that I am beginning to get old.

Despite Maud's melancholy, she found the spirit and energy to write another article listing England's crimes against the Irish people. It was published on July 16, 1916 in the *New York Sun* under the heading, "Irish Joan of Arc Comes to Defence of Sinn Fein." In the course of it, she wrote:

It is necessary for England to empty her jails of such apostles of liberty as Countess Markievicz, or as Professor John MacNeill, or as Mr. Arthur Griffith. It is necessary for her to try to efface the too recent memories of the bombardment of the open city of Dublin and of the wanton executions . . . of some of Ireland's noblest thinkers and writers who dared to . . . proclaim Ireland's right to nationhood and free government. . . .

With her odd penchant for giving to others the credit for fighting the school conditions in Ireland (previously she had given it to Hanna Sheehy-Skeffington), she now gave it to James Connolly, the man who "with his broken leg was dragged out of the hospital to be executed" for his role in the Easter Rising. After "three years of incessant agitation," she wrote, he had "succeeded in getting a bill passed . . .

permitting, with many restrictions, local Irish authorities to strike a half-penny rate to feed necessitous school children. This bill was passed in June, 1914, and owing to the war I believe it still remains a dead letter. . . ."

In July 1916 Maud persuaded W. B. Yeats to sign a petition asking the English government to spare the life of Roger Casement, who had been convicted of trying to provide arms for the Easter Rising. Quinn tried to save him through British Ambassador Spring-Rice, but all efforts were unavailing. Casement was hanged on August 3, 1916.

On July 29, 1916, Quinn wrote that he found Jules Blois a charming man; hoped Hughes would beat Woodrow Wilson in the coming presidential election; and thought MacBride's death "a better end than a small place-holder going on living in the past and drinking and talking out his life." He enclosed a copy of a poem published about MacBride's life and death.

Maud was glad to have it. She replied on August 16 that she was keeping all such material for Sean's sake. "He made a fine heroic end which has atoned for all. It was a death he had always desired."

She was determined to return with Sean and Iseult to Dublin in October. "I must have my boy brought up in Ireland. I must be near him. Besides, I feel my place is there."

There was another reason for returning. She wanted to help

the families of the thousands who have been arbitrarily arrested and sent to prison camps in England under the Martial Law of that murderer Maxwell. About 1500 of these are still without trial, shut up in prison camps not knowing of what they are accused. Many being members of the Gaelic League and in no way connected with Sinn Fein or . . . politics of any sort. Naturally, they lose their employment, and naturally, to the satisfaction of England, their families starve.

She reported that Yeats, who was with her in Normandy on that very day, was reading with Iseult the works of

Charles Peguy, Paul Claudel, and Francis Jammes. Yeats hoped that Iseult would some day write a book about these distinguished French Catholic poets. Meanwhile he was grateful to her for acting as his secretary while he worked on another book of memoirs.

Joseph Hone writes amusingly about this. "The thought that the lovely Iseult would 'civilise Dublin Catholics' by imparting to them an enthusiasm for Peguy, Claudel and Jammes almost reconciled him to Maud Gonne's project of getting back to Ireland." But as it was, Yeats left Normandy "filled with fears for that fabulous household, with its dogs, cats and the monkey which interrupted the conversations on literature, religion and politics."

Yeats was falling in love with Iseult. The intimation lurks in a letter he wrote Lady Gregory from Normandy during the same month:

I believe I was meant to be the father of an unruly family. I did not think that I liked little boys but I liked Shawn. I am really managing Iseult very well. The other night she made a prolonged appeal for an extra cigarette. . . . I have stayed on longer than I intended, but I think you will forgive me under the circumstances—as father, but as father only, I have been a great success.

Lady Gregory realized what was happening and encouraged it. She thought Maud too much immersed in politics to be a suitable wife for Yeats, that his marriage to Iseult would do less harm to his psyche, to her own friendship with Yeats, and to the Abbey Theatre

It is probable that Maud Gonne reached the same conclusion at the same time. It may have been an additional reason for rejecting another proposal of marriage from her constant suitor, now fifty-one. He was emboldened to renew his offer because one obstacle had been removed; Maud was now a widow.

Concerned with other matters, Maud asked Quinn on August 16 if he could help her obtain a position as correspondent for some American newspaper once she got to

Dublin. It would give her some degree of protection, she
thought, in a city under martial law, just as her connections
with French newspapers had protected her in France
against British intrigues.

Maud was convinced that England was deliberately covering up atrocities committed by her soldiers during Easter
Week, such as the murders in King Street and the "execution" of Francis Sheehy-Skeffington in Portobello Barracks.
She told Quinn that Irish-Americans should see to it that
such charges were seriously investigated by the same sort of
American committee that had investigated German conduct in Belgium. It would be of immense moral value to
Ireland and perhaps prod the English into settling the Irish
question.

In October of 1916 Maud moved to a small seventh-floor
apartment at 17 rue de l'Annonciation. "It is nearer
heaven," she wrote Quinn, "and has a roof terrace from
which the sunset on the chimney tops of Paris looks wonderful. I hope to live chiefly in Ireland now, so am only
keeping a pied-à-terre here."

In the same letter she enclosed a copy of "Easter, 1916," a
poem Yeats had sent to her to forward to Quinn, thinking
that French censors would be kinder to it than British ones.
This is the magnificent poem in which Yeats celebrates the
"terrible beauty" that the Easter Rising had effected in the
popular view of shrill Constance Markievicz, commonplace
Padraic Pearse, and vainglorious John MacBride. Their
deaths, the poet thinks, may have been needless, "For England may keep faith / For all that is done and said." But
for the moment it is enough "To murmur name upon
name" and to realize that "Wherever green is worn," these
people have been "changed utterly: / A terrible beauty is
born."

Maud did not think that either the French or English
censors would bother to black out the poem since it was
"not worthy of Willie's genius and still less of the subject.

England and Ireland are too far apart for a writer to be able to keep one eye on one and the other on the other without a squint. . . ."

In her next letter, written in November, she gave Quinn a bleak picture of conditions in Europe:

Great tracts of land are going out of cultivation everywhere for want of men to work them. . . . Germany with her genius for organisation is taking steps to meet the coming famine, and the great productiveness of the French soil and the work of her women will help France to meet the strain, but in Ireland with a hostile government, nothing I think can save us. . . .

Information from George Russell and others had convinced her England was willfully preparing another famine for Ireland like that of 1846–47. Nothing was being done to help Irish farmers increase their output or obtain agricultural machinery, and they were being forced to sell their products to the British military at low set prices.

Furthermore, all possibilities for employment were being squashed in order to force men to enter the Irish regiments, in which casualties were so great that the English dared not release the figures. Under these circumstances, she wrote,

I have decided on going to Ireland with Sean and Iseult. I feel it a duty to do the little one can for one's own country in the face of the present terrible situation. . . .

I am sending you the little book in which I jotted down all the money I spent that you sent me for charity. . . . I have still 520 francs in hand . . . with your consent I shall spend it in Ireland, probably in food for the school children. If I do that, may I give it publicity in your name.

Until this time Maud had not really doubted that she could go to Ireland, either directly or through England. She was shocked to learn otherwise. She had packed her belongings, received her passport, signed necessary papers at the English consulate, countersigned them at the French Prefecture, bought her tickets and reserved places on the boat, when she was informed by Major Lampton, head of the

British control bureau, that he had received orders from the English War Office to tell Maud Gonne MacBride that she could go to England but not to Ireland. Enraged, Maud promptly wrote Lloyd George to ask the reason for "this monstrous and stupid piece of tyranny." She also asked various Irish members of Parliament to inquire about it. And on November 24, 1916, she sent John Quinn a description of her woes:

In the meantime here I am stranded in Paris, living in a tiny attic on the 7th floor which I had taken to store my furniture in. I would go to London to agitate the questions there, but unofficially Major Lampton told me he thought it very doubtful if, once I was in England, the English authorities would allow me to return to France. Such is the liberty of the world we live in! O, why am I not in America with the children! . . .

CHAPTER XIX

Return to Ireland (1917–1918)

⚘ In March of 1917, Maud told John Quinn that her correspondence with Irish members of Parliament concerning her desire to reach Ireland was extraordinary, instructive, and futile. John Redmond, their leader, said he could not interfere in such matters. Tim Healy wrote that Redmond was the only person who could help, provided he wanted to. Stephen Gwynn told her that, being at the front himself, he could not do much, but if she were willing to support Redmond's policies on Ireland he would try. William Field, Hugh Law, and other members communicated Maud's desire to the War Office but "up to the present I am still an exile and likely to remain one. . . . It is not gay! About Xmas all got *la grippe* . . . and I got congestion of the lungs as well and was very ill. I am only just getting over it."

Conditions in Paris were very difficult. Coal was impossible to get and electricity was regulated; vegetables were double and treble in price; only stale bread could be sold. Meat, sugar, and butter were rationed and often difficult to buy. Thinking that the family would soon be in Ireland, she had neglected to lay in any supplies. However, she did not mind these discomforts, she said, because conditions in England would soon be worse than in France, and the worse they get the sooner the war will end which is the one great important thing. . . .

At last the worm (Redmond) has turned and wriggled. Lloyd George's refusal of Home Rule was too much even for him. If he had walked out of the House of Commons years ago it would have been better for his reputation and for Ireland. . . .

John Quinn tried to help Maud gain admission to Ireland by talking to the British Ambassador, but had to tell her, on March 14, that London had denied so many requests of the sort that the ambassador no longer tried to intervene.

In the same letter Quinn agreed with her that Yeats's poem on the Easter Rising was not up to his genius. James Stephens's poem, "Spring 1916," was far superior. He also said that if Maud had been able to get to Dublin, he might have been able to get her appointed Irish correspondent for some American newspaper.

As usual, Maud and her children spent the Easter holidays in Normandy at Les Mouettes, but this year their activities were different. They turned their garden into a potato and bean field, thinking that both products would help to replenish the dwindling food supplies. "If only we were in Ireland!" she wrote Quinn in April.

And then she gave him a fresh example of English despotism. After John MacBride had been executed, his sixty-year-old brother Joseph, who lived quietly with his wife and five young children and took no part in politics, had been arrested and deported to England without trial. Owing to the cold and bad food in prison, his health had broken down and he had been allowed to return home. But no sooner had his wife nursed him back to health than he had again been arrested and deported, this time to Oxford, where he was allowed to work at the Bodleian Library. A few months later, with a few other Irish deportees, he was removed to a little Gloucestershire village, and ordered to remain within a five-mile radius. No work or money was provided, and had it not been for the Irish Prisoners' Aid Society they would all have starved.

"English and French papers complain that the Germans feed very scantily the unfortunate people they deport— England doesn't feed them at all, which is certainly simpler," Maud wrote, but she did admit that "after a fuss was made in Parliament the English government has decided on paying for the board of the deported men." So long as such acts of tyranny were practiced against the Irish, she could arouse in herself little pity or indignation when she read the propaganda about the sufferings of Belgians, Serbs, and Montenegrins. She expressed her pleasure at the entrance of the United States into the World War, without noting that this propaganda had been a major cause of it. She thought that the inevitable peace conference could not "allow Ireland's claim to be put to one side. England is already beginning, through her creatures in the French press, to warn France against America's Utopian ideas of the rights of small nationalities, such as Ireland."

It was a long and episodic letter. She agreed with Quinn that the Home Rule Act was unworkable economically, and should be vigorously rejected by Ireland. She repeated her thought about John MacBride's death: "Through it, he has left a name his son can be proud of." She enclosed a clipping from an Irish nationalist paper reporting the statement of a minister that "very large numbers of children perish absolutely from want of food." And she thanked him for another generous contribution

enabling me to help a few of those who appeal to me and who I know are in need, for the war has almost ruined me, so that I cannot do much for people when so much is needed. Thank you again. I always say the money is from an Irishman in America for we cannot let America have you altogether.... Some day you will perhaps come and see us here when this hideous war is over—for hideous it is beyond words, and the danger of it is that in order to destroy German militarism a system of intolerable military despotism will be established everywhere. Do not think that England will give up her new army easily. The [upper] classes in England will need an army to hold in check these millions of men who have been taught by every means to kill, to bomb, to destroy and who will be hungry at the end of the war.

The submarine war is going on, though the papers had orders to say little. 5 fishing boats were sunk off this coast last week and though no coal can be bought in the district, every day we pick up little basketfuls of it washed up by the sea from sunken colliers.

Maud forgot these problems briefly when she read John Quinn's review of James Joyce's *Portrait of the Artist as a Young Man*. On May 12, 1917, she wrote him a one-paragraph comment on it:

Just received Vanity Fair with your very interesting and generous article on Joyce's book. I don't like the book as much as you do, though as self-analysis of a somewhat mediocre soul who has failed to see and to understand the beauty it has lived among, it is curious and interesting. The childhood parts are especially good. While he has portrayed himself with curious frankness and probably photographic accuracy, he has failed, I think, in drawing vividly any of the other characters. I am told that I know many of them and yet I have failed to recognise any. Those who know the young students in Dublin, the intensity and vividness of their lives (MacDonagh and Pearse, though both very exceptional men, men of genius, were the type our students follow) would find it hard to recognise the uncouth nonentities presented by Joyce.

Quinn's reply, in a letter dated July 17, 1917, was fair enough.

Joyce is not for all and does not appeal to all. One either likes writing of that kind or one doesn't, just as one person is attracted by a painting that repels another, and yet it may be a good work of art. . . . Ireland is a world in itself and has many types . . . and there is really no one type.

During that summer, Maud and her children were again at Les Mouettes, where she waited for a reply to her renewed application for permission to go to Ireland. No answer came from the British control office, but she was told unofficially by two Irish M.P.s that if she signed a paper promising to take no part in Irish politics she would be allowed to return. "Of course I refused," she told Quinn in a letter dated July 30, 1917. The matter again proved that the Irish Parliamentary Party was useless.

Maud, Iseult, and Sean lived on the potatoes they had

planted at Easter, on torpedoed fish, and other washed-up treasure. They occasionally heard naval guns, but otherwise life was peaceful enough. After the German parliament's declaration about peace, a repetition of President Wilson's program, she did not understand why the fighting was continuing. No longer did she believe that the militarists would control the world after the war; she thought now that the Socialists would take over to make future wars impossible. "I think that is what all the governments are really afraid to face," she wrote, but they would have to face it before long since all the soldiers were sick of the butchery. Even America would not tolerate much longer the continuation of this hell. "But you, I believe, still see beauty in war. I did once, but hospitals and broken hearts and the devastation and destruction of all art and beauty have changed me and I bow to every peace advocate. They are the real ones who are showing moral courage at the present time in Europe."

Maud thanked Quinn for sending her a collection of Japanese Noh plays. They had been translated by Ernest Fenellosa and polished by Ezra Pound. "Because of a slight prejudice I have against the affectation of Ezra Pound I had not thought I should care for it," she wrote, but actually read it from beginning to end with excitement and delight. She thought Pound, whom she had never met, had edited the book with great skill and taste.

In August 1917 Maud received a letter from the director in Paris of the British Passport Office which dashed her hope that the recent release of Easter Rising prisoners and their return to Ireland were good auguries for her own case. She could still have a visa for England but she would not be permitted to go to Ireland. Furthermore, if she accepted the visa to England, there was no guarantee that she would ever be allowed to return to France.

On August 3 Maud sent a letter to John Quinn enclosing a copy of the refusal and asking:

Can you do anything for me?... Why I should be singled out for their prosecution by the English government, I do not know, I have urgent personal reasons for wanting to return to Ireland. Above all, I want my boy to be educated there....

Do you think I risk being interned in England if we go and try, if from there we couldn't get to Ireland?... Iseult, Sean and I have made up our minds we won't pass another winter in Paris under present conditions. It is too sad.

If we are interned in England, please try and get us out. If you can make them give me a passport, that would be better still.

A week later Yeats came to France for a hectic two months. He gave a series of lectures in Paris and, of course, visited the MacBride family in Colleville. His first aim was to persuade Maud that the family would be better off in London than in Paris, even if they got no farther, but two other things were on his mind. One was to complete a Noh kind of play called *The Dreaming of the Bones*. The plot was based on an event in ancient Irish history wherein a guilty love facilitated the conquest of Ireland. Because of its subject, some Celtic-twilight lyrics, and a description of the atrocities committed against the Irish by invading hordes, the play may be considered Yeats's last expression of nationalist sentiment.

The third item on Yeats's mind this summer of 1917 was to propose to Iseult Gonne. There is no record of how Maud felt when he told her of his intention, but we can guess. Maud was too old to be surprised at anything human beings did; and it is not likely that she felt like mocking her old friend's desire to marry a twenty-two-year-old girl. Iseult was intellectual, widely-read, had a sophisticated knowledge of art, and had associated with brilliant writers; it seemed quite possible that she would enjoy being the wife of an author who was beginning to achieve worldwide fame. In addition, the marriage would help to end any questions about her birth. These were probably Maud's thoughts when she told Yeats that she did not object to his intention, though she did warn him that Iseult was not likely to take his proposal seriously. Iseult's reaction was odd; she seemed not to take the proposal in any way at all. She tried to avoid discussing it, and she certainly did not want to give any positive answer. On August 12 Yeats wrote Lady Gregory from Les Mouettes,

Iseult and I are on our old intimate terms but I don't think she will accept. She "has not the impulse." However, I will think the matter undecided till we part. They talk of returning to Paris at the end of the month and of going to London in middle of September. They hope to be allowed back to Ireland but do not yet know. At present there is refusal. . . . It is very pleasant here. Maud Gonne is no longer bitter and she and Iseult are on good terms now and life goes on smoothly. Iseult herself seems to have grown into more self mastery after months of illness from cigarettes. She has only had one outbreak so far and that was only one cigarette and a half and was secret.

Three days later Yeats sent Lady Gregory a description of the animals in the household—"the usual number of caged birds, a parrot, a monkey, a goat, two dogs, a cat and seven rabbits"—and added: "Iseult and I take long walks, and are as we were last year affectionate and intimate and she shows many little signs of affection, but otherwise things are as I wrote."

In a letter to T. Sturge Moore he described the menagerie as consisting of "three and thirty singing birds." The doors of their cages are open "so that they alight on the table during meals and peck the fruit from the dishes. There is also . . . a Javanese cock which perches on Madame Gonne's chair."

On August 21 Yeats wrote Lady Gregory:

Iseult has been ill and came down this morning after two days in bed, full of affection owing to a dream she had had in which I had sympathised with her in some nightmare circumstances. Yet I don't think she will change her mind. The little boy is now quite tall and is going to be very clever and to my amusement has begun to criticise his mother's politics. He has a confident analytical mind and is more like a boy of 17 than 13. Life goes smoothly after one outbreak from Maud Gonne, the result of my suggesting that London was a better place for Iseult than

Dublin. They go to London in the middle of September to try and get the government refusal to allow Maud Gonne to go to Ireland withdrawn. It has just been repeated however—so everything is very uncertain.

A few days later Maud wrote John Quinn: "I am anxious to get Sean to Ireland for his school term, which begins in September. Shall we be able to get there?... I may be stopped at Southampton. All is arbitrary and capricious in English official dealings with Irish people."

The political situation in Ireland was serious, she wrote, because the British government, which had freed Irish prisoners in order to conciliate American and Russian officials, was now rearresting them for having helped the Sinn Fein separatists to win a smashing victory over Home Rule groups in the recent elections. The economic situation was just as bad. Although Ireland was producing more food than she needed, it would not prevent Irish people from dying of famine "any more than the great food supply did in 1845." Because England was seizing the arms of the Irish Volunteers, there would be insufficient force to prevent Irish food from being shipped to England or commandeered for the military locusts swarming in Ireland.

I have sent the last £20 you sent me to the bank in Ireland, for nowhere I believe will help be more needed than in Dublin this winter. . . .

As soon as Sean is safe at school in Ireland, I want to turn my whole energy to feeding the school children, but the need and the difficulties are increasing in a terrifying way. God knows I don't ever want German domination in Ireland, but nothing can be worse than English. Don't you, who are of Irish blood, realise this? America, who has saved herself from it, does she not understand? Even in that interesting pamphlet of American opinion on the Irish question you sent me, many of the measured half-hearted declarations jarred on me. It is not in terms like that the fathers of your liberties would have spoken. When Wilson in his pronouncement for small nationalities mentioned Poland, why did he not mention Ireland too by name? Many French people noticed this and remarked on it to me.

During the next few weeks, while everyone was packing for the trip from Paris to London, Yeats accepted as final

Iseult's refusal of his marriage proposal. He wrote to Lady Gregory on September 8:

Iseult has always been something like a daughter to me and so I am less upset than I might have been—I am chiefly unhappy about her general prospects. Just at the moment she is in one of her alarming moods— deep melancholy and apathy, the result of having left the country—and is always accusing herself of sins—sins of omission not of commission—She has a horoscope that makes me dread melancholia. Only in the country is she amused and free of this mood for long. Maud Gonne on the other hand is in a joyous and self-forgetting condition of political hate the like of which I have not yet encountered.

"Political hate" was Yeats's term for Maud's passionate interest in Irish national freedom.

In a second letter Yeats told Lady Gregory that on the journey from Paris to Havre, Iseult was "very depressed," that at Havre she "went off by herself and cried." She was ashamed, he thought, at being so selfish as to refuse to marry him, and in thus breaking her friendship with him. "I need hardly say she had said nothing to me of 'not wanting.' Meanwhile she has not faltered in her refusal of me but as you can imagine life is a good deal at white heat."

Maud stepped on English soil—Southampton—with her family on September 17. She and Iseult had a difficult time. They were taken into a shed and searched for secret codes, while Yeats walked up and down the platform fuming under the drizzling rain and cursing the shame-faced, polite detectives. The boat train was held for them, but no sooner had they reached London than Maud was served with a notice under the Defence of the Realm Act forbidding her to proceed to Ireland.

Yeats had come to France carrying in his pocket an invitation from Mrs. H. T. Tucker to visit her and her daughter George Hyde-Lees at their country home. He had decided that if Iseult rejected him, he would accept the invitation and ask George to marry him. Now he wavered. With the Defence of the Realm Act barring Maud and Iseult from continuing to Ireland, he felt that Iseult was more than ever in need of his friendship. British hostility was not the only danger. There was the possibility that Maud would do something rash. And indeed it did seem at first that she would try somehow to smuggle her children, herself, and her menagerie into Ireland. But, to Yeats's great relief, she finally decided to take a flat in Chelsea for six months and study design at a London art school.

This swung Yeats back to his original resolve. On September 19 he wrote Lady Gregory that he had decided to be

what some Indian calls "true of voice." I am going to Mrs. Tucker's in the country on Saturday or Monday at latest and I will ask her daughter to marry me. Perhaps she is tired of the idea. I shall however make it clear that I will still be friend and guardian to Iseult. . . .

I have seen Iseult to-day and am doing as she wishes. All last night the darkness was full of writing, now on stone, now on paper, now on parchment, but I could not read it. Were spirits trying to communicate? I prayed a great deal and believe I am doing right.

Yeats kept his promise to guard and protect Iseult. At the Savile Club he met a friend who said he could have her appointed assistant librarian in the School of Oriental Languages. The pay was small but she would be among people of culture, and could supplement her income with her own writing. Hone writes in his biography that "When this had been arranged, Yeats burst into tears from sheer happiness."

Yeats and Miss Hyde-Lees were married at the Harrow Register Office in London on October 20, 1917. As they were about to leave for their honeymoon, Yeats asked his best man, Ezra Pound, to send a telegram about the wedding to Lady Gregory. Then, remembering the unpredictability and breadth of Pound's language when put to the test, he added thoughtfully, "*Not* a message that will be talked about at Coole Park for the next generation."

Yeats and George had been married less than a week when Yeats fell into a "great gloom." He felt that he had betrayed three people—Maud, Iseult, and George; then he thought, "I have lived all through this before." His wife experienced the same sensation of prior performance, and investigated it through automatic writing, a device new to her but familiar to many with psychic gifts. The person holds a pen loosely, allows his mind to drift, relaxes the will, and permits some invisible force to control his hand. The result is a script full of scattered images, sometimes coherent, sometimes not. In this case the message read: "With the bird, all is well at heart. Your action was right for both but in London you mistook its meaning." Yeats understood that the bird was Iseult Gonne; within a half-hour his rheumatic pains, neuralgia, and fatigue disappeared.

Mrs. Yeats, a friendly, kind, witty woman, discovered that she could write automatic script for several hours at a time, while spirits with strange names, whom her husband called "communicators," would answer his questions. With great delight Yeats wrote Lady Gregory on October 29, 1917: "From being more miserable than I ever remember being since Maud Gonne's marriage I became extremely happy. That sense of happiness has lasted ever since."

Whether it was indeed automatic writing that saved their marriage, or George's realization, conscious or unconscious, that her husband required extrasensory support is debatable. On many later occasions Mrs. Yeats showed similar sensitivity and tact; for instance, she knew almost before Yeats did, how much he required the friendship of such women as Olivia Shakespear, Lady Gregory, Lady Gerald Wellesley, and Margot Ruddock. George seemed to have this flair for resolving problems of human relationship from the beginning. She had been married less than two months when Yeats wrote Lady Gregory:

Iseult stayed here last night as she seemed too tired to go home and they have spent the morning talking dress. And now I find that George is giving Iseult a dress as a Xmas present. They made friends first for my sake but now it is for each other's, and as both, according to the new fashion for young girls, are full of serious studies (both work at

Sanskrit) it should ripen. My wife is a perfect wife, kind, wise, and unselfish. I think you were such another young girl once. She has made my life serene and full of order.

A letter Maud wrote John Quinn three days after Yeats's marriage is missing and we can only conjecture that she told him about it, and described her new flat at 265 Kings Road, Chelsea.

On December 8, she wrote again:

I am still held up in London, and longing to be among all my friends in God's own country, Ireland! I often see Arthur Symons who seems wonderfully well now and has regained something of his old brilliance. He took Iseult and me to see John's wonderful exhibition of paintings and there I heard that you had bought that splendid portrait of Symons. . . .

Willie Yeats and his wife are still in the country in Sussex. They only come to London occasionally for a day or two.

Iseult is working here as librarian at the School of Oriental Languages. She is learning Ganseril and Benjalee and seems very interested in the work. Sean is working with Ezra Pound until such time as the English Government will let him go to Ireland.

Quinn replied that he had received a letter from George Russell "telling me of W. B. Y.'s marriage, and saying you had liked her."

Maud celebrated her fifty-second birthday by giving two consecutive talks in London, under the auspices of the Workers' Suffrage Federation, on "Sinn Fein Ideals and Personalities." Sylvia Pankhurst was in the chair on both occasions. The indomitable suffragist leader was only a month away from the realization of her dreams. The act granting Englishwomen over thirty the right to vote was passed on January 10, 1918.

According to the *Irish Citizen*, Maud held her audience spellbound with her attack on the British government for refusing to allow her son to visit Ireland and stand beside his father's nameless grave; with her declaration that the Easter Rising and the Irish rejection of conscription proved that "in spite of shallow politicians Ireland is still determined to become a nation"; and her eyewitness account of the horrors of war in France. Maud lauded Francis Sheehy-Skeffington and James Connolly as the modern type of patriot, as exponents of a new definition of freedom which embraced the emancipation of women, the struggle to solve social problems, the improvement of conditions for workers, and the feeding of school children. The reporter commented that Ireland "leads the way in a true conception of Freedom as once it led in Education and Religion."

By combining a concern for children with a demand for national freedom, Maud herself fit into the definition of a modern patriot. When she learned in the fall of 1919 that the newly established St. Ultan's Hospital for Children was starting to use goat's milk for its patients, she dashed off a letter to the *Irish Citizen* urging support for this venture, pointing out the superiority of goat's milk to cow's milk (it was cheaper, and goats were less likely to have tuberculosis), and recalling that it was much used in France for delicate infants. In Paris she had often seen groups of goats being milked. The goatherd would play on pipes to attract attention, whereupon women would hurry out with jugs to fetch the fresh, warm milk for their babies. "Would it not be possible to arrange something of this sort in Dublin?" Maud asked.

In the December 1919 issue of the same magazine, Madame MacBride commented on a discussion that had appeared in a Dublin newspaper concerning the advisability of putting child street beggers into reformatories. Maud thought the idea was "criminal." She could never forget the convulsive sobbing of two little girls who were being admitted to the Bridewell for seeking charity while she was waiting for transportation to Arbour Hill Military Prison.

As a mother, if I had not food to give to my child, I would prefer to defy the law and keep it in bed or let it wander free in the streets where it would have the chance of getting food given to it—than to send it weak from hunger into a crowded class room where medical inspection is not allowed and the rules of hygiene ill observed, and proper meals not provided.

She expressed the hope that it would be possible to establish in Ireland Day Industrial Schools similar to those in England which provided two meals a day, playgrounds, baths, medical inspections, and at least half a pint of milk per pupil per day. From a national point of view, she thought, "no money is so well spent as money on the mental and physical development of the children and of making their school life attractive."

She condemned at the same time the continued use of corporal punishment in Irish schools. "Schools should be run by attraction, not by compulsion"; a teacher in France or Germany "who could not keep order without resort to physical force would be dismissed."

She tied it all together in her last paragraph. If schools were better, and there was more employment in Ireland—both would be true if Ireland were free—then children would not be on the streets begging for food. To punish such "innocent victims of foreign rule" by putting them into a reformatory was "an outrage to humanity."

By this time Maud's limited stock of patience was exhausted. She decided that she would get to Ireland no matter what laws she broke. Using the knowledge of make-up and disguise gained in her brief stage career, she donned a short tweed dress and red hat, put rouge on her cheeks and cushions in strategic areas, and transformed herself from the stately Maud Gonne to a buxom, middle-class matron. With her son Sean beside her, she took in succession the train to the English port of Holyhead, the boat across the Irish Sea, and the train to Dublin. Coming out of Westland Row station, she saw Helena Molony waiting for her, according to plan, but she did not stop for fear of detectives. She passed her friend, noted with pleasure that she did not penetrate the disguise, and proceeded to the home of Dr. Kathleen Lynn, who had acted as medical officer with the rebel battalion at St. Stephen's Green during the Easter Rising. When Helena arrived at Dr. Lynn's, saying that Maeve (Maud's pseudonym in the Daughters of Erin) must have failed to make good her escape, Maud was already removing her rouge.

Dublin Castle knew immediately when Maud bought a house at 73 St. Stephen's Green, but wisely left her alone. She, too, was ready to observe a truce. She needed time to furnish the house she had moved into—and to mourn the death of Lucien Millevoye, who died in Paris of pulmonary congestion on March 25, 1918. At the age of sixty-seven he was still a Deputy from the 16th Arrondissement of Paris, as well as chairman of the French army's committee on aviation and editor of *La Patrie*. The resonant obituary in *Le Gaulois* lauded him for his patriotism and mentioned the death in battle the previous year of his son Henri.

It is difficult to measure the depth of Maud's grief at Lucien's death, for she always tried to make it seem that public affairs were her sole concern. It is reasonable to assume, however, that she was shaken; Lucien, after all, had been her first and most enduring love. This assumption is strengthened by the fact that among the family photographs there are two of Millevoye, and one that is probably of Maud's first child by him. It took effort and care to preserve these pictures through numerous changes of residence, not only from city to city but from nation to nation. In the process, many of Yeats's letters were lost—but not these photographs.

Maud's desire for a truce with the British government was frustrated by a wave of great political change. The policies of those Irish nationalists who sought Home Rule by peaceful means had been discredited by uncertainty as to when it would be made effective, and by the certainty that northern Ireland would have no part in it; many of their leaders, indignant at having been unjustly jailed after the Rising, now accepted physical-force doctrines. As a consequence, the political and military wings of the extremists were joined in October and November of 1917 when Eamon de Valera became both president of Sinn Fein (Arthur Griffith graciously accepted the vice-presidency) and commander of the Irish Volunteers. Several by-elections showed the way the wind was blowing.

Lloyd George, prime minister, missed their significance completely. Concerned solely with the need for more manpower, he obtained passage on April 16, 1918 of a bill that would make conscription applicable in Ireland. All the country rose in anger. Within a week the Irish parliamentarians had left Westminster in protest, two million Irish had signed a declaration to resist conscription, and a one-day general strike was held.

The prime minister, alarmed by the fury he had released, now listened to advice—but it was bad. Henry Duke, chief secretary for Ireland, urged that all known nationalist leaders be taken into custody. It was obvious, he said, that they were conspiring with the German government, which had declared that it would support Ireland's claims at any peace conference following the war's end. In addition, an Irishman had been picked up bearing a message from Germany to Sinn Fein leaders. The British were repeating the error they had made in evaluating the 1916 Rising; because they themselves were locked in a death embrace with the Germans, they assumed that everyone else was involved. They could not believe that two separate wars were in effect.

The swoop started the night of May 17, 1918, and within a few days seventy-three prominent Sinn Fein leaders had been arrested and deported. Among them were Arthur Griffith, de Valera, William Cosgrave, and Constance Markievicz. The most unfortunate one was Maud's brother-in-law, Joseph, who for the third time in two years was arrested, deported, and imprisoned without trial. Arthur Griffith wrote from Gloucester Prison in July, "He is the oldest of the prisoners here, and the confinement is visibly affecting him." On July 3 all major patriotic organizations were proscribed: Sinn Fein organizations and clubs, Irish Volunteers, Cumann na mBan, and the Gaelic League. By December 1918 over five hundred persons had been arrested.

Though Maud Gonne had not been back in Ireland long enough to take any part in politics, it was inevitable that she should be one of the first picked up. She was on every Dublin Castle list, and her home was the last one that Constance Markievicz had visited before her own arrest.

On Sunday evening, May 19, 1918, Maud dined with the George Russells at 70 Rathgar Avenue. She was returning to her own home on St. Stephen's Green with Sean, now fourteen, and Joseph King, an M.P. who was investigating conditions in Dublin, when four detectives surrounded the group and unceremoniously hustled Maud into a police van. Through the barred window she could see her son running after it.

Maud spent the night at the Bridewell, and the following day was transferred to Arbour Hill Military Prison, where she had the honor of being the first woman to be held prisoner there, a fact that should have pleased all her military relatives but probably didn't. Then, escorted by a British officer, "pleasant enough but officious," Maud was taken to England and incarcerated in Holloway Prison. She was not told why she had been arrested; no charges were preferred against her; and it was many days before she learned about the "German plot" in which she was supposed to be involved.

In the same prison with Maud were Constance Markievicz, Mrs. Hanna Sheehy-Skeffington, and Mrs. Kathleen Clarke, widow of Tom Clarke, a leader of the Irish Republic that had been proclaimed on the steps of the Government Post Office on that fateful Easter Monday of 1916. The one worst off was Mrs. Clarke, who was ill, had trouble downing her food, and was worried about the fate of her five children.

But the person who took imprisonment the hardest was Maud Gonne—an ironic circumstance for one who had so often and so blithely told Irish peasants that jail was preferable to starvation. She had many reasons for discomfort and anxiety. She could not forget the sight of her son running after the Black Maria that took her away. She was not permitted to write checks so that he could be provided for. She could not receive letters, and she refused to receive visitors unless she was permitted to talk politics with them. Since her fellow prisoners were resolved not to request that special meals be purchased and sent in, she did the same. But it was the *experience* of imprisonment that was traumatic, the condition of being locked in day and night, of being unable to go and do what she pleased when she pleased. It was a new and shocking sensation to her hawklike nature, and she never forgot it. It was those months in Holloway Jail that fueled, for the rest of her life, the conviction and intensity that she brought to her campaign for releasing, or at least making more comfortable, all political prisoners.

The only solace was that she and Constance Markievicz were permitted to receive potted plants. Because the plants languished if kept always in the cells, they took their prized patches of color to the exercise yard on alternate days and left them there overnight. For further color, they sometimes hung bright swatches of cloth on the pots.

The psychological and physical punishment proved too much for Maud. After five months of imprisonment, she was so seriously ill that on October 21, Dr. F. W. Tunnicliffe of King's College Hospital was summoned to Holloway Prison to examine her. He reported that she had been suffering from intermittent fever (101.4 degrees at night to 97 in the morning) and from loss of weight, and that she had a marked family history of pulmonary tuberculosis. There were remains, he said, of pulmonary disease at the apex of her right lung, certainly tubercular in nature, and at the base of her left lung, indicating partial collapse of the left lower lobe with thickened pleura. The report concluded:

In my opinion Mrs. MacBride's condition at the present time is due to recrudescence of her former pulmonary tuberculosis. . . . If the disease is to be arrested she requires active medical and open air treatment in a suitable climate, without delay.

First to hear the distressing news was Iseult Gonne. But, since she was living with the Ezra Pounds in Kensington while her mother was in jail, it was Ezra who communicated the information to W. B. Yeats and John Quinn. Yeats, as it happened, was living with his bride at Maud's home on St. Stephen's Green, for when she had learned that he was looking for lodgings in Dublin so that his first child might be born in Ireland, she had offered him her house at a nominal rent.

Yeats and Quinn swiftly notified every important person they knew of the danger to Maud Gonne's life. By November 7 Quinn had been informed by the British War Mission in New York City that her health was not as bad as reported, that she was out of prison, and could enter any sanitarium in England—but not elsewhere: "Chief Secretary has endeavoured to get her permission to travel either to France or Switzerland but objections made by both countries." On November 8 Quinn transmitted this information to Iseult Gonne, together with an offer of 50 to 100 pounds to facilitate a trip for Maud to Switzerland or elsewhere. In the same letter he told Iseult that he had noticed her pieces in the *English Review:* a poem, "The Shadow of Noon" (April 1918), and a one-page imaginative essay, "Landscape" (June 1918). Both of these melancholy and fanciful pieces lack the precision of language and thought that had become a fixed characteristic of the work of the man she was obviously imitating, W. B. Yeats.

On November 12 Quinn received a cable from Pound saying that Maud was indeed out of prison but, "Fanatic desire to return to Ireland most undesirable." Quinn cabled back, "Please impress Madame Gonne my strong conviction climate Ireland wholly unsuitable her condition." When Ezra Pound showed her this cable, the result was "Peals of laughter from that unfortunate female."

By this time Maud had left—unopposed—the nursing home in London where she had stayed five days, and was again demanding clearance for Ireland. It was not a place, Pound thought, to be "considered a health resort for consumptives." She was staying at Yeats's flat in the Woburn Buildings with Iseult and the "gnome-like" old cook, Josephine Pillon, who had served her in Normandy. A glimpse of Maud's appearance, her mood, and her relations with Iseult is given by Brigit Patmore, who visited the family at this hectic time. Born in Ireland of landed Ulster gentry, Brigit moved freely in London literary circles of the early 1900s after her marriage to the grandson of the famous Victorian poet, Coventry Patmore. Maud, she wrote,

could not have been old, but who knows what political passions and frustrations had lined her face and drained beauty from the chalice?

Maud paced up and down the room in a kind of distraught dream. With characteristic generous hospitality Iseult had bought cutlets (not easy to find in those days).... Once she turned to Maud and said, "Take off your hat, darling."

Her mother took it off absent-mindedly and Iseult said to me, "The shape of her head is lovely, isn't it?"

On another page Brigit accurately observes that Yeats's "apparent ease and calm covered an absurd diffidence and shyness"; and he "was used to women who were not aggressive but strong and full of confidence ... like Maud and Iseult Gonne" and his wife George.

Ezra Pound, because he was as inclined to extreme opinions as Maud, and because he was unaware of how much British propaganda he had absorbed, found it easy to condemn her and all her works. In a letter to John Quinn written four days after the end of World War I, Pound declared that the Easter Rising had been an attempt to stab the allies in the back; that the arrest of Maud and others was to prevent the rebels from making another try, already organized, during the spring military offensive; that Maud was not arrested because of charges that she was implicated in a German plot. He told Quinn that she was released solely on grounds of ill health, not because of pressure or in the belief "that she was a safe person to be at large or in Ireland." What made her case worse was that she had gone to Ireland without a permit, in disguise and during wartime. He thought that the Abbey Theatre and the works of Yeats, Synge, and others had created a broad sympathy for Ireland which the revolutionaries had dissipated.

> I give it up. M. G. seems as able to ignore facts in politics as W. B. Y. does when it comes to evidence of psychic phenomena. . . .
>
> Seagan [Sean] was quite intelligent when she brought him from France, but the months in Ireland have ruined his mind and left him, as might be expected at his age, doomed to political futilities. . . .
>
> She is still full of admiration for Lenin. . . . The sum of it is that I am glad she is out of gaol, and that I hope no one will be ass enough to let her get to Ireland.

On November 23, 1918 Maud boarded a boat for Ireland and got to her home at 73 St. Stephen's Green without trouble. On December 2 Ezra Pound informed Quinn that he had just received a note from Iseult saying that she "had fixed it up with the Lord Mayor and Maud is to be left in peace."

A rather different picture of Maud's condition in jail and of how she left it appears in the account she gave thirty years later to feature writer J. Doran O'Reilly. In this version, the imprisoned Irishwoman rejects offers to bring her meals from outside because "I am now the unwilling guest of the English Government. They brought me here by force, let them support me." She wants to go on a hunger strike in order to force her way out but abandons the idea when Constance Markievicz and Kathleen Clarke, in a spirit of solidarity, insist on joining her. So this gallant patriot, who has long been interested in the power of the spirit to control the body, and has conducted experiments in the area with her distinguished friend W. B. Yeats, now uses it to reduce her weight. Actually, she is eating as much food as ever. When she becomes almost a skeleton, the prison doctor orders her to be removed to a nursing home. Since it is not attached to the prison, her son Sean can visit her freely. Together they plan her escape to Ireland. Maud goes to early mass one morning and meets there, by prearrangement, an Irish girl who is employed as a maid in the home of a friend. When the maid goes home for a holiday, Maud, posing as her old grandmother, accompanies her. The deed is accomplished.

Maud's impatience to return to Ireland had awkward consequences. When she knocked on the door of her own home, Yeats felt it necessary to refuse admission. His wife was seven months pregnant, had recently undergone a severe attack of influenza, and now was suffering from pneumonia. It was no time, he argued, to admit an unexpected guest who might bring down upon them police raids, searches, and confusion.

The discussion between the two friends was difficult, almost acrimonious. Yeats did not tell his wife that he had turned Maud away, but promptly found another home. By Christmas 1918 Maud was back at 73 St. Stephen's Green.

Anne Butler Yeats was born on February 26, 1919. On that day Yeats began writing a poem, "A Prayer for My Daughter," in which he repeated the fear of the future he had expressed a month before in "The Second Coming":

> Things fall apart; the centre cannot hold;
> Mere anarchy is loosed upon the world,

> The blood-dimmed tide is loosed, and everywhere
> The ceremony of innocence is drowned;
> The best lack all conviction, while the worst
> Are full of passionate intensity.

In this new poem he prayed that his daughter might be beautiful but not so beautiful as "to make a stranger's eye distraught" or hinder her from making friends. He hoped that she would learn in school "light-hearted courtesy," live "Rooted in one dear perpetual place," and never succumb to the kind of hatred to which Maud Gonne and Constance Markievicz had been prone.

> An intellectual hatred is the worst,
> So let her think opinions are accursed.
> Have I not seen the loveliest woman born
> Out of the mouth of Plenty's horn,
> Because of her opinionated mind
> Barter that horn and every good
> By quiet natures understood
> For an old bellows full of angry wind?

He concluded with the hope that the man his daughter married would bring her to a home

> Where all's accustomed, ceremonious;
> For arrogance and hatred are the wares
> Peddled in the thoroughfares.
> How but in custom and in ceremony
> Are innocence and beauty born?

The poet who had sympathized with the Irish peasantry in the 1890s and with the Dublin working masses in the great industrial struggle of 1913 had apparently forgotten that the kind of "arrogance and hatred" peddled in the streets was often less potent and vicious than the kind distilled in the Big Houses of the world.

It would also seem that, with this poem, W. B. Yeats had said everything he had to say about "Mad" Gonne. It would not be true. Though less than before, she continued to delight and torment his inner vision.

CHAPTER XX

The Troubles (1919–1922)

𝕴 In February 1919, only eleven months after the death of Lucien Millevoye, Maud Gonne received a second blow—the death of her fifty-year-old sister, Kathleen Pilcher, who had spent her last weary and lonely years in a Swiss pension. In the same year, Kathleen's former husband, Major General T. D. Pilcher, retired from military service and began writing such books as *Lessons from the Boer War* and *A General's Letters to His Son*.

It was a period when it seemed that men like General Pilcher would never again be in power. In the Communist whirlwind sweeping from the steppes of Russia, many decent and intelligent persons saw intimations of a world in which generals, admirals, and other militarists would no longer be permitted to practice their profession. Iseult was not one of these, but she did tell W. B. Yeats something she had heard from George Russell: that the Bolsheviks had executed only four hundred people in their drive for power.

An indignant Yeats wrote directly to Russell, quoting a Labor Party M.P. who had said that the present Russian government was worse than the former autocracy, that the Marxist system of values was "the spear-head of materialism," and led inevitably to murder. He told Russell that he hoped Ireland, "despite its lunatic faculty of going against everything which it believes England to affirm," would resist any tendency to accept the Marxist revolution. "Do you ever remember a European question on which Ireland did not at once take the opposite side to England? Well, that kills all thought and encourages the most miserable kind of mob rhetoric."

But in Ireland it was not the Communists but the Sinn Feiners who seemed to threaten destruction of the established order. In the elections of December 14, 1918, Sinn Fein ran boldly on the issue of an Irish Republic entirely disconnected from England, and swept the Home Rule party out of existence, taking seventy-three seats in the House of Commons—seats which it was pledged not to occupy—while the Irish Parliamentary Party took only seven.

A new and independent Irish parliament, called Dail Eireann (Assembly of Ireland), was established. When it convened on January 21, 1919, only twenty-four members were present; the others were in jail or in hiding. The score was somewhat better at the second session, held on April 1; fifty-two members were present, and Eamon de Valera was elected president. Cabinet seats in the underground government were filled by Arthur Griffith, Cathal Brugha, Count George Plunkett, Eoin MacNeill, Michael Collins, and William Cosgrave. Countess Markievicz was named secretary of labor, and thus became the first woman cabinet minister in any Western European government.

Maud Gonne MacBride seems not to have been considered for any office. Though everyone recognized the strength of her patriotism, there were still uneasy feelings about her break with John MacBride, the legitimacy of her children, and the fact that she had only recently returned to Ireland.

Looking on the officeholders as instigators of sedition and treason, the British government in the summer of 1919 found and again jailed Constance Markievicz. According to

Elizabeth Coxhead, Maud Gonne visited Constance in prison, taking with her an automatic pistol concealed in a bouquet of flowers, "a gesture fairly common among those visiting prisoners at the period." Apparently too common, for the authorities found the pistol and confiscated it. Maud attended the trial of the Countess on December 2–3, 1920. The charge was that of organizing the Fianna na hEireann, the Irish boy scouts, back in 1909. Constance was found guilty and spent the next eighteen months in Mountjoy prison studying Gaelic and gardening.

For many years George Russell's Sunday evenings were a great attraction to young Dublin artists and writers. In the winter of 1918–19, a young man named Henry Francis Montgomery Stuart was brought to one of them by a Trinity College Fellow who was tutoring him for admission to the school.

Francis Stuart was six feet tall, incredibly handsome, a would-be poet, with a head full of Celtic visions. His family on both sides were Scottish Presbyterian, natives of County Antrim, in the ancient province of Ulster.

Francis was born in Australia on April 29, 1902. When his father, who ran a sheep station, died four months later, his mother returned to Ireland, bringing him and his English nurse to live with her unmarried sister, Janet Montgomery, in County Meath, about thirty miles from Dublin. Francis Stuart's love for this nurse and his aunt, the only serious reader and Irish nationalist in the entire clan, were the only bright spots in a difficult childhood. From 1912 to 1915 he attended three different preparatory schools in England, and in 1916 entered Rugby. His problems were always the same: academic difficulties compounded by apathy and inattention.

At Russell's home, Francis Stuart saw Iseult Gonne for the first time, and was deeply impressed by her beauty. In fact, until the following day, he thought she was the famed

Maud Gonne. The next time he saw Iseult, it was at one of Maud's Tuesday evenings. He found the "tall girl in a sky-blue dress with a tasselled shawl" who met him at the door undeniably attractive. But her mother, he thought, was "oblivious" of nonentities and "effusive" toward important people.

Francis and Iseult met again at a cottage in Glenmalure, in County Wicklow, which Maud had recently purchased for Iseult with funds from the sale of Les Mouettes. At that meeting Francis was with a young British officer, his companion on a walking tour of the area. On the following day he returned alone and handed Iseult a book of Yeats's poems that he carried with him. Iseult read out loud some poems she had heard Yeats chanting while in the process of composing them.

Within a few months Iseult and Francis decided to live together. They would rather have married but saw little hope of obtaining family consent. The Montgomerys, all staunch Protestant unionists, were unlikely to sanction Francis's marriage to a Catholic of equivocal birth who was related to a notorious Irish nationalist; it was equally certain that Maud Gonne would not want to see her twenty-four-year-old daughter marry a seventeen-year-old would-be poet.

The lovers took things in hand. On January 4, 1920, leaving Ireland by different routes, they went to London and rented a flat over a grocery store on a narrow lane off Tottenham Court Road. During the next three months they received several letters from Helena Molony, speaking for Maud Gonne, that convinced them that it would be prudent to marry. They returned, Francis received a smattering of instruction in the Roman Catholic faith, and in April 1920 they were married in University Church, only a few doors away from Maud's home on St. Stephen's Green.

Iseult became pregnant the following summer. In January 1921 Francis went to London to sell a jewel that his family had given her as a wedding present. The trip was sensible, for he could get a better price in England than in Ireland, but staying two months in London was not. After sending back most of the money obtained from the sale, he spent this time in witless and futile pursuit of a Russian ballerina.

Francis Stuart took little interest in baby Dolores when she was born in March 1921, and even failed to attend her christening. When she sickened and died the following July, he still paid no attention; he seemed completely engrossed in republican politics and his motor bike. It is easy to deduce that these interests were largely attempts to escape discomforts of his situation and to blur the realization that he was too immature to handle the responsibilities of marriage. He was shocked when Iseult confessed that her relationship with Ezra Pound had been more than friendly. He was bothered by his poverty, by Iseult's reliance on her mother for advice and assistance, by the constant card playing and cigarette smoking in which mother and daughter indulged, by the rigidity of the Church he had joined. In *Black List: Section H*, the longest of Stuart's autobiographical novels, he wrote that the young married couple was

hemmed in on all sides, by his mother-in-law and her wide circle of admiring acquaintances (one of whom . . . lived in the same house and, he imagined, made her reports), by the curfew lately imposed on the city, and by some of their own habits such as the card playing and Iseult's general neglect of the flat, which he occasionally tried to straighten out in her absence.

Aware that Francis and Iseult were having marital difficulties and that Iseult was not adjusting to the loss of her child, Maud took them abroad with her in late August to hear some Wagner at the newly built Munich opera house. She returned in a month, but the other two stayed away much longer, visiting Nuremberg, Dresden, Prague, and Vienna.

During the trip, Iseult Gonne Stuart wrote some revealing lines in her notebook. Sensitive, impractical, aesthetic, insecure, guilt-ridden, constantly striving for perfection, she wrote in November 1922: "I renounce smoking entirely for 9 days, and handling cards entirely and letter games entirely. I make vow for 9 days to bring to mind and accomplish as closely as can be all duties big or small, inward or external and to have an outward serene manner." The following January, less than three years after her marriage, she wrote: "Somehow . . . I think of us both as moths who had loved each other on the flowers of the roadside, flowers tarnished by dust, then the wind rose and we were whirled in clouds of dust each a different way." Iseult was pre-Raphaelite in more than appearance.

A good many persons besides Francis Stuart dedicated themselves to the illegal, infant Irish Republic. By the middle of 1920 it was operating a land bank, land arbitration courts, labor arbitration boards, and an industrial commission. A government loan of £250,000 had been oversubscribed, and, thanks to the Republic's influence, few men were seeking service in the Royal Irish Constabulary. To maintain law and order, the British government recruited ex-soldiers who were too unruly or incompetent for humdrum civilian jobs—the infamous Black and Tans, so called because they wore army khaki and black leather belts.

Guerrilla warfare was encouraged by such events as the death on October 25, 1920 of Terence MacSwiney, lord mayor of Cork, after a seventy-four-day hunger strike, and the hanging, the day after the burial, of Kevin Barry, an eighteen-year-old medical student who had participated in the ambush of some British soldiers.

The British fought hard to maintain control of the country. Near midnight on September 26, 1920, a British patrol stopped a car going through Rathmines, and ordered the passengers out. The driver was sixteen-year-old Sean Mac-Bride. The others were Constance Markievicz and Maurice

Bourgeois, French writer, translator of Synge, and secret agent for the French government. The three were taken to the city prison. On the following day the British military and police entered Maud's flat in her absence and ransacked the rooms. They did not look for the owner and released Sean soon afterward, but Madame MacBride (as she was now generally called) was not grateful. For years afterward she fumed about the atrocious treatment of her possessions.

Sometime in 1920, Maud Gonne met an extraordinary woman, then seventy-six years old, named Charlotte Despard. She was the sister of Sir John French, who had become lord lieutenant (viceroy) of Ireland in 1918 and, as such, had been active in rounding up the Sinn Fein leaders who opposed conscription.

Charlotte was a wealthy middle-aged widow of a British colonel when she first entered public life. This occurred in the 1890s after a visit to a large London workhouse where the callous neglect of the inmates so enraged her that she ran for the office of Poor Law Guardian at Kingstown in Surrey. As such she became familiar with the problems of the poor, and on friendly terms with the Social Democratic Federation and the Independent Labor Party. She spoke with James Connolly on a platform in Edinburgh, joined Emmeline Pankhurst's militant suffragette movement, helped to found the Women's Freedom League, and adopted the pacifist and Socialist ideas of her friend George Bernard Shaw. Imprisoned four times for her activities, she became an abomination to the middle-class and upper-class families of England. Mrs. Vera Ryder, who lived near Mrs. Despard's home, recalls in her description of her Edwardian childhood* that whenever she and her nanny passed Mrs. Despard's little house, they would hurry along

as though it were a fever hospital with germs jumping out of it.... If, as occasionally happened, we met Mrs. Despard on the road and there

*See bibliography.

could be no turning back, nannie put on her most disapproving expression... and dragged us past as fast as we could go. From surreptitious glances beneath lowered eyes we were agreeably surprised at the witch's appearance. She had shining white hair which shone through a flowing black chiffon veil and sandalled feet peeped from beneath long voluminous black skirts; really most attractive for a witch....

As early as 1909, Charlotte Despard had shown an interest in Irish affairs and on November 19, 1913, at the height of the Dublin labor struggle, she was one of the speakers at a huge mass meeting held in the Royal Albert Hall, London, to raise support for the strikers. Other speakers were G. B. Shaw, labor leader Ben Tillett, James Connolly, and Miss Sylvia Pankhurst.

After the 1916 Rising, Mrs. Despard joined in efforts to improve conditions for the Irish rebels in English jails. A few years later, when she went to live permanently in Ireland, it was inevitable that she and Maud Gonne should become staunch friends. Both were firebrands, advocates of direct action, and rebels against the Establishment in which they had been born and raised. Both believed in a republican goal for Ireland, and both sought to aid political prisoners and their families. Mrs. Despard became a frequent visitor to 73 St. Stephen's Green and eventually made it her home.

Together, the two women toured various areas in the south of Ireland where the British had imposed martial law. Maud wrote John Quinn on February 21, 1921,

The English may batter us to pieces but they will never succeed in breaking our spirit.... Mrs. Despard is a most remarkable woman and intensely Irish in feeling....
... with her I was able to visit places I should never have been able to get to alone, in the martial law areas. It is amusing to see the puzzled expressions on the faces of the officers and of the Black and Tans, who continually held up our car, when Mrs. Despard said she was the Viceroy's sister.

Conditions in Dublin city, she said, were equally bad.

Hardly a night passes that one is not woke up by the sound of firing.... One night last week there was such a terrible fusillade just outside our house, that we all got up thinking something terrible was happening. That morning, when curfew regulations permitted us to go out, we only found the bodies of a cat and dog riddled with bullets....

Sean is working at his law course in the National University. There again it is hard for boys to work, with raids and arrests among the students going on continually.... One quiet boy of 17, a divinity student, Lawlor, was beaten to death by the Black and Tans.

Maud enclosed an article which she hoped Quinn could get published in some U.S. newspaper. She wondered if he could find one that would hire her to write such articles on a regular basis, for she needed the money. Owing to the present rate of exchange for the French franc, "I am almost ruined."

Her article, titled "Devastation," opened with the assertion that "Devastation is England's trade mark in Ireland, broken masonry her contribution to civilisation." The heart of the article was a description of the sacking by British soldiers of Cullinswood House, "a beautiful old 18th century house where Patrick Pearse made his first great educational experiment." Pearse's "saintly mother" had turned it into an apartment house which was the chief source of income for her and her two daughters. With Mrs. Despard and a correspondent from Le Temps, Maud went to see "this incredible manifestation" of English civilization. Soldiers were

engaged in sacking the house. We could see them on the roof working with pickaxes, and from a distance could hear the crashing of the broken masonry as the chimney stacks fell to the ground. Inside the now frameless windows one could see khaki-clad figures with picks and crowbars working at destruction like maniacs. Others were seated on windows....

Maud saw a tenant, the widow of an Indian civil servant, talking with an officer.

She was greatly distressed at the wreckage of her home and furniture. The officer said the destruction was justified by what they had found in the house when they raided the evening before . . . they had found a revolver. . . . Mrs. S. said she certainly had nothing seditious in her flat. The officer shrugged his shoulders and said he "was sorry but she should not live in such a rotten house. . . ."

Quinn sent the article to literary agent Curtis Brown, who regretted that he could find no market for it.

Such destruction, of which both British and Republican forces were guilty, was taking place throughout all of Ireland. The sight of it impelled Maud to write to Arthur Griffith, pointing out the urgent need for an organization that could cope with the resulting human deprivations. Griffith responded to her plea, and doubtless to the pleas of others, by asking the women of Ireland to form the Irish White Cross. Most of the funds it collected were raised in the United States. Shiploads of food and clothing were also dispatched.

This was the sort of work that Maud, a member of the executive committee, was interested and experienced in— rebuilding burned down homes and keeping the children of political prisoners fed and clothed. Her instinctive approach to such problems was always personal, never really organizational. When Mrs. Desmond Fitzgerald asked for help in getting permission to visit her husband in Arbour Hill military prison, Maud wrote not to an official but to W. B. Yeats. He pulled the proper strings with his customary alacrity. In her letter of March 21 thanking him, Maud mentioned that she had been to the Abbey Theatre on St. Patrick's Day and had seen Lady Gregory's *Aristotle's Bellows*—"a charming fantastic little play," and spoke of her concern for "my Sean as the raids and arrests of every day particularly of students is going on worse than ever. . . . He got through his law exams very creditably . . . one of the first four." She did not forget to send her love to Mrs. Yeats.

The tradition that Maud Gonne's home was a refuge for anybody on the run or in need of financial help began about this time. One of the earliest persons to take advantage of it was Eithne Coyle (now Mrs. O'Donnell). On the evening of Halloween 1921, Eithne slipped out of Mountjoy Prison with several others, slithered over a wall, and eventually took refuge at 73 St. Stephen's Green.

"Maud gave us a big welcome," Eithne has written this biographer. "She saw the report of our escape in the papers and was wondering how she could contact us. She was a charming hostess and she put her beautiful house at our disposal." Another visitor, Constance Markievicz, gave Eithne a five-pound note to tide her over until she could communicate with her relatives. Everyone was kind and friendly, with the exception of a caged black monkey on the ground floor who snarled and spit at Eithne every time she passed.

In 1921 the Dail Eireann sent a delegation, headed by Arthur Griffith, to work out a peace treaty in London with Lloyd George's government. The treaty, signed in December 1921, provided that an Irish Free State should be established with dominion status, that Britain should retain control of three naval bases, that Northern Ireland should have the right to opt out of the new state (its parliament in Belfast promptly did), and that a commission should be set up to adjust the existing borders in accordance with the wishes of the inhabitants. It was also specified that members of the Free State government would have to swear allegiance to the Crown. The majority of Irishmen were tired of the Black and Tan atrocities and favored ratification. So did the Dail, by a vote of 64 to 57. De Valera did not, and resigned the presidency. He was succeeded by Arthur Griffith.

Joesph Holloway took time off from reviewing Dublin plays in his diary to write a friend that the peace treaty was

only a makeshift and settles nothing. By it, Ireland is as far off as ever from the freedom she has longed through centuries for. It is generally accepted that it was signed to avoid the further assassination by the

foreign savage brutes who hold a strangle hold on our beloved land, and
not by the delegates' free will. . . .

The same opinion was held by almost all women
nationalists. Their umbrella organization, the Cumann na
mBan, met on February 5, 1922 and rejected the treaty by a
vote of 419 to 63. All the women who held seats in the Dail
Eireann, including Mrs. Margaret Pearse, Mrs. Tom
Clarke, and Countess Markievicz, spoke against ratification.

Maud took the opposite stand. She thought the treaty
was a great improvement upon Home Rule and a stepping
stone to complete independence. This was flatly asserted
by her son, Sean MacBride, only a few years ago in a signed
letter that appeared in the *Irish Sunday Independent*, February 3, 1974. His testimony helps to correct the impression one might get from Maud's autobiographical writings
and speeches that she never sympathized with the Free
State. In fact, at about this time she accepted an assignment
from Arthur Griffith to go to France as a public relations
agent for the Free State. She obviously thought that a Free
State victory would end the wave of outrages and assassinations that had been going on and prevent a long and sagui-
nary civil war. At the same time she tried to conciliate the
bitter-end Republicans by publicizing evidence given her
by de Valera and others describing atrocities that were
being committed against Catholics in the North.

Maud was in Paris on January 17, 1922 when a huge Irish
Race Congress was held there. She found the opening reception somewhat out of tune with the assembly's mission,
which was to gather moral and financial help for the young
state from all the Irish people scattered throughout the
world. She was particularly irked by seeing the Duke of
Tetuan sitting on a raised throne on a red-draped dais.
Though a lineal descendant of the patriot who had left
Ireland in 1601, he knew nothing about Ireland except that
it was a good place to buy horses. Many of her old friends,

among them W. B. Yeats, Douglas Hyde, Constance Markievicz, and Eamon de Valera, were at the congress. But
she was glad to get away from the festivities and political
intriguing to return to Ireland.

Once there, at the request of the Irish Republican Army,
she began to cope with the problems of feeding and housing
a large number of Catholic refugees from the North. The
IRA had put them in Fowler Hall, Parnell Square, which
was owned by an Orange order and empty except for some
office furniture. Since the most pressing need was for beds,
Maud called on Arthur Griffith to ask him to move some in
from evacuated British barracks. Griffith, looking ill and
harassed, was unresponsive. He said that the IRA was not
the government and had no right to bring in refugees from
the North. Maud replied that the refugees had come of
their own volition, like those whom the French government
had housed in public buildings in Paris in 1914.

Griffith then objected that Fowler Hall was not a suitable
place. "What place," Maud asked him, "could be more suitable than the property of an Orange institution to house its
victims?"

Griffith's final argument was that the IRA was simply
looking for trouble. The first object of his government was
to establish order; only when that came about would Lloyd
George permit a plebescite in the North. Maud got nowhere
by answering that the problem was one of humanity, not
politics.

A few days later she talked with Michael Collins, who
had won a great reputation fighting the Black and Tans, but
was now supporting ratification of the treaty with England.
He urged her to encourage Catholics to remain in Ulster.
"They have to hold their own corner there until we can get
the plebiscite which we were promised in London. We
know that so many will vote themselves into the Free State
that it will make a separate government in the North impossible. What the White Cross should do is build houses for

the people whose homes have been destroyed in the po-grom."*

The outbreak of full-scale hostilities between the Free Staters and the Irish Republican Army was inevitable. On June 28, 1922, Michael Collins and his Free Staters attacked the IRA headquarters in the Four Courts in Dublin with field guns and shrapnel provided by the British. On the morning of June 30 the handsome Georgian building caught fire and in the afternoon the garrison of 150 men surrendered.

During the two days of shelling, Maud Gonne called on the Lord Mayor of Dublin, and was told to get together "some of the women who are not afraid and who want peace" to urge a truce at the Four Courts. She had just assembled such a group when word came of the surrender. Plans were changed, but not the objective. Half the women visited the Republicans, who proved ready for a truce, the others saw Michael Collins and Arthur Griffith, who were not. Though Griffith came personally to see Maud at the door of the council chamber, he still insisted, "We are now a government and we have to keep order." The two old friends did not meet again. Griffith's death in August 1922 helped to end any emotional attachment Maud had for the Free State.

Her son Sean and her son-in-law Francis Stuart had both anticipated her in rejecting it. In 1918, when he was fourteen, Sean had joined the Fianna na hEireann, the boy scout group founded by the Countess Markievicz; in 1920, while awaiting a raid by Black and Tans, he learned how to fire a machine gun; in 1921 he was carrying out missions for IRA general headquarters, and taking dispatches from Griffith and Collins, the treaty negotiators in London, to the Dail Eireann in Dublin.

Francis Stuart had gone to the Continent and, surpris-

*Article by Maud Gonne in *Capuchin Annual 1943*, Dublin.

ingly enough, smuggled some guns from Belgium to the
IRA. He was then sent south as a courier, but was captured
in August 1922 when he and some companions tried to steal
an armored car.

Maud, now fifty-eight, and too old to indulge in such
exploits, turned her home on St. Stephen's Green into a
makeshift hospital for wounded Republicans. Before he
was jailed, Francis Stuart helped by carrying out slop pails,
bringing up food trays, and running errands. When Mrs.
Charlotte Despard acquired Roebuck House, a spacious
Victorian mansion outside Dublin, it was not only Maud
and her menagerie that moved into it. It became a refuge for
newly released and indigent Republicans; and headquarters
of a newly founded Women's Prisoners' Defence League, of
which Madame MacBride was secretary and Mrs. Despard
was president. The organization, consisting of mothers,
wives, and sisters of political prisoners, collected food and
clothing for the prisoners and their families, and got permission for relatives to visit the jails. It arranged for children to be led to church in elaborate processions to pray for
the release of their fathers and brothers and in various other
ways it publicized prison conditions and atrocities.

Every Sunday, week after week, Maud Gonne and Mrs.
Despard, both robed in flowing black, headed a procession
of women demonstrating against the arrest and imprisonment of Republicans. The march would end on the "ruins
corner" on O'Connell Street, where the 1916 shelling had
reduced the Gresham Hotel to rubble.

When four Republican prisoners were executed, the Defence League held a protest meeting outside the home of the
Free State minister for defense. Maud tells about this tense
event in her autobiography.

The Free State soldiers were drawn up inside the railings; some shots
had been fired over our heads; a woman's hat had been pierced by a
bullet. I heard an order given and the front line of soldiers knelt down
with rifles ready—some of the young soldiers were white and trem-

bling. I got up on the parapet and smiled contempt at the officer. He had curious rather beautiful pale grey eyes and a thin brown face. We gazed at each other for a full minute. The order to fire was not given. Later I was told I was brave and had saved many lives.

This is vintage Maud Gonne.

Another Defence League tactic was to harass meetings of the Dail. On one occasion Mrs. Charlotte Despard so flagrantly interrupted a speech by the minister for home affairs that the speaker felt compelled to order her removal. The *London Times* for September 21, 1922 reported that Mrs. MacBride, seated beside her, "was also requested to leave, and as she declined to do so she was removed."

W. B. Yeats was taking an opposite path. In December 1922 he became a member of the Senate established under the Free State constitution. Many people thought it was fitting recognition for one who had done so much to bring dignity to Ireland, but his acceptance of this honor created a lasting breach with Maud. She thought he was thereby signifying his support of a state that flogged young Republican soldiers who sought only to free Ireland "from the contamination of the British Empire." She considered it an additional indignity when, at about the same time, Yeats received an honorary Doctor of Letters from that bastion of British cultural aggression, Trinity College.

The break did not come suddenly (chronology shows that Maud herself was close to the Free State position at that time) nor was it ever total, but there was a definite cooling, and the two met thereafter only at infrequent intervals.

CHAPTER XXI

In Defence of Prisoners
(1923–1929)

𝒩 IN THE EARLY 1920s the Free State government, now
headed by Griffith's successor, William T. Cosgrave, made
a vigorous effort to repress the dissidents. It banned Republican meetings and publications, proscribed such organizations as the Women's Prisoners' Defence League, and
arrested demonstrators by the hundreds. Writing to Olivia
Shakespear on January 5, 1923, W. B. Yeats thought prospects for tranquility were improving. "The irregulars are
evidently breaking up and only fighting to get a little better
terms." But even while penning this letter, he got contra-
dictory news that caused him to end it abruptly.

I cannot write any more as I have just learned that Maud Gonne has
been arrested and I must write to Iseult and offer to help with the
authorities in the matter of warm blankets. The day before her arrest
she wrote to say that if I did not denounce the Government she re-
nounced my society for ever. I am afraid my help in the matter of
blankets, instead of her release (where I could do nothing), will not
make her less resentful. She had to choose (perhaps all women must)
between broomstick and distaff and she has chosen the broomstick—I
mean the witches' hats.

As it turned out, the blankets were not needed. Maud,
described by the *London Times* as "one of the most prominent Republicans in the country," was kept overnight at
Mountjoy prison, and released the following day. The brev-

ity of her incarceration did not temper her wrath. She wrote a long letter to Max Wright of the *Daily Express* in which she said that conditions in Mountjoy were scandalous. She was "grateful to the ignorant young ape of a Free State officer" who arrested her for letting her obtain an up-to-date picture of prison conditions. She had many abuses to report.

Miss Taft, the secretary of the Prisoners' Dependents Society, a perfectly legal charitable organisation, was arrested at the same time and as unjustifiably as I was. She is still in prison. I was released because I happen to be well known abroad and in America, and Mrs. Despard hastened to make my illegal arrest known to the press. My arrest is typical of hundreds of the arrests now taking place. If anyone is in a house that is being raided and the . . . Free State officer does not happen to like his or her face he arrests at pleasure without warrant or order. The prisoner is then lodged in jail *in secret*, no communication with the outside world permitted, no solicitor allowed in, no redress possible.

There is no proper medical attendance in Mountjoy. The Doctor does not come around daily as with ordinary prisoners; he only comes when sent for and then only after long delay. . . . The overcrowding is shocking. . . . Disorder and drunkenness seem the rule of the officers, so-called guards, in Mountjoy.

There are 43 women prisoners there—two or three in every cell. The men I hear are even worse off than the women. I will be glad if you will make these facts public.

If you want to see me I will be in O'Connell Street tomorrow between 12:30 and 2 o'clock in the ruins entering names on a register of those who protest against the reprisals on defenceless prisoners.

Maud was again arrested in April, this time for twenty days. The *London Times* reported that she and three others were seized because they were planning to conduct a poster parade to protest the imprisonment of Republicans. As Maud recalled it in her conversations with O'Reilly twenty-five years later, the arrest took place because she was assembling a group of women to go to the Shelbourne Hotel and tell an emissary of the Pope who was staying there about the horrible conditions in Ireland.

In prison, she immediately went on a hunger strike, becoming thinner and weaker, but remaining good-humored. When the doctors wondered why, she said, "Why not? I'm on the winning side. If I live, I will get out and start where I left off. If not, my death will be a great blow to the Cosgrave government."

W. B. Yeats reacted as he always did. He visited Cosgrave and told him that, while Constance Markievicz seemed to thrive on imprisonment, Maud Gonne was too delicate for such treatment. Cosgrave muttered that women, doctors, and clergy had no business in politics and should stick to tending the sick. But since it was obviously impossible for any Irish government to allow the "Irish Joan of Arc" to die in jail, Maud was released.

She was borne out of prison on a stretcher and taken to Roebuck House. Within a week she was back at her accustomed indoor tasks, tending refugees, and directing projects for making jam and seashell ornaments as ways of providing work and funds for the families of political prisoners. Out of doors, Maud resumed her street-corner talks, and took part in demonstrations and vigils at prison gates.

After Republicans won thirty-four seats in the elections of August 27, 1923 and refused to take them because of the required oath of allegiance to King George, the government cracked down harder. Meetings of the Women's Prisoners' Defence League were banned, but Maud produced a portable platform and held impromptu assemblies where they were least expected. Finally the authorities gave up, feeling, as Maud put it, "those damned women make more trouble than the meetings are worth."

From those days come numerous reports of Maud's magnetism as a public speaker, how she would lead her Defence Leaguers holding a huge bouquet of flowers, "looking radiant," and filling her audience "in some strange fashion . . . with a sense of irresistible power." This language did not appear in descriptions of demonstrations published by the *London Times*. All it said when the Free State legislature met on September 19, 1923 was that a number of Republican women, including Mrs. MacBride and Mrs. Despard, marched outside with banners calling for the release of Republican prisoners. After some argument with police, "the women left Molesworth Street and transferred their attention to St. Stephen's Green, where they were allowed to 'demonstrate' in peace."

In its issue of October 23, 1923, the *Times* published a photograph of the two leading "intransigents," Mrs. Mac-Bride and Mrs. Despard, standing at the head of a demonstration. Maud, in black and carrying a large pocketbook, holds a poster reading "Freedom or the Grave. Mountjoy Prisoners on Hunger Strike for Release since October 15th."

The strike of 400 prisoners in Mountjoy spread to other prisons, and within two weeks 8,000 prisoners were involved. The last to join was Constance Markievicz, arrested again on November 20, 1923. On the same day a Republican named Dennis Barry died in Newbridge prison after going thirty-four days without food. It was the last straw. The government began releasing the prisoners; and by the end of 1923 almost all were out, including Francis Stuart in November and Constance Markievicz in December.

Stuart was not yet twenty-two. During his imprisonment a small collection of his poems, *We Have Kept the Faith*, appeared. Yeats, who may have had mixed emotions about a youth who had courted successfully where he himself had failed, recognized Stuart's talent and induced the Royal Irish Academy to award the book a prize. Francis was stunned to be visited by the famous poet and to hear "this strange and rather chilling figure with his eagle glance" discuss his work. Yeats's generous sponsorship continued. When Stuart and some of his friends founded a periodical called *To-Morrow* (it lasted only two issues), the first issue contained an editorial written by Yeats, though signed by others, and the second contained a controversial poem titled "Leda and the Swan." Iseult Stuart also contributed to each issue.

Like many other Republicans of the period, Stuart insisted on Ireland's need to be free but had little interest in the kind of political or economic structure this required. He was a Republican mainly because it provided some bond with Iseult and her mother. He was never officially a member of the Irish Republican Army, carrying a membership card only for identification in tight places. After his release from prison he settled down with Iseult in a cottage in Glencree, County Wicklow, where he meditated, read, and tried ineffectively to write more poems.

Yeats, on the other hand, was at the peak of productivity. During 1923 he published three books (memoirs, poetry, and plays) to critical acclaim; accepted the Nobel prize for literature in Stockholm; and completed a draft of *A Vision*, a philosophical work he considered his masterpiece. It describes a Great Wheel of twenty-eight incarnations that takes some two thousand years for a single revolution, and through which all persons pass. As examples of phase 16 Yeats names Blake, Rabelais, Aretino, Paracelsus, and Maud Gonne. According to his theory, if such individuals subordinate their intellect "to the *Body of Fate*, all the cruelty and narrowness of that intellect are displayed in service of preposterous purpose after purpose till there is nothing left but the fixed idea and some hysterical hatred." He includes in this category beautiful women who "walk like queens" and who "are gentle only to those whom they have chosen or subdued, or to the dogs that follow at their heels . . . perhaps if the body have great perfection, there is always something imperfect in the mind, some rejection or inadequacy of *Mask:* Venus out of phase chose lame Vulcan."

Yeats took his duties as a Senator seriously. He was head of a committee that promoted research in Gaelic language, music, folklore, and ancient poetry. As chairman of the coinage committee, he was largely responsible for obtaining the.beautiful designs of the present Irish currency. His persistence and eloquence were decisive in getting a new literary copyright law passed. He advocated reforms in the schools, denounced censorship, and feelingly expressed his views on the differences between the Catholic and Protestant communities of Ireland. In the *Irish Statesman*, Yeats declared that Ireland was not the preserve of Catholics only. "Ireland is not more theirs than ours. We must glory in our difference, be as proud of it as they are of theirs." Concerning the legalization of divorce, Yeats said presciently,

> If you show that this country, Southern Ireland, is going to be governed by Catholic ideas and by Catholic ideas alone, you will never get the North. . . .
> I think it is tragic that within three years of this country gaining its independence we should be discussing a measure which a minority of this nation considers to be grossly oppressive. . . . We against whom you have done this thing are no petty people. We are one of the great stocks of Europe. We are the people of Burke; we are the people of Grattan; we are the people of Swift, the people of Emmet, the people of Parnell. We have created the most of the modern literature of this country. We have created the best of its political intelligence. . . .

This is Yeats's prose at its most persuasive and most sensible. It should be remembered, however, that the people whose intelligence he was lauding never managed during their long years of rule in Ireland to build a political, economic, or cultural society broad enough to comprehend the Catholic natives.

Even in appearance William Butler Yeats was becoming impressive. "A smiling public man" approaching sixty, he no longer resembled the black folded umbrella to which George Moore had once compared him. His figure had broadened, and was snugly molded by the black velvet coat he put on for evening wear. There was elegance in his

silver-buckled shoes, in the wide black ribbon attached to
his eyeglasses with their tortoise-shell rims, in the gold ring
he wore on his finger. "More marked than these accessories," Joseph Hone wrote in his biography, "was the elegance of his bearing, the noble carriage of his head, the
harmony of his gestures; something of the ease and grace of
a *grand seigneur* in his manners."

Maud Gonne for her part was willing to work with any
organization that opposed the Free State, no matter what
other opinions it had. When a "Workers Party of Ireland"
was established under Communist auspices, she did not
hesitate to accept an invitation from it to deliver a lecture on
the evils of British rule. And during the last six months of
1925 she contributed a regular column to *An Phoblacht* (The
Republic), issued weekly by a left-wing semi-Marxist faction within Sinn Fein. The column, under the head of
"Political Prisoners' Committee," shows how closely she
kept track of everything that was happening in jails both
North and South.

She revealed, for instance, that Peter Keane had been
placed in solitary confinement at Maryborough prison because he had left the chapel and gone on a work stoppage
after a political pastoral talk had been given at mass. She
thought this action should set an example for all those who,
though often revolted by the Free State's injustices, did not
have the spirit to make their indignation known. In a succeeding issue she had the satisfaction of announcing that,
partly because of her publicity, Keane had been released
from solitary confinement and given outdoor work. Then
she named five other prisoners who were still confined because they too had protested "altar politics."

On October 9, 1925 Maud reported that several minor
but welcome changes had occurred in some prisons. Prisoners were allowed to possess pencil and paper, study Irish
grammar, and use needle and thread. The Prison Board had

sought out and hired two wardens who could speak Gaelic. To enable visitors and prisoners to communicate better, a new structure had been set up resembling the one used in Portland prison when Maud had been there in 1895. Previously, prisoners had been seen "across a wide sort of counter and, if the warden was amiable, by dint of stretching one could just shake hands. . . ." She remembered one prisoner who was "weak and infirm and suffering from rheumatism during his last imprisonment in Mountjoy . . . it was difficult for him to stretch across the counter; but he would never forego it, and the old worn face would light up with joy when he succeeded in touching the white hand of his wife, whom I often accompanied on her visits to Mountjoy."

In the same column Maud reported that on the previous Monday twenty-four women carrying posters protesting prison conditions had marched from the ruins of O'Connell Street through the chief streets of the city, and that "Everywhere the people looked with sympathetic interest, and well-known citizens made a point of saluting, and even of walking and chatting with the poster carriers." It speaks volumes for the depth of Maud's devotion, conversion, and redemption, if we can use these terms, that the daughter of Colonel Thomas Gonne and Edith Frith Cook should feel gratified because "well-known citizens" of a decaying metropolis condescended to chat with her raggle-taggle group of agitators.

There was never a shortage of matters to protest about. During one week, Sir James Craig in the North jailed a dozen Catholics who were preparing a memorial for an IRA martyr named McKelvey; while Mr. Cosgrave in the South jailed members of a committee who wished to honor the memory of Liam Mellowes. Both patriots had been executed in Mountjoy jail on December 8, 1922. Maud asserted that the actions were typical of "the thorough accord" existing between the leaders of North and South.

When people collecting funds for imprisoned Irish Republicans were attacked, while others selling poppies for the benefit of wounded British soldiers were not, Maud expressed her indignation in *An Phoblacht*. She did not mind that Irish people gave generously to poppy sellers even though

a rich Empire should be able to support its own wounded soldiers without appealing to the charity of Ireland.... Suffering will always appeal to Irish hearts. But it is a little too much that these crowds of Britishers should attack Irish women in the streets of their own capital, when they are collecting for Irish prisoners of war....

Nearly all our collectors were attacked. Mrs. Despard in Grafton Street had her collecting box knocked out of her hand by a man, while a woman tried to tear off her black lace veil. Mrs. Sheehy-Skeffington was threatened by a gentleman motorist sporting a Union Jack, who brandished an iron spanner over her head. I, myself, while passing through College Green at 12:30 P.M., was set upon by a crowd of rather well-dressed men and women who tried to take my collecting box and would have succeeded in knocking me down but for the intervention of the police... and not before my shoulders and shins were bruised.

Maud Gonne was involved in only a minor way in the controversy about Sean O'Casey's play *The Plough and the Stars*, which opened at the Abbey Theatre on February 8, 1926. Hanna Sheehy-Skeffington led the attack, charging in *The Independent* that the play, though given "in a supposedly national theatre... held up to derision and obloquy the men and women of Easter Week."

O'Casey replied in the *Irish Times* that it was a simple fact that Citizen Army soldiers and the tricolor were occasionally seen in public houses; that the rebels sometimes showed signs of fear; that Nora Clotheroe, in voicing fears for the safety of her son, was speaking for all mothers.

The debate peaked at a public meeting held on March 4, 1926, at which almost all of Dublin's literati and nationalists were present. O'Casey declared that he had not slandered the heroes of the Easter Rising; he had never intended to portray the conventional type of hero and indeed had no use for him. Madame MacBride's only comment was that she hadn't seen the play, but from what O'Casey himself had said, he had no right to introduce a real hero, Padraic Pearse, into it; and that from O'Casey's own words one could understand why the protest had arisen.

Sean O'Casey had a relatively high opinion of Maud Gonne. He thought Constance Markievicz "lagged far" behind her "in dignity, character, and grace, and couldn't hold a candle to her as a speaker." But his description of Maud at this event, dressed in a "classical" way with a dark blue veil covering her hair, was far from complimentary. He wrote in *Inishfallen, Fare Thee Well* that Maud no longer resembled the spirit of Ireland who walked like a queen but the Shan Van Vocht,

the Poor Old Woman, whose voice was querulous, from whom came many words that were bitter, and but few kind. This was she of whom it had been said that men could thresh out, on a dark night, a full barn of corn by the light from one tress of her hair. This was she for whom Yeats had woven so many beautiful cloths of embroidered poetry.... No ring of glory now surrounded that crinkled, querulous face. Shadows now were all its marking, shadows where the flesh had swelled or where the flesh had sagged. This is she who, as Yeats declared,

Hurled the little streets upon the great.

She had never done that, for her knowledge of the ways of little streets was scanty, interesting her only when they issued from their dim places headed by a green flag. She never seemed to have understood Yeats, the poet.... Here she sat now, silent, stony; waiting her turn to say more bitter words against the one who refused to make her dying dream his own. There she sits stonily silent, once a sibyl of patriotism from whom no oracle ever came; now silent and aged; her deep-set eyes now sad, agleam with disappointment; never quite at ease with the crowd, whose cheers she loved; the colonel's daughter still.

Two months after the play opened, Joseph Holloway saw Maud Gonne, Charlotte Despard, and Hanna Sheehy-Skeffington leading a band of women carrying placards to protest the performance. They were standing on the curb in front of both entrances to the theater, "with policemen in numbers about. . . ."

If Maud's eyes were "agleam" this year, it must have been from delight, not disappointment. In January 1926 her son Sean married Catalina Bulfin (called Kid), daughter of author William Bulfin, and eleven months later the couple had a daughter, Anna. Catalina, who was tall and thin, a young edition of Maud Gonne, had been active in the Republican movement with Sean for three years before their marriage.

On those infrequent occasions when Yeats saw Maud, he did not sense that she was experiencing a "dying dream." The ravages of time upon her person—she was now over sixty—were obvious but they served only to fuel his memories. Even as he saw her "present image . . . hollow of cheek as though it drank the wind," he recalled the "Ledaean body" of her youth. She seemed to stand before him "as a living child" when he walked "Among School Children," the great poem he produced in June 1926.

Between May 1926 and March 1927 Yeats wrote a series of poems under the general title of "A Man Young and Old" that are full of Maud. They speak of the heart of stone in the girl "who smiled and that transfigured me / And left me but a lout"; of Maud's bitter kindness because it was "the same for all," of the "wildness" of her daughter, which resembled that of a hare in the woods but was now replaced by a "distracted air."

Iseult had good reason to be distracted, for her marriage was going badly. The birth of a son, Ian, in 1926, and the coming of her mother-in-law to live with the family, did not improve conditions, for Francis Stuart was not very fond of her. In any case nothing seemed able to divert Francis from his endless probing into esoteric works. Yeats wrote Lady Gregory that Francis Stuart was "silent unless one brings the conversation round to St. John of the Cross or a kindred theme."

Early in 1929, in a desperate attempt to start a new life, Iseult and Francis Staurt, with money supplied by Maud Gonne, bought a thick-walled granite structure resembling a medieval castle and became chicken farmers. Laragh Castle, as it was called, was located at the southeastern end of the Vale of Glendalough, County Wicklow, a few miles from the ruins of a famous sixth-century monastery. Outwardly at least, it seemed to be an ideal place for someone of Stuart's complex temperament to earn money, write, and resolve his inner struggles.

Though Yeats visited the Stuarts in July 1929, he made no attempt to see Maud Gonne, writing Olivia Shakespear that they had "been estranged by politics this long while." Despite his success, he was finding life rather gloomy, moaning that Olivia was almost the only friend he had left.

In 1927 an eighteen-year-old lad named Francis MacManus came to Dublin from Kilkenny and stayed on to become a novelist, biographer, editor, and director of features for national Irish radio. One of the first sights he saw in Dublin was Mrs. MacBride talking before a crowd of some three hundred people at her favorite location, a side street near the Parnell monument. Even before he could glimpse the speaker, he heard her voice.

It was a voice no man forgets. Never had I heard a voice like it; not from any woman, unless perhaps from one of the renowned Abbey actresses. . . .

She appeared to be a tall woman, dressed from head to foot in wispy, lacy black. Black, they say, is absence of colour. She made it vivid as scarlet or turquoise. She had clear, defined, most lovely features, and in her white, drawn face her eyes were lively. She gestured neatly with a precise economy. She moved her head and held her shoulders with a bearing that seemed to belong to a queenly discipline. . . . What she said I never remembered as words but only the effect of it: an effect of fluent, stern, and even slightly theatrical speech; and more than that, an effect of intense feminine vitality and of great hope. I can recall that . . . she could use a worn rhetorical name like "Cathleen ni Houlihan" so that it meant something living. . . .

I saw her walking up the street with the carriage of body that was a perfect physical equivalent of that sybilline voice. She held herself erect; her pace was stately; her wispy black clothes fluttered. People turned to look after her as I would see them turning to look in the many years to come. . . .

Dublin was a battlement on which she, Helen, walked triumphant.

Maud had plenty of subjects to talk about. There was, for one, the arrest and imprisonment in August 1927 of her son Sean. The charge was implication in a conspiracy to murder Kevin O'Higgins, Free State vice-president, minister for justice, and minister for external affairs. O'Higgins, only thirty-five, was probably the most brilliant and fearless of those who came to power during the civil war, and might well have changed the course of history if he had lived. He was shot as he was walking, alone and unguarded, to attend mass in the Dublin suburb where he lived. Sean was discharged by a district justice on the ground of insufficent evidence, but promptly rearrested by the Civic Guard. After it was proved that he had been on the Continent at the time of the murder, he was released.

The passage of new restrictive legislation was another subject. A Public Safety Act empowered the Free State government to ban any association that sought to overthrow the government by force; to conduct searches almost at will; and to establish courts authorized to inflict death or penal servitude for life upon persons convicted of the unlawful possession of arms. Another new law required that every candidate for election should, when nominated, promise to take the oath of allegiance as prescribed by the Constitution. This second law would have forced de Valera and his followers out of politics. De Valera concluded, therefore, that the oath was an empty political formula which could be taken by members of his organization, now called the Fianna Fail, "without becoming involved or without involving their nation, in obligations of loyalty to the English Crown."

On July 15, 1927, in her sixtieth year, Constance Markievicz died. She had long seemed tired, old, ill, and
heartsick. Of her own will she had been separated from her
husband and child for some time; the man she admired
most, James Connolly, had been dead for eleven years; her
beloved sister, Eva Gore-Booth, had died the year before.
Yeats's judgment upon her was severe; he felt that her fight
had been "folly" since "The innocent and beautiful / Have
no enemy but time," that she had dragged out "lonely
years / Conspiring among the ignorant." Constance had no
chance to refute this; the poem, "In Memory of Eva Gore-
Booth and Con Markievicz," containing these lines was
written three months after she died in a free ward of Sir
Patrick Dun's Hospital. She received a splendid patriotic
funeral, with flags, banners, and bands. The clergy, army,
government, political parties, trade unions, and women's
groups were well represented. Madame MacBride and Mrs.
Charlotte Despard marched at the head of a delegation from
the Women's Prisoners' Defence League. Eamon de Valera
said in his funeral oration that Constance had rejected "ease
and station" to serve the weak and the downtrodden. "Sacrifice, misunderstanding and scorn lay on the road she
adopted, but she trod it unflinchingly."

This was precisely the kind of end that Yeats envisioned
and feared for Maud, who was never far from his mind and
voice. At his first meeting with C. M. Bowra, classical
scholar, he mentioned that he had seen Maud Gonne
"watching a British battleship and hoping it would blow
up."*

This conversation with Bowra took place at George Russell's home in Dublin. That Yeats should visit AE unexpect-
edly was part of the odd love-hate relationship that existed
for decades between the two dedicated Theosophists.

On April 1, 1928 Yeats sent Lady Gregory a comparison

*Cecil Maurice Bowra, *Memories 1898–1939*.

between Ezra Pound and Maud Gonne. Ezra, he wrote,

has most of Maud Gonne's opinions (political and economic) about the world in general, being what Lewis calls "the revolutionary simpleton." The chief difference is that he hates Palgrave's *Golden Treasury* as she does the Free State Government, and thinks even worse of its editor than she does of President Cosgrave. . . .

Maud would not have thought this amusing. She did not consider that her attempt to improve living conditions for political prisoners was a matter for jest, or that it was trivial to explain why members of the Irish Republican Army were breaking into banks in England. Her seriousness on such matters emerges clearly from two leaflets which she had a hand in writing and distributing at this time.

The first leaflet, signed by Maud Gonne MacBride as "Hon. Secretary, Women's Prisoners' Defence League," 47 Parnell Square, recapitulated recent Irish history, and argued that, in view of all that had happened, four IRA men recently arrested for breaking into a Manchester bank should be considered prisoners of war and treated as such. That goal could be achieved if "the thirty millions of the Irish Race living in Free Countries" rose in their wrath and demanded "the release of Irish prisoners of war as slaves of England."

The second leaflet, "The Whole Truth," was signed by Charlotte Despard, Maud Gonne MacBride, Hanna Sheehy-Skeffington, and Linda Kearns as "Members of Political Prisoners Committee." It narrated a complicated tale of prison brutality and subsequent cover-up. The story, when arranged chronologically, goes as follows:

In 1925 Eamon de Valera called into being a Political Prisoners Committee to look after the interests of Republicans in English and Irish jails. The committee issued a leaflet describing the brutal treatment accorded in Mountjoy prison to George Gilmore (later one of Ireland's most famous Communists), and named the persons responsible.

In May 1928, two women, Mrs. MacDermott and Miss
Jackson, were tried for having printed and distributed the
committee's leaflet. When they were found not guilty, they
were returned to jail for a new trial and were assaulted there
by a number of convicts deliberately loosed upon them (it
was charged) with pokers, tongs, and sticks. While holding
the door of a small office against the attack, Mrs. MacDermott received an "internal strain" that caused her to be sent
to a hospital where she lay for three weeks in a critical
condition. She was unconditionally released on July 15, but
was soon removed from her home and returned to
Mountjoy for the new trial.

In the courtroom Mrs. MacDermott and Miss Jackson
denied any involvement in writing, printing, or publishing
the leaflet, and refused to recognize the court's jurisdiction.
On July 20 a "packed" jury found them guilty of conspiracy
and seditious libel.

And now the signers of "The Whole Truth" were demanding a public inquiry into the prison system where
"such regrettable indiscretions" could take place.

Madame MacBride discussed this and related matters at a
large Republican meeting held in Liverpool at St. Martin's
Hall. Afterward she attended a concert arranged for her by
Murt Curran, "Irish Dancing Adjudicator," at the Irish
Club on Gay Street. Mr. Curran has written me that she
watched with delight the children doing Irish dances. "She
had a charming personality and you could feel quite at ease
in her company. We had tea together, and I always look
back with pride to have had the honour of meeting such a
great Irish Woman and Patriot."

Though Maud constantly condemned the actions of the
Free State government, she was fair enough to investigate
what was perhaps its greatest achievement—the development of a system for generating electricity based on the
Shannon River. Between 1925 and 1929, when the main
power station at Ardnacrushna, near Limerick city, was

being built, she visited it in the company of the radical writer Richard Michael Fox. He recorded that when the "tall, graceful figure with flowing black robes" stood on the dry bed of the channel between the huge concrete dams, the scene resembled a perfect allegorical meeting "between Romantic Ireland and the modern industrial era."

CHAPTER XXII

A Patriot Is Honored (1930–1936)

FRANCIS STUART WROTE some twenty novels which, because of their high autobiographical content, provide us with many interesting, if biased, views of his wife, Iseult Gonne; his mother-in-law, Maud Gonne; and their friend, W. B. Yeats.

In 1930, when he was twenty-eight, Francis launched himself from Laragh Castle in all directions, geographically as well as metaphorically. At Lourdes and at the Cistercian Abbey at Rosencrea he explored the world of the spirit. In Dublin he lived as a recluse. In London, using Liam O'Flaherty's flat as a base, he engaged in heavy drinking and numerous love affairs. He frequented racetracks in the "mad hope of large winnings." In such a life the birth in 1931 of a daughter, Katherine, made little impression.

Stuart's first novel, *Women and God* (1931), was an outpouring of sophomoric attitudes toward love, religion, and society; but his second, *Pidgeon Irish* (1932), was a success, both financially and critically. It was reviewed on the first page of the *New York Times* book review section. Yeats praised the book, which held the first intimations of Stuart's recurring theme of victory in defeat, for its "cold exciting strangeness, attained less by beautiful passages, though there are such passages in plenty, than by construction, characterisation and a single dominating aim."

Five months later there appeared *The Coloured Dome*, a novel that maintained that only when a person has endured "the vulgar, sordid and sometimes ludicrous suffering of the world" can he learn to surrender his attachment of life. Yeats, again impressed, wrote Olivia Shakespear on July 25, 1932:

It is strange and exciting in theme and perhaps more personally and beautifully written than any book of our generation; it makes you understand the strange Ireland that is rising up here. What an inexplicable thing sexual selection is. Iseult picked this young man, by what seemed half chance, half a mere desire to escape from an impossible life, and when he seemed almost imbecile to his own relations. Now he is her very self made active and visible, her nobility walking and singing. If luck comes to his aid he will be our great writer.

Yeats personally visited Stuart to tell him that the Irish Academy of Letters that he and George Bernard Shaw had just formed had selected his book for an award. In *Blacklist*, published in 1971, Stuart describes Yeats on this occasion. The character "H" represents Francis Stuart himself.

Yeats stopped just inside the door, raised his leonine head... and announced with an emphasis that made H momentarily suppose it was what he had come to tell them, "I didn't ask for Maud. I thought it might be unwise for us to meet."

The lock of hair falling over the imposing brow and brushed back by a pudgy finger, the full short lips, the black ribbon from the glasses to the lapel of the jacket, the folds of the waistcoat over the slight belly bulge, the mixture of deliberation and absentmindedness, all was being registered by H as manifestations of the first, and possibly only, great writer ever to come his way....

Between 1933 and 1939 Francis Stuart published eight more novels, as well as a play and an autobiography. Their number and lack of quality disclose that he was badly in need of money. His only successful book was a guide to horse racing and the art of picking winners called *Racing for*

Pleasure and Profit in Ireland and Elsewhere. It was the product of a passion which had begun in childhood, when he was "lifted up in order to give my shilling bet to a bookmaker at a small country meeting called Bellewstown."*

After a dozen years of marriage, Francis had come to resent everything about Iseult, but could find no effective retort when she told him he would be unable to make any headway in his studies of the Christian mystics until he learned to pray. "Find a priest and be guided by him," she said. "Learn humility, and don't imagine that by indulging in extravagances and going to extremes you'll solve your problems."

He disliked Iseult's way "of keeping the sexual act from impinging too clearly on everyday consciousness. For her it was a weakness, an aberration, best confined to night and darkness, or disguised by musical accompaniment, never indulged in too deliberately but, if possible, slipped into by chance and quickly forgotten." He even disliked her habit of making "the final moves, a habit that had remained from the days of his utter ignorance, when it was hard for him to take the initiative."

Because he felt that Iseult was unduly attached to her mother and quoted her excessively, Stuart developed a facile and malicious interpretation of Maud's character and personality. He told his wife that Maud was the kind of woman "who fastened on causes as an outlet for passions which weren't fulfilled through her senses." These causes, he said, had "a puritan lack of complexity" that was alien to him. "Having failed in her relationship to her three men (Yeats, Millevoye, and, later, MacBride) her mother found in nationalist passion an emotion to fill the void."

Stuart had no patience with Maud's growing rheumatism. In various European spa towns, he trudged around looking at cathedrals with Iseult while Maud took

*Letter from Stuart to author, dated August 27, 1974.

mud baths and drank the water from the hot springs. "She who had once inspired Yeats's love poetry now only asked for some amelioration of the aches in her joints."

In Vienna, Francis became friendly with a balding, middle-aged Jew. When he told Iseult about him she was displeased.

Like her mother, who, through Iseult's father, had belonged to the anti-Dreyfus, Boulangist faction in France, she disliked the Jews. H sensed that this hostility was more than just political, especially with Iseult. She lived too much in the mind, by moral or spiritual judgements, not to distrust what he was beginning to see was the Jewish character: humble where she was proud, realist where she relied on abstract principles, revelling in the sense which to her were tiresome

By sense, Stuart probably meant sensuality.

Iseult told Stuart that "Uncle Willie" was "mean and a snob," and would have accepted a knighthood from the British government if she and her mother hadn't talked him out of it. Iseult was angry because Yeats had rented 73 St. Stephen's Green for a very small sum while Maud was in jail, and then let his pet rabbits eat up the plants in the back garden. "Having just married a rich wife it wasn't as if he couldn't have paid her properly."

This portrait of a petty, back-biting, anti-Semitic, puritanical Iseult Gonne is markedly different from the portrait one gets from other sources. She remains a person who lacked interest in domestic affairs, smoked excessively, and played patience endlessly; she might very well have been ill-suited for marriage to anyone. But she was the product of a well-bred and cultivated French society; she was well read, versed in comparative religions, a good conversationalist in both French and English, and had a strong sense of French realism and an analytical mind. Best of all, she was outgoing and generous; she would not speak badly about anyone, even her husband. If her marriage was doomed from the start, it was not because of the difference in their ages, but because her background of metropolitan

French culture was so markedly different from his. It can be said about both Iseult and Maud Gonne that they married not merely the wrong man but the wrong country.

What attracted W. B. Yeats to Iseult was not only her resemblance to her mother, but her own qualities of ability, culture, and determination. Yeats lacked many of the attributes that make for pleasant social discourse, but he did have the virtue of seeking the company of intelligent and capable women.

During the early thirties, Francis Stuart, W. B. Yeats, and Maud Gonne inhabited widely disparate worlds. Yeats had become remote from Dublin, spending much time in Italy nursing various ailments. The days when he would chastise Irishmen for their ignorant nationalism had long passed. On the rare occasions when he was in Ireland, Dubliners were dazzled by his attire of

quiet corn or brown tweeds, with bright blue or dark green shirts, always with matching handkerchief. He had an air of quiet elegance, his long white-blue hair crowning a face often sunburnt and always carefully shaved, his movements graceful and dignified, especially his salute, a slow raising of the hand as if in blessing, "a compromise between that of Mussolini and the Pope."

Yeats had added arguments against Catholic doctrines and many more against Marxist ones to his thoughts on the glories of his spiritual ancestors. He wrote to a friend, "Damn Bertrand Russell. He's a proletarian. He has a wicked and vulgar spirit." Among modern philosophers, he disliked Herbert Francis Bradley, and admired Henri Bergson except for "the Jewish element," and his "deification of the moment."

In April 1933 Yeats met Eoin O'Duffy, a former police chief, who wanted to form an Irish group similar to the German Nazis. Yeats was ready to be impressed by O'Duffy. Not long before this he had written, "If I were a young man, I would welcome five years of conflict for

re-creating unity among the educated and would force de
Valera and ministers in all probability to repudiate the ignorance that has in part put them in power." Yeats saw in
O'Duffy the man who could accomplish this task, and
wrote some marching songs for his men. One contained the
significant lines:

> What's equality? — Muck in the yard:
> Historic Nations grow
> From above to below.

Before the end of the year Yeats realized that the Blueshirts
were demagogues and deliberately altered his words so that
they became quite unsingable.

As Fascist, Nazi, and Bolshevik terror increased, Yeats
ceased to speak in favor of any existing government. He still
believed in the rule of an elite possessing superior genes,
education, leisure, intelligence, and a sense of social responsibility, but refused any longer to discuss this or any
other public issue. Not even the pleadings of Ethel Mannin
could shake him in this resolve. Ethel tells the story in her
book of memoirs titled *Privileged Spectator*.

Yeats met her through the doctor who performed a
Steinach operation upon him in 1934. That Yeats should
have desired this experimental method of restoring his sexual powers says much about his respect for their importance and his contempt for orthodoxy in medicine as in
religion, nationalism and other concepts.

Yeats found Ethel Mannin so attractive and interesting
that he saw her many times during the next five years (his
last) and wrote her at least twenty-two letters. She was a
divorcée with a thirteen-year-old child when he first met
her, possessed of a Madonna-like face and light hair that she
parted in the middle. Born in London in 1900 of working-
class parents, she had left school at fifteen to become a
stenographer; at seventeen she was editing a house organ
and a sports periodical; at twenty-two she wrote her first

novel. Eventually she produced the incredible total of 41 novels, 23 nonfiction books, 6 books of short stories, 6 autobiographical works, and 3 plays.

Ethel was a Socialist, agnostic, pacifist, and proud member of the Independent Labor Party. Her friendship with Yeats was odd in view of the "wide disparity in our ideas, Yeats with his innate mysticism, and I with my then inveterate materialism." The friendship had to overcome not only a difference of thirty-five years in their ages but Yeats's habitual formality, which made conversation with him as difficult for Ethel as for many others. When she asked him to add his signature to a protest against Nazism by Nobel prize winners, he answered in a letter postmarked April 8, 1936:

If the Nobel Society did what you want, it would seem to the majority of the German people that the Society hated their Government for its politics, not because it was inhuman—that is the way their newspapers would explain it. What victims of the Russian Government had been given the peace prize and so on?

He went on to say that with growing age and a deepening sense of reality, his horror at the cruelty of governments was growing steadily greater, and that he considered no form of government more moral than any other.

If Yeats's faith in politics and government had vanished, his belief in the rebirth of the soul and other transcendental concepts remained as strong as ever. In his poem "Quarrel in Old Age," he asserted that Maud Gonne's essential self, the "lonely thing / That shone" before he met her, still survived "beyond the curtain / Of distorting days," still trod "like Spring" because everything that now lived had existed before. In "The Results of Thought," Yeats perceived that Lady Gregory and Mrs. Shakespear were victims of the same malady that had distorted Maud Gonne's "wholesome strength," namely, old age; but he knew that the weight of time's "filthy load" bore no relationship

to the secret self each one carried within her. In "Stream
and Sun at Glendalough," the product of his visit to the
Stuart chicken farm in the Wicklow mountains, he spoke of
being distracted from his enjoyment of nature by memory
of the "stupid thing" he had once done—proposing marriage to Iseult, who (he thought) was now happily married.
He wondered what motion of sun or stream had brought
him to this moment of pain and perception.

On rare occasions Yeats would have dinner with Maud
Gonne. Because of the chasm in their political opinions, he
would try to limit the talk to gossip about old friends and
similar matters, subjects that Maud would indignantly reject, feeling that Irish politics was still of major importance.
In his biography of Yeats, Joseph Hone gives a brief but
accurate description of these occasions, as well as a picture
of how Maud lived at the time.

She had an old-fashioned house in the suburbs of Dublin called
Roebuck House, which she shared with Mrs. Despard, a ninety-year-
old suffragist and a sister of the first Earl of Ypres. Roebuck House was
a court and a paradise for animals, and, going up the short avenue, one
was assaulted by dogs of dubious temperament. But having faced these,
any person could walk on and ask for dinner or asylum for life; she
would give either. Whatever the reason—Mrs. Despard perhaps—
Yeats seldom visited Maud Gonne at Roebuck House. From time to
time they would meet and dine at a restaurant in Dublin, and, as
politics was always a dangerous subject, he would try to amuse her
with stories about the bright young people whom he knew in London.
Not very successfully; she did not care for his "butterfly" talk; she
thought it out of character.

In February 1932, Eamon de Valera finally became
prime minister of the Free State. At first Maud did not find
that de Valera's success changed anything, though her son
and Catalina had worked for his victory and Sean was now
his secretary. Exemplar of the "fanatic heart," she considered it still necessary to appear regularly on her favorite
corner near Findlater's grocery to demand better treatment
for Republican prisoners; and continued to wait outside

Mountjoy prison to provide immediate relief to prisoners when they were released.

Many Dubliners now considered her a hopeless crank and eccentric. Memories of her hapless marriage to John MacBride and her irregular life in France still clung to her. Once, as she waited outside Mountjoy, a taxicab driver yelled at her, "Go home and take care of your bastards!" A more pleasant anecdote is told by Mary Colum. Once, when she had returned to Dublin from the United States, a friend pointed out to her a tall old woman, dressed in black with floating veils about her head, who was addressing a political meeting on College Green. The friend said, "Did I not tell you that we have the most beautiful ruins in Europe? There is the most beautiful ruin of them all."

As time went on, Maud became increasingly pleased by de Valera's actions. He abolished the oath of allegiance to the British king and, pending independent arbitration, annulled the provisions of the 1921 peace treaty that provided for the payment of land annuities to the United Kingdom Exchequer. The British responded by slapping a high tariff on imports from Ireland. When de Valera placed a similar tax on British imports, an economic war ensued that lasted five years.

Maud welcomed the breakdown of the economic negotiations with England "because we now know where we are." She also wanted to cancel Trinity College's right to three seats in the Irish legislature. "What has it ever done for Ireland?" she asked.

In October 1932, at a meeting of the Women's Republican Prisoners' Defence League—which had been declared illegal under Cosgrave, had continued as the "People's Rights Association," and had now revived and expanded its old name—Maud Gonne went so far as to say, "Thank God we have men like Eamon de Valera . . . who cannot be bullied, cajoled or bribed. We are now definitely waging an economic war against Britain, and it is the duty of every man, woman and child to take part in it." No one, she said, would be going hungry because of it; the new government would insure that, within a year, everyone in the entire nation would be employed.

She told a book dealer named Fowler that the economic war England had started would enable Ireland to build up her own industries and eventually solve her unemployment problem. In the same letter she thanked him for sending her the money obtained from the sale of her copy of the Yeats-Ellis edition of William Blake. She still had a number of autographed Yeats books but did not think the time was right for selling them.

She implied that she had no high opinion of contemporary Sinn Feiners who lived "in too rarefied an atmosphere for poor mortals like myself." They were unwilling to help political prisoners, to boycott goods manufactured in England, to work with groups containing both Catholics and Protestants, or to initiate work on their own. "Caste rules," she wrote Fowler, "prevent them working with the rest of their countrymen, and the day of Caste is passing."*

In the spring of 1932 some of Maud's friends thought it was time to stage a public tribute "in recognition of her fifty years' heroic efforts in the cause of Irish independence and of Irish political prisoners." Maud got wind of the movement, and in an open letter that appeared on March 15, in the *Irish Press*, she begged her friends "to stop all talk of thanks or honours." She felt that, though "we women, by publicity, have perhaps succeeded in shortening some imprisonments" and "have stopped the beating of political prisoners in the black dungeon in Maryborough... we failed conspicuously in sparing Ireland the disgrace of the medieval torture of prisoners in Arbour Hill."

Tribute was paid nevertheless. A committee was organized with Sean MacGlynn as chairman, and an appeal

*Letter in National Library of Ireland.

for funds, accompanied by a description of Maud's public career, was sent to various Republican groups. At the presentation meeting, held early in December 1932 in a hall on North Frederick Street, Miss Brigit O'Mullane opened the proceedings by referring to Madame MacBride as "one of the greatest Irishwomen that ever lived." She said that Maud had resisted any effort to give her an automobile or to have a life-sized portrait hung in the National Gallery. Indeed, it was with the greatest reluctance that she had consented to accept as "trifling mementoes of the Tribute" a gold wrist watch and a gold key brooch symbolizing her efforts over many decades to open prison doors. "John Brennan" (born Sidney Gifford and now Mrs. Czira) said the key symbolized, in addition, Maud's efforts to open the mind of the Irish people to the concepts of nationalism. Before Cumann na mBan and the Irish Volunteers came into existence, Maud had established the Daughters of Erin. George Gilmore declared "it was hardly possible to exaggerate the good work done by the Women's Prisoners' Defence League in looking after the comfort of the prisoners and making things hot for the jailers." There were four more speakers, including Helena Molony.

Maud expressed her thanks for the "loving comradeship" in the same clear, youthful voice that was hers until she died. She said that she was glad to see young people entering the Republican movement, but was perturbed by the failure of de Valera's party, Fianna Fail, to keep its promise to end coercion; it had permitted the arrest in Cork of the son of Tomás MacCurtain, who had been murdered by the British. Maud then presented silver medals to thirty-three members of the Women's Prisoners' Defence League and small purses to others who had assisted in its work.

If this event did not remind Maud that she was now sixty-seven and that her career was over, the number of deaths that occurred during the previous decade should have done so. The list included John Quinn, who had written to her for the last time on August 29, 1921; Standish O'Grady, Edward Martyn, Darrell Figgis, and Katharine Tynan. Among those who died 1932 alone there were AE's wife, Violet Russell; Sir Horace Plunkett, who had done a great deal for Ireland when one stopped to think of it; and Lady Gregory, who had done much for W. B. Yeats, and therefore for Irish literature. Maud knew well enough that she herself might be considered as having done more, since she had been the subject of so many of Yeats's poems, but she thought it of little moment.

What she thought of seeing Yeats and herself embalmed in a "novel" written by George Russell is unknown. Called *The Avatars*, it appeared in 1933, and was greeted with critical indifference.

In addition to the deaths of her friends, there were numerous other signs of change in Maud's life: the aching in her bones and the wrinkles in her face; the flight of AE to London, following a long Irish tradition; and the departure to Ulster of Mrs. Despard, after selling her share of Roebuck House to Maud. Sean and Catalina continued to live there with her and their children—Anna, then age seven, and Tiernan, age one. Maud took great pleasure in their company, and in the visits of Iseult's two children. All of them called their grandmother "Madame."

Some things didn't change. Maud continued to fight for a system of school meals to be established in Dublin, similar to those in Paris and Brussels. In a brief, dignified, and informative letter to the *Irish Press*, issue of October 7, 1933, she described this system.

The parents buy dinner tickets from a central office, and those who can justify, through unemployment or other causes, that they are unable to pay, get the tickets free. Great stress is laid that the children should not know who pay or who do not. . . .

In the three countries I visited, the children were provided with a comfortable hot meal properly served, consisting of two courses meat (or fish) with vegetables and bread and dessert pudding (or cheese or fruit). . . . I hope our children in Ireland will soon get the same advantages other children have.

Maud's honeymoon with Eamon de Valera did not last long. She began to feel that abolishing the oath of allegiance and eroding the office of governor-general were not enough. On the other hand, de Valera's actions in restoring to military tribunals the right to try rebels and in banning the Irish Republican Army were too much. But she knew it would take time before most Irish took her leftward turn. At a protest meeting held in 1935, she said she was not despondent about recent political defeats of anti-de Valera Republicans in Galway and Wexford. She had learned from long experience that the Irish were a rather slow-moving people. It took them ten years to learn that the Republic would never be reached through William Cosgrave; it might take them just as long to discover that de Valera was the same kind of misleader. As for General O'Duffy's action in taking 2,000 Irishmen to help christianize Spain, "When," she asked, "would the people learn to have sense and to use their own reason?" Despite that, when the League of Nations imposed sanctions against Mussolini for invading Ethiopia, Maud protested the fact that the Irish Dail followed suit. At a November 1935 meeting on College Green, she declared that the sanctions were being imposed at the behest of England against a country with which Ireland was just beginning to do a profitable trade.

Here we are, who call ourselves a Christian nation, ready to try to starve Italian women and children for the sake of a nation, Ethiopia, whose civilisation is based on a system of slavery forbidden by our Church and forbidden by God.

Mr. de Valera, she continued, had tried to deceive the people concerning the Covenant of the League. It required that if sanctions failed, military operations would follow and this meant in essence that the League was Britain's tool for engineering another war; it was up to the Republicans to see to it that the Irish were not deceived. The Union Jack was burned at the close of what the newspapers termed an "anti-imperialist" rally.

At the end of 1935 a reporter from the *Irish Times* interviewed Madame MacBride on the occasion of her seventieth birthday on December 20. In response to his questions, Maud went over familiar biographical ground—her conversion to national and social reform when she saw the homes of evicted peasants turned to rubble; her periods in jail—"dozens of times"; her hunger strike; and her belief that the younger generation "is taking an interest in the ideals for which I have worked, and, what is very important, they have a better understanding of economics than those who have gone before them."

Age did not slow down either her mind or her actions. In 1936, after speaking at two meetings in Northern Ireland, she was arrested at Lurgan by the Royal Ulster Constabulary and shipped back across the border. Anticipating such action, she had been careful to buy only a one-way ticket.

CHAPTER XXIII

Death of an Irish Poet
(1937–1938)

🌿 IN HER EARLY SEVENTIES Maud Gonne MacBride continued to air her views on a wide range of topics. Her
instruments included a four-page monthly called *Prison Bars*
and other publications of the Women's Prisoners' Defence
League, letters to editors, magazine and newspaper articles,
public speeches, interviews, and a book-length autobiography.

The first copy of *Prison Bars* appeared in May 1937, cost a
penny, and bore the coy notation, "Edited by a Woman of
No Importance." Its basic point was that brave, honest
Irishmen were in jail on both sides of the partitioned country only for wanting an independent republic of thirty-two
counties with equal rights and opportunities for all. A typical issue (December 1937) attacked de Valera for exempting
certain cases from jury trial; discussed the rise in the cost of
living; deplored the heavy emigration to England; demanded monetary reform; and publicized the fact that men
in the Glass House (the Curragh prison) were not allowed
to receive such books as William J. Moloney's *Casement's
Forged Diaries* and Dorothy Macardle's *The Irish Republic*.
The same issue contained a poem by M. Barry O'Delany
and a partial reprint of a leaflet "got out by James Connolly

and Maud Gonne in 1897 which, because enough people heeded it, helped to stop a famine in the West of Ireland."

In June 1938, the Women's Prisoners' Defence League distributed a four-page pamphlet headed "An Appeal to Our Race." Signed by its secretary, Maud Gonne Mac-Bride, it described the persecution of Catholics going on in the North; named the political prisoners in the Belfast jail; and quoted the English Council of Civil Liberties on the lack of civil liberties: "rule of law . . . virtually abolished," "any person may be arrested without warrant on suspicion," "prisoners denied . . . access to all outside aid."

The pamphlet called on the government of the twenty-six Southern counties to demand the release of the Irish Republican prisoners in Belfast, and asked Irish diplomats and the Government Information Bureau to publicize in foreign countries the persecution in Ulster. The pamphlet did not mince words:

This persecution ranges from economic pressure driving Catholics from their employment, starving and penalising their schools, depriving them of fair representation on all public bodies, to the naked horror of pogroms, shooting of old people and children in the streets of Belfast, burning and looting their houses, wrecking their churches, desecrating their graveyards, and bombing their meeting halls.

In a letter to the *Irish Press* dated August 6, 1938, Maud suggested that a relief fund be established to assist the families of political prisoners in the North and Catholics deprived of their jobs because of religious discrimination. "A little help is of more value than much sympathy." She hoped that people of all shades of political opinion, both Catholics and Protestant, would contribute to the fund. "We should not remain indifferent to the distress of our own flesh and blood." Had any of her Cook or Gonne relatives read this sentence, they would have scratched their heads in bewilderment.

At a protest meeting on this general subject, Madame MacBride alleged that sectarian bitterness, which had been started in the North by England and the Orange Order and supplied with a ritual by the Freemasons, paved the road to atheism and should be combatted. Meanwhile, the Orangemen permitted persons who placed bombs in Catholic churches to go unpunished. The task of the twenty-six counties was to show England that the continuing partition was dangerous to Britain.

Ideas like these could never mesh with those currently held by William Butler Yeats. He refused to become excited about the abuse of Catholics in Ulster or the refusal to allow political prisoners to read nationalist literature. He jested about partition, writing Maud that he found the inhabitants of the lost province of Ulster so disagreeable that he hoped that it would never be reunited with the rest of the country. Maud was not amused, and categorized him as irremediably "contaminated with the British Empire."

Maud's concentration on prisoners and partition did not keep her from examining broader issues. In one issue of *Prison Bars* she discussed "Faith and Fatherland." She thought that:

If we are to create Ireland a savior nation of the world, she must... build on Truth Divine, not the false teaching of Marx, Hitler, Chamberlain, Cosgrave and de Valera. We must destroy the present system, root and branch. We can do this by a determined effort to co-ordinate the spiritual with the material.

But in the main she was sympathetic toward new ideas, whether Communist or Fascist. She did not allow her friendships to lag with Charlotte Despard, George Gilmore, and Dublin artist Harry Kernoff even after they had joined an Irish-Soviet Friendship Society and made a trip to the Soviet Union. When they returned, she listened to them eagerly and said she wished she could have gone with them.

Kernoff remembers that about this time he sold her one of his most effective prints, "The Unknown Prisoners." He thinks that the people who heard her speak on street corners listened with the respect due to a historic patriotic symbol. They were not bothered by rumors concerning her illegitimate children, partly because Maud, as a member of the Ascendancy, could not be expected to observe the conventions that bound ordinary people. The masses never took seriously her conversion, or that of any other Ascendancy figure, to Catholicism.

James Connolly's son Roderic recalls that she showed no reluctance in accompanying him on a trip to Ardlaugher, County Cavan, when he was spreading the Marxist word. She was greatly moved when a man came up to shake her hand and tell her that he had once walked fifteen miles to hear the beautiful Maud Gonne speak on behalf of the Land League.

While presiding at a meeting of a technical school debating society, Maud made some flat assertions about the then current depression and the problems facing Ireland. According to the *Irish Press* of October 24, 1938, she said that, while not approving of dictatorship, she had to admire the wonderful work that Hitler had done in raising up a fallen and humiliated race. She hoped that the German example would embolden Catholic Ireland to end the persecution of 400,000 of its people by the Orange Secret Society.

She also wished that Mr. de Valera, who had done wonderful work for Ireland, would realize that he must make his policies conform to the laws of economics. Until a nation smashed the banking circles and obtained control of its own finances, it could never obtain its national freedom.

Maud examined these issues in two long articles published the same year. Like many others, she had discovered that the deep economic depression and the threat of another world war were the result of international capitalism and that Ireland's only recourse was effective neutrality.

"Fascism, Communism and Ireland" was published in *Ireland Today* (Vol. III, No. 3); the second article appeared in the provincial newspaper, *The Kerryman*, June 18, 1938. In both, Maud deplored the fact that most of humanity was being forced to take sides either with the Fascists or the Communists in the conflict that was building up. As a former nurse in World War I, she knew that "once war starts there is no limit to horror, and no mitigation."

England, she stated in the first article, had prepared the way by grabbing and holding an inordinate amount of the world's territory, leaving the other nations penniless and competing with each other. It was now increasing its culpability by entering into an "alliance with the Jewish money powers," improving her proficiency "in their unholy science of Usury.... Ireland is... at the mercy of International Capitalism, represented for us by the Bank of England. His Holiness the Pope plainly points to International Capitalism as the cause of the world unrest, which is leading both to Communism and to War...."

International Capitalism, Maud continued, "finances Communism and Fascism alike so that, when they hurl themselves at each other, neither should be lacking the implement of destruction." The world

has reaped the harvest of production subsidised by interest-bearing loans. Production has outrun its limits... the time for destruction—War—has arrived—surplus goods and surplus men must be destroyed, that is business....

Ireland may not want to be either Communist or Fascist, but let us have the courage to look at the good points where the two contrary systems agree.

1. Each system insists on a planned economy.... The Five Years' Plan and labour corps have the same objective, increased production... the standard of living in Fascist and Communist countries has been raised, while in Ireland it has fallen.

2. A rigorous control of finance. No money allowed to be exported.... No rents paid to absentee landlords, and land not used productively is confiscated....

3. The care of children, the health of prospective mothers and the health of workers are *State affairs*....

In *The Kerryman* article, Maud urged Ireland to take immediate practical steps to insure that when the war came and she declared her neutrality, it would be respected.

> The people don't want to be involved in the unholy horror of war so all candidates speak of neutrality, but are silent as to the means of securing it. . . . Switzerland has just got hers guaranteed by the League of Nations and 52 nations who adhere to it.
>
> Neutrality to be respected must make its value apparent to all. In his public utterances Mr. de Valera only stresses the value of Ireland's neutrality to England . . . the other nations and we, ourselves, want to be assured that our ports will not be used to shelter English battleships, and our aerodromes used by English war planes. . . .
>
> Has Mr. de Valera plans for getting recognition of our neutrality? . . .
>
> Has he mobilised our race abroad to endeavour to secure the backing of America? If secured, it might peacefully end Partition, for even Orangemen might prefer joining our Neutrality to Conscription and the probability of seeing their shipyards and mills blown sky high. . . .

In October 1938, the London firm of Victor Gollancz published Madame MacBride's autobiography, *A Servant of the Queen*, at ten shillings sixpence. Maud told an *Irish Press* reporter that she had been impelled to write this book

> because I would like to leave my own record of the historic events with which I have been associated for over half-a-century. The part of my life with which I have dealt in the book covers the Land League period. . . . I may write a second book dealing with events up to the present.

Contemporary reviewers found the book an entrancing record of adventure and romance, written by a woman who had devoted her life to the service of the Irish people. E. T. Keane of the *Irish Independent* approved of the way she handled matters of a possibly intimate character "with frankness but with discretion," and thought that no student of Irish affairs from the eighties on could afford to neglect the book.

Attesting to the continued fascination of Maud's flamboyant figure and the importance of W. B. Yeats, *A Servant of the Queen* was reissued by Golden Eagle Books, Dublin, in 1950 and by Gollancz, London, in 1974. Again the reviewers were kind. The exception was Maud's son-in-law. In *Hibernia*, issue of April 12, 1974, Francis Stuart found the opinions contained in her book as simplistic and self-righteous as when he had heard them spoken originally. He thought that the woman portrayed in the autobiography— "utterly fearless and truthful," able to silence opponents "with a few quietly-spoken words"—existed nowhere but in her own heated imagination. In the same way that he had winced at the time, he winced again when he read Maud's references to Iseult as "the charming child I adopted" or "my lovely niece."

Stuart felt that the book communicated true emotion only when Maud described the peasant evictions she had seen. He conceded that her presence at these barbarous events probably did much to give the peasants heart and hope. He also agreed with Maud's conviction that no real change in the social or national structure could be achieved without the use of force. The only Maud Gonne he really liked to remember was "the tall, haggard and slightly bent figure in her black robes hurrying through the poorer streets of Dublin on her errands of mercy. And, on another level, one that seems to have meant little to herself, as the muse of the earlier Yeats."

For the biographer of Maud Gonne, the book is, of course, indispensable, even though it ends with her marriage to John MacBride in 1903; and she lived fifty years thereafter. For much of the information she gives—her friendship with Millevoye, for instance—there are simply no other sources. At the same time the book is infuriatingly *wrong* in matters both small and large. Maud supplies almost no dates, and the few she gives are erroneous. She mentions important people, like her faithful English nurse and her French governess, without supplying their names or gives only surnames.

The book is unbalanced. Maud spends several pages telling how she defeated the attempt of a large, red-faced passenger to eject Dagda from a railway compartment; but says almost nothing about her collaboration with Arthur Griffith during the early days of Sinn Fein. Nor could she ever resist her tendency to rewrite history, either to make events more dramatic and suspenseful or to increase the importance of her role in them.

To be sure, there is never a misstatement of fact; lying was beneath her dignity. But the parts played by other people and other organizations in the events she describes are largely absent in her recital; complementary, objective data are few. In the end, by portraying herself as a single-minded, selfless, tireless advocate of Irish independence, as a humble servant of Queen Cathleen ni Houlihan, Maud becomes incredible. What is worse, she fails to do justice to her real concern for evicted peasants, hungry school children, and prisoners. Her genuine tireless benevolence is submerged in melodrama.

In these years of 1937 and 1938, Maud saw less and less of William Butler Yeats, the Irish poet who had spent most of his life in England and was spending the end of it in Rapallo, Majorca, and southern France. It was not by choice; a dropsical condition which had prevented him from running for re-election to the Senate in 1928 was becoming worse. He made few other concessions to it. He returned to Ireland in October 1936 to attend a meeting of the Abbey board of directors; gave poetry readings in London over BBC in 1936 and 1937; produced an important anthology of English verse for the Oxford University Press; completed the final version of his great metaphysical work, *A Vision*; and continued to write magnificent poems, many of them with inevitable references to Maud Gonne.

In August-September 1937 he wrote "The Municipal Gallery Revisited," one of his most moving poems, in which he memorialized Arthur Griffith, Kevin O'Higgins,

Lady Augusta Gregory, Hugh Land, and John Millington Synge. He could not refrain from mentioning Sarah Purser's oil painting of Maud Gonne MacBride:

> Before a woman's portrait suddenly I stand,
> Beautiful and gentle in her Venetian way.

In "Beautiful Lofty Things," he recalled "O'Leary's noble head," Standish O'Grady speaking to a drunken audience, Augusta Gregory in her eightieth year, and

> Maud Gonne at Howth station waiting a train,
> Pallas Athene in that straight back and arrogant head.

A bust of Maud done by a young sculptor named Lawrence Campbell inspired his last published tribute to her. In "A Bronze Head," Yeats compared her appearance in black robes with the way she had appeared many years before:

> No dark-tomb haunter once; her form all full
> As though with magnanimity of light,
> Yet a most gentle woman; who can tell
> Which of her forms has shown her substance right?

In some unpublished verse he recalled that the sight of her in her youth often aroused in him a premonition of the terrors she would endure. Propinquity to her youthful wildness brought his own

> Imagination to that pitch where it casts out
> All that is not itself; I had grown wild
> And wandered murmuring everywhere, "My child, my child!"

It was appropriate that Yeats's last poems about Maud should display both bafflement about her true nature and solicitude for her welfare.

In January 1938, a year before he died, Yeats began planning an occasional publication to be called *On the Boiler*. He expected to put into it a denunciation of compulsory free education; a belief that the duty of the masses was to earn the favor of the king and lord mayor; and a conviction that *no* political system was any good for Ireland, that she should count the "able men with public minds" within her borders, estimate how many more of them she could expect in the near future, and then shape her system to them. "It does not matter how you get them. Republics, Kings, Soviets, Corporate States, Parliaments, are trash...."

The delight Yeats felt when he thought of the shock these ideas would give to democrats and professional do-gooders is evident in the last letter he wrote Maud Gonne (on June 16, 1938). In answer to her request for permission to say certain things about him in her autobiography, he wrote:

Yes of course you can say what you like about me. I do not however think that I would have said "hopeless struggle." I never felt the Irish struggle "hopeless." Let it be "exhausting struggle" or "tragic struggle" or some such phrase. I wanted the struggle to go on but in a different way.

You can of course quote those poems of mine, but if you do not want my curse do not misprint them. People constantly misprint quotations....

When I came back from the south of France in, I think, April I was ill for a time. When I got better I thought of asking you to dine with me, then I put it off till *On The Boiler* is out.... Perhaps you will hate me for it. For the first time I am saying what I believe about Irish and European politics. I wonder how many friends I will have left. Some of it may amuse you....

God be with you.

Late in the summer of 1938, Yeats asked Maud to come and visit him at Riversdale, his home at Rathfarnham, near Dublin. He could rise from his armchair only with difficulty when she entered. Two old friends, one seventy-three, the other almost that, they reminisced nostalgically about events decades old. As she was leaving, Yeats said, "Maud, we should have gone on with our Castle of Heroes." Maud was so deeply touched that she could not reply.

Neither realized, then or ever, that in a sense a Castle of Heroes had already been built and would endure so long as men read English poetry. It was not the one Yeats and Maud Gonne had envisaged, but it had its own power, insuring that a goodly assemblage of Yeats's relatives, lovers, friends, colleagues, acquaintances, and enemies would, thanks to his art, become familiar to thousands of people who had never set foot on Irish soil. Most inhabitants of the castle had lived active lives; some had accomplished much in politics and the arts, others little; but all of them had been magnified into something strange and wonderful. Among them are: Yeats's father, brother, sisters, George Pollexfen, George Russell, Lady Gregory, Florence Farr, Frank Fay, A. E. F. Horniman, John and Ellen O'Leary, Sarah Purser, Roger Casement, Sir Charles Gavan Duffy, Oliver St. John Gogarty, Arthur Griffith, George Hyde-Lees, Sean O'Casey, Kevin O'Higgins, Lionel Johnson, Edward Martyn, George Moore, T. W. Rolleston, Olivia Shakespear, John M. Synge, Constance Markievicz, Katharine Tynan, Dorothy Wellesley . . . and, perpetually, immortally, eternally, Maud Gonne.

A few weeks after their last meeting, Yeats saw a newspaper item saying that the police had found a letter from Maud Gonne MacBride on the person of an IRA captive. He threw up his arms in elation, exclaiming, "What a woman! What vitality! What energy!

He wrote Sir William Rothenstein, asking him if he would make a drawing of her. "No artist has ever drawn her and just now she looks magnificent. I cannot imagine anything but an air raid that would bring her to London—she might come to see the spectacle."

W. B. Yeats died on the afternoon of January 28, 1939, in a hotel in Cap Martin, on the Riviera, and was buried temporarily in a cemetery facing the sea, high above the little village of Roquebrune. T. S. Eliot called him one of the few poets whose times cannot be understood without him. I prefer the simpler eulogy with which A. Norman Jeffares concluded his biography of Yeats: "He made himself a great poet." In so doing, Yeats created an entire world, and became its chief ornament.

CHAPTER XXIV

Waiting for Release
(1939–1944)

EAMON DE VALERA's ability to back the country into full independence improved as time went on. He obtained approval by plebiscite of a new Irish constitution, effective in December 1937, that provided for the establishment of the state of Eire and the abolishment of the office of governor-general. A few months later de Valera negotiated a package deal with England under which she evacuated three military bases she still held and Ireland made a lump sum payment to end the land annuities problem. Each country then reduced its tariffs on products imported from the other, and the economic war was over. In the June 1938 elections, Fianna Fail gained an absolute majority, which meant that it no longer needed the votes of the Labour Party. Maud Gonne's friend Dr. Douglas Hyde, Protestant and eminent Gaelic scholar, was named to fill the new office of president.

Some elements of the Irish Republican Army, finding these actions too little and too late, showed their displeasure by setting off a series of bombs in England. The British government responded by passing a law which enabled it to return to Ireland, without bringing charges, any Irish who were suspected of being engaged in terroristic activities. The following month more than fifty men were deported.

The total number arriving in Dublin seeking lodging and other forms of assistance ran to many more than that, for some deportees were married and had children.

Joe Deighan, appointed by the IRA to handle the problem, quickly established a small "Deportees Committee" of which Madame MacBride, almost seventy-four, of the Women's Prisoners' Defence League, was named treasurer. Sheila O'Donoghue, who represented Cumann na mBan, keeps as a souvenir a letter Maud sent her on August 26, 1939 with a pound note from a former detainee. The letter reads in part: "He sent it because he had just got a job! Isn't it decent of him. . . ." Then comes an inevitable and inimitable Maud Gonne touch. "Your baby is a real darling. So glad I saw her and she condescended to smile."

The steps taken by the de Valera government to repress the extremists were as firm as the British ones. Dozens of IRA men were brought before a special military tribunal, sentenced to jail (the crime consisted usually of a refusal to answer questions), and shipped to Mountjoy, Arbour Hill, or a hastily constructed internment center at the Curragh. When the accused was allowed a legal defense, he often asked for Sean MacBride, who achieved prominence in a case that arose on December 16, 1940 when some guards fired into a line of prisoners at the Curragh, killed Barney Casey, and wounded several others. To many, the massacre seemed

unprovoked and inexcusable, an exercise in brutality hushed up by the government. At the subsequent inquest Sean MacBride was allowed to ask a single question—"Why was Barney Casey shot in the back?" The inquest was adjourned at once.*

In another much-publicized case, MacBride defended Maurice O'Neill, who had been holed up in a house in Donnycarney when police attacked and a detective was killed. MacBride pointed out that the police had not identi-

*J. Bowyer Bell, *The Secret Army*, pp. 214–215.

fied themselves before firing, and that without an autopsy
there was no evidence that it was O'Neill's bullet that had
killed the detective. The special military court was uncon-
vinced; on November 12, 1942 O'Neill was hanged.

While Maud's son was making a career as legal defender
of a revolutionary underground, her son-in-law was becoming a member of a cultural underground that few intellectuals of the time would have joined. Before World
War II, Francis Stuart toured Nazi Germany giving lectures on his works under the sponsorship of Die Deutsche
Academie. After the war started, he accepted a permanent
post at the University of Berlin and remained there
throughout the entire war.

His reasons for taking this step have been capably
analyzed by his biographer, J. H. Natterstad. The only
war that counts is the one that takes place within the conscience, imagination, and psyche of the individual, not between nations, parties, or sects. Today—he is still alive—
Stuart points out that no writer of imagination and psychic
complexity can possibly become a genuine fascist.

Before Stuart left for Berlin, he was asked by the IRA to
inform the German authorities that the arrival in Ireland of
a German liaison officer and a radio transmitter would be
appreciated. In response, Captain Hermann Goertz, after
being briefed by Stuart, made a parachute landing on Irish
soil and turned up at Laragh Castle, one of the places he
had been told would serve as a refuge. Iseult allowed him to
remain, and purchased some civilian clothes for him at a
Dublin department store. This led to her arrest in May
1944 by the Irish secret service, but she was released on
July 1 after a special court failed to find her directly involved in intelligence activities. However, many liberals
and other anti-fascists were displeased by the Stuart association with the Hitlerites. Had they been able to read a book
Stuart wrote in 1940 accusing England of forging the

diaries that stamped the 1916 martyr, Roger Casement, a homosexual, they would have been even more offended. The book concluded in this fashion:

Casement's name is now immortal in the history of Ireland—raised high over the reach of the repugnant slander of English forgers. And the German victory, on which he placed so much, is at the moment I am writing these words almost complete.

Perhaps one day, no longer lying far away, Irish and German soldiers will stand together before Casement's unmarked grave in the Pentonville prison in order to honor the great patriot who has done so much to further friendship between the two nations.

The complexity of Francis Stuart's reactions is indicated by the fact that, in 1941, shortly before Germany attacked Russia, he was thinking of going there because Stalin possessed the "dark Dostoyevskian stature that Hitler lacked." He didn't go because he met a twenty-six-year-old girl named Gertrud Meissner, born in Danzig of Kashubian Catholic parents, who worked in the office where he was a part-time translator of German news broadcasts to England.

When Germany surrendered in May 1945, Francis went to Paris and tried to get permission from the Irish Embassy for Gertrud to return with him to Ireland. He was refused and wrote Iseult for money. In her reply dated October 17, 1945 she urged him to come home immediately, said his mother and aunt were willing to give him financial assistance, and implied that he was simply obstinate in refusing to return home alone. "But you see, Darling, why I keep reiterating in all my letters that if and when it is possible for you to come home you should do so at once. So long as you must stay abroad they are glad and willing to help, but it would really be an untenable position for you and me if it became possible for you to get home and you refused." She never mentioned his companion.

In November 1945 Stuart and Miss Meissner were ar-

rested and jailed by French occupation troops, but were
released after seven months without any charges being
made against them. They lived for the next three years in a
small crowded flat in Freiburg, Germany, dependent much
of the time on food parcels from America. From these experiences, and intense brooding on the nature of depriva-
tion, suffering, and hostility, Francis emerged with two of
his best novels, *The Pillar of Cloud* (1948) and *Redemption*
(1949).

What Maud thought about her son-in-law's political
opinions, activities, and wanderings during these years no
one knows. She probably considered his desertion of his
family, to which she was greatly attached, more reprehen-
sible than his attitude toward Nazi Germany, for she re-
tained the ancient Republican doctrine: any nation that was
an enemy of England was automatically a friend of Ireland.
Ireland was the center of her thinking; the immediate and
pressing tasks were to end its partition and to rescue those
Catholics under the heel of the Orange majority in the
North. In the *Capuchin Annual 1943* she argued that Ireland
should have resigned immediately from the League of Nations when it refused to allow the partition of Ireland to be
discussed at Geneva.

The death of William Butler Yeats created no great stir in
the English-speaking world. Most intellectuals believed
that his talent, like that of several other Nobel prize winners, was essentially parochial. Few persons, including
Maud Gonne, expected his fame to rocket as it has. When
the idea was broached of publishing a book of tributes to his
memory, it acquired support partly because of the belief
that it might help to solidify his reputation. The book,
called *Scattering Branches* and edited by Stephen Gwynn,
was published in 1940 by Macmillan and contained articles
by Sir William Rothenstein, W. G. Fay, and C. Day
Lewis, among others.

Maud Gonne's article deserves quoting at some length. Concerning the Castle of Heroes, she wrote:

It was to be in the middle of a lake, a shrine of Irish tradition where only those who had dedicated their lives to Ireland might penetrate; they were to be brought there in a painted boat across the lake and might only stay for short periods of rest and inspiration. It was to be built of Irish stone and decorated only with the Four Jewels of the Tuatha de Danaan. . . .

The Four Jewels, as Willie explained, are universal symbols appearing in debased form on the Tarot, the divining cards of the Egyptians and even on our own playing cards and foreshadowed the Christian symbolism of the Saint Grail, whose legends Willie loved to trace to Ireland. . . .

Willie loved symbols, to crystallise his thought. . . . He is gone, and I am a prisoner of old age waiting for release. The Ireland I live in is very different from the Ireland of our dreams, because our dream is not yet achieved. . . .

Nations like men are created in . . . the image of the most Blessed Trinity—the People, the Land, and, from their love proceeding, the Spirit of Life, its creative force which alone can make Nations separate entities. In each generation that Spirit chooses its instrument of expression from among the people, and when it speaks through them, their words and acts have extraordinary significance and extraordinary power.

Without Yeats there would have been no Literary Revival in Ireland. Without the inspiration of that Revival and the glorification of beauty and heroic value, I doubt if there would have been an Easter Week. . . .

Yeats's aloofness and his intolerance of mediocrity, a spiritual pride which is dangerous, tended to keep him apart from the first person of the National Trinity, the People. He hated crowds, I loved them. His generous desire to help and share my work brought him into contact with crowds and with all sorts of people, men from the country and men from the towns, working for Ireland's freedom. I hardly realised then how important that contact was to him and sometimes felt guilty at taking so much of his time from his literary work. . . . After my marriage and during my long sojourn in France, he lost this contact and . . . found himself among the comfortable and well-fed. . . . In London we parted; my road led to jail with Constance de Markievicz, and Cathleen Clarke, but Willie's road was more difficult, a road of outer peace and inner confusion, discernible in his later work. He was too old to cut a way for himself and for Ireland out of the confusion which, after the imposed Treaty of 1921, spread like a wizard's mist over the country. . . . The Spirit of Ireland needs young instruments for its expression. . . . Willie Yeats, like myself, had passed the allotted span of human activities.

Maud's tribute gains in honesty in that she fails to mention Yeats's many years of unrequited passion for its author, and in her frank assertion that the man who had once expressed in immortal words the spirit of Ireland had in the end become faithless to it.

Maud got her first intimation of what it means to be immortalized by a great poet when Joseph Hone interviewed her concerning his proposed biography of W. B. Yeats. In answer to a letter requesting further details, she told him on July 20, 1939 that Yeats joined the Irish Republican Brotherhood before she did.

I was sworn in by Mark Ryan much later. I think about 1896 or 1897, When I left the G.D. because I thought it had Masonic affiliations, Willie and William Sharp (Fiona Macleod) thought of forming a mystical Celtic order, and together wrote some beautiful lines for its ritual. . . . He was very interested in Irish mythology and in the Grail legends. I used to translate d'Arbois de Joubainville's *Mythologie Ireland* for him.

On February 17, 1942, Maud wrote again:

What must you think of me not having replied to your letter. In the past year I have been ill with heart trouble which not only prevents me getting out, but often makes me so lazy about writing.

About the letters, alas, I have not been able to find any. As I told you a box of papers where I think many letters I had of Willie's was left in Paris with Mr. Carney, when during the last war I came to Ireland. . . . When the Carneys left Paris, the box was sent to the concierge of the flat I had occupied in Paris who promised to keep it for me, but I never got there to retrieve it, and now in this second war, and the German occupation of Paris, I doubt if it still exists. Another lot of letters of Willie's and from Pearse and Connolly were all burned when the Staters shot up my house in St. Stephen's Green in 1922 and made a huge bonfire of all my papers. It was a terrible loss to me in writing my memoirs.

Now in her mid-seventies, Maud was being repeatedly plagued by illness, something she pretended to accept with Christian resignation, but in truth resented bitterly. She did her best to ignore the ailments of age by working on the second—unfinished—volume of her autobiography, *The Tower of Age;* and by chatting with her family and whatever friends managed to get to Roebuck House. One of Maud's chief complaints against the war was that the resulting shortage of gasoline prevented more frequent visits.

In the spring of 1943 Maud was pleased to get a letter from Ella Young, her old friend, who was now living in California. She answered on June 8, 1943:

The muscles of my heart gave out and for over a year I just can't walk. But lying in bed I don't suffer and can write and read happily enough while I wait for the last big adventure which awaits even the most adventurous and to which I am impatiently looking forward. . . .

I live with Sean and his family. Grandchildren are great darlings. Barry O'Delany still in the land of the living and though well over 80 hobbling around, she was delighted at your remembrance of her. . . .

Five months later, on November 21, 1943, Maud Gonne wrote Ella a letter full of her ideas, interests, and activities at the age of seventy-eight.

Our fairy Godmothers bestowed on you and me the gift of happiness so we never know boredom. . . .

It is lovely thinking of you in a land where flowers bloom all the year, writing the book I am longing to read, and in your garden, so happy, bringing beauty to life out of the Dear Dark kind earth. . . .

You remember saying how the world was passing out of the cycle of the Cup into that of the Stone, and that for us born of the Cauldron it would be hard to understand. It was terribly true, and though I am very happy I am feeling the limitations of those 4 cycles of Willie Yeats's Tarot corresponding to the seasons and to the cycles of Celtic mythology and am longing for the cycle outside all limitations. To get into that will be such a wonderful adventure.

In one chapter of *The Tower* I have tried to show how humanity has tried 3 experiments in civilisation, and each produced great wonders, but died when human misery became too great. The first, Slavery, left as monuments the Pyramids and went down before Christ's Revelations of the brotherhood of man, the fatherhood of God. The 2nd, Feudalism, based on possession of the Land, went down when the lot of the serfs became as bad as that of the slaves, but left as monuments Cathedrals and all the Golden Art of the middle ages. The 3rd, Capitalism, based on money, the medium of exchange of the wealth produced by labour and the land, is dying today because the lot of the unemployed has become worse than that of slaves and serfs, and is, ironically, dying from its greatest monument, the conquest of Space— the air plane; and the World is waiting for its 4th experiment in Civilisation which I think will be based on production. . . .

Though I can no longer address great crowds making them articulate, but always pulling from them *more* than I gave, as one always does when one gives oneself to the *people*, or to the *land*, I still am in communion with the Spirit, the 3rd person of the National Trinity, and I am quite happy lying in bed, thinking and drawing.

It is months now since I have been able to go even into my garden. My only grief now is that I am so useless to Ireland and all the friends I love. . . .

Iseult often comes and stays. She is the same lovely wise thing, as ever; she tells me of her joy in the land and the mountains but is a little lonely, for both her children are at school. She had to send them, because at Glendalough where she had taught them herself for some years she could not get teachers for subjects beyond her own power to instruct in, and she can't afford to take a house in town. To live in town would have been hard for such a wild one who loves the mountains, so perhaps it is best as it is. Ian is a lovely boy, tall as Iseult now, and his great delight is in carpentry and design. He is at a Benedictine School near Limerick where it is taught, but hates being away from Iseult. Kay is at a Loretto school in Bray and so can occasionally get home for week ends. She is a very vivid child, but not as beautiful as Iseult. We call her the witch, and she is very charming. . . .

Sean, who managed to do his exam for the bar while he was "on the run," took silk last month and is now a senior Council; . . . he is making a name for himself but I wish he wasn't working so hard. He has a power of concentration rather rare here, and he really loves Law. . . .

Hone's book on Willie is as dry as the dust of Trinity College; but it contains valuable data for someone who may yet write a living biography. For years I didn't see Willie, but just before he left Ireland on his last journey, I went out to Riversdale to tea with him, he was very ill; before I left he startled me by saying suddenly, "Maud, you and I should have built the Castle of Heroes, when I come back we might do it still." . . .

Willie never returned, and if he had we were both too old to make that dream materialise, but I was surprised and very happy that he remembered it. As we said farewell I felt that the long years of misunderstanding and estrangement since he became Senator of the Free State had vanished, but I did not think I was likely ever again to see him in this world. . . .

Do you remember the two carved wooden statues of St. John and St. Matthew you gave me? I put them on top of the dresser in the dining room, and a lovely golden Buddha in the centre. They didn't like it and persistently turned their backs on him. . . . The dresser is too high for the maid to dust; *they turned of themselves*. At last I said it was wrong to make them unhappy and cross, so I took the golden Buddha and put him in the drawing room, and brought a statue of the Blessed Virgin from my bedroom and put her in the centre, and they stand quite straight and look happy. . . .

There are such queer things impossible to explain, and more impossible to deny . . . the liveliness of those beautiful carved wooden statues you gave me is one of them.

As this letter indicates, Maud was still obsessed by the idea that the Irish soil was part of a mystic trinity, and had to be guarded. In 1944 an attempt was made to quarry stones from Tara, the abode of Celtic royalty, in order to mend roads; it was stopped because of a protest by the artist and patriot Art O'Murnaghan. The incident reminded Maud of an earlier threat to Tara, back in 1899 and 1900, when a mad Englishman had started digging in the belief that Noah's ark was buried there. She and Arthur Griffith had stopped this sacrilege by publishing an article about it in the *United Irishman*. The fact that Tara was twice threatened and twice saved was convincing proof, Maud wrote in the *Irish Ecclesiastical Record*, organ of Maynooth University priests, that Tara was waiting for some great event that would make real all that poets have dreamed and saints have prophesied about Ireland.

CHAPTER XXV

Symbol of Irish Patriotism (1945–1949)

IN 1938 YEATS'S FRIEND Ethel Mannin bought a two-room cottage in Connemara, near Mannin Bay, mainly because she fancied that an early ancestor must have been responsible for giving the bay its name. After a lapse during the war, Ethel began to visit her cottage two or three times a year. Given her temperament and passion for meeting prominent people, it was inevitable that she should become acquainted with Madame MacBride. Maud, in turn, was impressed by her youthful energy, beauty, writing ability, friendship with persons she knew, knowledge of Celtic lore, and interest in prison reform.

Between 1945 and 1952 Maud wrote more than two dozen letters to Ethel, which show that she was persistently and deeply disturbed by her advanced age and its sad concomitants—chronic ailments and the death of friends. She was depressed also by the increasing number of political prisoners in the world, and by their treatment. On the other hand, she found pleasure in new friends, and maintained her interest in Irish politics; engaged in controversy about the failure to feed starving German children after World War II; and continued to deplore the tendency of Irish youth to enter the British armed forces.

Her ailments were real enough. After falling and breaking her hip, she endured "a long nightmare of pain" in the hospital. On the day before she entered, she read a newspaper account of a chemical that had been used as a humane killer of cattle landed from a wrecked boat in Scotland; in her delirium she pleaded for an injection of the same substance. She was saved from death only by "the love of my friends and the skill of Irish doctors and nurses," but she had no sooner returned home, without even a limp, than she contracted pneumonia. She wrote Ethel, "I am better again but what is the use of being better when one is 80?" Because the muscles of her old heart no longer worked properly, she could not even indulge in one of her main pleasures—tending the garden and walking about the grounds.

Maud was deeply shaken by the death in 1946 of Hanna Sheehy-Skeffington, her "dearest friend" and "the woman I admired most on earth. Her loss to Ireland is terrible and Dublin won't be the same place without her."

To some extent, Ethel Mannin helped to fill the void. Maud admired her bravery in facing the loneliness of her cottage in winter, and felt honored when Ethel dedicated a book about the cottage, *Connemara Journal*, to her. Maud wrote that, if she were fifty years younger, she would be in love with Ethel's husband, Reginald Reynolds (a Quaker who had written a book on prison reform), though she was not one "to fall in love much, being too much taken up with winning freedom in Ireland." She frequently invited Ethel to Roebuck House to meet the "crowd of children who are my joy," her son Sean "and his wife Kid, who took a fearless part in our fight for freedom. Sean was the lucky boy when he got her to marry him."

She asked Ethel to tell her about the last time she saw Willie Yeats, and described her own last meeting with him.

Politics had separated us for such a long while, we got on each other's nerves over them and neither wanted to see the other, but at the last we had come together again, and the last time I saw him at Riversdale he was planning things we would do together when he returned—but he seemed to me so ill, I felt unhappy for I didn't think we would meet again in this life—not that one should feel unhappy about death for the *pattern* will be clearer to us I think after.

Ethel Mannin's friendship proved to Maud that there existed a closely knit spiritual fraternity (consisting of herself, Hanna, Yeats, Iseult, "and others whom we may never have met in this life") which was not circumscribed by limitations of space or time. Its members required no signs or passwords to recognize each other. This mystic bond "explains why you, whose life is so full and active, feel at home and happy with an old useless woman of 80." One of the principal activities of this "great fellowship of love" consisted of "protesting against crime and cruelty," especially when it was directed against children.

In many of her letters Maud said that there was a "mysterious livingness" in the soil of each country, that she had actually heard it sing, and that it was "the source and origin of most of the old folk songs of nations, which later great musicians have woven into their symphonies." In the same way that the Irish land had preserved Ireland as a nation, German soil would similarly preserve Germany from those who were trying to destroy it. Maud spent some time trying to work these ideas into a book, but suspected, rightly enough, that she would never finish it.

After the fall of Hitler's empire, she wrote a letter to a Dublin newspaper urging that food be shipped to feed German children. Despite a flood of dissenting communications, Maud maintained that the children's hunger was not an inevitable consequence of the war but the result of action by "self-appointed apostles of Peace and Liberalism." In a letter to Ethel, Maud said that "John Brennan" had found homes for 400 such children in Ireland, had raised a thousand pounds to transport and support them, and now asked if Ethel knew of any way in which England might be induced to lift its embargo against bringing the children out of Germany.

After spending two pleasant evenings with Richard Ellmann, eventual author of major studies of W. B. Yeats and James Joyce, Maud decided that he was "quite sincere in his admiration for Willie's work." She wrote Ethel:

> He has that painstaking American thoroughness in research which should make the book he is writing valuable and interesting, so I told him all I could about Willie's early years when I first knew him and I hope removed a misconception many people have that Willie's real devotion to Ireland started with his love of me; it did not, he got that from his child days in Sligo and the influence of those mountains and lakes.
>
> I think possibly Mr. Ellmann is pro-British *though he said nothing to make me think this* and therefore unconsciously he may be inclined to underestimate Ireland's influence on Willie's thought and work.

"My obsession about prisoners holds me!" she burst out in one letter. She was concerned not only about Irish political prisoners but about all the soldiers from defeated nations who were being held in prison camps, and the consequent "mountains of hatred" that their captivity was piling up in the world. Struggling for solutions, she once got the notion that perhaps they could be rescued only by strengthening their own wills. Will to Maud was an extraordinary force, without which thought and emotion were futile. "It seems to me the strongest and most mysterious force in ourselves, and I have watched extraordinary experiments in hypnotisms, the imposition of another's will on the hypnotised person."

When she read that several Republican prisoners were trying to get their freedom by going on hunger strikes, she wrote Ethel that "Hunger strikes always get me down, unless I happen to be the hunger striker. . . . It is a different matter when young lives are at stake." She said she was trying to make clear in an article she was writing that "every act of wanton cruelty turns like a boomerang against the nation who allows it."

The article appeared in the *Irish Times* in the form of a letter to the editor. Those who were unable to serve, Maud wrote, were not entitled to demand anything. Being almost eighty and bedridden, she could only *request* that young Sean McCaughey and others with him on a hunger strike in Portlaoise prison should be immediately released, for only then could people in the South demand, without hypocrisy, that the ill-treatment of prisoners in the North be stopped. Catholic Ireland, as the center of a vast spiritual empire, had the special duty of revising its penal system to bring it into accord with Christ's words: "I will have mercy, not sacrifice, for I am not come to call the just but the sinners."

For Maud to plead for compassion toward prisoners was typical; for her to consider Catholic, not Celtic, Ireland as the center of the universe, and to admit publicly her physical frailty, were novel.

On May 11, 1946, the day after this letter appeared, Sean McCaughey died. The case made a great sensation. *Hibernia* referred twenty-five years later to "the brilliant manner" in which Sean MacBride exposed at the inquest "the horrific conditions under which the de Valera-Boland group held their political prisoners; even the prison doctor admitted he would not treat a dog as McCaughey had been treated." In a letter dated May 15, 1946 Maud sent Ethel Mannin a full account of what took place at the inquest.

I have hardly seen Sean these past days, for in addition to his own work he had tremendous work on the McCaughey inquest. Death seems the one thing able to tear momentarily at least the prison secrecy which makes prison reform so hard to obtain.

If you have read the pretty full newspaper reports of that inquest, you will . . . have seen that twice Sean walked out, and it was only his request for an adjournment so he might appeal to the High Court for an order to oblige the Coroner to fulfill his function of ascertaining the cause of the fatal hunger strike that frightened the Coroner into allowing cross-examination to continue. . . .

Maud took advantage of every opportunity to discuss prison conditions. When a barrister named Shiels insisted that the prisons were now devoid of "Georgian and Victorian harshness," she wrote in a long letter to the *Irish Times:*

I wish Mr. Shiels had been more precise about the reforms he praises. . . . He tells us: "concerts are given." I suppose this refers to the Christmas concert ordered for prisoners in Mountjoy by Mr. Fitzgerald Kenny, Minister for Justice in the year when he substituted margarine for butter in the diet. I know the Christmas concert is still given, because I learned this year that a prisoner under sentence of death in the condemned cell was forbidden to attend it, and the thought of his loneliness stood between me and sleep, so that next morning I sent him the largest box of chocolates kind friends had sent me in hospital. I hope he received it, because Mr. Shiels tells us that prisoners may receive parcels at Christmas. He also tells us that "classes for prisoners are contemplated." . . . How long are we to go on "contemplating" reform?

She urged that everyone read a report about conditions at Portlaoise (Maryborough) prison recently released by a committee of Labour Party members. They had the good sense to proceed on the assumption that "prisons should be schools of citizenship, instead of factories for the perpetuation of a criminal class."

By 1947 Eamon de Valera had been in office thirteen years, and his popularity had declined. To boredom with his policies was added the continuance of wartime scarcities, difficulties in industry and transportation caused by fuel shortages, and the hardships of a wet summer in 1946 and an ensuing cold winter.

It was time for a new departure in politics. Its natural leader was Sean MacBride, now forty-three. From earlier Republican groups, which had never taken root among the masses, he formed a party called Clann na Poblachta (Republican Family) that sought to carry de Valera's foreign policy one step further and break all of Ireland's ties with Britain, end partition, and make radical internal changes within Irish society. Typifying this movement to the left was a medical doctor named Noel Browne, ten years younger than MacBride, and son of a former member of the Royal Irish Constabulary. After most of Browne's family had been swept away by tuberculosis, and he himself had become a victim, he made its eradication in Ireland the prime business of his life, and met with sensational success. In 1947 he became an ally of MacBride in his attempt to form a coalition with Fine Gael (formerly the Free State Party), the Labour Party, and various independent forces. The unlikely combination of poor and wealthy farmers, manual workers and industrialists, conservatives and radicals succeeded in defeating de Valera and his Fianna Fail. Maud thought the government called for the general elections in February 1948 because of its "amazing and inexplicable rage" when Sean was elected a member of the Dail at a by-election. She described the campaign in a letter to Ethel Mannin dated February 10, 1948. "Not only my grandchildren but every young thing I know were working, talking and thinking of nothing but the elections. She said that

Dev punished the whole country with a general election in winter, which has not added to his popularity.

He had his general election and neither he nor anyone else is satisfied with the results! Of course Clann na Poblachta could not hope to win, for it is *new* and had no organisation. . . .

I haven't seen Sean except for rare moments for the past month for he has been away speaking all over the country, but this house has been like an election office, the phone ringing continuously, typewriters clattering, and voluntary workers in and out of every room continuously.

Then came the news of Gandhi's assassination, which upset me badly for I looked on him as the wisest and best man on this earth. . . .

By winning ten seats in the election, the Clann got a great deal of influence in the new coalition government. Sean MacBride was named minister of external affairs, and Noel Browne minister of health. John A. Costello, attorney-general during the last six years of the Cosgrave administration, became prime minister.

As one consequence of his position, Sean MacBride escorted the body of William Butler Yeats when it was transferred, at Mrs. George Yeats's request, from Roquebrune to Ireland on the Irish corvette *Macha*. Sligo city officials and numerous friends and admirers of the poet watched the interment in Crumcliff churchyard. Maud Gonne, almost eighty-three, was not among them. Her condition had become such that she could not see "more than one or two friends a day." In December 1948 she wrote identical letters to the *Irish Press* and the *Irish Times* on the deplorable ignorance of Irish children about their patriotic past. The situation today, she said, was no better than in 1932, when she had visited a Dublin school and engaged the children in questions about the signers of the 1916 Proclamation of Independence. Not one child had been able to name them all. A few had hardly recognized the names of Pearse and Connolly. Subsequently, she had proposed giving every classroom, by courtesy of the Prisoners' Defence League, a copy of the Proclamation, run off from the original block that Connolly had used. The minister of education had refused the offer. Maud hoped that, once some policies were changed, the names of the Proclamation signers would become as familiar to Irish children as the names of Washington and Lincoln were to American ones.

With this letter Maud was acknowledging that she held a unique position as a historic, living symbol of Irish patriotism, and was accepting the duty of fostering national pride. That position was foreshadowed earlier in the year when a life-size photograph of Maud, taken in May 1893 by a man named Werner, was displayed in the annual exhibi-

tion of the Photographic Society. The *Irish Press* called it
"one of the showpieces" of the exhibition, "very much of its
period, with drapings and railings and hints of fernery in
the background. Maud Gonne, standing erect, comes out in
all her beauty. The only criticism one might make is that it
lacks some of the fire one has seen in other photographs of
the period."

Maud's position in Irish history was enhanced in 1948 by
the publication, in nine consecutive issues of the *Sunday
Chronicle*, of a glowing biography written by J. Doran
O'Reilly. O'Reilly called Maud "a grand old lady on whose
delicate frame the hand of time has pressed heavily, but left
untouched the keen intellect and buoyant good humour."
He termed her "a happy philosopher... optimistic and still
dynamic... glad to have numbered among her friends the
men and women who led the nation—John O'Leary, Yeats,
Griffith, Connolly, Pearse, Countess Markievicz, and the
others."

"It was false," he wrote, to picture Maud as

a severe lady, erring on the side of zeal, who... wore "widow's weeds"
in commemoration of her husband....

She was not, and is not, a sombre person.

She told me: "I have always found that there is a silver lining in the
blackest cloud. I have enjoyed my life in spite of its disappointments
and crosses...."

Now Maud Gonne spends her day writing or reading, and her evening
receiving visitors or sitting in the family circle by the fire. She goes to
bed late.

She smokes almost continually. "More cigarettes than are good for
me," she says laughingly....

Most of O'Reilly's biography is a rerun of *A Servant of the
Queen*, but it does describe one activity not mentioned there
(because it happened many years after the autobiography
ended), namely, the workshops Maud established, with the
assistance of the Irish White Cross, for girls who had fled the
troubles in Northern Ireland. Maud knew that they wanted

work more than charity, and guaranteed to the White Cross that the workshops would provide the girls with more funds than if they took relief.

In a short time the workshops, where garments for women and children were made, were providing employment for as many as 100 girls. Maud Gonne herself supervised and advised. . . .

Formal inauguration of the Republic of Ireland took place on Easter Monday 1949—thirty-three years after that fateful Monday of 1916. *Life* magazine published pictures of important figures leaving the Pro-Cathedral after mass on that day; among them was Maud Gonne MacBride, leaning on the arm of her son, and wearing a black coat and veil. Jubilation was restrained, for many people felt that a truncated Irish republic was not quite what the founders had envisaged. A patriotic song inherited from the nineteenth century was sardonically altered to read, "God save the southern part of Ireland / Three-quarters of a nation once again."

On May 3, 1949 Maud wrote Ethel Mannin that her new book, *Innisfail, the Isle of Destiny*, reminded her of "the appalling and terrifying feeling of crumbling old age" that she had felt in Connemara and North Mayo many years before. These sights had helped her to understand the apathy and defeatism of the people living there.

You and I can get away for a time till we recover vitality, though the beauty of the land draws us back to it again, while many of them cannot . . . I thought . . . it was good for you for a time to get away from Connemara to your English mother. I too had an English mother, though she died when I was four. Her blood in me makes me able to understand English people and to appreciate the good qualities in them you write of even while my Irish blood obliges me to fight their governments. . . .

This is the only place the author has found in Maud's writings where she has a kind word to say about the English.

During the year 1949, Maud read Francis Stuart's *Re-*

demption and Ethel Mannin's *Every Man a Stranger*. The hero
of Stuart's novel was an Irishman who, while living in wartime Germany, found his wife at home unable to "open her
heart to him at the time of his need . . . as his wife she could
not accept Margareta. To be a wife is to be incapable of the
final, unjudging friendship." Iseult was further described
as a woman with a "small, pale face," "vague remote smile,"
and a distaste for sex. Maud and Iseult waited impatiently
for Ethel's book as "something to take away the nastiness"
of Stuart's. When it arrived, Maud found that the pages in
it that dealt with the fall of Nazi Germany were "master-
pieces of literature." She complimented her friend on her
courage in condemning the hate that had been loosed
against Germany in the name of peace and justice; many
people in Ireland, she thought, would agree with Ethel.

When Ireland appointed a woman to be an ambassador,
Maud wrote Ethel Mannin on November 21, 1949 to express her delight. "Until we have more women taking a
direct share in political life we shall never get a peaceful
world—not that we are better than men but being born
fosterers of life we have a greater instinct to protect life."

On August 24, 1949, November 19, 1949, and January
17, 1950, Maud Gonne recorded some reminiscenses which
were broadcast over Irish radio. Her voice was strong and
mellow, showing no signs that the speaker was eighty-four.
She talked about the activities of the Daughters of Erin, the
campaign for school meals, the importance of women's voluntary organizations in social and nationalist movements,
and the evictions of 1886 when the evictors had often found
her and her horse getting in the way. She took the opportunity to enunciate two of her principal doctrines. The first
was something she believed in as a young girl and still
believed as an old woman. "Force is the only remedy for a
people who have let a stranger get hold of their land." Talk
was good in its place, "but, if it has not force behind it, it
cuts no ice." Her second conviction was that "The Irish are

the best soldiers in the world and the worst diplomats while the English are just the contrary. We are as God made us and must use the talents he has endowed us with."

The recordings were made at Roebuck House under the direction of Francis MacManus. He had just seen in the *Capuchin Annual 1949* a new photograph of Maud Gonne taken by Adolf Morath, and observed the "astounding reticulation of lines" in her face, "map of a lifetime's joy and . . . sorrow." What he had not expected to see was her spirit shining through them as "luminous" as in the days

when Yeats compared her complexion to the apple blossom through which the light falls. What nobody had told me about was the serene wisdom, even the good humour, with which she accepted what the years had brought. . . .

Her hair, fine as silk and still glossy, was whorled over her ears in an antique way. It sat on her head like a cap so that little of the forehead showed. Deep furrows lined her cheeks in close parallel and when she smiled her face was all laughter. Above the fine aquiline nose, the calm, bright eyes were lively as a young girl's. . . .

There was witchcraft in her voice. She was aware of it. She had not forgotten the virtue of control and of contrast, the effect of deliberate phrasing followed by a rapid conversational snatch, the exaltation of the rise in pitch, and the solemnity of words spoken slowly in a monotone as she spoke them, for the dead. . . . Oratory had come to be suspect . . . it had been one of the chief instruments of the popular frenzies that maintained dictatorships. But this old woman whose devotion had been pure and who had learned to speak as orators once spoke, was able, for those minutes, to restore innocence to a fallen art and to make it worthy and even necessary. . . .

While Maud smoked her Sweet Afton cigarettes, she chatted with MacManus about such matters as reform of the prison system, and the tendency of the younger generation to lose touch with "the heroic past." As he was leaving, MacManus observed a sudden lifting of Maud's body which, owing to the ravages of age, had taken, from the shoulders down, the form of a sickle. Viewing "that straight back and arrogant head," he remembered the countess who, in a play that combined poetry, folklore, and patriotism, had pledged her life to save a famished people.

The recordings took their toll. Maud broke down during the last session and for a time had to go without seeing any visitors at all. "It's awful to be old and deaf as I am!" she moaned in a letter to Ethel on an occasion when she had to put off a visit from her.

But Maud's memory remained good, her convictions strong, and her thinking unimpaired. In the same letter she asked Ethel,

Do you happen to know if English prisons are overcrowded with war criminals at present? . . . I heard a rumour that England shipped a lot of her war criminals to Palestine to be policemen there, just as in 1795 she sent her war criminals to Ireland [the Peep o Day boys] and in 1919 sent them here as the Black and Tans. . . .

When she read Ethel's latest book, *Bavarian Story*, she commented, in writing more crabbed than ever, "I am not sure, had I been a German after the treaty of Versailles, that I would not have become a Nazi, except for the Nazi exclusion of women from a share of direction of affairs." The book reminded her of the time she had toured Bavaria with Iseult, a holiday made possible only because of the favorable rate of exchange. She had "tried to make a little restitution by giving as much as I could to the collections held for the wounded or the orphans between the acts at the Opera House."

CHAPTER XXVI

Death of a Charmer (1950–1953)

🌿 DURING THE LATTER part of its period in power, Fianna Fail brought forth a comprehensive health plan that was promptly shot down by the medical profession as an infringement of the people's right to choose their own doctors; by opponents of governmental centralization; and by the Catholic hierarchy, which considered those provisions that made maternity and child care available to all mothers regardless of means as an invasion of family rights.

In March 1951, Dr. Noel Browne, minister of health in the coalition government, produced a mother and child welfare scheme that proved even more offensive to the Church. When Browne received no support from his colleagues in Clann na Poblachta, he became convinced that his party had lost its idealism and integrity. In April 1951, after a sharp interchange of letters between him and MacBride, he resigned his position in the coalition government.

Mr. Costello, seeing his forces weakened by the controversy, tried to improve his position by calling in May 1951 for a general election. Roebuck House again became a center of frenzied activity. A monthly titled *Our Nation* was inaugurated in order to improve Sean MacBride's fortunes. Maud contributed four sections of her unfinished memoirs to it, but all in vain. Clann na Poblachta won only two seats. De Valera's Fianna Fail again took over the reins of government, together with the nation's problems of inflation, unemployment, emigration, adverse balance of payment, and inadequate social insurance.

In the 1957 elections the Clann na Poblachta received so few votes that its demise became inevitable. MacBride left Irish politics to carve out a brilliant new career, becoming in sequence secretary-general of the International Commission of Jurists; head of Amnesty International, an organization devoted to liberating political prisoners in every country; and United Nations Commissioner for Namibia (South West Africa). In 1974, in recognition of his defense of civil liberties and efforts to free political prisoners, he was awarded the Nobel Peace Prize—the first Irishman to win this honor. If his mother had been alive, she would have regretted that he never became prime minister of Ireland, in which position he could have helped to end partition; but would have been enormously pleased at the *reasons* why he won the Nobel prize.

Sean's brother-in-law has led a different kind of life. With Gertrud Meissner he lived in a Paris attic for a few years, then moved to London in 1951, where Gertrud worked at a variety of uninspiring jobs while Francis turned out four novels. The last, *Victor and Vanquished* (1958), is again autobiographical. But now the man who leaves his wife in Ireland to teach in Germany becomes the young guardian of a baby girl he inadvertently acquires on the way to Berlin, and the German girl with whom he finds love and peace is Jewish.

When Iseult Gonne Stuart died in March 1954, Francis was free to marry Miss Meissner. In 1958 he returned with her to Ireland, where he continues to write. In *Memorial* (1973) he refers a few times to Iseult (Nancy); on one occasion the protagonist looks at an ancient Rolls-Royce he once owned, and remembers the "long drives with Nancy over what seemed perpetually wet roads... and, when I now opened the door, did the air really smell of tears and tobacco? . . ."

To her grandchildren, Maud Gonne was a friendly and comforting figure, equally adept at repairing broken toys and healing scraped knees. When she came downstairs (after morning tea served late in bed, and after finishing another letter to the editor), she was always ready to unbend her towering figure and engage in eye-to-eye conversation based on equality and common interests. But to a child who happened to meet her in the dark, the sight of this giant woman could be a traumatic experience. James Plunkett, novelist and musician, recalls that one evening

> I turned the corner of a quiet road in Clonskeagh and found myself face to face with a ghost. It was a very tall, very thin old lady, dressed from head to foot in black drapes, with a wolfhound on a lead. Then she passed me, an apparition in October twilight. She was Maud Gonne MacBride, once the symbol of Romantic Ireland, now so incredibly old to my young eyes that I thought of Oisin when his foot touched mortal ground and all his years in the blinking of an eye descended with the weight of an avalanche on top of him.

Her age was not always so frightening. When the American critic Van Wyck Brooks and his wife visited Dublin, Brooks asked Monk Gibbon to introduce him to Maud Gonne. To Gibbon she had always seemed to be "a firebrand, committed always to opposition; a fanatic who, when she and Mrs. Despard settled in my father's parish about the time of the Black and Tans and he called upon them, met him on the doorstep and explained to him that, if he came in, he must speak either French or Irish because they refused to sully their lips with the English language."

Reluctantly, Gibbon arranged for a visit, and was told by Maud's daughter-in-law that she now stayed in bed all day, occasionally getting up about eight o'clock to receive visitors.

When Gibbon and the Brookses arrived at Roebuck
House, they found Maud Gonne downstairs, "sunk in a
huge deep armchair by the wood fire, awaiting us. The
broad-browed face was more deeply lined than any face
that I have ever seen. Her long, thin, heavily veined hands
rested upon her lap. She was a tall, frail old lady...."

Gibbon had seen the photograph of Maud shown at the
Mansion House during the Photographic Society's exhibit.
She had then seemed simply a "fine, handsome young
woman such as every Edwardian drawing-room delighted
in." The photograph left him unmoved but now she capti-
vated him.

> I think what won my heart finally was when Mrs. Van Wyck Brooks
> asked her how it came about that she, an English army officer's daugh-
> ter, should have become the prophetess of Irish nationalism. She
> thought for a moment and then said, "Well, when I was still quite a
> little girl I used to go riding through the country on a pony beside my
> father. It was the time of the evictions and I used to see people standing
> in front of their unroofed cottages from which the police held them
> back, and weeping bitterly. I thought to myself, "When I grow up I'm
> going to change all that. Yes, I'm going to change all that."
>
> As she said it the years vanished and we seemed to be looking into the
> heart of a little girl of nine who saw herself in imagination as another
> Joan of Arc....
>
> She seemed all grace and charm, an enchantress of men's hearts
> despite her eighty years, and when we rose to go it was I, her detractor,
> who raised her heavily-veined brown hand and kissed it.

Little did Mr. Gibbon know how well-worn that story was,
how practiced that hesitation.

Another account of Maud in her old age comes from
Michael Mac Liammoir, who used to visit her when he was
in his forties. A brilliant actor, producer, and author, he
wrote in *Put Money in Thy Purse*, a book concerning the film
Othello that he made with Orson Welles:

> Tea with Madame Gonne MacBride. This ceremony, however fre-
> quent, has invariable effect on me of romantic pleasure. Her heroic and
> now cavernous beauty, made sombre by the customary black draperies

she wears, is also illumined by an increasing gentleness and humour; she has now what seems a faint far-away amusement at life.

Although she will die a partisan . . . that portion of her mind which Yeats described as "all but turned to stone" is somehow delicately perceived by herself, and as delicately passed by, as one passes by in time of peace a monument celebrating the tragedy of war. . . .

I sit and watch that fragile body bent with age, the restless hands, the smiling head held a little to one side, the gold-flecked eyes that grow alternately dim and brilliant as she talks, and I think: "There before my eyes she sits, the 'phoenix' who *'lived in storm and strife,'* she who was *'beautiful and fierce, sudden and laughing'*; there is the *'dim heavy hair'* that's *'streaked with gray'* the *'eagle look,'* the lips *'with all their mournful pride'* "; and I am faintly surprised to find that the *"one flaw"* that he had celebrated, more beautifully than any of her perfections, seemed to me untrue. . . . Well, to me her hands are beautiful. . . .

She is perhaps the only person in the world now who is as beautiful as the poems that were made for her, and they are the best of her generation. No one so single-minded has ever lived, I think. When . . . I told her about the *Othello* film, she said: "How splendid—perhaps you and he can learn about films and make them for Ireland one day."

She likes sherry, tea, cigarettes, and the society of her son, Sean, and his wife; she likes poor people, wild birds, speculative ideas, and a horizon beyond her windows that is ragged with mountains; and when one goes away she comes smilingly and very slowly to the door to wave good-bye. . . .

A year before Maud died, she talked for three hours to Virginia Moore, who was working on her invaluable study of Yeats's mystical ideas, *The Unicorn*. It was the spring of 1952. As Miss Moore tells it, Maud was wrapped in a robe of black silk brocade with three huge ornate silver buttons, and sat by a coal fire, under the oval portraits of herself and her mother done by the Irish painter Wall.

There were countless wrinkles. I grew faint with the pity of time's ruining power. Almost I could not look. But, as she talked, I felt the upsurge of a vibrant, almost childlike personality. For ten years heart trouble had kept her immobile, she said. "Old age is hell. So boring." . . . Yes, there had been a close bond between her and Willy; she had loved him, "but not that way," and had *never* intended to marry him. Really, he had not been as unhappy as people thought. . . . Had I

ever seen invisible things? Yes, like Willy, she had been able to slip out
of her body, but didn't know about it now—it took so much concentration. Exhausting! Her favorite poem by Willy was "The Two Thorn
Trees."... And then her last words: "I shall see him again"—smiling.
"Oh, yes, I shall see him again."

The poem to which Maud referred was "The Two Trees,"
published in 1893, which begins, "Beloved, gaze in thine
own heart."

Elsewhere, Miss Moore puts her finger on that element
in Maud's personality that made Yeats so protective: she
had "a freeborn, innocent, not wholly mature quality in
her...." She was "a woman incapable—as a child is
incapable—of guile, of pretense, of mask."

On January 22, 1950 Maud Gonne wrote M. J. Mac-
Manus, literary editor of the *Irish Press*, to congratulate him
on the brilliance of his article "The Landlord Wore a Suit of
Chain Mail." It reminded her, Maud said, of the evictions
she had seen in 1885, after her return from France, and it
proved again that Irish landlords were the worst col-
laborators in infamy that ever lived. Her only criticism was
that he had not stressed sufficiently the fact that the evictors were an integral part of English policy, a deliberate
attempt to annihilate economically a nation England had
been unable to destroy by military massacre for two previous centuries.

MacManus reviewed Maud Gonne's autobiography
when it was reprinted in May 1950. He found it as fascinating as before, and said in his review that Maud looks on the
British Empire as the symbol of the Devil on earth.

Maud responded on May 3 by writing that his words had
been too kind; she was really "a very ordinary girl and my
life was only interesting because I belonged to Ireland and
Ireland is Innisfail so it is a great privilege to belong to the
Isle of Destiny." This concept of Ireland as Innisfail was
much on her mind.

On January 21, 1951, Maud wrote again to M. J. Mac-Manus to say she liked his article on Arthur Griffith. She thought he should do a biography of Griffith, and volunteered to give him what information she had. She said that John MacBride had got Griffith his job as assayer in South Africa, but that Griffith had relinquished it because of homesickness. "John and Arthur were *lifelong friends.*" The passage of time—several decades—had finally made it possible for Maud to mention without heat or rancor people with whom she had had marital or political differences.

In May 1952, less than a year before she died, Maud saw an item in the Dublin newspapers referring to the possibility that the land commissioners were about to acquire a portion of Tara Hill for a housing development. She reacted immediately, writing to the editors: "I want to add my old voice to urge safeguarding what Professor MacAllister in his learned book on Tara says is 'the most beautiful site in Europe.'"

On October 9, 1950, Maud wrote Ethel Mannin that she was "slowly recovering from a bad congestion of the lungs which I thought was going to release me from the Prison House of old age—but no, I am recovering!" She was glad that Ethel and her husband were working for pace—"for *Peace and Freedom* are the only worthwhile things to strive for, and they are *indivisible.*" She was still ill in December when she turned eighty-five. This and the absence of a maid prevented her from sending out any Christmas cards, she wrote Ethel Mannin on January 23, 1951. She wrote also about Ian, the son of Iseult and Francis Stuart, who was just beginning his career as a sculptor.

I love seeing you and Reginald *always.* You are so good to look at and both so interesting—and doing so many of the things I would love to be doing, were I not afflicted by the appalling *futility* of old age—85....

How lucky Willie Yeats was to escape into the freer life of the spirit.... He was one year older than I was.

You speak of dock strikes, rent strikes, etc. I think Ireland is not

doing too badly, when I compare it with the Ireland of my girlhood. . . .
There has been tremendous progress, and reconstruction work is going on
relatively quickly. Sean has great plans for afforestation and land rec-
lamation to end emigration. . . .

I think Ireland is going to produce a 3rd Golden Age which will
probably make her a leader of the *Peace* thought in this world of confused thinking. You, I think, like myself, believe in Ireland's destiny.
India is already leading *Peace*.

How kind of you lending Ian a room. . . . He is a dear boy, but I
don't want him to stay *too long in London*. I want him to come back and
make his outhouse famous as a *Studio in Glendalough*. Glendalough has
such great traditions!

When Maud received Ethel Mannin's latest book, *The
Wild Swans*, consisting of three tales based on the ancient
Irish, her sight was so bad that she had to read it slowly,
but the stories blended past and present so beautifully that
she could not put the book down until she had read every
word of it. In handwriting so tremulous as to be almost
illegible, she wrote Ethel on July 6, 1952 that they must
both belong to Innisfail because their minds seemed to
work on the same pattern. Ethel's book belonged to the
second Golden Age, the Christian one which, with an
"amazing continuity of thought," had developed from the
Pagan one. The inevitable successor, on the island of the
Shamrock, was "a third Golden Age which, I think, began
with Willie Yeats and the Irish Literary Renaissance." Here
at last, almost by chance and in her very last year, was
Maud's admission that she realized the literary magnifi-
cence of the period in which she had lived, and the extraordinary quality of the poetry she had helped to inspire.

Death was a welcome visitor to Maud when he finally
came to Roebuck House and took her by the hand. She was
four months past her eighty-seventh birthday, and had
been completely bedridden for six months. Her death on
the evening of April 27, 1953 was caused more by age than
anything else. At her bedside were Sean and Kid MacBride
and their two children.

On the following day hundreds of people walked up the broad driveway to pay their last respects. Madame lay in a brass-bound bed with her hands crossed as if in sleep; a black mantilla covered her hair. "Even in death," said the *Irish Times*, her features displayed "the regularity that gave her in life the beauty that was renowned."

At six that evening, her body was moved to the Church of the Sacred Heart, in Donnybrook. Requiem mass was celebrated at ten the next morning. Numerous members of the clergy, including the Acting Nuncio, participated in the services. The chief mourners were Sean and Catalina Mac-Bride, and their children, Anna and Tiernan; Iseult Stuart and her children, Katherine and Ian; relatives of John Mac-Bride; Mr. and Mrs. Eamon Bulfin; Eamon de Valera; ministers for external affairs, finance, defense, etc.; the speaker and members of the Dail; the lord mayor of Dublin; members of the judiciary and diplomatic corps; leaders of various political parties; and numerous government officials. Also present was the director (called governor in Ireland) of Mountjoy jail. Maud would probably have ordered him removed if she could have done so.

The coffin, draped with the national flag, was borne from the church to a hearse which led a procession of cars through the city. A large group of IRA and Cumann na mBan members joined the procession as it moved across O'Connell bridge. Some of the IRA men carried the coffin to the Republican Plot in Glasnevin cemetery. In his funeral oration The O'Rahilly praised Maud Gonne's courage, love of justice, and persistence. "Injustice was one of the things she could not tolerate," he said. "She realized that only by freeing Ireland from English rule could the lot of the Irish people be improved."

In addition to the expected condolences from political figures, Sean MacBride received messages from peasants who had suffered eviction many years before, former political prisoners, Irish communities in the United States, France, Canada, and elsewhere, and the Anti-Partition

League of Britain. The Madame Markievicz Memorial
Committee cancelled a scheduled meeting as a mark of respect.

It was an impressive funeral but lacked the panoply that
had attended the one given Constance Markievicz a quarter
of a century earlier. Maud, after all, had not participated in
the Easter 1916 Rising, had not been a government minister, and her family had not lived at Sligo for three centuries.

But there were other reasons for the relative quiet that
attended Maud's passing. It was the wrong time to die. She
had lived too long; all the organizations and publications
that she had founded had vanished, together with almost all
her colleagues. Besides, old-fashioned patriotism was in a
slump. The Irish Republican Army was again blowing up
buildings in London, but no one quite knew why. Emigration and poverty were continuing, and people were still in
jail, but there was nothing new or exciting about such circumstances.

Many people had forgotten what Maud, decades earlier,
had done for Ireland. Some confused her with Countess
Markievicz. Her association with W. B. Yeats, which was
to establish her fame for all time, did not seem important
since Yeats's own reputation had not yet reached its zenith.
In 1953 the torrent of general and specialized studies about
him was just getting under way.

All this made it possible for the *London Times* to brush off
the news of Maud's death in twenty-nine lines. The paper
said that she had been for many years "one of the most
colourful figures in Irish politics" (true but unimportant);
that she was eighty-eight years old (false); and that she had
been born near Glengariff, on Bantry Bay (false). There
was no mention of her friendship with Yeats.

From that date to this, there has never been a serious
attempt to make an even-handed assessment of Maud Gonne's role in Irish history. Did she alter its course in any

significant way? The general answer, I think, is that Maud took the same road that the Irish Republic as a whole has taken. Whether her activities helped or hindered depends on how highly one values Irish national independence, and how one sees the actions of the nation thereafter.

There is no question that Maud *tried* to make basic alterations in Ireland's political, economic, and social life. In millions of written and spoken words, she spread the gospel of separatism among many thousands of English, Irish, French, and Irish-American listeners and readers.

It is true that Irishmen no longer flock to join the British army. They work, instead, by the thousands in Liverpool and other English cities of commercial and industrial importance. To Maud the change would seem no improvement. As for her gospel that nothing meaningful can be accomplished without violence, it is doubtful that many have been converted by her preaching or example; and those who have are not proving helpful in removing the great remaining blight on the Island of Destiny: the inability of Protestants and Catholics, those with property or jobs and those without either, those in power and those without, to mend their differences.

Though Maud thought long and seriously about political problems, she turned out in the end to be more of a propagandist than a fresh political thinker or effective organizer. At best, she broadened roads which pioneer scholars of Gaelic language and culture had carved out, which nationalists like Arthur Griffith had paved, and which extremists like Padraic Pearse and James Connolly had stained with their blood.

In the area of economics, she was more successful. She publicized the need of evicted farmers for food and housing (without offering any scheme for land reform); she sympathized with the workers in the Dublin industrial struggle of 1913. She often used the national cause to strengthen her appeals for better conditions in prisons, for the liberation of

Republican prisoners, and for a system of free meals for school children.

She certainly had an effect on the nation—not perhaps as much as she thought she did—but anyone who displayed her energy, ability and perseverance could hardly leave it unaffected. Sometimes that impression was made accidentally—the help her Daughters of Erin gave to the formation of the Abbey players comes to mind—but it was there. Without investigation, it may be assumed that she helped to insure that political prisoners in Ireland today are treated less brutally than they were a half-century ago (although recent reports from Northern internment centers give one pause); that Irish school children no longer go hungry; that rural and urban poor are better protected by government and society than they used to be. It is not difficult to argue that, in the end, Maud Gonne turned out to be more successful as a philanthropist than patriot.

Maud Gonne's death aroused emotion mainly in the hearts of her family; of a few surviving friends like Helena Molony, "John Brennan," and Mrs. Sheila O'Donoghue; and of former prisoners who remembered gratefully the aid she had given them and their families. That emotion surfaces clearly in a fifteen-minute radio program broadcast by Irish Radio on the day of the funeral. Written and movingly narrated by Michael Mac Liammoir, it incorporates cello music, the Gregorian funeral chant, tributes by The O'Rahilly and Helena Molony, the acting of Siobhan McKenna, and the voice of Maud Gonne herself transferred from her recordings.

On that same day, an article appeared in the *Irish Times*, signed "Nichevo," which described Maud as a woman with a one-track mind, "who could, or would, talk about nothing except the manifold sins and wickedness of the British in Ireland," and who, when the British left, transferred her hatred to the Free State. For all that, Nichevo said, she had something that other women lacked—perhaps charm, perhaps femininity, or "it may have been that indefinable quality known as breeding. For, no matter how violent or unreasonable Maud Gonne may have been from time to time, she was always, and obviously, a lady."

Nichevo thought that Maud's life in Ireland

must have been pretty drab after all the gaiety and colour she had known on the Continent. The "Madame" affectation, if you like, and the classically-cut kind of nostalgic yearning for something she had thrown deliberately away in order... "that she might become one of those little stones on which the feet of the Queen rest a moment on her way to freedom." She had sacrificed much in the cause of a hard taskmistress, and her little personal foibles were as harmless as they were naive.... There was a touch of magic about her, which persisted even into the sourness of frustrated old age.

After reading this column, Maud's daughter-in-law, Kid, dashed off a letter to the *Irish Times* angrily protesting the accuracy of the last five words.

I have lived 26 years with Madame, and sourness and frustration are two things I should never have remotely connected with her. Sourness is for people who have not achieved, or who lack appreciation for, their achievements, and are small enough to mind, but in Madame's case there was plenty of appreciation from the people about whom she cared. All over the country there are people who bless her name. Frustration is for little people.... Nothing ever really stopped Madame once set on a course, as various Governments and people have found out from time to time.

She was an outstanding personality while as yet in her teens, and remained so until the hour she drew her last breath. She was also a great, kindly, lovable human being. May she rest in peace.

Few women have received so mighty an encomium from a daughter-in-law.

On May 2, 1953, Iseult Gonne Stuart sent a letter* from Laragh Castle to her husband in London, to give him the details of Maud's death. As usual, Iseult called Francis by

*Original in the Morris Library, Southern Illinois University at Carbondale.

his nickname, Grim; referred to Maud not as her mother but as Moura; and still refused to admit that there was a reason—Miss Meissner—why Francis refused to come home. When Iseult wrote this letter, she was already suffering from the coronary thrombosis of which she died a year later.

Dear Grim,

I meant to write to you for your birthday but Moura's death put all out of my mind. That you did not write to me a few words of sympathy has made me feel very sad.

Now I write to you for two reasons: the first, which I have long had in mind, is to ask you would you care to come and spend a few days with us? . . .

The other reason is to tell you about Moura's death, one of those really beautiful things one reads of in holy books and doesn't quite believe in. She had gone through a lot of pain and misery the last two or three months. She was saying to me only a few weeks ago how disgusting and despairing it was that all that, instead of spiritualising her, only made her selfish and materialistic. As it is also my experience with this rotten heart illness, I could only wretchedly agree. Then the day before her death, after she got the last sacraments, she had some kind of mystical experience, and looked radiantly happy and young. One of the last words she spoke was: "I feel now an ineffable joy." Then she went to sleep breathing lightly like a child and died that way the next day. Nobody knew the exact moment she ceased to breathe.

Maud Gonne may well have died the way Iseult says she did—looking like a saint, radiantly young, feeling an ineffable joy. She probably did "go gentle into that good night." She was old, tired, sick; she had earned her rest. But one cannot help thinking that this is not the way she *should* have died. She should have fought to the end—intransigent, rebellious, indomitable. No doubt, she would have preferred the kind of death Iseult describes—but, as we know, Maud Gonne was never very good at knowing what was best for her.

Bibliography

Adam, Madame Edmond. *My Literary Life*. New York: Appleton, 1904.
————. *The Romance of My Childhood and Youth*. New York: Appleton, 1902.
Adam, Villiers de l'Isle. *Axel*. Dublin: Dolmen Press, 1970.
Barker, Dudley. *Prominent Edwardians*. New York: Atheneum, 1969.
Bax, Arnold. *Farewell, My Youth*. London: Longmans Green, 1943.
Bell, J. Bowyer. *The Secret Army: The IRA, 1916–1974*. Cambridge: M.I.T. Press, 1974.
Birmingham, George A. *Benedict Kavanagh*. London: Edward Arnold, 1907.
————. *Hyacinth*. London: Edward Arnold, 1906.
Blake, John Y. F. *A West Pointer with the Boers*. Boston: Angel Guardian Press, 1903.
Bloom, Harold. *Yeats*. New York: Oxford University Press, 1970.
Bowra, Cecil Maurice. *Memories 1898–1939*. Cambridge: Harvard University Press, 1966. (Reprint)
Brown, Malcolm. *The Politics of Irish Literature*. London: George Allen and Unwin, 1972.
Clarke, Austin. *A Penny in the Clouds*. London: Routledge and Kegan Paul, 1969.
Cole, Howard N. *A Surrey Village and Its Church*. Tongham: F. H. Brown, 1973.
Colum, Mary. *Life and the Dream*. New York: Doubleday, 1947.
Coogan, Tim Pat. *The I.R.A.* London: Pall Mall Press, 1970.
Costigan, Giovanni. *A History of Modern Ireland*. Indianapolis: Bobbs Merrill, 1969.

Cousins, James Henry and Margaret E. *We Two Together*. London: Luzac, 1951.

Coxhead, Elizabeth. *Daughters of Erin*. London: New English Library, 1968.

———. *Lady Gregory, A Literary Portrait*. London: Secker and Warburg, 1961.

Crowley, Aleister. *The Confessions of Aleister Crowley*. New York: Hill and Wang, 1969.

Daly, Dominic. *The Young Douglas Hyde*. Dublin: Irish University Press, 1974.

Denson, Alan, ed. *Letters from AE*. London: Abelard-Schuman, 1961.

Deutsch-Brady, Chantal. "The King's Visit and the People's Protection Committee," in *Eire-Ireland*, Autumn 1975.

Dodds, E. R., ed. *Journal and Letters of Stephen Mackenna*. London: Constable, 1936.

Donoghue, Denis. *Yeats*. London: Collins, 1971.

Donoghue, Denis, and J. R. Mulryne, eds. *An Honored Guest. New Essays On W. B. Yeats*. New York: St. Martin's Press, 1966.

Eglinton, John (W. Magee). *A Memoir of AE*. London: Macmillan, 1937.

Ellis-Fermor, Una. *The Irish Dramatic Movement*. London: Methuen, 1939.

Ellmann, Richard. *The Identity of Yeats*. New York: Oxford University Press, 1954.

———. *James Joyce*. New York: Oxford University Press, 1959.

———. *Yeats—the Man and the Mask*. New York: Macmillan, 1948.

Ervine, St. John. "Some Impressions of My Elders." *North American Review*, February-March 1920.

Fox, R. M. *Rebel Irishwomen*. Dublin: Progress House, 1935.

Gibbon, Monk. *The Masterpiece and the Man, Yeats as I Knew Him*. New York: Macmillan, 1959.

Goldring, Douglas. *South Lodge*. London: Constable, 1943.

Gregory, Lady Augusta. *Journals*. Lennox Robinson, ed. London: Putnam, 1946.

Gwynn, Stephen, ed. *Scattering Branches*. New York: Macmillan, 1940.

Harding, James. *Boulanger—France's Demagogue on Horseback*. New York: Scribner's, 1971.

Healy, Chris. *Confessions of a Journalist*. London: Chatto and Windus, 1904.

Henn, T. R. *The Lonely Tower, Studies in the Poetry of W. B. Yeats*. London: Methuen, 1950.

Hobson, Bulmer. *Ireland Yesterday and Tomorrow*. Tralee: Anvil Books, 1968.

Hogan, Robert, and James Kilroy, eds. *Lost Plays of the Irish Renaissance*. Newark: Proscenium Press, 1970.

Holloway, Joseph. *Joseph Holloway's Abbey Theatre*. Robert Hogan and Michael J. O'Neill, eds. Carbondale: Southern Illinois University Press, 1967.

Hone, Joseph. *W. B. Yeats–1865–1939*. London: Macmillan, 1943.

Howarth, Herbert. *The Irish Writers: Literature and Nationalism. 1880–1940*. New York: Hill and Wang, 1958.

Jackson, T. A. *Ireland Her Own: An Outline History of the Irish Struggle*. New York: International Publishers, 1970.

Jeffares, A. Norman. *A Commentary on the Collected Poems of W. B. Yeats*. London: Macmillan, 1968.

———. *W. B. Yeats* (Profiles in Literature Series). London: Routledge and Kegan Paul, 1971.

———. *W. B. Yeats—Man and Poet*. New York: Barnes and Noble, 1966.

Jeffares, A. Norman, and K. G. W. Cross, eds. *In Excited Reverie—A Centenary Tribute. W. B. Yeats 1865–1939*. London: Macmillan, 1965.

Jochum, K. P. S. "Maud Gonne on Synge." *Eire-Ireland*. Winter, 1971.

Joy, Maurice, ed. *The Irish Rebellion of 1916*. New York: Devin-Adair, 1916.

Jullian, Philippe. *Dreamers of Decadence—Symbolist Painters of the 1890's*. New York: Praeger, 1971.

Kee, Robert. *The Green Flag*. London: Weidenfeld and Nicolson, 1972.

Kelly, Tom. "I Remember." *Capuchin Annual*. Dublin, 1942.

Kilroy, James. *The Playboy Riots*. Dublin: Dolmen Press, 1971.

Levenson, Samuel. *James Connolly*. London: Martin Brian and O'Keeffe, 1973.

Loftus, Richard J. *Nationalism in Modern Anglo-Irish Poetry*. Madison: University of Wisconsin Press, 1964.

Lynch, Arthur. *Ireland: Vital Hour*. London: Stanley Paul, 1915.

———. *My Life Story*. London: John Long, 1924.

Lynd, Robert. *Books and Writers*. London: Dent, 1952.

Lyons, F. S. L. *Ireland Since the Famine*. New York: Scribner's, 1971.

Macardle, Dorothy. *The Irish Republic*. New York: Farrar, Straus and Giroux, 1965.

MacBride, Maud Gonne. *A Servant of the Queen*. London: Gollancz, 1938, 1974.

McCann, Sean, ed. *The Story of the Abbey Theatre*. London: New English Library, 1967.

McCormack, W. J., ed. *A Festschrift for Francis Stuart*. Dublin: Dolmen Press, 1972.

McFate, Patricia Ann. "AE's Portraits of the Artists: A Study of The Avatars." *Eire-Ireland*. Winter 1971.

Macken, Mary M. "W. B. Yeats, John O'Leary and the Contemporary Club." *Studies*. XXVIII Dublin, 1939.

Mac Liammoir, Michael. *Put Money in Thy Purse*. London: Methuen, 1952.

MacLysaght, Edward. *The Surnames of Ireland*. Dublin: Irish University Press, 1973.

Mannin, Ethel. *Brief Voices*. London: Hutchinson, 1959.

———. *Jungle Journey*. London: Jarrolds, 1950.

———. *Late Have I Loved Thee*. London: Jarrolds, 1948.

———. *Privileged Spectator*. London: Jarrolds, 1938.

———. *Stories from My Life*. London: Hutchinson, 1973.

———. *Young in the Twenties*. London: Hutchinson, 1971.

Marecco, Anne. *The Rebel Countess*. Philadelphia: Chilton, 1967.

Martin, F. X., ed. *Leaders and Men of the Easter Rising*. London: Methuen, 1967.

Moore, George. *Hail and Farewell: Ave, Salve, Vale*. London: Heinemann, 1911–1914.

Moore, Virginia. *The Unicorn. William Butler Yeats' Search for Reality*. New York: Macmillan, 1954.

Murphet, Howard. *When Daylight Comes: A Biography of H. P. Blavatsky*. Wheaton, Ill.: Theosophical Publishing House, 1975.

Natterstad, J. H. *Francis Stuart*. Lewisburg, Pa.: Bucknell University Press, 1974.

Nevinson, Henry W. *Changes and Chances*. London: Nisbet, 1923.

Ni Eireamhoin, Eibhlin. *Two Great Irishwomen—Maud Gonne MacBride, Constance Markievicz*. Dublin: Fallon, 1971.

O'Brien, William. *Forth the Banners Go: Reminiscences of William O'Brien*. Dublin: Three Candles, 1969.

O'Brien, William, and Desmond Ryan, eds. *Devoy's Post Bag, 1871–1928*. 2 v. Dublin: Fallon, 1948 and 1953.

O'Casey, Sean. *Drums Under the Windows*. New York: Macmillan, 1950.

———. *Inishfallen, Fare Thee Well*. New York: Macmillan, 1949.

O'Faolain, Sean. *Constance Markievicz*. London: Jonathan Cape, 1934.

Orwell, George. *Dickens, Dali and Others*. New York: Reynal and Hitchcock, 1946.

Patmore, Brigit. *My Friends When Young—The Memoirs of Brigit Patmore*. London: Heinemann, 1968.

Pearl, Cyril. *Dublin in Bloomtime*. New York: Viking, 1969.

Plunkett, James. Article in *Conor Cruise O'Brien Introduces Ireland*. Owen Dudley Edwards, ed. New York: McGraw-Hill, 1969.

Pound, Ezra. *Selected Letters 1907–1941*. D. D. Page, ed. New York: New Directions, 1971.

Reid, B. L. *The Man from New York, John Quinn and His Friends*. New York: Oxford University Press, 1968.

Rhys, Ernest. *Everyman Remembers*. London: Dent, 1931.

———. *Wales England Wed: An Autobiography*. London: Dent, 1940.

Richardson, Mary R. *Laugh a Defiance*. London: Weidenfeld and Nicolson, 1953.

Rodgers, R. W., ed. *Irish Literary Portraits*. New York: Taplinger, 1973.

Rolleston, C. H. *Portrait of an Irishman*. London: Methuen, 1939.

Rothenstein, William. *Men and Memories; Recollections of William Rothenstein*. 3 v. New York: Coward-McCann, 1931–1940.

Russell, George. *Letters from AE*. Alan Denson, ed. London: Abelard-Schuman, 1961.

Ryan, Desmond. *The Rising*. Dublin: Golden Eagle Books, 1949.

Ryan, Mark F. *Fenian Memories*. Dublin: Gill, 1945.

Ryder, Vera. *The Little Victims Play—An Edwardian Childhood*. London: Robert Hale, 1974.

Sachs, Emanie Louise. *The Terrible Siren*. New York: Harper, 1928.

Seiden, Morton Irving. *William Butler Yeats, The Poet as a Mythmaker, 1865–1939*. East Lansing: Michigan State University Press, 1962.

Sheehy-Skeffington, Francis. *Michael Davitt*. London: T. Fisher Unwin, 1908.

Shirer, William L. *The Collapse of the Third Republic*. New York: Simon and Schuster, 1969.

Skelton, Robin. *J. M. Synge and His World*. New York: Viking, 1971.

Skene, Reg. *The Cuchulainn Plays of W. B. Yeats*. London: Macmillan, 1974.

Steegmuller, Francis. *Cocteau*. Boston: Little Brown, 1970.

Stephens, Edward. *My Uncle John* [Synge]. London: Oxford University Press, 1974.

Stephens, Winifred. *Madame Adam (Juliette Lamber)*. New York: Dutton, 1917.

Stock, Noel. *The Life of Ezra Pound*. New York: Pantheon, 1970.

Stuart, Francis. *Black List, Section H*. Carbondale: Southern Illinois University Press, 1971.

———. *The Coloured Dome*. London: Gollancz, 1932.

———. *Memorial*. London: Martin Brian and O'Keeffe, 1973.

————. *Pigeon Irish*. London: Gollancz, 1932.

————. *The Pillar of Cloud*. London: Gollancz, 1948.

————. *Redemption*. London: Gollancz, 1949.

————. *Things to Live For: Notes for an Autobiography*. London: Jonathan Cape, 1934.

————. *Victors and Vanquished*. London: Gollancz, 1958.

Thompson, William Irwin. *The Imagination of an Insurrection: Dublin, Easter 1916*. New York: Oxford University Press, 1967.

Tynan, Katharine. *The Middle Years, 1892–1911*. London: Constable, 1916.

————. *Twenty-five Years: Reminiscences*. London: Smith Elder, 1913.

Unterecker, John. *A Reader's Guide to William Butler Yeats*. New York: Farrar, Straus and Giroux, 1959.

Van Voris, Jacqueline. *Constance de Markievicz. In the Cause of Ireland*. Amherst: University of Massachusetts Press, 1967.

Whittington-Egan, Richard, and Geoffrey Smerdon. *The Quest of the Golden Boy. The Life and Letters of Richard Le Gallienne*. Barre, Mass.: Barre Publishing Co., 1962.

Wilson, Colin. *The Occult*, A History. New York: Random House, 1971.

Yeats, J. B. *Letters to His Son, W. B. Yeats, and Others—1869–1922*. Joseph Hone, ed. New York: Dutton, 1946.

Yeats, W. B. *The Autobiography of William Butler Yeats*. New York: Macmillan, 1916.

————. *The Collected Poems of W. B. Yeats*. New York: Macmillan, 1956.

————. *Explorations*. New York: Macmillan, 1962.

————. *The Letters of W. B. Yeats*. Allan Wade, ed. New York: Macmillan, 1955.

————. *Letters to Katharine Tynan*. Roger McHugh, ed. Dublin: Clonmore and Reynolds, 1953.

————. *Letters to the New Island*. Horace Reynolds, ed. Cambridge, Mass.: Harvard University Press, 1934.

————. *Memoirs*. Denis Donoghue, ed. London: Macmillan, 1972.

————. *Selected Prose*. A. Norman Jeffares, ed. London: Macmillan, 1964.

————. *The Speckled Bird*. William O'Donnell, ed. Dublin: Cuala Press, 1974. 2 vols.

————. *Uncollected Prose by W. B. Yeats, 1866–1896*. John Frayne, ed. New York: Columbia University Press, 1970.

Young, Ellen. *Flowering Dusk*. New York: Longmans Green, 1945.

Zwerdling, Alex. *Yeats and the Heroic Ideal*. New York: New York University Press, 1965.

Index

429

Irish Republican Army (IRA), 340,
341, 342, 348, 358, 373, 386,
387, 388, 417, 418
Irish Republican Brotherhood ("the
Organization"), 21, 68, 112, 125,
131, 132, 142, 149, 266–268,
294, 392
Irish Socialist Republican Party, 117,
118–119, 151
Irish-Soviet Friendship Society, 377
Irish Times, 10, 155, 209, 210, 234,
352, 374, 400, 401, 402, 417,
420, 421
Irish Transvaal Committee, 153, 154,
155, 157
Irish Volunteers, 286, 294, 295, 312,
320, 321
Irish White Cross, 337, 340, 404–405
Irish Women's Franchise League,
256, 275
Irish World, 126, 128, 129–130, 136,
161–162, 183, 184, 222

Jameson, Ida, 44–45, 47
Jeffares, A. Norman, 385
John, Augustus, 250, 268, 285
Johnson, Anna (Ethna Carberry), 170
Joyce, James, 205, 224, 237, 258*n*,
263, 264, 281, 308, 399
Jubilee, Queen Victoria's, 116–123,
125, 128

Kavanagh, Rose, 71
Kee, Robert, 268
Kelly, Father Peter, 51–52, 54, 73
Kelly, Tom, 207–208, 218, 267
Kernoff, Harry, 277
Kickham, Charles Joseph, 142
Kruger, Paul, 155, 160, 161, 178

labor struggles, 278–280
Ladies' Land League, 170, 171
Lane, Sir Hugh Percy, 241, 280–281,
383
La Patrie, 66, 117, 143, 182, 200, 319
Larkin, James, 278, 279, 280
League of Nations, 373
League of Patriots, 37, 39, 65

l'Irlande Libre, 100, 115–116, 140, 200,
262
Lloyd George, David, 304, 306, 320,
338, 340
Lyman, W. W., 259
Lynch, Arthur, 176, 189, 190, 199,
200
Lyons, F. S. L., 221

MacBride, Anna, 354, 372, 416, 417
MacBride, Anthony, 176
MacBride, Catalina (Kid) Bulfin, 255,
354, 368, 372, 416, 417, 421
MacBride, Major John, 153, 154,
176–177, 178, 197–198, 210,
226–232, 237, 238, 241, 256,
266–268, 295, 296, 298, 300,
302, 306, 381, 415
  Maud's marriage to, 201–206
  U.S. tour of, 180–181, 182–185,
  187–188, 235
MacBride, Joseph, 306, 320–321
MacBride, Sean, 33, 218, 223, 233,
236, 240, 252, 255, 256, 261,
262, 264, 269, 270, 277, 279,
288, 290, 293, 300, 311, 316,
321, 325, 326, 334–335, 336,
337, 339, 341, 354, 356, 368,
372, 387, 393, 394, 400, 401–
403, 409–410, 416
MacBride, Tiernan, 372, 416, 417
McCaughey, Sean, 400
MacCool, Finn, 21
McCullough, Denis, 237
MacDermott, Sean, 294
MacDonagh, Thomas, 294, 295
McFadden, Father, 51, 52, 53, 66, 74,
102
Mac Liammoir, Michael, 412–413,
420
MacLysaght, Edward, 8
MacManus, Francis, 355–356, 407–
408
MacManus, M. J., 414, 415
MacManus, Seamus, 207, 209, 218
MacSwiney, Terence, 333
"Mademoiselle" (governess), 15, 33,
38

MAUD GONNE as a young beauty.

WILLIAM BUTLER YEATS. Portrait by J. B. Yeats.
(Courtesy of the National Gallery of Ireland.)

ISEULT GONNE.

ISEULT GONNE STUART
in later years.

MAJOR JOHN MACBRIDE.
(Courtesy of the National
Library of Ireland.)

SEAN MACBRIDE as a
young man.

MAUD GONNE in her early sixties, with one of her favorite dogs.

Maud Gonne in old age.